A CONSPIRATORIAL LIFE

A Conspiratorial Life

ROBERT WELCH, THE JOHN BIRCH SOCIETY, AND THE REVOLUTION OF AMERICAN CONSERVATISM

Edward H. Miller

The University of Chicago Press CHICAGO AND LONDON

The University of Chicago Press, Chicago 60637
The University of Chicago Press, Ltd., London

Published 2021
Paperback edition 2023
Printed in the United States of America

32 31 30 29 28 27 26 25 24 23   1 2 3 4 5

ISBN-13: 978-0-226-44886-2 (cloth)
ISBN-13: 978-0-226-82650-9 (paper)
ISBN-13: 978-0-226-44905-0 (e-book)
DOI: https://doi.org/10.7208/chicago/9780226449050.001.0001

Library of Congress Cataloging-in-Publication Data

Names: Miller, Edward H. (Edward Herbert), author.
Title: A conspiratorial life : Robert Welch, the John Birch Society, and the revolution of American conservatism / Edward H. Miller.
Description: Chicago : University of Chicago Press, 2021. | Includes index.
Identifiers: LCCN 2021017533 | ISBN 9780226448862 (cloth) | ISBN 9780226449050 (ebook)
Subjects: LCSH: Welch, Robert, 1899–1985. | John Birch Society—Biography. | Right-wing extremists—United States—Biography. | Conspiracy theories—United States—History—20th century. | Conservatism—United States—History—20th century. | United States—Politics and government—1945–1989.
Classification: LCC E748.W436 M56 2021 | DDC [Fic]—dc26
LC record available at https://lccn.loc.gov/2021017533

♾ This paper meets the requirements of ANSI/NISO Z39.48-1992 (Permanence of Paper).

TO JACK MILLER

Contents

Introduction

We live in the age of Robert Welch—whether or not we know who he is, what he did, or why he matters. So shouldn't we know something more about a man whose worldview is absolutely everywhere?

The day Joseph R. Biden took the oath of office from Chief Justice John Roberts and became the forty-sixth president of the United States, Donald J. Trump still had not conceded. Election fraud by the Democrats, Trump tweeted for two whole months, stole the election from him and the American people. But this claim was pure myth. Court after election commission after court found no evidence to support Trump's words. A full 75 percent of Republicans didn't believe that Joe Biden legitimately won the 2020 election, laying the groundwork for Donald Trump to incite an insurrection to steal it for real.

The QAnon conspiracy theory—which holds that Democrats in the Deep State undermined Trump's presidency in order to cover up their child-sex racket, and claims Representative Marjorie Taylor Greene among its more prominent adherents—is favorably viewed by nearly one-third of Republicans, while polling shows that violent anti-democratic sentiment is rampant in the conservative movement.

And when Republican lawmakers had a chance to draw a bright line between their party and the conspiracy theorists and the insurrectionists during Trump's impeachment trial, the vast majority voted to acquit.

The QAnon conspiracy theory had no basis in reality. Trump's election fraud conspiracy theory had no basis in reality, but his supporters and some Republican leaders echoed the false charge. Trump's entire political career—and a great deal of his popular appeal—lay in conspiracism of a kind that owes something to Robert Welch.

Trump's entry into politics began with another conspiracy theory. In 1989, after a female jogger was raped and beaten nearly to death in New York City's Central Park, Trump took out newspaper ads calling for the death penalty for the five Black and Brown teens accused of committing the crime. Even after DNA evidence found they were not guilty, Trump still insisted they were. Similarly, Trump amplified early and often the completely baseless claim that Barack Obama was born in Africa and thus ineligible to serve as president. Yet Obama was born in Hawaii. Trump's lie stirred up long-standing racial hatreds, and his followers believed his false claim.

Trump put forward many other conspiracies and lies. He characterized all Mexican immigrants as rapists and drug runners, and told his supporters that he would build a border wall and make Mexico pay for it. Trump dispensed with one of his rivals, Ted Cruz, by alleging that Cruz's father was somehow involved in the assassination of President John F. Kennedy. Trump based this claim on a *National Enquirer* photograph showing Cruz's father and Lee Harvey Oswald standing together several months before the assassination.

These lies led to others and to wild overstatements. Trump threatened to jail his Democratic challenger in the 2016 presidential election, former secretary of state Hillary Clinton, for using a private email server while serving in her official capacity. Although illegal, her actions hardly were unprecedented or verifiably malicious. But this distinction did not deter Trump's supporters from cheering "Lock Her Up" at political rallies. Trump was swept into the White House in the November election by riding a wave of anti-immigrant sentiment, assaulting traditional alliances, and appealing to nostalgia with promises to "Make America Great Again," summoning a mythical past where American manufacturing was second to none and where Black, Brown, and female people "knew their place."

Trump didn't necessarily know the historical background of his claims and rhetoric. One of his campaign slogans was "America First," the name of an organization that Welch joined in the 1940s to keep America out of World War II. Trump's isolationism and Welch's isolationism weren't exactly the same, but they rhymed.

"Our politics today seems more vulnerable to conspiracy theories and outright fabrications," George W. Bush observed in 2017. The forty-third president was right. But the onset of his presidency had contributed to their rise; in 2000, the Supreme Court, not the American people, ruled that he had won over Al Gore. Some people saw a conspiracy: elites had manipulated the vote. How did such a calamity come to pass? It was as if Welch had scripted it.

On election night, Fox News announced that Bush had won Florida and was thus president-elect. ABC, NBC, and CNN followed suit. Then Gore conceded. John Ellis, Bush's first cousin, who was appointed by Roger Ailes to run Fox News's decision desk, yelled out, "Jebbie says we've got it!" "Jebbie" was Bush's brother, the governor of Florida. Gore then unconceded, telling George Bush over the telephone, "Your little brother is not the ultimate authority on this."[1]

But that wasn't all there was to fuel conspiracy theories. Confusion and irregularities at the polls were reported throughout that day. Gore had won the national popular vote by more than a half of a million votes, and relying on this, he contested Bush's win in Florida. Florida's Supreme Court then called for a manual recount. That count went on for thirty-six tension-filled days. Then, the US Supreme Court struck down the recount by a five-to-four vote. The five justices who gave the presidency to George Walker Bush based their decision on the equal protection clause of the Fourteenth Amendment—one of the strangest decisions in judicial history. The Fourteenth Amendment had been passed to provide rights to African Americans during Reconstruction, not to decide a presidential election. Those five justices had been appointed by Republicans: either Ronald Reagan or George Herbert Walker Bush, George Bush's father. Justice John Paul Stevens—who had also been appointed by a Republican, Gerald Ford—dissented, writing, "although we may never know with complete certainty the identity of the winner of this year's presidential election, the identity of the loser is perfectly clear. It is the Nation's confidence in the judge as an impartial guardian of the rule of law."[2]

Welch never did believe the political playing field was level. And now he had plenty of company.

Of course, many Americans have believed conspiracy theories, dating back to the nation's founding. And conspiracy theories are not limited to the Right. After he was elected president in 1992, Bill Clinton talked with his friend Webster Hubbell about a job in the Justice Department. They were close friends, golfing buddies, and Clinton trusted Hubbell. "If I put you over at Justice, I want you to find the answers to two questions for me. One, Who killed JFK? And two, Are there UFOs?" The president was "dead serious," Hubbell said.[3]

But by 2020, something was different. Conspiracies were not whispered about anymore. They were everywhere. Supporters of Senator Bernie Sanders claimed that mainstream Democrats had conspired to deny Sanders the presidential nomination—more than once. Conspiracies about the Clintons continue to come from all sides. Some think they killed Jeffrey Epstein, Vincent Foster, and others. Some, including former Clinton labor secretary Robert Reich, suggested that Trump faked his own contraction of the coronavirus. Today, all of us are strapped into the roller coaster in the fantastical theme park of Welch's political imagination. And we can't get off.

...

Who then was Robert Welch? To some, he was a genius: a child prodigy who was reading at age two. He attended the University of North Carolina when he was twelve. He created the Sugar Daddy and other childhood confectioneries. He founded the John Birch Society, the most successful anti-Communist organization in the history of the United States.

To his detractors, he was at best a prophet of doom who predicted that the country was on the verge of a Communist conspiracy engulfing all aspects of American life—education, religion, the government. His star flew high but petered out by the late 1960s when the John Birch Society was no longer a force to be reckoned with.

Many Americans first learned of the candy maker after March 20, 1961. That day, Senator Milton Young of North Dakota stepped up to the rostrum of the US Senate; read thirteen pages of Welch's book, *The Politician*; and reported that Welch called former president Dwight David Eisenhower a Communist.

Now in most periods of American history, Welch's bizarre thesis would have made him a pariah. Welch would have been pitied as somebody suffering a pathology. He would have been disqualified as an irresponsible purveyor of unreasonable ideas.

But these were not usual times. The Cold War was at its height, and Americans were very anxious. They were stocking food and building bunkers. They were getting ready to "duck and cover" in the event of a nuclear attack from the Soviet Union that might come any moment.

Times were tense.

Thus, Welch was not just seen as unreasonable. He was considered a danger to the country. After all, he was calling the man who planned D-Day, defeated Hitler, and won World War II a Red. Welch embodied extremism in the body politic, according to the consensus. He became associated in the public mind with the Ku Klux Klan, the racist White Citizens' Councils, and even George Lincoln Rockwell's American Nazis. The Anti-Defamation League called him a covert anti-Semite. Others said there was nothing covert about him.

Welch's problem was that most of what he said about Communism seemed absurd. His analysis sounded delusionary and made all anti-Communists appear ridiculous.

Welch's early life helped make him a conspiracist. He was born in a postbellum South that was very suspicious of the North. His ancestors feared the loss of their social status, the loss of their slaves, the loss of their jobs, and the decline of their White supremacy. And even after he had left the South, as a young candy manufacturer working in an industry without patents and fearing that his latest confectionery invention could be pilfered by the competition, Welch was always in a state of hypervigilance. That Welch's original business was unsuccessful contributed to his insecurity. And after he went into business with his brother, James, whom he'd taught everything he knew about the candy business, he discovered James never considered him a business partner but simply an employee who deserved a daily wage but no more.

In the early 1950s, Welch watched with great interest Senator Joseph McCarthy's investigations into Communist infiltration of government. Welch came to echo and even amplify the allegations of treason from McCarthy and other Republican public officials, such as Senator William Jenner. Secretary George Marshall was one of the most honorable men in the country, but Senator Jenner called Marshall "a front man for traitors" and suggested that Marshall tricked the American people into World War II. Jenner set the stage for McCarthy's attacks on the army, which set the stage for Welch's assaults on the former head of the army—Dwight David Eisenhower. Amid numerous allegations of espionage, McCarthy attacked Secretary of State Dean Acheson and Marshall as part of "a conspiracy on a scale so immense so as to dwarf any previous such venture in the history of man." Daily calls for Acheson's resignation became the norm for the Republican Party.

In 1951 during this feverish climate, Welch wrote *May God Forgive Us*, but his conclusions were feverish and fantastic. General Douglas MacArthur had been fired by Stalin, Welch wrote. American diplomats had given away Poland, Yugoslavia, North Korea, and China.

In 1954, Welch wrote *The Life of John Birch*. Welch found in the tragedy of Birch's death evidence of secret Communist sympathizers within the US government who had ensured the ascendancy of Mao Tse-tung to power in China. Welch called Birch the first casualty of the Cold War. During Birch's short but courageous life, wrote Welch, he had given everything and told the American people everything they needed to know about the treachery of the Chinese Communists. He had died so that Americans could understand the evil of the Chinese Communists. In death, Birch became a martyr for liberty and a saint to anti-Communist hardliners. "In one blade of grass lies the key to all creation, could we only understand it," Welch wrote, "and in the forces that swirled around John Birch lay all the conflicts of philosophy, and of implementation, with which our whole world is now so imperatively concerned." Communist China, not America, was in charge, observed Welch. A Washington cabal was sabotaging Chiang Kai-shek, and high-level American officials were delivering China into the hands of the Communists. Birch had known this to be true.

In Birch, Welch had his hero; but he needed a villain, and he found that villain in Eisenhower. According to Welch, after Stalin's 1953 death, the Soviet Union faced a crucial moment. "Not since the siege of Stalingrad had the whole Communist tyranny been in so much danger of being wiped off the face of the earth," Welch wrote in *The Politician*. "Just one thing" saved the Soviet Union: the election of Eisenhower, "the most completely opportunistic and unprincipled politician America has ever raised to high office." Welch covered Ike's quick rise in the army, his support for a premature second front, his reluctance to attack

Berlin, and his strong commitment to unconditional surrender. According to Welch, as president, Eisenhower virtually destroyed the Republican Party, failed to roll back the New Deal, and settled for the status quo in Eastern Europe. Welch also suggested that Eisenhower worked to destroy McCarthy. According to Welch, Ike was a "dedicated, conscious agent of the communist conspiracy." Welch had the same view about Marshall, who "since at least sometime in the 1930s . . . has been a conscious, deliberate, dedicated agent of the Soviet conspiracy."[4]

But in calling Ike a Commie, along with suggesting Marshall, Acheson, and other Communist spies had infiltrated the American government—indeed they made up the nation's deep state—Welch was just getting started in weaving his tapestry of conspiracy.

He saw Communist conspiracies lurking in international organizations, colleges, high schools, and the government itself.

The Communists had infiltrated the country's public health departments, Welch believed. Fluoride was being used to enervate the hearts, minds, and bodies of Americans to the coming Communist occupation.

Although the Venona documents—Soviet diplomatic material from World War II decoded by the American government—indeed highlighted that Communist spies *had* infiltrated the American government, Welch went further and said American domestic and foreign policymakers were treasonous.

Welch called Sputnik I a hoax. Welch believed Vietnam to be a "phony war," in which both sides were being not run from the White House but from the Kremlin. Welch said the civil rights movement was a conspiracy of the Communists. The creation of the United Nations, he was sure, was just the beginning step toward one world government, with Communists and American officials working behind the scenes.

Welch's conspiracies fed postwar America's growing suspicion of government, a general mistrust, and belief in cover-ups in high places, including even the existence of UFOs and government involvement in the 1963 assassination of John F. Kennedy. In the John Birch Society's magazine *American Opinion*, the ardent anti-Semite and John Birch Society member Revilo Oliver wrote in "Marx-manship in Dallas," the Soviets killed Kennedy, a debunkable theory. But Welch peddled the theory like pushcart peanuts. And many bought the nuts.

The Communists killed not only Kennedy but also Martin Luther King Jr., alleged Welch. King was more valuable to the Communists as a dead martyr than a living human being, he proposed. Then Welch claimed the Communists killed JFK's brother Robert Kennedy in June 1968. But Sirhan Sirhan shot Robert Kennedy.

But that wasn't all. In later years, Welch actually moved away from conspiracy theories involving the Communists, whether American, Russian, or Chinese. He soon concluded that Communism was just another name for the conspiracy begun by the Bavarian Illuminati in 1776. The Illuminati, believed Welch, had survived and thrived through the centuries. His worldview became even more fantastical from there. The Trilateral Commission, the Council on Foreign Relations, and the Bilderbergers were the true puppet masters of America's foreign and economic interests, and foreign policy was the product of the devilish desires of these globalist bodies.[5]

But Welch was wrong. Although elites in these organizations were influential in his day and continue to be powerful, they do not run the show. Errors by our foreign policymakers and elected officials, whether in Vietnam, China, or elsewhere, provide the best evidence. The US government continues to be run by extremely fallible elected men and women—under "the consent of the governed." Our divided civic life and contemporary partisan warfare certainly testify to that.

In the long run, Welch's kind of conspiracy has grown only stronger. More people believe extreme theories. It used to be that Welch's commitment to conspiracy theory made him, as well the John Birch Society, easy to dismiss; this may be why no historian has written a full-scale biography of Welch. Pieces of the story are included in the scores of books on American conservatism, but they tend to focus on the Society's marginalization and its waning importance to postwar conservatism after 1966.

When Donald Trump won the presidency, historians began revising the standard narrative of American conservatism.

That standard narrative holds that the Welch conspiratorial style waned when the patron saint of American conservatives, William F. Buckley, kicked him out of the conservative movement in the early 1960s. Other journalists and academics wrote off the John Birch Society and Welch as irrational and paranoid. Because of his penchant for conspiracy theory, Welch threatened the America that Buckley wanted to build. Historians largely embraced Buckley's vision that making conservatism "intellectually respectable" was absolutely necessary to its success: Buckley purged extremists, and these excommunications made possible the rise of the age of Reagan. According to the usual narrative, Welch and the Society became particular liabilities to the Republican Right after Barry Goldwater's tremendous defeat in the presidential election of 1964. But Welch was a far more flexible and important a figure to the Republican Party than historians have realized.

Like the fundamentalists of the 1920s, many Birchers did disengage when it became an embarrassment to be associated with the Society. Welch's followers were seen as crackpots, deplorables, losers who did not fit into the modern world. But the Society was only taking a lower profile. Now the ideas of the John Birch Society are everywhere—even in the White House. Even in your own house.

After tasting fame in the early 1960s and finding it bitter, Welch thereafter preferred to remain on the sidelines—the rightward fringe of acceptable conservatism. Welch was uninterested in claiming credit for contributions to the conservative movement. Welch became completely satisfied in establishing ad hoc committees that opposed the Equal Rights Amendment, abortion, high taxation, and sex education. He sustained the relevance of the Society for its espousal of any issues that the Reagan revolution of the 1980s cared about. The ideas of the John Birch Society paved the way for the conservatism of the twentieth century, shaped events in the twenty-first century, and will continue to do so far into the future.

Welch's story also needs to be told because historians have got the conservative movement all wrong. For about two decades we have falsely bought into a narrative of American conservatism as a mild-mannered phenomenon. Books like Lisa McGirr's seminal and classic study *Suburban Warriors* have made the tones of American conservatism sound like the Beach Boys; but it has always sounded like death metal. Historians have generally jettisoned Richard Hofstadter's darker vision of American conservatism, but Hofstadter got a lot right.[6]

Despite the predominant story that the suave, prolific, and "responsible" right of Buckley purged the conservative movement and thus saved it, Welch was never excommunicated, and his style of American conservatism remained extremely potent. Thus, rather than a story of rise, fall, and impotence, this book is a story of survival, growth, and significance. This book asks how the Society was able to survive and play a decisive role in establishing the rightward terminus of conservative opinion in the 1970s. After Goldwater's debacle, Welch applied many of the same strategies as Richard Nixon and Ronald Reagan to reinvent his brand of conservatism. Despite a decline in membership between 1966 and 1970, the Society grew in the 1970s and solidified its position as the primary institution on the rightmost flank. In the late 1960s and 1970s, Welch changed course and spun a richer tapestry for the Society than its traditional narratives of patriotism and conspiracy. He championed new issues—often less controversial and more practicable ones—to retain membership, foster growth, and refashion the Society. Welch also adopted the tactic from socially conservative activists of advocating single-issue campaigns focusing on traditional values. Welch added economic issues to his agenda in the 1970s, helping to push the country to the right by providing much of the support behind the anti-tax movement at both the federal and state levels.

Welch's uniqueness and the depth of his influence on the transformation of the Republican Party—and by extension of America—has never been fully appreciated. Here, thanks in part to access to Welch's personal papers—papers that have never been drawn on before—we can remedy that. And thanks in part to Donald Trump, it's time to get the Right right again.

The roots of Welch's conspiracy thinking formed in a family of southern, formerly slave-owning yeomen distrustful of Yankee merchant elite, who after the Civil War saw an eastern conspiracy in everything and began to see a conspiracy of international bankers. Let's go meet the men and women and places that forged Welch—and transformed forever the United States of America. We start our trip in North Carolina. It's going to get bumpy.

1

Chowan County, North Carolina, 1700–1899

Early settlers to North Carolina's Chowan County, which sits at the junction of Albemarle Sound to the south and the Chowan River to the west, tended to believe that with hard work, persistence, and a little bit of luck, a good life was possible. But their environs were not completely auspicious. The muggy climate and mosquitos made life miserable. Roads were bone-shaking, rough-hewn trails. The earliest settlers hacked down trees, established clearings, and built their farms with rudimentary utensils: the scythe, the sickle, and the hoe. They sowed wide acres, but the soil was very stubborn, contained many stumps, and required hand hoeing. Wooden plows splintered, snapped, and busted. Horses and mules expressed unhappiness with the stumpy landscape by balking, bucking, and throwing their hapless riders to the ground.

Edward Welch was one of them. He was one of a band of four emigrant brothers from Wales. Edward brimmed with hopes and dreams to get ahead and make his mark in the world. He arrived in Chowan County sometime in the early 1700s. By 1790, the largest city of Chowan County, Edenton, contained 150 homes and 1,600 souls, including 1,000 slaves. Wealth in Edenton was not well distributed. Five men—none of them Welch—owned approximately half of Edenton's slaves.[1]

And yet, the decades after the American Revolution were a time of wonder, adventure, and opportunity for millions. Immigration from Europe surged, and the new nation's population doubled every twenty-five years. Most who pulled up stakes and ventured to this experiment in democracy and individualism looked ahead with optimism. They cleared land, planted seed, sowed crops, bought slaves, and flourished. Settlement was scattered, and plenty of land was available. For many new arrivals, the West beckoned. But Edward was not as footloose as some of his countrymen. He married Rachel Hollowell, and the couple had three sons: Willis, Miles, and William. Edward acquired 130 acres of waterfront land about eighteen miles from Edenton off Cannon's Ferry Road. He never left. Family lore held that Edward obtained the land from the king and later fought in the Revolutionary War, but no documentation supports either claim, and the former is possibly a family witticism.[2]

Edward focused on more than worldly affairs. He was a man of faith, a Baptist when Baptism was under attack. Chowan County was considered a refuge for Quakers and Baptists being driven out of Virginia. Edward probably held serious doubts that the Anglican clergy was a force for moral and social good, and probably scorned their willingness to drink and duel as proof. Other Chowan County citizens were concerned that the community's spiritual life had reached its lowest point. Edenton then was more likely to be visited by fortunetellers, circuses, menageries, and phrenologists than clergymen. "There seemed but little religion" at Edenton, observed an aspiring preacher. The *Edenton Gazette* protested the young men "lolling in tavern piazzas and . . . gaping and sauntering about the public rooms." Others complained about "the midnight revels of sailors, or men who emulate their manners," and claimed "the Sabbath is profaned by noisy and wanton sports, and our streets so thronged by clans of Negroes, that the fair sex find it difficult to pass, without being jostled."[3]

Like his brother Edward, David was concerned that Enlightenment rationalism had overtaken American churches. Both brothers sought a more emotional Christianity. They were makers of the Second Great Awakening, which swept the United States in the first half of the nineteenth century. Baptists, Methodists, and Presbyterians flocked to revivals, which embraced a new evangelism and ebullient piety. The spirit was palpable. Missionaries graced southern parlors. Subscriptions to religious journals soared. More and more men and women kept devotional books near their bedsides. Camp meetings—often with hot suppers—were everywhere.

In Chowan County, David became the first pastor of Ballard's Bridge Church, where he frequently held revivals. He taught that salvation was not God's preordained judgment but up to the free will of the individual. He stressed the need for adult baptism, but only when the individual made the conscious decision to be "born again." Pastors like David fostered the young nation's individualistic spirit, passion for civic involvement, and confidence. A person's destiny was entirely self-determined in this country.

Edward's son, Miles, followed his uncle David, who died in 1783, into the clergy at Ballard's Bridge. His Baptist faith was central in his life, and his King James Bible was his most treasured possession. Miles's pastoral service lasted from 1826 to 1837, the year of his death. Miles lived up to his pledges against worldliness. He didn't take a nickel for preaching the Gospel. He wanted neither wealth nor status. He sought redemption through Christ. And he believed that his slaves should be availed the same thing as Whites. His church contained a gallery in the rear for slaves to hear his sermons.[4]

Miles's revivals—when souls experienced the power of the spirit and conversion—must have been something to witness. Folks reached ecstatic states of consciousness. Knees buckled. Bodies trembled. Joyful voices cried out. Miles probably warned his flock to flee the wrath of God to come. He distinguished the righteous from the unrighteous and believed in original sin. He was probably quick to evaluate and condemn the morals of offenders. Since the Bible was inerrant, Miles prohibited dancing, scorned drinking, encouraged the chastisement of the sinful. He ostracized drunkards, believing the dirt farmer's cheap pleasure—the little brown jug—was a curse. Yet those who were read the riot act from Miles rarely turned away from their church family. They grew despondent without its spiritual fellowship.[5]

The Welches believed in primogeniture. Family success was made possible by hard work, but careful family—and estate—planning were also important. Up until the outbreak of the Civil War, Robert Welch's male heirs—Edward, Willis, William Drew—made careful wills to centralize land holdings and prioritize the first-born males who received the bulk of the land. But second, third, and fourth children got secondary holdings, such as farming equipment and draft animals. The upshot was a family whose male heirs—despite clear advantages over their siblings—lent support. If any grudges were held through the generations, the bare genealogical record does not yield any evidence.[6]

By all accounts, Miles enjoyed living next door to his brother Willis, who was also a pillar of Chowan County. In their twenties, the two built a large, white frame house near Cannon Ferry. According to family oral history, fire consumed the home in the early nineteenth century, but the family quickly rebuilt, and the new house—Robert Welch's eventual birthplace—became the family gathering spot for generations. Family members remember that Wayside Farm, as it came to be known, contained an extensive grapevine, which reportedly originated from the Mother Vineyard on Roanoke Island. Although Edward bequeathed his son Miles the bulk of his estate, Willis apparently received enough for a marriage proposal, and on November 28, 1828—just weeks after Andrew Jackson was elected president of the United States—he married Nancy Byrum in Gates, North Carolina.

The Welches were yeomen gentry and full-time farmers when farming was the most sought-after vocation in the South. Indeed a man became a lawyer or a doctor to get a piece of land and become a planter. A contemporary of Miles wrote, "as soon as the young lawyer requires sufficient to purchase a few hundred acres of rich alluvial lands, and a few slaves, he quits his profession at once, though perhaps just rising into eminence, and turns cotton planter." They were all fiercely proud of being farmers and proud of their hero, Thomas Jefferson, who was one too. For Jefferson, agriculture was the basis of American life, and farmers were simply the best citizens alive.

Chowan County folks were Jeffersonian in their economic outlook as well. They helped neighbors with logrolling, stump grubbing, and barn raising. They believed in small government and were suspicious of an encroaching federal one. They saw much public funding as scandalous waste. Matters of roads, of schools, belonged to the states and localities.[7]

They also loved President Jackson. As fighting Democrats, they faced down their foes with the same ferocity that Jackson reserved for the Bank of the United States. They probably saw the bank as Jackson did: an affront to American frontier democracy and a pet project of some serpentine banking elite, which sought to foreclose upon the homes of their loved ones and hold hostage the American people. As the market system ascended, their hatred toward the bank belied their fear of uncertainty. Their views may have been exaggerated, but their fears were very real. Many of Robert's forebears came to embrace what Richard Hofstadter later called the "paranoid style"—that impersonal forces were boxing them in and conspiring against them.

Also like Jackson, the citizens of Chowan County hated tariffs. In those years, manufacturing boomed in the Northeast. The West experienced growth from immigration and expansion. But the South fell backward, and many saw the tariff as the source of the problem. Some envisioned a northern cabal since their cotton was not protected by the tariff, but Yankee manufacturers, who bought southern cotton for their own textile goods, were so protected.

Some Chowan citizens grew increasingly concerned that this northern mercantile elite was becoming too powerful. Its network seemed to extend to Washington, extracting government subsidies of credit and transportation and producing economic dislocations. Rumors circulated even that Washington would abolish slavery. Southern preachers grew more suspicious of the northerners' supposed philanthropy, commercialism, and seemingly ubiquitous itinerant preaching. Some spoke of an eastern conspiracy of elites intent on stealing what little wealth remained in the South and the West.[8] Talk of conspiracy by the northern mercantile elite infused the southern planter elite's discourse, and even entered the Welch household.

After all, like Jackson, Willis owned slaves—one of whom shared a name with "Old Hickory." Willis was yeomen gentry, lived as a courtly southern gentleman, and his Jacksonian worldview informed his view of slavery: the federal government had no business meddling in what was a local issue.

We do not know how well or ill Willis treated his slaves, but as a whole, force defined the relationship between master and slave. Often driven by sexual desires, planters treated their property according to their whims. Another sordid aspect of the institution was the possibility at any time of familial separation. At slave auctions, children sobbed uncontrollably as their mothers were sold to speculators and fathers stood by helpless. For most, it was the last time they ever saw their loved ones.[9]

During Edward's middle age, the institution of slavery appeared to be dying in the United States, but Eli Whitney's invention of the cotton gin reinvigorated it. More than fifty times more efficient than handpicking, the cotton gin separated seed from fiber and produced overnight a revolution. Whitney's machine made the snowy fiber profitable again, and the South, and Chowan County, now bowed to King Cotton. Willis personally believed slavery to be biblically sound, and no evidence suggests that he entertained any guilt about owning slaves. If he had doubts, passages from the Bible condoning the "peculiar institution" probably assuaged them.[10]

Other southern churchmen went even further. They said that slavery was a positive good; it contributed to human progress. They held that Blacks were better off in America than Africa. Slavery gave planters the opportunity to shed their worldly worries, helping them to live more cultivated lives of the mind. It also liberated Whites from the factory floor—a powerful argument in an age of White supremacy.

As slavery grew in numbers, and arguments for slavery grew too, Chowan County citizens developed the tendency to imagine slave insurrections. During the War of 1812, some worried that with the young men away, Blacks might revolt. One warned every resident "who has not arms in his house; immediately procure them" to defend against enemies—here, Blacks—"which may spring up in our bosom!"[11] A historian of Chowan County called such fears "groundless": "The Negro population gave no cause for alarm during the war." That such fears may have been delusional, however, did not make them any less real. Many still slept at night with guns under their pillows.

Chowan County newspaper accounts by Whites present a community under great duress and often besieged by attacks from Black runaways. In February 1819, the *Gazette* reported the capture of "General Jackson," "the desperate and noted ringleader of the band of runaway Negroes, who have for a long time been depredating upon the property of the good citizens of the Town and County." A short time later, armed citizens located a hideout for runaways in a hollow gum tree large enough "to contain six persons with much comfort," and killed their leader "Jack Stump" in a fierce pistol exchange.

In 1831 Nat Turner led a slave insurrection in Southampton County, Virginia, only seventy miles away. His fellow insurgents—a band of fifty or sixty Blacks—used firearms and axes to slaughter fifty Whites, including women and children. The Nat Turner revolt left the planter class frozen with fear. Panic consumed Chowan County. Nineteen Blacks were arrested and jailed in Edenton. As a local historian observed, "the white reaction was, as usual, disproportionate to the seriousness of the situation. The Negro slave was never so sinister as his master imagined." Again, that that reaction was disproportionate did not make Chowan citizens feel any less surrounded or vigilant.[12] Again, more Chowan citizens grasped tightly their guns at night. They probably prayed more often because it seemed that they were all surrounded by an invisible force.

In 1834, Willis and Nancy Welch welcomed their son, William Drew, into the world. Rising tensions between North and South predominated throughout his youth and reached a fatal crescendo with the election to the presidency of an Illinois lawyer named Abraham Lincoln in 1860. Civil War engulfed the nation, and the Welch family sided with the Confederacy. Their greatest fears had become reality. The Welches and their neighbors, who sold tickets for lavish balls to raise money for the boys in gray, sought to preserve their property, which included their slaves.[13]

In April 1861, just after the newly inaugurated president issued his call for 75,000 volunteers in response to the firing on Fort Sumter, my great-great grandfather George O. Miller, a shoemaker from Hingham, Massachusetts, signed up to end slavery in the United States forever. For the Confederacy, twenty-seven-year-old William Drew enlisted as a private. Drew was part of the first Civil War regimen to be raised in North Carolina. He belonged to the "Chowan Dixie Boys," the first volunteer regiment's Company M. After the war, they were memorialized as the "Bethel Regiment" for their contributions to the Confederate victory in the Battle of Big Bethel. Like George O. Miller's for the North, William Drew's service for the South was short. Mustered out in November 1861, he returned to Chowan County, acquired land worth $1,500 in 1870, and married Fannie Hollowell Welch. The couple's two sons followed: Robert Henry Winborne in 1871, and William Dorsey in 1873.[14]

When the Civil War ended, emancipation afforded human dignity to freed slaves but wiped out their former masters' investment.

The Welches' slaves were a major source of the family's wealth and status, and when both disappeared, family members grew even more anxious. The Millers also suffered great hardship. All four of George's brothers served for the Union. Two suffered lifelong disabilities, and another, Henry Felt, was killed in action. But matters were worse for the Welches. If the Welches had invested in Confederate bonds, those moneys were lost forever. During Republican-led Reconstruction, the Welches identified the Party with misrule, military occupation, and government by carpetbaggers; as a result, they became even more firmly ensconced in the Democratic Party.

Like many southern counties after the war, Chowan County was in shambles. Population fell; fewer persons lived there in 1870 than 1820. Thick green weeds covered fields where fleecy cotton fiber once grew. Farmers had trouble locating seed. Livestock grew sparse and spindly. Rampant inflation shut down banks and corner stores. The county avoided the large-scale pillaging and foraging that ravaged other communities, but education remained inadequate and roads—dusty in the summer and muddy in the fall and spring—were still bone shaking. Antebellum estates may have escaped looting but their value plummeted, and they were often sold to buyers who divided them into smaller holdings.

With their slaves departing, the Welches needed to do more physical labor. In 1874, William Drew died, leaving behind a widow, two young sons, and his elderly father, Willis. In their prime working years—their thirties and forties—brothers Robert and William lived through decades of much hardship. The rise in sharecropping gave the family a stable and cheap workforce, but the crop lien system made farming supplies more expensive. Interest rates skyrocketed after the war, and cotton prices fell. As a result, farmers were often in debt. They planted more and more cotton to cover the debt. They also began offering merchants some of their cotton as collateral. This produced a vicious circle since crop prices were still falling, encouraging farmers to grow more cotton, and pushing them further into debt. Some exasperated yeoman farmers became sharecroppers themselves.[15]

Citizens of Chowan scorned the "better elements" of the North and saw an eastern conspiracy in everything. Elite bankers were taking advantage of the remaining wealth in the South. We do not know whether Robert or William harbored any of these views, but many North Carolina farmers came to view the merchants, bankers, and railroad promoters—increasingly based in the postwar North—as the enemy and issued their wrath accordingly. They believed international bankers conspired against them. As their voices grew louder and more heated, they became conspiratorial, overly suspicious, and apocalyptic. The style harkened back to the fantastical hyperbole of an earlier time. It evoked the irrational conclusions of some Pilgrims and Puritans who claimed that the Church of England wanted to beat back the Protestant Reformation and restore Roman Catholicism throughout the land. It drew on the ideology of the American Revolution and its popular yet exaggerated claim that King George wanted to enslave colonists. This newest manifestation evoked the antebellum hot mind that worried about a cabal of financiers, abolitionists, and members of the Republican Party seeking to eradicate slavery and enslave the South. Both North and South during the period of 1850 to 1866 saw conspiracies: slaveholders observed that abolitionists were fomenting slave insurrections, while abolitionists in the North were highlighting that the "Cotton kingdom" of the South was omnipotent.[16]

"Once thought of as the backbone of Society, farmers by the 1880s had come to be considered hicks, hayseeds, and wool hatters, ignorant country bumpkins left out of a modern, rapidly industrializing Society," observed historian Milton Ready. "Farmers had little place. Something had gone terribly wrong for them," he added. They blamed the 1873 financial collapse—what became known as the Great Crime of 1873—on financial kingpin Jay Cooke, the chief financier of the Civil War in the North, after his company, heavily invested in railroads, fell apart. The economy deteriorated, a panic ensued, and farmers suffered miserably. Farmers concluded that boom and bust cycles usually meant nothing but bust for them.[17]

The farmers became activists for the cause of inflationary politics, calling for the issuance of greenbacks, or "cheap money," which, they concluded, would allow them to pay their debts. When President Ulysses Grant vetoed a bill in 1874 to issue more greenbacks and, with an 1875 measure, defiantly withdrew greenbacks in circulation, farmers saw more evidence of a conspiracy of Cooke, J. P. Morgan, and other devilish financiers of the North.[18]

Massive amounts of capital financed steel, manufacturing, the burgeoning railroad industry, the refining of petroleum. Morgan halted a drain of gold from the federal treasury by establishing an international syndicate. Farmers in deep debt and suffering from depressed prices were trapped in a downward spiral and, unfortunately, sought out scapegoats. Farmers accounted for their plight by blaming international Jewish bankers. The Jewish international conspiracy, they said, had its inception in Europe. Many Americans came to embrace simple solutions.

In truth, impoverished farmers were caught up in more complicated circumstances. The sequestration of their slaves had given way to sharecropping, the crop lien system, and tenancy. Tenancy, the 1888 *Progressive Farmer* averred, was "a worse curse to North Carolina than droughts, floods, cyclones, storms, . . . caterpillars, and every other evil that attends the farmer." Between 1865 and 1895, farm prices dropped by one-half. The international cotton market also had a detrimental impact on American farmers. Filling the vacuum caused by the stoppage of American cotton exports during the Civil War were Brazil, India, and Egypt. Soon, a superabundance of the fleecy fiber pushed down prices, increased farmer debt, and accelerated loss of land. Along with the various economic depressions throughout the 1870s, 1880s, and 1890s, farmers cursed the integration of the international cotton community.[19]

Robert became a great success in selling his staple market items. Diversification of crops underlay his success. He traveled on horseback to manage operations and directed his hired hands, both Black and White. Unlike his father and grandfather, who grew only cotton, Robert raised corn and pigs too. Farmers like Robert appreciated corn's versatility because the yellow grain could be fed to the pigs. His religion, however, prohibited distilling the corn into liquor. He slaughtered his hogs and sent the hams to market. Robert and his brother William rose above the hardship surrounding them and became a terrific success. Whereas many farmers struggled during the 1890s—as the populist revolt and the divisive election of 1896 attested—for Robert and William, it was the Gay '90s.

With improving financial conditions, Robert also proved to be lucky in love. In 1896, he met Lina Verona James, who had moved in

August 1895 to Chowan County from Pasquotank County to serve as principal and schoolteacher of Warwick High School, a one-room country school in Edenton. Lina James was an accomplished piano player, a devotee of English literature, especially Chaucer, Shakespeare, and Dickens. She had attended Murphreesboro College and graduated from North Carolina Normal where she studied literature, art, and music. Lina's family tree resembled the Welches'. Her father had won laurels as a soldier for the Confederacy in the Civil War but died soon thereafter. Her widowed mother remarried.[20]

Lina Verona James had classic features. Strikingly attractive with intense and intelligent eyes, taut thin lips, and jutting jaw. Her stern visage masked her vivacity, spontaneity, and love for life. In one photo, she appears as the quintessential Gibson girl with a flamboyant dark ribbon in her hair, an embroidered linen dress, and a tight collar of ruffled lace. She was loquacious and loved singing hymns and playing the piano. She had flawless manners and spotless etiquette, and enjoyed hosting dinner parties. She was devoted to her Baptist faith, reading and committing the Bible to memory. Robert was smitten, Lina fell equally in love, and the couple married on September 29, 1898. They made a handsome pair. Robert was well muscled, square jawed, with chiseled features, baby-blue penetrating eyes, and jet-black hair cut tight. Her positivity and liveliness were the perfect complement to Robert, who could be gruff, austere, taciturn, despondent. Lina lightened Robert's burdens; she could make him laugh. They enjoyed each other's company, reading newspapers and periodicals, and discussing great books from the Western canon. They sat before roaring fires reading classic literature, singing happy ditties, and sharing tales of ancestors long gone. By all accounts, Robert appreciated the education he received from his marriage. They were deeply in love.[21]

By the late 1890s, conditions for farmers had improved. With the discovery of gold in South Africa and Brazil, global gold output tripled in production from 1880 to 1890. More gold meant more money in circulation. Robert's brother had even more success. He entered politics on the heels of the populist movement, which had revolutionized North Carolina politics. The Populists, or the People's Party, grew out of the Farmers' Alliance and assailed Wall Street, the harvester trust, the barbed wire trust, and anybody or anything else that seemed to have farmers in thrall. They called for a graduated income tax, nationalizing the railroads, and the free coinage of silver. As economic problems had flattened farmers throughout the 1880s, northeastern North Carolina became an epicenter for this agricultural movement, and Leonidas Polk became a central figure in it. With his flowing black beard, stern visage, and chiseled features, Polk said that cause of the farmers' plight rested with the merchants and railroad titans. Polk became the president of the Southern Farmers' Alliance with 90,000 strong in 1890 in North Carolina. He spearheaded the national effort to establish warehouses for farmers to store their crops when prices fell. Polk helped bring farmers into the legislature, which in 1891 established North Carolina State University, an agricultural college, and formed a state railroad commission, which checked rates and practices.[22]

Polk likely would have been the Populists' presidential contender in 1892 had he not died; instead, James Weaver assumed the mantle of leadership. In the 1880s, the Democratic Party of North Carolina restricted the suffrage rights of Blacks, proclaiming itself "the white man's party." Populists tread carefully on race and acquired power in North Carolina by "fusing" with Republicans, especially Black ones, into a highly successful political coalition. In 1894 a fusion government took over both houses of the state legislature—the first defeat of the Bourbon Democrats since Reconstruction. This government rolled back some anti-suffrage provisions, leading to increased Black turnout in the gubernatorial elections of 1896. The return of Blacks to the electorate was only brief, however.[23]

As the 1890s progressed, the Democratic Party—both in North Carolina and nationally—increasingly co-opted the populist message and platform. In the presidential election of 1896, William Jennings Bryan stole the Populists' thunder by making free silver the central campaign issue. Populism's decline produced a new racial order in the South. As late as the 1880s, Blacks helped elect Black state legislators in North Carolina and Virginia. Redeemers—Democratic southern White supremacists—made the case that political power in the hands of Blacks threatened the physical safety and racial purity of White women. Voting for Populists or Republicans, they said, was a danger to White supremacy. Starting with Mississippi in 1890 and South Carolina in 1895, southern states introduced literacy tests and poll taxes to take voting rights away predominately from Black citizens. By 1906, all southern states had moved to eliminate the African American vote. Literacy tests and poll taxes were backed up with violence. One North Carolinian threatened to disfranchise Blacks if he had to "chok[e] the Cape Fear River with bodies of [N]egroes" and did gun down Blacks in the street. After 1900, as few Blacks risked their lives to vote, the South became solidly Democratic. As late as 1940, only 3 percent of African Americans in the South were registered voters.[24]

Robert's brother William, a Democratic state representative from Black-majority Chowan, was elected in 1898, served one term, and supported a successful constitutional amendment that eliminated Blacks' voting rights and cemented White rule. The *News and Observer* of Raleigh cheered: "From the mountains to the sea there is no disagreement or discord that seriously impedes the united and harmonious work necessary to insure success. Silver men, gold men, expansionists, anti-expansionists, dispensary men, prohibitionists and advocates of saloons have buried their differences in order to make permanent white supremacy in North Carolina." William himself observed: "The situation in Chowan is favorable" and "the Democrats are for it to a man and a good many Republicans and Populists will vote" for the amendment. "The negroes admit that the amendment will be adopted," Welch proclaimed, likely hoping to dampen Black voting.[25] Representative Welch was less cavalier and hyperbolic and more humble about the amendment's importance and implications than were some other backers. "This is a fight for the salvation of the white race," observed Representative Carroll of Alamance County. "Every white man who . . . still love[s] the Anglo-Saxon race and the state of North Carolina more than they do the negro and the Republican Party, will . . . vote for permanent White Supremacy."[26]

2
Stockton, 1899–1910

The son of Lina Verona James and Robert Henry Winborne Welch, Sr., Robert Henry Winborne Welch, Jr. was born on December 1, 1899 in Chowan County. Robert grew up happy and healthy. Among his siblings—two brothers and three sisters—Robert was unquestionably his mother's favorite. That circumstance likely contributed to a fateful sibling rivalry with his younger brother James.[1] Robert and James fought unmercifully.

In 1903, Robert Senior and his brother William purchased a 500-acre piece of property 9 miles from Elizabeth City, near the village of Woodville in Perquimans County. Stockton—named for Commodore Robert F. Stockton of Mexican-American War fame—was Robert Junior's boyhood home. It was handsome with elaborate ornamentation inside and out.[2] Stockton is "one of the most attractive home places in northeastern North Carolina," observed an Elizabeth City newspaper, years later. In 1911, Robert Senior described the house as "located nearly in the center of a sixteen-acre lot and has 238 trees of almost every variety known to the forests of this section, as the grove was trimmed up out of the natural forest almost 100 years ago. The entire lawn is set with native grass." Stockton is a testament to the great reverence for the "Lost Cause" of the Confederacy during Robert's childhood. "It is one of the few of those large plantations which survived the wreck of that fateful war that abolished the institution of slavery. . . . Today there are all the conditions of the 'fo de war' time, save only the slave," wrote the *Tar Heel*. "The broad verandas and lofty columns of the old mansion give it a stately appearance. . . . The old home in many ways gives evidence of the splendor and opulence in which [a] typical Southern gentleman lived. A visit to the old home impresses one with an idea of those conditions which prevailed in the South 50 or 75 years ago, and the likes of which the world never saw before and, in all probability, will never see again. Those days, with their peculiar customs, had their advantages, but many were the disadvantages. The Stockton homestead is approached by a broad avenue, which is lined by beautiful shade trees on either side. The spacious yard is dotted with majestic trees, which form a beautiful grove. . . . This grove was a rendezvous for the social pleasures of that olden time," the paper wrote nostalgically.[3] Robert Senior loved Stockton. He remarked in 1921 that it would take about $100,000 for him to sell it.

Built after the style of Thomas Jefferson's Monticello, the homestead has four Doric columns on its portico "project[ing] a monumentality that the diminutive proportions belie," as one observed. "The entrance featuring Greek key motifs opens into a formal hall. . . . All interior woodwork is distinguished by Greek Revival Motiffs." The central block extended to three rooms to the rear and included the dining room and kitchen. The north wing contained the sitting and drawing rooms, where young Robert read by candlelight in the evening; the southern wing held Lina's beloved piano. Imagine nine-year-old sandy-haired Robert bounding up its front stairs in overalls and barefoot to hear his mother play.[4]

It could be dangerous for a child growing up on a plantation at the turn of the twentieth century. He could get hurt, lost in the woods, thrown from a mule, trampled by a wild boar, or injured by another boy's firearm. Robert enjoyed exploring books more than exploring verdant forests and riding horses. But he and James were never lonely; their community was very close-knit, and neighbors came together to raise a barn, marvel at a new piece of machinery, and celebrate July Fourth in style. As a five-year-old, with book in hand, he loved to sit on the edge of Stockton's porch, dangling his feet, and perhaps eating a ham sandwich, his favorite snack. On scorching summer days, he skinny-dipped at the mile-wide Little River. Robert giddily rode horses and romped through rolling meadows alongside cousins and other playmates. Under the shade of an oak tree, Robert read Dickens.

He loved *A Tale of Two Cities* and enjoyed reading *A Christmas Carol* in season. Into the wee hours of the morning, he read Shakespeare. At nine, the boy with a great big imagination from all the books he read probably staged his own reenactments of his heroes from history and literature. Perhaps on one occasion, he pretended to be Natty Bump, the lonely, audacious figure from James Fenimore Cooper's *Last of the Mohicans*. Maybe the next moment he was Thomas "Stonewall" Jackson standing defiantly on a hillock and inspiring confidence for the Confederacy. For his next act, maybe he staged the Battle of New Orleans and played the pugnacious and valiant Andrew Jackson, marching into the city for a belated but resounding victory.[5]

The Welch household encouraged southern ways, routines, and attitudes. The family deeply admired the forebears who took up arms against the North. Baptist faith was also central to the household. Robert Senior, Lina, and the children bowed down and said their prayers every morning, noon, and night. Robert Senior gave the blessing before each meal. Lina played Bible hymns on her piano. Some orchard owners transformed apples and peaches into brandy, but these Welches were not into fruit juices. Robert Junior's parents never smoke or drank, and their faith prohibited swearing, drinking, and smoking. But eventually Robert resisted and became a heavy smoker of cigars. "When I was 25 years old," Robert recalled, "and had never smoked even one cigarette in my life, I bought a box of Robert Burns cigars and deliberately set out to learn to like them. My success at that task was remarkable!" He smoked up to twenty cigars a day for fifty years, with few breaks. The adult Robert also drank, typically two Manhattans or Black Russians when eating out.

Yet as a child, he constantly sought his parents' approval. While he could do no wrong in his mother's eyes, the opposite seemed true in his father's. When he was five years old, Robert watched as his father handed his mother a cotton bloom. "I'll bet it's the first cotton bloom this year in the whole county," his father said. His mother was excited: "That's wonderful, Mr. Welch. It's a sign of a good crop to come." Robert came up with an idea: if one cotton bloom could make his mother happy, imagine what a whole bunch would do? When he came across more of the little white flowers he retrieved a large basket to collect as many that would fit. But when he returned home and saw his father's livid face, he knew that something had gone horribly wrong. Robert had picked hundreds of blooms before they formed the cotton bolls, which was the family source of income. Robert was dumbfounded. "Don't be too harsh with Robert," Lina asked of her husband. Saying nothing, Robert Senior walked out to the barn and continued the work of his day. Robert spent the next thirty years trying to gain his father's approbation. Robert came to hope that academic achievement or financial success would bring the approval from his distant, aloof, and demanding father that his mother granted unconditionally.[6]

Robert Senior had grand expectations for Robert Henry Winborne Welch, his oldest and brightest child. Patriarchy mattered in this time and place, as did primogeniture, which afforded Robert ample advantages over his brothers and sisters. From a young age, he was expected to strive and thrive, and to be better off than his parents. "The danger of slippage," as Bertram Wyatt-Brown wrote, "was never far from the thoughts of wary elders" in the postbellum South. "Anxiety to preserve and ambition to recover family fortunes were constant refrains in advice to the young."[7] Robert and his siblings heard the stories of their grandparents' poverty and loss of status. Reminders of "slippage" were all around Robert—dilapidated homes, hungry neighbors, and thin livestock—and only fortified the warnings of the importance of providence, self-reliance, and entrepreneurialism. For Robert, like many young men throughout the postbellum South, the past was a heavy weight to carry and one not so easy to escape. Failure to live up to expectations could bring shame and guilt.

It would be an understatement to say that Lina's love for her son Robert was unqualified. Lina's idolatry gave Robert the sense that he was worthy of something special and beholden to make his way in the world. As Sigmund Freud said, a "man who has been the indisputable favorite of his mother keeps for life the feeling of a conqueror." Lina proudly dressed the cherubic toddler in fashionable sailor suits with fine brass buttons, nautical collars, and short pants that met at the knee. When he grew a little older, she donned him in the Little Lord Fauntleroy style: knickerbockers, buckled shoes, and ruffled shirt.

The student was extremely precocious, but even Lina—who was a hard-driving teacher—must have been thunderstruck by his progress. Robert was reading children's books on his own by his third birthday.

Lina exposed Robert to mathematics at the age of three, and he took a liking to the subject. At age four, Robert was learning his multiplication tables and reading. He was doing algebra at six and was proficient in Latin at seven. He completed many of his lessons in arithmetic, language, and literature in the large davenport-like swing on the porch. Lessons began in the morning after a hearty breakfast. They continued until Robert broke for a nap. In the midafternoon, Robert resumed his studies. In the summer, he often took his little rocking chair to the south side of the house and placed it down in a patch of thick, green grass. He sat in the sun reading until the intense sun forced him inside. He would return to the same spot in the cooler hours of the afternoon for three more hours of study.

His favorite subject was history, and he became mesmerized by the tales of soldiers, political leaders, and other great men. At the age of five or six, he became enchanted with the adventures of Julius Caesar after reading Ridpath's *History of the World*. One evening during supper, he asked his father: "Do you think Kazar was a good man or a bad man?" "Who's Kazar?" his father asked his mother. "Oh, you know Kazar," Robert answered. "He was a very famous Roman general. In fact, they thought he wanted to be king. Everyone knows who Julius Kazar was."[8]

Lina did not fear that Robert would become too bookish or refuse to follow his father into farming. Lina committed her life to passing on to her offspring her joy of learning—what Robert later called "the romance of education." Her husband was very proud of her learning and her accomplishments and believed that the proper role of a wife was to bring culture to her children. Her passion for learning surpassed his, and he probably found it peculiar that his son was beginning his intellectual journey at such an early age. Robert Senior relaxed by playing cards, listening to red seal records on his cabinet Victrola, and reading *Harper's Magazine*, *Cosmopolitan*, *Review of Reviews*, *New York World*, and Elizabeth City's *Independent*. Yet it was unfashionable and unmanly for fathers to loiter over the cradle or become involved in domestic affairs, save to deliver punishments, which could be fearsome. Robert, unlike his brother James, was not subject to his father's wrath. Lina intervened to restrain Robert Senior when it came to punish Robert, but not her other offspring. But the love was abundant in the Welch home. Robert Senior never enjoyed disciplining any of his children.

Other family members impressed virtues upon the boys. Robert was reminded of the importance of financial security and sensibility with money by both his father and his Aunt Viola, who was a frequent visitor. Aunt Viola reminded him, "Just money cannot make any teacher, or any other worthwhile human being happy."

The Welch family enjoyed a very positive reputation in the community. By the second decade of the century, Robert Senior was hailed in his local newspaper as "one of the most successful farmers and one of the best citizens in Northeastern North Carolina." Robert Senior was known to be hard working, honest, and a keen businessman. In 1921, the *Independent* observed there is an "unmistakable air of prosperity about Stockton." He appreciated straight-talking folks who presented their views without dissembling. Robert Senior also loathed braggarts. "My father used to say of a certain neighbor: 'if I could buy him for what he really is worth, and sell him for what he thinks he is worth, I'd be a millionaire.'" Lina was known as a good mother and a fine teacher. The papers carried no stories of idleness, scandal, or malfeasance around the Welch name.[9]

In addition to his wise diversification into both livestock and produce, Robert Senior's investment in machinery played a factor in his success. As the farm increasingly became a factory, the availability of time-saving and back-saving machines was a double-edged sword for farmers. Farmers became even more tied to banking, manufacturing, and railroading, as they bought costly machines to plant and gather their produce. Successful use of the new equipment required prudence, stellar organization, and a large amount of luck. In bad times—frequent depressions, a volatile global arena—poor administration of farm machinery could wreak much havoc. Farmers often blamed the bankers and the railroads rather than themselves for their failures. Robert's efficiency meant he could pay off his debts faster than most farmers. He observed, "I will have to confess that though born on a farm and working on one all my life, I never owned a piece of machinery to do farm work till a friend sent me *The Progressive Farmer* to read about three years ago. Since then I have . . . bought farm machinery. How have I succeeded with the machinery? Well, to make a long story short it is all paid for, though I started seven years ago several thousand dollars in debt."

The bulk of the farm chores went to Robert's younger brother James. "Everyone else had chores, but not Robert," observed one sister. "We didn't interrupt Robert because Robert was studying or reading, or Robert was taking a nap." That Robert received a dispensation accelerated the sibling rivalry between him and James. As someone who came to understand the relationship related: "James would wait until Robert was napping, and then do something deliberately to wake him up. Robert then would begin the chase. James would go running all over the house and finally out a window onto the porch roof and down the lightning rod onto the yard below, always two steps ahead of his pursuer. Finally Robert would give up and go back to his room to continue his studies or even try to nap again. On cue, James would return to his self-assigned task of harassment and the Tom and Jerry chase would begin anew. Eventually, Robert would catch his tormentor and tie him to the pump or lock him in one of the storage rooms under the house." "In the end," Robert's sister explained, "it was always James who got the whipping" from father.

Robert Senior was a hard worker and an even more intense manager. He rose before dawn and roused James and the hired hands from their comfortable slumbers. By early dawn, James was wrestling livestock, milking cows, and watering the animals. He weeded the garden and rotated the crops. James and the men worked the land until dusk. As James grew older, he was assigned even more responsibilities, including for the farm machinery. During the 1910s, James ran the family steel mule—the gasoline engine tractor. James and his father appreciated such new mechanical wonders, which replaced the last century's binder, corn planter, gang plow, and manure spreader. The mechanized dynamos and the manure allowed them to cultivate more fields faster, hire fewer workers, and strain fewer work animals. The new equipment was unpredictable and unreliable, however. James often found himself back in the nineteenth century when the equipment broke down, shocking wheat, plowing cotton, and tilling corn while peering at the backside of a mule or horse.

Childhood games stoked the boys' competitive fires as well. They invented a game like Monopoly. They divided up sections of the house as property and used acorns for monopoly money. One sibling recalled that James proved to be the better businessman and financier, winning most matches. This greatly perturbed Robert, but this fact was a harbinger of their business careers. As somebody who knew the family well remembered, "Robert was the theoretician, the philosopher, and the salesman. James was the practitioner, the businessman, and the financier."

Robert's sisters did not begrudge Robert's high intelligence and enjoyed it when he delivered lectures or explained things to them. They loved his recitations of poetry, but one later recalled her mother was perhaps too approving of Robert, suggesting that the result was that later he thought he could do no wrong. "It's a wonder we weren't all jealous of him because of all the favoritism he received," one sister recalled, "due to his high intelligence. But we weren't, with the exception of James, who felt a natural brotherly competition. Actually, we were all very close and felt no animosity toward him at all, simply because he gave us no occasion to." But Robert never suffered fools at any point throughout his life. Another sister observed that "he tended to give you an inferiority complex when you were around him. If he told you something once and you didn't remember it, that was bad. If he told you something twice, and you still couldn't repeat it, you were a dumnkopft."[10]

3
Elizabeth City, Raleigh, Annapolis, 1910–1919

By age seven, Robert had not spent much time with children of his own age. For this reason, Lina sent Robert to the public school in Woodville, about one mile and a half away. Woodville was a village of approximately three stores, the community church, and modest homes. Each day, Robert walked to the one-room schoolhouse, toting his lunch in a pail. There, Miss Wood taught boys and girls who were Robert's age, but also some who were much older. One of those older boys was Trim Wilson, who needed to learn algebra, but Miss Woods, whose own education was limited to high school, had never learned algebra. Seven-year-old Robert spent the next six months teaching algebra to Trim and Miss Woods alike.[1]

In autumn 1910, Lina concluded that Robert was ready for high school. The nearest one, however, was ten miles away in Elizabeth City. Ten-year-old Robert, his father, and mother, traveled by horse and buggy to the Raleigh Hotel there. Years earlier Robert's great-great-great grandfather had made many trips along the same stumpy and bumpy roads. He would unload his bulging bales of cotton on ships bound to England, received pounds sterling for his efforts, and returned a richer man. Now, Robert kissed his mother goodbye; for the school year, he would live alone in the Raleigh Hotel during the week. His parents would pick him up on Friday night, travel to Stockton for the weekend, and drive him back on Monday morning.

The year must have been filled with wonder, adventure, and fun. The citizens of booming Elizabeth City had turned a swampland into a thriving but anxious community of canneries, brickyards, and textile mills. The river town's population had trebled with the advent of the Elizabeth City and Norfolk Railroad in 1881. Boatyards and machine shops were quickly constructed. Trade also picked up considerably along the Dismal Swamp Canal, which connected Albemarle Sound with Norfolk and the Chesapeake Bay. Many residents were hardworking and law abiding, but many wondered how long the good times would last.[2]

His year at the Raleigh was not like the boarding school experiences that children of northeastern elites underwent. He had no peers to share his fears and dreams. He was a ten-year-old living by himself in a shantytown hotel replete with transients, hustlers, prostitutes, vagabonds, and drifters. Elizabeth City also had a reputation for danger and mystery. Less than ten years earlier, the town had become notorious for the sudden disappearance of nineteen-year-old Nell Cropsey. The killer was never found despite numerous suspects, the involvement of various detectives, bloodhounds and psychics, and the case remains unsolved to this day.[3]

Robert kept his eyes in books and on the bustle of the city. Despite probably being lonely, he powered through and used his great concentration to hush his insecurities and strive for excellence in his work. His ability to surmount the challenges of adult life at ten gave him confidence and a sense of belonging in the adult world. He probably devoured Doctor Palemon John's *Republican Weekly*, the *North Carolinian*, and W. O. Saunders's *Independent*. He also saw things that he had only before read about, and the world opened up before his eyes. The wharf bustled as railway workers packed fish and fowl with ice into baskets and barrels and out onto trains. On schooners and mothboats, dockhands packed fresh catches of rockfish, hogfish, Spanish mackerel, sturgeon, and oysters with fresh ice before shipping them out. He saw the railroad yard with the telegraph poles, stacks of tires, switches and steam. Sawmills with their bigtooth blades buzzed piney-smelling logs all day. Bobbin spinners made goods at a frenzied pace. He saw the textile workers bringing industry to the South, suffering browned lungs in the process. Canners and oyster shuckers found merriment and debauchery in the thirteen saloons, while minstrel and vaudeville shows entertained crowds at the Academe of Music.[4]

Robert successfully passed the tenth-grade examination at Elizabeth City High School and entered as a junior. A newspaper described him as "in knee britches and looking more like a child than a college youth. . . . In fact, he is so very youthful in appearance that he was pronounced immune when the hazers set about their pranks." Another newspaper observed: "The lad has a marked predilection for mathematics, finding the solution of pons asinorum and other difficult problems in this line as simple as the multiplication table was to him at the age of four." This first year away from home shaped his character and made him a stronger person. His two years living alone fostered his enviable drive and his indomitable spirit in the face of dubious odds.[5] It was never to leave him.

At twelve, Robert became the youngest student ever to enroll at the University of North Carolina. He intended to enter the previous year, but President Venable recommended to his father that Robert wait another year. "One September a small lad disembarked at Carrboro and coming on up to the Hill as a member proceeded to register as a member of the class of '16," reads the 1916 *Yackety Yack*, the University of North Carolina yearbook. As a freshman he weighed only 75 pounds; at graduation, he weighed 126 pounds and stood five feet, nine inches. Robert belonged to the Tennis Association, the Philanthropic Literary Society, the YMCA, the Historical Society, and the Albemarle Club, a student club that studied social and economic issues in his home county. He played extended chess games with his Latin teacher, Professor Henry, on many occasions, both tending to lose track of time and miss classes to finish games. But Robert had few close friends at the university. Nothing suggests that school friends visited him or that Robert frequented their homes. Critics of Welch later said his precociousness was exaggerated by the John Birch Society. But he was a real child prodigy—a twelve-year-old freshman at one of the top universities in the country. The pictures show a child among young men.

And he flourished, at least intellectually. "Math was Bobby's hobby for his first years in college," observed the *Yack*, "but later, he decided to try a little philosophy—not with the same success he had in math, however." Throughout his life, when he mastered something, whether it was candy making or mathematics, he moved on to subjects that were not necessarily his wheelhouse. His progeny would possess the same genius for math and science. He developed a passion for solving differential equations. He then mastered German, devouring Faust and everything he could get his hands on by Johann Wolfgang von Goethe. About Faust, he later wrote, its "philosophic penetration into the questions of living make it one of the worlds masterpieces." He memorized German songs and sang them with a schoolmate. He also learned French, which opened a whole new world. Then everything changed. Learning French made him feel like a free man in Paris. "I began to feel an aroused intellectual curiosity about the world that was coming on me pretty fast. This was triggered off, I think, by my exposure to French which, since it is the language in which much of the culture of civilization had been written, opened up to me a pursuit of classical literature that I hadn't known even existed."[6]

During his first year, an English class with John M. Booker sparked his interest in poetry. Students found Booker's classroom exciting and life changing. The author Thomas Wolfe called him the "Hegel of the corn patch." Booker made a deep impression on Robert and helped make a realist out of the young boy, despite teaching Hegelian idealism. He resembled Oliver Wendell Holmes with his white mane, fur mustache, and gaunt face.

That year, the poet Alfred Noyes came for a reading of his work. Robert sat in the rear of the 800-seat college chapel as Noyes recited his poem "The Barrel Organ," his voice reaching a powerful crescendo with the line: "And now it's roaring cannon down to fight the king of France." The line apparently stuck with Robert, and his interest in poetry gradually evolved into a "love affair" and a "daily compulsion." He later said: "in a busy life of many ups and downs with interest scattered over business and family and books and games and travel, I have derived more pleasure from my long friendship with the poets than from any other source." Why did Robert become so enchanted with poetry? "There are few of the great sweeps of human thought or emotion that have not been crystallized by some poet in a single line," he observed. "There are languages full of beautiful short lyrics which tell a story; of grief or joy of triumph or despair. There are stories to express every reflection on human life and its impenetrable destiny. The poets thus put for us more forcefully, poignantly, and precisely than we can ever do in prose, the thoughts for which we grasp in our contemplative moods."[7]

He loved reciting Jean de La Fontaine's *Fables*, and later wrote: "to say that it would be worthwhile learning the French language just to read La Fontaine's *Fables* would admittedly be a slight exaggeration—but the idea is not a bad one." Gustave Nadaud's *Chansons* gave him the same satisfaction. Philosophy, at least as taught by Professor Horace Williams, gave him no such pleasure. Students and faculty adored Williams, but Robert was disappointed with his relativism. "How much was 3 times 3?" Williams asked the class. "Nine," the class dutifully replied. "Is it, really? Why couldn't we make it two or seven, or anything else we want? Numbers are merely concepts. They exist only in the mind. They may reflect something thought to be absolute, but nevertheless they are wholly the product of man's brain. Since numbers are wholly created by man, he can make them into anything he wishes. If he decide that 3×3 = 2, and if everyone agrees to accept that concept, then 3×3 does indeed equal 2." Slouching in the back of the room, Robert was having none of Williams's intellectual aerobics and "nihilistic indoctrination." Robert wrote in his notepad: "H-O-G-W-A-S-H" and flashed it for all his schoolmates to see. Williams caught sight and was not pleased. The incident did help endear Robert among his peers. Robert later said he should've been even more forceful in rejecting "that egghead nonsense because while it's possible to change number's names, it is simply not possible to change the entity of the same numbers. What we call three multiplied by what we call three equals what we call nine. You can change the names, but you don't change the reality."[8]

After graduating from college at sixteen in the fall of 1917, Robert went on his first date. He remembered: "She was 16. I was 16. . . . She was something ethereal, to be treated with the deference and homage due a fragile princess. . . . I felt that I hardly dared to breathe." The two ate ice cream cones "on a hot afternoon." "I walked with her up the path to her front door and thrilled to her smiling thanks and the handshake as we said goodbye. Thomas Moore was not only right when he said there 'is nothing half so sweet in life as Love's young dream.'" His ability to memorize poetry or literature, or sit down for hours to work out a math theorem, even as a teenager, would never leave him, and it would sweep his wife off her feet. It would also later captivate many followers in the John Birch Society, who would follow him cult-like on his many adventurers.

Robert then went to Raleigh, where he took courses toward a master's degree. But he soon lost interest, left graduate school, moved to Durham, and landed a job at Liggett & Myers Co. as an invoice checker. Robert did not inform his parents of this change of plans until after the fact. After five months of laborious, intellect-deadening work, Robert headed home to Stockton. There, his father pressed him to decide on a career. The United States was on the verge of entering World War I, and Robert wanted a piece of the action.[9] That romantic understanding of war captivated many American teens of the era. Robert was no different.

Robert Senior was a member of the local draft board and had a personal relationship with his congressman. He mentioned to his son that a commission in the navy and an appointment at Annapolis would be an excellent career choice for a boy filled with patriotism. The congressman supplied the application, but another boy got the appointment, and Robert got the unenviable distinction of being the first alternate. His only hope rested in the unlikely chance that the other boy failed the entrance examination, which he did, while Robert passed with flying colors. Robert entered the US Naval Academy in the summer of 1917. He would be a cadet! His dreams were coming true. He was going to see the world. Or so it seemed.

Because the navy needed more officers to supply ships transporting doughboys to Europe, it compressed the training program from four to three years for the duration of the war. In the summer of 1917, Robert was sworn in as a first-year plebe and became part of the largest entering class in the academy's history. The spirit was palpable. The curriculum, however, was provincial and had dire limitations. The dry, unrewarding courses failed to offer satisfactory training for anything beyond a naval career. The curriculum focused on electrical and marine engineering for engineer officers, and gunnery navigation and seamanship for deck officers. No courses in economics, biology, geography, the social sciences, ethics, or the fine arts were offered. And Robert found it terribly dull.

Instructors possessed only a little more knowledge than the students and were products of the Naval Academy as well. Instructors sought obedience and conformity, and rote learning was the preferred method. Instructors aimed not to produce supple and searching minds but students bursting with information and facts. The emphasis was on building character. Martinets dominated the cadets every hour of the day, and students were completely isolated from civilian life. Every decision was made for Robert, from his waking moment to his goodnight prayers. He felt stifled.

He grew bored. He personified a rare but emerging trend at the Naval Academy: the cadet with a college degree. Yet Robert's internal mental process was not frozen, but rather stimulated by the academic environment of the Naval Academy.[10] His imagination grew amid the daytime drudgery and regimentation. He dreamed of escaping mustard gas attacks, slaying Germans, saving his friends, and other heroics on the front. All the stories he read from his youth must have come flashing back to him, and he envisioned himself saving his fellow countrymen. Or his country, and that dream would never be extinguished. He was a man in motion. His mission was to save America. In that aspect, his mind never left the academy.

He contributed to the war effort by growing vegetable gardens. But he soon grew disappointed. Robert had thought the great war was going to be the navy's fight, but it was General John J. Pershing's army that made the most important contribution. Rather than heading "over there," Robert avidly read about the heroics of Pershing's army during the Meuse-Argonne offensive and, in the fall of 1918, the accounts of Alvin York, who single-handedly captured thirty-two Germans. But Robert thought he was supposed to be Alvin York. What the hell happened?

Robert could be irascible and was prone to caustic outbursts of temper. Throughout his life, he delivered eviscerating comebacks that punctured the thought processes of his adversaries. If his verbal comebacks burned, his letters could be stilettos that froze their victims. He also learned to channel his antipathies into fiery letters which, more often than not, were not sent but thrown into a drawer. Yet for a young man with a felicity with words and a biting, even poisonous, pen, no evidence suggests that he ever complained when his dreams were dashed. These types of disappointments must have produced some psychological crises, but we can only imagine their true effect.

Overall, the Naval Academy helped Robert broaden his experience and worldview. What captivated him most was the chance to travel and the prospects of adventure. He revered the traditions of the academy, loved the fresh uniforms and the military bearing of the plebes. But the spit-and-polish martinets and the haughty attitudes of some of the officers left him unimpressed. Both officers and upperclassmen could make the academy a grim place for some cadets. As the military historian E. B. Potter observed, some officers encouraged "the relentless weeding-out of the unfit. Plebes were subjected to 'running' by the upper classes. This, when kept within bounds, was a mild form of hazing involving no physical contact but plenty of harsh words and onerous regulations, all calculated to discourage the faint-hearted."[11] Upperclassmen penalized plebes with demerits for failing to demonstrate proper dinner etiquette, failing to stand at attention, or possessing a smudge of dirt on their uniform. Dress that line, soldier! Straighten that cap! Drop and give me twenty! Hold my mount! Dress that belt buckle! You are weak! Worthless! They were the mass men without individual spirit that Robert most loathed. They seemed enchained. Robert was a free spirit with a hint of adventure and mischief. A Huckleberry Finn.

Plebes were required to demonstrate a cheerful demeanor. They could get demerits for failing to rise early enough in the morning to warm up the toilet seats for the upperclassman. Demerits were granted if an upperclassman did not like the general bearing of the plebe or a physical characteristic like the shape of his nose—perhaps testifying to the reality of reprehensible and altogether false stereotyping about Jews in early twentieth-century American life.[12]

As a pledge, Robert was nonplussed upon receiving a demerit. But he refused to have his spirit broken or his individuality lost, and he relished the opportunity to demonstrate that it did not bother him whatsoever. He enjoyed it. Hardly an apple polisher, Robert accumulated so many demerits that his father wrote him: "I know it is exceedingly difficult not to get a few demerits, but you should be on your good behavior at all times. That is what you are in training for. A man who is careless in one of the smallest things cannot be a captain in the U.S. Navy or make a success. I am very anxious that you can lead your class this coming year at the Academy, and the record you are making now will count for or against you to a certain extent."[13] Robert listened and made the effort to accumulate fewer demerits in the second half of the school year. But the regimentation must have been excruciating for this young buck with a maverick streak.

Scholastically, Robert thrived at the academy, earning stellar marks. He rose early and studied until reveille. He discovered that his peers liked him because he was smart. He became popular and sought-after because he was very willing to assist his fellow cadets with their studies. Many cadets struggled with mathematics, which assumed prior knowledge of algebra and geometry. For Robert, this was second nature, and he earned the nickname "Savvy" for his skill as a tutor.

He met some of the closest friends in his life at the Naval Academy. Robert's best friend was Hillard "Hid" Walmer, after whom Robert later named his second son. For years, classmates were just too much older than Robert to make any sustainable bond. Because of this, Robert never took Hid for granted and realized earning a best friend was something that didn't happen every day. The feeling was obviously reciprocal because when Robert gave Hid the opportunity to read "Castles in Spain," a novel that Robert was writing, Hid was absolutely thrilled. "Savvy," Hid said, "I was very proud the day last summer when you took me to the torpedo room and read your manuscript to me for I realized then, probably for the first time, how much a book means to the author who has created it wholly in his own mind. I knew then that it was only to one you considered a real friend that you could show your work to then."[14]

When the Germans put down their weapons at eleven o'clock on the eleventh day of the eleventh month in 1918, Robert was still training to become an officer. But he had decided that he did not want to have a career in the navy. The prospect of an entire lifetime of regimentation filled him with dread. Robert had dreamed of traveling to all the wonderful locations that he had read about in books, but over his three years at Annapolis, Robert ventured no further than the Chesapeake Bay.

What is more, Robert knew by then that the navy was not about to help him pursue a life of the mind—and he had resolved to be a writer. He needed to get out of the navy, but because he was fourth in his class, he was in demand as an officer. It looked like he was stuck. But Robert came up with a strategy. While Robert was from humble stock, many of his friends looking to get out as well had fathers who were high-ranking officials in Washington. Robert timed the submission of his resignation letter to coincide with a more "connected" student's letter. The strategy worked. A few weeks later, Robert received a letter informing him that his termination notice had been approved and his services in the navy were no longer necessary. Nineteen-year-old Robert returned to Stockton and commenced to write.

On June 13, 1919, he received word from Henry D. Perkins, the managing editor of the *Norfolk Ledger,* that the paper would be happy to publish his "Headline Jingles," which were weekly news summaries put to verse. The ledger paid him two dollars for each column, which gave the reader a sense of where Robert stood on the issues of the day.[15]

Newspapers were undergoing a seismic change. Yellow journalism—with its sensationalist headlines, exaggerated imagery, and invented facts—had peaked. A new brand of objective reporting and professional standards—always more a broad goal than a reality—was on the rise. As journalism professionalized, it branched into reportage, analysis, and opinion; Robert's Headline Jingles combined all three. Robert criticized President Woodrow Wilson, assailed the Democratic Party, and attacked socialism: "The plan to nationalize the roads/We think is just Plumb foolish/Although some brotherhoods may balk/And act a wee-bit mulish/The country as a whole is not/Inclined to socialism,/And laziness and envy work/In vain for communism." He attacked government benefits and labor union strikes: "We haven't Rockefeller's gold,/Nor any private yacht,/But still the shirt upon our back,/And fifty cents we've got/We'd rather have as our own,/And work to dodge the poorhouse,/Than have them issued out to us/From any public storehouse./In Oakland, California, there/Is now a labor union/Of clergymen who will not preach,/Nor even hold communion,/Unless they get their lawful share/Of neighbors' hams and chickens./If angels take the cue, and strike,/Won't heaven be the dickens!" His predilection for conspiracy and that events were "staged" shone through as well as his tendency to draw questionable connections. He seemed to suggest that the introduction of an income tax law produced labor strikes: "The actors in Chicago and/ New York took to their legs/About the time the government/Took some few million eggs/We wonder of the two events/Have any slightest connection/ Our own experience on the stage/Has prompted that reflection."[16] Indeed while Robert was writing his Headline Jingles, a nonsensical conspiracy theory grew that the creation of the Federal Reserve Agency banking system under President Woodrow Wilson was the work of bankers to further their self-interest.[17]

Headline Jingles were sort of an entrance examination into the world of reporting, and Robert passed. Other newspapers in the vicinity soon began running his news summaries in verse. *The Raleigh News and Observer* offered Robert a full-time job. But Robert declined because he sought a profession that could secure him greater financial security than he believed journalism would. Robert Senior was not amused by his son's inability to commit to a career. Since his son had already forgone a lifetime of financial security in the navy, Robert Senior worried that his son was floundering and foundering.

But an Annapolis friend whetted Robert's appetite for high adventure and travel, telling him of an exciting new government program called "Super Cargo" that promised enchanting trips around the world. The friend told Robert he had seen things he had never dreamed of. Robert was mesmerized and wanted to join up. The lucky chosen few would ride on a Merchant Marine ship as government observers and needed to fill out only a few forms to apply. "Gosh Savvy, with your record at Annapolis, it'd be a snap for you to get in. You're just the type they're looking for," observed Robert's friend.

His Annapolis buddy roused Robert's dream of distant ports and adventure. Robert figured he had nothing to lose because the program was for only two years. He applied enthusiastically and received the approval letter two weeks later. But seven days before the ship left port, Congress canceled the program. His dreams of combat, world travel, and high adventure twice dashed, he fell into a depression. Robert had squandered a guaranteed lifetime job in the navy and abandoned a full-time job as a newspaper flak for absolutely nothing. Worse still, he didn't know what to do next.[18]

4

The Candyman, 1919–1927

One evening at Stockton while his brothers and sisters cleared the table and cleaned the dishes, his father wanted a word with Robert. Robert Senior gave him a strong dose of reality and told him to go back to school and study something more practical than math and poetry, "something a man could use to make a living." The conversation was tense, and Robert, taking offense, made an emotional case for studying math and poetry.

"Well son," his father said "you've got a tough decision to make. And I know you'll make the right one. But you've got to make it soon. You know we don't have a lot of money, and your brothers and sisters are entitled to go to school too, which is quite a drain on our means. But if you feel you'd like to go back to college, and if you think that would help you settle on a career, we'll find the money, somehow, to do it. Think it over."

Money was becoming more important to him. As he put it, he wanted to "make more dough than papa" and "gain in the fight for an honored place." "Deep inside he had to admit that his father was right about math—and poetry—and English literature—and history," observed a later advisor to Robert Welch. "It was becoming increasingly obvious to him that the man who achieved economic security" could follow his dreams of intellectual inquiry. For Robert, the road to riches led to the palace of wisdom.

Robert decided to become a businessman but wasn't sure where to start. He believed that the study of law was a good springboard, however. When the day came to start his company, he reasoned, a legal education would be essential. He knew he wanted to start his company in the industrial North, where the postwar economy was roaring in the 1920s. With his dreams of combat and world travel dashed, the fiercely ambitious nineteen-year-old decided to pursue a legal education at Harvard Law School. "If there be a more successful school in our country or in the world for any profession," President Charles W. Eliot of Harvard observed, "I can only say that I do not know where it is. The school seems to have reached the climax of success in professional education."[1]

But Robert needed money. Fortunately his experience at the Naval Academy set him up for a thriving tutoring job on the side. In addition, many of the law and business school students in Cambridge intended on practicing their trade in Mexico and wanted to learn Spanish. Robert spoke Spanish fluently. He charged one dollar per student each class. Thirty students enrolled, and the class met three times each week. Soon Harvard undergraduates and other area students learned of a bright young man from the South who knew Spanish fluently and was a fine instructor. Robert's small business grew. He was soon making house calls. One high school student, badly burned in a fire, fell behind in his studies. Robert raised his rate, and three afternoons each week, visited the Corey Hill Hospital in Brookline, tutoring the patient for $2.50 an hour. He was a climber, hungry and shrewd.[2]

The winds of change were blowing hard at Harvard Law School when Robert Welch arrived. Less than ten years prior, instructors "stressed knowledge of judicial precedents. Students were to find out what the law was, not what it ought to be. And the law in those times of rapid change had to be an agent of stability, not of social reform," observed the historian James Patterson.[3] But in Robert's day, many of the faculty were active progressives, and that became a problem for him. Robert was already a reactionary—an old man in a young man's body.

As was the case throughout his life, the iconoclastic and contrarian Robert spoke out. In 1911 and 1912, Harvard Law professor Roscoe Pound in the *Harvard Law Review* wrote a three-part article that declared law a "social institution which may be improved by intelligent human effort." Pound explained that in their decision making, judges ought to consider the broader societal impact. But Robert was already a zealous originalist when it came to the Constitution and thought it folly to try to improve social institutions, which could never be perfected. Such talk of utopia was the discourse of the Communists, and hogwash, Robert thought. An even louder progressive voice on the law school faculty was Felix Frankfurter, and Robert's strong aversion to this future Supreme Court Justice's politics trimmed Robert's sails further to the right.[4] Frankfurter was just like the cadets and the officers at the Naval Academy, he probably thought. Myopic, bureaucratic fools all. Whether it was the army or the academy, they were not free. And Welch was bucking like a young stallion. He wanted to be let loose.

His Headline Jingles belied his developing position that Wall Street speculators and eastern monopolists threatened the people. He loathed the excess supply of meddlesome legislation and rejected the Volstead Act, which prohibited the sale of alcoholic beverages. A law could never slake a thirst, he thought. Why bother with passing the law?

During 1919—a year of strikes, violence, and other labor agitation—Robert thundered against boycotts and expressed great reluctance about the usefulness of unions. Partly due to his White male privilege, he demonstrated little regard for securing social justice for the underprivileged and remonstrated against an encroaching federal government. He supported government when it abetted small business, however. He believed that austerity, self-denial, and hard work brought material improvement. Penury was the fault of the individual, who lacked self-discipline or a strong enough work ethic. The poor, he believed, were alive because of the genius and industry of the rich manufacturer.[5] But he was also no rigid advocate of laissez-faire economics. He tolerated indirect business subsidies. He vehemently supported balanced budgets and a national debt so long as it was diminutive, but he still opposed large federal expenditures, especially for social welfare programs. Whether monopolists or government bureaucrats, such men were enslavers or slaves to centralization, Welch thought. He wanted to be free of them all.

Unlike big business, which wanted to keep its cheap labor, Robert generally supported governmental restrictions on immigration. Robert felt nostalgic for an America filled with Americans of Anglo-Saxon and northern European heritage. Although he, as well as every American other than Indians, came from immigrant stock, Robert supported the passage of immigration restrictions in the 1920s—quota systems implemented by the Immigration Acts of 1921 and 1924. For him, these laws safeguarded the existing racialist hierarchy: Anglo-Saxons, northern Europeans, southern and eastern Europeans, and then Asians. "One hundred percent Americans" recoiled that the New Immigration was bringing "the wretched refuse" to America's "teeming shore," as the base of the Statue of Liberty declares.

We do not know whether Robert harbored these nativist or xenophobic views, as the archival record is unfortunately silent. But we do know that he revered the Republican presidents of the 1920s—Harding and Coolidge and Hoover—who all held to Republican liberalism: an individual's moral qualities played the decisive role in failure or success. Their suspicion of foreign immigration was based on cultural fears that non-Anglo-Saxon foreigners may infuse the country with values that were inconsistent with Americanism. As the country returned to peacetime after years of war, the Immigration Acts of 1921 and especially 1924, which passed in the US House of Representatives by a margin of 323 to 71, belied a nation that was becoming provincial and ingrown, and American immigration dwindled significantly.

By his twenties, when he strayed from the Baptism of his youth, Welch had shucked off any residue of anti-Catholicism and the canard of its authoritarianism, love of hierarchy, and suspicion of democracy. And he had many Catholic friends in his adopted Boston and loved all those whose religious views were contrary to his own budding Unitarianism. He saw this as the real message of Jesus Christ, who was his Savior. As it would happen, approximately 50 percent of future John Birch Society members were Catholic. His prejudices remained cultural.

His Americanism cast suspicion on so-called hyphenism, whether German American, African American, or Italian American. In wartime America, many German Americans faced an onslaught against their ethnic institutions and language and were pressured to Americanize. Welch cheered that development. Hamburger became liberty sausage and sauerkraut liberty cabbage. Nativism became confused with patriotism. It was America first.

In this context, mainly because of ideological differences, Welch lost interest in finishing the law degree. He never intended on practicing law anyway. When Felix Frankfurter openly demonstrated his affinity for the Marxist concept of labor and capital relations by arguing that conflict between the two was unavoidable, Robert had had enough. So it was back to the drawing board for Robert.[6]

One night, he sat at his desk in his dwelling on Oxford Street in Cambridge. He wrote through the night, asking himself a central question: "what is the surest and shortest road to financial success?" He then narrowed the inquiry: "what specific goods in demand would be best for me to start manufacturing without either capital or experience?" According to Welch's later associate: "as the sky began to show the first streaks of dawn, Robert stared at the notes in front of him. One word remained amid the maze of dark lines scratched across the pages. That word was "'CANDY'." As he went to bed, a Latin phrase, the motto of North Carolina, popped into his head: Esse quam videri. To be rather than to seem. "Just think," he observed nearly out loud as he slipped into his dreams, "I'm in the candy manufacturing business."[7] But his real dream was still dedicating his life to intellectual inquiry. Economic security would be his means to becoming a philosopher gentleman. But in the meantime, making a killing in business in the 1920s surely beat the regimentation of the academy, whether it was the Naval Academy or Harvard University Law School. In business, he would be free from serfdom, he thought.

He awakened in the afternoon the following day. He was serene. He was confident. He was completely relaxed. Then his mind snapped to attention. Harvard Law seemed ancient history. He bounded down to John G. Gale's candy shop in Harvard Square. Gale made a delicious creamy fudge, which Robert believed to be superior to any other candy. He purchased several trays of the fudge and brought them back to his apartment, cut them into small squares, wrapped them in tinfoil, boxed them, and sold three squares for $0.10 each in drugstores throughout Cambridge and Boston. The tasty fudge was a big hit, and Robert purchased the recipe from Gale for $150.[8] He was a candyman now. He was free. Now it was time to get to work.

Robert first rented 1,500 square feet of an empty loft over a garage on Cambridge's Brookline Street. The loft had no heat, no water, and no electric lighting. Robert bought three copper kettles, a secondhand coke stove, and some lumber to make tables. He hired a young boy to assist him in pouring the fudge, and his girlfriend Marian, his soon-to-be fiancée, wrapped it. She was perfect. He knew she was the one. Avalon Fudge and the Oxford Candy Company were born. After doggedly tinkering with his formula, Avalon fudge became the signature product of the new company.

Robert needed more manpower, however. He frantically wrote home and inquired about the availability of his brother Edward, then tending his father's farm. Edward soon arrived, and while his epilepsy prohibited full use of his talents, the brawny and peppy twenty-year-old was a loyal, dependable, and indefatigable hand. Edward gave his all, performed consequential tasks that Robert found awkward, and helped establish a sound foundation for growing success throughout the decade. "My brother Edward, when all his characteristics and total character were duly weighed, was the finest human being that I've ever known," said Robert.

His dramatic concern for practical considerations coincided with the successful courting of Wellesley student Marian Probert, who became his wife as well as astute advisor and also a proficient candy wrapper at Oxford Candy Company. Marian was the beloved daughter of an Akron, Ohio, family. Like Robert's mother, Marian had an affinity for the liberal arts, majoring in English literature with a secondary interest in music and history. Robert's friend went with Marian's roommate, and Marian and Robert met for a blind double date. Marian was bright, poised and sophisticated, and deeply enchanted by Robert's command of the English language, his deep love of history, but also appreciated his humble roots as a poor country boy. Marian was far more athletic than Robert. Though Robert admitted a love for hitting golf balls because it lessened his anxiety, anybody who sized up his swing saw that Robert was clumsy to a fault. Though Marian favored brains over brawn, their second date was due to take place on the tennis courts. But Boston was hit with an early November snow squall, probably to Robert's benefit, and the match was called off in favor of fireside conversation. If it was not love at first sight, the couple were extremely interested in each other.

Marian rarely quibbled that Robert was a nineteenth-century man living in the twentieth century. She too was fiscally and socially conservative. Marian was a strikingly beautiful young woman and had many suitors. While some of them danced the Charleston, zoomed her through Harvard Square in their new automobiles, and downed bootleg liquor during Prohibition, she was captivated by the bookish Robert: a romantic, a dreamer, and a child at heart. (He savored Harold Gray's Little Orphan Annie comic strips.)[9]

For three years, Robert spent three afternoons or evenings a week courting Marian on the Wellesley campus. They embodied the hoary maxim: she went to Wellesley, while he went to Harvard. Theirs was like *Love Story* without the sad ending. Toting box lunches, they canoed Lake Waban near the campus. They discussed history and literature on the college green or sat in one of the "spoon holder" park benches. They also enjoyed sitting by a roaring fire in the living room of Tower Court, Marian's dormitory. Parietal rules banished Robert by 9:45 p.m., however.

Off-campus, they enjoyed tea dances at Copley Plaza. All done up in an elegant dress with white gloves, Marian cut a stunning figure and relished the opportunity to display what she had learned in dancing school. On the dance floor, lumbering, oafish Robert exuded a lack of confidence that undoubtedly further endeared him because he was jaunty in almost every other activity. On one occasion, he good-naturedly encouraged Marian to find a more dexterous partner, rather smartly giving the Copley attendees some reason to believe that if he was a clod, at least he was a gentleman. A proud wallflower, he sat stone-faced while Marian did indeed glide across the Copley dance floor with other men. Robert was not jealous, though. He was so confident. Cocky even. He knew he had gotten the girl.

After the first year of courtship, the two became engaged on the porch of her home in Akron on a sunny August 6, 1920. Robert could not afford a ring, but it did not seem to matter to Marian. He kissed his bride to be for the very first time that day. It was also on that very day that Robert Welch kissed a girl for the first time in his life. He would not kiss another woman for the remaining years of his life. He was a devoted husband, but never considered his monogamy any bit a sacrifice on his part. He thought he had struck gold. Marian was a dream walking.

As was customary for that particular time, Robert believed that women should be subordinate and docile. He wanted a female companion who was dependent enough to support his aspirations but also clever enough to appreciate his mind. He wanted a partner who would support his learning and had a demonstrated interest in books. Marian was not submissive but was content with her position as the subordinate. Robert expected her to lighten his burdens and cheerily soothe his troubles and anxieties. She remained engaged in his intellectual interests but was careful not to provoke his jealousy by engaging in any overzealous academic pursuits, even while showing an obvious cultivated taste for music and literature. Both wholeheartedly embraced the nineteenth-century belief in "separate spheres," which confined women to the home as doting wives and nurturing mothers.

The young couple needed parental consent. Robert's parents found Marian to be lovely and consented without the slightest reservation, encouraging Robert only to finish law school and secure employment before marriage. His paternal grandmother also quickly approved the selection, but jested to Robert: "why in darnation did you have to go and find a Yankee?" Marian laughed about the remark then and for the remainder of their happy marriage.[10]

Marian's choice of mate was not as popular for the Proberts, who saw Robert not as a doer but as a dreamer. They apparently never thought he was the kind to follow through. They found Robert's dabbling in lofty intellectual pursuits silly and feared that his romantic yearnings for a life of the mind would make it challenging for him to keep down full-time employment. The Proberts wondered why anybody who did not want to practice law would attend law school? How could he afford his big dreams of world travel and build a large home that was worthy of their daughter? But the Proberts also knew that their daughter, headstrong like Robert, had already made up her mind. They hoped only that she would come to her senses before the wedding day.

Despite her parents' admonitions, the couple married on Saturday, December 2, 1922, and spent the following day wrapping and mixing Avalon fudge. The reluctance of Marian's parents to endorse the partnership only deepened Robert's conviction to secure a fortune and prove his new in-laws wrong. Robert increased the number of tutoring students he took on, to the detriment of his new career.

Despite brotherly help and Robert's own unflagging work ethic, he continued his descent into debt into 1922, and he leaned on his parents for financial assistance. He wrote his mother: "Father knows all about the drafts now—the one for $25 and the one for $50—as they were drawn over a week ago. I'm almost positive that they will be the last I shall draw. They were for equipment, for which I couldn't spare the money." He needed the loan for more tables in the shop: "you see, with hot weather coming on, we have to let the candy stay on the tables 2 days instead of one, which means many more tables. And with my business growing anyway, I just had to have some right away." Despite the debt, he was making great progress during these early years of entrepreneurial seed sowing.

His candy was moving and his business growing: "I had to be at the shop from 5 to 6 this afternoon to give candy to a man who is going all the way around Cape Ann with it for the first of next week. He came and took 102 boxes between the time I wrote the 'afternoon' and the 'to' in that last sentence. . . . I am getting started towards getting on my feet, and because I have established very good credit. My next big step along that line will be being able to buy sugar direct from the refineries, which will save me over a cent a box on my candy."[11]

Robert entered the candy manufacturing business during the golden age of the industry. The key to success was selling high-quality, low-cost products to consumers, which required mass production. The movement toward a mass economy occurred not only in the candy industry but also in many others, including the auto industry and the sports industry. Consumer-oriented goods like Coca-Cola, Ford motor cars, radios, and Hershey bars became synonymous with American life and demonstrated the possibilities of mass production.

The candy industry abandoned the practice of cooking fifty-pound batches in coke-burning furnaces before wrapping the confections by hand. Confectioners had relied on kettles, starch boards, hand cutters, shallow trays, and hand printers. But no longer did they need to print the mold by hand, then fill it, then shake starch from the molded center, before cooling the center. Everything could be done by machine. Like most industries, candy makers rationalized business operations and streamlined the entire process. Candy makers embraced the scientific management and standardized production techniques of Frederick Winslow Taylor, who turned the chaotic and inefficient factory system into a model of productivity and efficacy. The greatest proponent in the candy industry of the creed of scientific management was Milton Hershey. His story read like a tale from Horatio Alger. Like Henry Ford, who didn't invent the car, Hershey did not invent the candy bar but perfected it, at least in the eyes and in the palates of millions of American youngsters who saved their pennies and bought his mouthwatering milk chocolate.[12]

Hershey had little education but was full of initiative and persistence, specializing early in penny candies for the children of his neighborhood. His trip to the 1893 Chicago World Exposition changed the candy business forever. There, Hershey became enamored with the sparkling new German chocolate machinery on display, with its promise of product standardization.[13] He bought the machinery, purchased 1,200 acres of farmland in Pennsylvania, and established an empire. Just like Ford, Hershey's motto was to produce a quality product that was affordable to everybody. Also like Ford, Hershey pioneered attractive and progressive labor policies for his workers who lived in the gorgeous model town of Hershey with its aroma of milk chocolate endlessly wafting through the air.[14]

He revolutionized the chocolate industry with this recipe, but also foreshadowed the suspicion and paranoia that was to engulf the candy industry. Bodyguards, secret recipes, suspicious demeanors, eccentric behaviors, padlocks, and private eyes were all part of the life and legend of many twentieth-century candymen and chocolate kings. Many walked a fine line between deception and detection to conceal their recipes or to steal from their competitors. In twentieth-century America, reclusive, eccentric, and paranoid confectioners were found not only in the pages of novels.[15] And Robert Welch was an important one.

Hershey's plant was a cross between Frankenstein's laboratory, the fictional world of Willy Wonka, and a Cold War warehouse. Security guards patrolled the grounds. Everything was on a need-to-know basis, and absolute secrecy was essential. Hershey was a benevolent despot, a mercurial boss who was prone to firing employees. He produced the slightly sour milk chocolate bar that Americans deemed heaven-sent, and made it on a mass scale. After World War I, with competitors focusing on their export business, Hershey saturated the American market.[16]

There were two important factors in the rise of candy as an industry. First, the 1906 Pure Food and Drug Act safeguarded consumers from harmful, unhealthy, and contaminated food, including candy, and introduced more purity in manufacturing confections. Second, drawing from their experiences in wartime, candy manufacturers marketed their product less as a luxury item for the rich but as an energy food for the masses. World War I doughboys in France longing for home wanted candy bars, and American candy makers, especially Hershey, supplied them in bulk. One-, five-, and ten-cent candy bars came to encompass more than 50 percent of the market. The convenience of the candy bar led to the invention and popularity of scores of varieties. Bars containing nuts with their potential for quick energy led to the ascendancy of new firms. From 1914 to 1919, candy sales tripled to $447,726,000. The candy industry grew even more thereafter.

Robert was part of the revolution not only in production but also in distribution. Like the nineteenth-century market revolution in which the construction of roads, canals, and railroads changed how goods were moved to consumers, the early twentieth-century mass consumption economy altered the ways that candymen got their goods out. Jobbers or wholesalers, a new profession, became crucial to distribution. Manufacturers like Robert needed to develop good relationships with jobbers, who delivered the manufacturer's products to retailers: drugstores, newsstands, and food shops.[17]

One problem candy manufacturers had yet to solve was the problem of spoilage amid summer heat, which caused sales to plummet. In the summer of 1923, to stay afloat Robert needed to find part-time work as a truck salesman, not least because Marian was pregnant with their first child. By the fall, Robert was back working full time in his candy business. Mixing and packing fudge up to twenty hours each day, Robert often collapsed in exhaustion on a pile of sugar bags. Then he'd awaken, rub his eyes, and begin a new day. He'd often pile the candy into his model T Ford roadster, travel on a darkened road to Gloucester—sixty-five miles away—to meet at dawn a jobber for the daily handoff. Then Robert returned to Boston, using the cash from the jobber to buy sugar, chocolate, and other commodities. By midmorning he'd be in the shop again, and the team would make more product during the day. He skipped many meals, gulped down others, and grew gaunt. By 6 p.m., the tables were covered with fudge, cooked and settling. The workers "scored" the fudge into squares, cutting the final product by hand. Then flying fingers wrapped the fudge, and packed it aboard

Robert's model T, and Robert was out again and off to Worcester or Gloucester. And so it went. On many occasions, the flow of cash was so tight that Robert needed to pawn essential office supplies like the typewriter to pay his workers, redeeming the items after he was in the black again. He lamented at one low point that his rent for his apartment was behind five months. As he put it later, "I was in debt and getting in debter all the time."[18]

But his will was indomitable. More important, the postwar economy was on his side. The flu pandemic between 1918 and 1920 and the recession of 1920 through 1921 dampened some enthusiasm, but the economy quickly recovered and for seven years sprinted ahead. Techniques of mass distribution and production, more efficient methods of organization, and the widespread availability of consumer products accounted for the boom. The economy roared. Americans embraced economic nationalism, abandoned the reformist spirit of the progressive era, and backed the conservative Republican politics of the Harding, Coolidge, and the Hoover administrations. Robert found complete agreement with the statement by Calvin Coolidge: "the business of government was business." Other Republican conservatives favored the Republican "retrenchment," which defended free-market capitalism, Americanism, and helped make business—big and small—thrive. Republican administrations in the 1920s implemented tariffs. The popular Fordney-McCumber Tariff of 1922 highlighted that Americans believed that foreign policy under the idealistic President Wilson suffered from overextension, and the nation's proper course was to pull back from foreign commitments that might hurt business at home.

In 1918, only 15 percent of American households paid income taxes. Eighty percent of all tax revenue derived from the richest 1 percent. In the 1920s, Republican leaders introduced economic policies that dramatically cut the taxes of the rich. Led by Treasury Secretary Andrew Mellon and business tycoons John Rockefeller and Henry Ford, the Coolidge administration argued that high taxes on the affluent discouraged investment and economic growth. Tax cuts, Mellon argued, acted as an incentive for business owners to reinvest their savings for their companies and employees and spurred economic activity. Mellon's policies cut the marginal tax rate for individuals from 73 percent to 25 percent—comparable to the difference between the Lyndon

Johnson administration and the Reagan administration in the 1960s and 1980s, respectively. Congressional Republicans lowered not only income taxes but also estate tax, the surtax, and excise taxes; they abolished the gift tax and the excess profits tax. As a result, capital investment expanded, as in the ingenious candy machines that Robert Welch and other candymen purchased.[19]

Robert's early investment in cooling equipment made him one of the earliest to solve the problem of spoilage of fudge in the summer. Despite its high quality, Robert's fudge, like all fudge manufactured in "candy kitchens," started to dry within forty-eight hours; within one week, it was hard as a brick. Robert was largely successful because he could produce, deliver to market, and sell Avalon fudge within the forty-eight-hour window. But he reasoned that if he could extend the lifespan of Avalon fudge beyond forty-eight hours, he would be able to broaden the reach of his market and accumulate a great fortune. Robert was one of the first to come upon a successful method. He would cool the product in a cork-lined room with a combination of ice and electric fans that blew cold air on the fudge. Girls wearing heavy skirts and warm sweaters then hand dipped the cooled fudge in a thick chocolate coating. Although the process changed the texture of the fudge, it extended its shelf life, and it tasted the same six months later.[20]

In the second half of the 1920s, Welch moved his operation to Albany Street, where in 10,000 square feet of factory space, he constructed a large electric-powered chocolate-coating room and an equally large refrigerated room. Welch installed a large enrober, and its 40-foot cooling belt and single maw increased production and greatly improved sanitation by replacing the hand labor of dipping. While he initially feared this increased mechanization would affect quality, Robert acquiesced when he realized that the enrober did the work of 40 employees.

Imagine Robert hovering in fascination over the conveyor belt as it carried his Avalon fudge to the liquid bath of chocolate coating. Then watch him mesmerized as the belt went through a cooling tunnel before sending his coated candy to the packers. He added a second enrober, and then another. Robert initially cooked 140-pound batches of fudge in copper kettles over open-fire gas stoves. Borrowing even more capital thanks to Mellon's policies, Robert bought more stoves and kettles, until he was cooking or cooling 10 tons of his signature fudge.

Another innovation, from Austria, was vacuum-cooking equipment, which was a major improvement over open-fire cooking. Robert purchased one machine in the mid-1920s, as well as motor-driven stirrers and scrapers, gas stoves, and a mechanical cutter.[21] Finally Robert purchased a large automatic steel mogul, which had revolutionized the process of shaping the center of the candy.[22]

Robert dreamed of pursuing a life dedicated to intellectual inquiry, but realized that economic security would need to come first. Throughout the period between the birth of Robert's first son Robert Henry Winborne Welch on November 22, 1923, and the birth of his second boy Hillard "Hid" Walmer Welch on December 4, 1925, Robert had demonstrated to colleagues and competitors an unfettered persistence, a willingness to work, and a keen ability to secure close relationships with jobbers. His talents allowed Avalon fudge to move quickly and grow steadily. Many jobbers as well as competitors, who became his close friends, were impressed by this "man on the come."

By 1925, the Oxford Candy Company employed 70 workers and shipped Avalon fudge as far as Ohio and New Jersey. Growth surged in 1926 with Robert's creation of the Sugar Daddy, whose uncoated, high-cooked caramel on a stick became a childhood favorite. Its cream base and double wrapper prevented melting in the summer and dodged the usual decline in sales for the season. Sugar Babies were later created entirely by accident when a batch of Sugar Daddies melted, and the bite-sized sweets were born. In 1927, the Oxford Candy Company employed 160 people and enjoyed record profits. Robert Welch was on the verge of becoming a millionaire, and possibly a millionaire several times over.[23]

5
Professional Breakdown and the Great Depression, 1928–1940

Despite riding the prosperity of the roaring twenties, dark clouds loomed on Welch's horizon. Welch had accumulated significant debt investing in his wondrous machines. He exacerbated his problem of buying on credit when he purchased a Chicago factory just as the stock market crashed. Meanwhile, a foreign competitor nearly cornered the cocoa bean market, sending chocolate prices skyward. The perfect economic storm—unmanageable debt, a stock market debacle, and surging chocolate prices—bankrupted Robert Welch. On the cusp of fame and fortune, Welch lost everything when his candy company folded at the end of the decade.[1]

In the 1930s, Robert tried in vain to pay back his creditors with two attempts to restart his company and a stint at E. J. Brach, the nation's largest candy manufacturer. Robert lamented, "my pretty bubbles are exploded and vanished, my rainbows have changed into thin air." But the bitterest blow was yet to come: in 1935, Robert reluctantly went to work for his brother, James. Although Robert himself admitted that James was a better businessman and financier, the two were lifelong rivals. As a child, James, who was six years younger, agonized Robert by distracting him from his readings. Pugnacious Robert once reciprocated by locking James in a closet.[2]

A decade before, Robert had tapped eighteen-year-old James for the position of factory superintendent at the Oxford Candy Company. He taught James everything he knew about the candy business—to the point that James started his own eponymous candy company. As head of the sales department of James O. Welch, Robert spent the next twenty years working for his baby brother. As a condition of employment, James insisted that Robert file formal bankruptcy proceedings on his own company. Robert felt humiliated.

James's company thrived, with sales soaring from about $200,000 in 1935 to $20 million in 1956, by which time it—with Robert as its employee—was producing 1.5 million Sugar Daddies. Robert found it a bitter pill that his brother's company had reaped the great fortune from his invention. Robert did earn 10 percent of the profits on the Sugar Daddy, but that percentage dwindled as time passed, becoming a source of tension between the brothers.

While Robert bade his own dreams goodbye when he went to work for James, he dedicated himself to helping James build a great fortune. Developing close relationships with often cynical and cunning New Deal bureaucrats, Robert aggressively garnered singular benefits that competitors did not enjoy—often through ruthless means. Incredibly competitive and bellicose, Robert possessed a single mindedness of winning at every occasion, which he usually did.

By the 1930s, Welch's political philosophy was fully maturated, and in 1934, he wrote an article called "A Weight on My Shoulders." While it went unpublished, the article demonstrated Robert's gloomy vision of the state of American life and his longing for a bygone era that government interference and rampant immigration had destroyed. He wrote: "the America that I was born in; that was given to me by courageous and farseeing men, many of whom died for that purpose; that I grew up in, went to school in, and loved more every year . . . is being made over into a carbon copy of thousands of despotisms that have gone before."[3]

Robert, a staunch Republican, shared the antipathy that many businesspeople harbored toward Franklin Delano Roosevelt, who occupied the White House between 1933 and 1945. The gravity of the Depression, the popularity of his policies, and the charisma of the Democratic Roosevelt made a Republican renascence altogether impossible in the 1930s. Classical liberalism had been the ideology of Republican hegemony between 1896 and 1929, but in the 1930s, the American people called for greater government involvement in the economy.

Perspectives abounded about the woes of the Depression. Keynesians advocated massive federal spending to alleviate the unprecedented downturn. American Marxists, who claimed erroneously that the engines of American capitalism had used up its capacity to locate domestic markets for investment, preferred a planned economy and working-class control of the means of production. An older generation of unalloyed and proud progressives saw underconsumption, oversavings, and massive inequality as the products of corporate monopolies, which needed breaking up. Meanwhile, economic historians cast blame on the harsh terms of the Treaty of Versailles, which overwhelmed a weakened Germany unable to pay reparations, placed too much promise on Great Britain, and had too much faith in America, which lacked the political will to embrace collective security. With the decline of the business cycle, a predictable downturn morphed into a catastrophic depression because nations built up insurmountable tariff walls and depreciated their currencies.

Robert Welch keenly supported the argument that the New Deal dampened business confidence, inhibited the entrepreneurial spirit of American individualism, and depleted business investment. He believed that the business cycle would have naturally recuperated before World War II if the New Deal had not unleashed irresponsible fiscal policies that lessened business confidence and assaulted businessmen personally. But Welch's spirit was wounded, not broken. He felt forlorn and despondent, but not hopeless. A deep believer in the cycles of history, he expected that the pendulum would swing back. But "that man in the White House," as many conservative business leaders called Franklin Roosevelt, had to be retired back to Hyde Park.

What frightened Robert the most about the Democratic Party under Roosevelt was its alliance with a militant labor movement. Led by the bushy-browed John L. Lewis, the Congress of Industrial Organization (CIO) conducted militant strikes in the mid-1930s and organized millions of workers. Embedded within the New Deal and the CIO was the powerful Communist Party (CPUSA), which comprised 25 percent of the CIO unions. Between 1934 and January 1939, the CPUSA claimed its membership grew from 26,000 and 75,000.[4] But despite its influence on immigration policy, foreign policy, and middle-class organizations throughout the 1930s, the "CIO" Communists never ran the Democratic Party. Still, Robert fretted that the intelligentsia were also influenced by Communism in the 1930s, propagating Marxism throughout the media, schools, Hollywood, newspapers, magazines, and other cultural organs.

Welch cursed the day that the Democratic Party came to dominate the cities with its new approach to immigration. The better elements had once checked the influence of the masses, but democracy was rampant in the 1930s, machine politics denigrated the civil service, and the quid pro quo arrangement was commonplace. Class conflict, once checked by Republican rule, sectional politics, and ethnic animosities, roared back to life in the 1930s and became the most pressing matter in American politics. The president, Welch and the men of the Right claimed, exacerbated class tensions, especially with his vitriolic 1936 inaugural address, which attacked "economic royalists." Welch and others on the Right never failed to remember that Roosevelt had called America's business leaders the "resolute enemy within our gates" and taunted the wealthy with the cry that in 1936, they will "meet their master."

FDR probably overstated his radical intentions, but there was some truth to the fear that class conflict was reaching a boiling point in the 1930s. The "brains trust" of the New Deal experimented with both state capitalism and social democracy—two principles that the Right found were incompatible. The National Recovery Administration (NRA) especially received Robert's ire because it entailed a partnership between business and government. Robert feared the NRA's patriotic mobilization, its "Blue Eagle" marches, and its implication that unrestrained free market competition should be abandoned for the duration of the downturn. Robert berated the NRA's control of prices and industrial output. He attacked the NRA's section 7a, which allowed workers to organize unions. By giving unions and industry the ability to curtail price reductions as "unfair competition," the NRA essentially promoted cartels. Robert viewed such a program as an unfortunate encroachment into state capitalism and the wholesale corruption of classical liberalism; he even suggested it reeked of fascism. The Supreme Court ultimately ruled the NRA unconstitutional in 1935—one helluva good day for Robert Welch.

Other businesspeople too were turned off by Roosevelt's early reforms, such as the Emergency Banking Act, and his reforms of Wall Street, including the Glass-Steagall Act. But if the first New Deal quickened a business executive's pulse, the Second New Deal—those measures passed after Roosevelt's 1936 election victory—hardened his arteries and produced angina. Roosevelt started to shift his sails to the left in 1935 with the Supreme Court's ruling on the NRA. Businesspeople saw FDR's Tennessee Valley Authority, which built dams to halt deforestation and flooding and bring cheap electricity to a seven-state region, as "fascistic." Others called it "creeping socialism" in concrete and worse. Conservative firebrand John T. Flynn observed, the "great government power" brought all the old progressives "with their plaudits and offerings to the foot of the throne."[5]

A right-wing Republican response to the New Deal gradually developed, dominated by midwestern reactionaries like those of the nominally bipartisan American Liberty League, including the conservative Republican J. Howard Pew of the Sun Oil Company. The Liberty League extolled the wonders of free markets, individualism, and the Constitution. Newspapers also contributed to a growing resistance to the New Deal, including Colonel Robert R. McCormick's right-wing *Chicago Tribune*, and the media empire of William Randolph Hearst, with twenty-eight newspapers, thirteen magazines, and eight radio stations. The Chicago Tribune Company owned other large papers as well as the Mutual Broadcasting System, which featured the star power of conservative radio commentator Fulton Lewis Jr., who had a listening audience of 16 million—the biggest in the United States. Together, the Hearst and McCormick–Patterson publishing empires in 1935 held 20 percent of the daily circulation and 36 percent of Sunday circulation nationwide.[6]

The tail end of the 1930s saw a rise in right-wing fortunes as Roosevelt's Supreme Court–packing scheme and the 1937 recession alienated some in his base and represented the twilight of his New Deal. In 1937, despite 14 percent unemployment, the gross national product and industrial production reached 1929 levels. It looked like the economy was improving. But then these indices dropped 20 percent. Roosevelt's nationwide support fell significantly. Meanwhile militant sit-down strikes in the automobile industry appeared to signal that Communists were taking over the trade union movement. Gallup polls showed that two-thirds of the public favored the use of presidential force against them, despite Roosevelt's refusal to do so. As Congress grew more conservative and perturbed with FDR's autocratic tendencies, his New Deal stalled.

Robert was ecstatic when the returns from the 1938 elections came in. The Republicans had gained six seats in the Senate, and eighty seats in the House. The GOP now had the strength to challenge the New Deal. Robert was confident the issues he cared about had won the day: the Constitution, the economic catastrophe of the New Deal, and the Communist influence in labor unions. Republicans even gained an advantage because they were working with conservative Democrats to probe the National Labor Relations Board and the Works Progress Administration, two ominous bodies in FDR's socialistic scheme. These investigations engendered the Hatch Act, which prohibited federal employees from participating in partisan politics. This in turn poisoned urban patronage machines and augured the end of the New Deal.[7]

Another of the signs of a backlash against the New Deal was the appearance of Martin Dies's House Un-American Activities Committee in 1938. Then in the summer of 1939, Stalin surprised the world by joining forces with Hitler in the conquest of Poland. Soon anti-Communist legislation was enacted, including the Smith Act of 1940, the country's first peacetime anti-sedition act since 1798. The Red Scare of 1939 was paving the way for further assaults on Communism—something Welch would make the most of.

Welch cheered as a conservative coalition of midwestern Republicans and southern Democrats bolstered the reactionary offensive. Under pressure, Roosevelt abandoned Keynesian economics and, at the Right's urging, reduced budget deficits. John Maynard Keynes persisted in his demands that federal spending reach massive levels to combat the Depression, but Keynes's pleas fell on deaf ears. Roosevelt dodged criticism from his left on such matters by relaying the message that he had to mollify the Jeffersonians of his party. Democrats whose principles were more in line with the Right on many issues—individual liberty, free markets, racial and ethnic conservatism—were heartened by Roosevelt's change of course. But the reactionary alliance was short-lived. As World War II loomed, southern Democrats, who supported intervention, fell in line behind Roosevelt. Although Robert's spirits had been buoyed by the revival of the Right in the late 1930s, the winds of war stalled that drive, as the crisis brought political consensus—if only temporarily.

6

America First, 1940–1945

The war in Europe was a crucible for Robert Welch, who made important connections to the Republican Right as a member of the America First Committee (AFC). He came in contact with the ideas and men who opposed the war. In this time, Senator Robert Taft was unquestionably the leader of the GOP's conservative wing, which opposed New Deal "socialism" and intervention in European wars. Welch backed Taft's unsuccessful candidacy for the Republican presidential nomination in 1940. Welch also vehemently defended the AFC's star, Charles Lindbergh, who ironically crossed the Atlantic in 1927 but argued against intervention in the 1930s. Welch argued in 1940 that a conspiracy was afoot to shut down the pronouncements of the handsome and charismatic aviator.

Robert was a North Carolinian turned Bostonian, but his foreign policy position was far more midwestern than eastern. Many of his fellow Bostonians were committed interventionists, in both world wars. They made their living in the polyglot and cosmopolitan East and benefited immensely from trade and capital between New York and London. But Robert was not among them. At a candy manufacturer, Welch's employment depended on dairy from the Midwest and sugar from southern climes. His cultural and business ties were different from those of his neighbors and peers.

Welch's foreign policy derived from a traditional Republican view that emphasized a serious conflict between the East and the Midwest. The Midwest resented the East as arrogant, exploitative, abusive, and most ominously, Anglophilic. Britain had long been a major investor in the East and on Wall Street, which was seen not incorrectly as a major exploiter of the Midwest. Like Taft, Welch was sympathetic not to national corporations or financial institutions but to the small businessperson and the small farmer who supplied his milk and worked as his father and grandfather had. Robert identified with the rising self-employed professional classes too. He later went to bat for dentists when he raged against fluoride as a Communistic device that threatened their livelihood. He went to bat for doctors when he raged against universal healthcare. He looked out for the small businessperson because he had been one of them. National corporations made up half of all industrial production in the United States, but there were still 600,000 smaller corporations and 7.5 million smaller businesses. These were Robert's white-collared professionals. They were shopkeepers. They were traders. They were innkeepers and lawyers. Workers living in small rural towns and working in small plants also found a home in his cohort. Not all of them were of the Right, but since Robert and many of the Right sympathized with their plight, he eventually became their voice in American politics.

The Great Depression and the crisis of capitalism accounted for the birth of many Republican rightists. In that time, Welch saw the rise of anarchy and Communism and, like many of his ilk, responded by imbibing the classical liberalism found in the books of Ludwig von Mises and Friedrich Hayek, and the popular Americanism of John T. Flynn whose oeuvre included thirty books—mostly attacking the New Deal and FDR's foreign policy, which Flynn concluded was even worse than Woodrow Wilson's unmitigated idealism. Flynn savaged the Reciprocal Trade Agreements Act, which secured freer trade, and assailed the Destroyer Deal and Lend Lease as steps toward dictatorship, foreshadowing an American war that was really England's fight. For Flynn, Roosevelt's recognition of Russia in 1933 was an egregious sin, only made worse with the wartime alliance and eventual concessions at Yalta.[1] For Robert Welch, Flynn was the consummate answer to Roosevelt, and their views begin to echo each other's.

As much as this faction of the Right abjured intervention in the Atlantic and Europe, the Republican Party had long championed an Asia First policy in the Pacific—one whose effects are evident in American conservatism even today. Robert agreed, seeing an Asia First policy as critical for stopping the domination of China by Japan as well as curbing the ambitions of the "Old World" empires of Britain, France, and Germany. As a former navy student at Annapolis, he supported a strong naval defense to protect the Western Hemisphere, but especially to wield an offensive and aggressive big stick in the Pacific. Such a policy, which long defined the Republican Party, tangled America in the Spanish American War, through which it secured the Philippines and Guam, as well as Hawaii, eventually fueling conflict with Japan. Contrary to much myth making, the Republican Party was not isolationist at the beginning of the American century.

And yet, Republicans like Welch followed George Washington's suspicion of multilateral arrangements and "entangling alliances" with Europe. Welch had deep isolationist tendencies when it came to Europe, largely because of what he saw as the absurdity and waste of America's involvement in World War I. He thought the conflict did not "make the world safe for democracy," but only put the Bolsheviks in power in Russia. His conclusions were only buttressed with the findings of the Nye committee in 1934 and 1935, which concluded that New York bankers and the armaments industry were responsible for American involvement in that war.

Welch agreed with Republican foreign policy of the 1920s, which rejected Wilsonian idealism, its "Europe First" commitments, embrace of national determination for the colonized, and reduction of tariffs. Welch favored unilateralism and protectionism, as the twenty-first-century Republican does. He loathed Wilson's League of Nations and then the United Nations as a threat to American sovereignty and a globalist power grab. The tumult of the 1930s, and the rise of fascism in Germany and Italy, confirmed to Welch, as it did many Republicans, the folly of the First World War. Welch saw little point in magnanimous foreign aid and backed protectionist policies, seeing Europe as toxic and decadent.

A "great debate" ensued with Hitler's invasion of Poland in September 1939 and the fall of France in June 1940: should America hunker down, or should it openly aid its allies?[2] The America First Committee, or AFC, wanted to hunker down and opposed US aid to Britain.

Americans have largely forgotten the vitriolic debates waged over

US involvement in World War II, now mythologized as a "good war." Arthur Schlesinger called "those angry days" the "most savage political debate in my lifetime." Joseph P. Kennedy, Henry Ford, and anti-interventionism's biggest star, Charles Lindbergh, argued that appeasement with Hitler was the best course. He blamed the push for US involvement on the "British, the Jewish, and Roosevelt administration." Lindbergh's appalling words live in infamy. The "greatest danger to this country lies in" the Jews' "large ownership and influence in our motion pictures, our press, our radio, and our government," observed Lindbergh at an America First rally on September 11, 1941, in Des Moines, Iowa.[3] Lindbergh's star fell after the Des Moines address. It haunted him, as it should have, for the remainder of his days.

President Roosevelt had already turned on Lindbergh before the address. "If I should die tomorrow," Roosevelt told Secretary of the Treasury Henry Morgenthau Jr. one year earlier, "I want you to know this. I am absolutely convinced Lindbergh is a Nazi."[4] Herbert Hoover, Roosevelt's Republican challenger in 1932, agreed. "Lindbergh's anti-Jewish speech is, of course, all wrong," observed Hoover. "It will hurt all of us who are opposed to war."[5] John T. Flynn, chair of the New York branch of the AFC, called the speech stupid, but most leaders gave Lindbergh "qualified support," as the historian Wayne S. Cole observed.[6]

The historical record is silent on whether Welch responded to Lindberg's Des Moines speech, but Welch wanted America to stay out of the war and opposed aid to Britain. It was Europe's fight, he thought.

Welch's interests were also personal. Welch, just like Ambassador Joseph P. Kennedy Sr., another Boston businessman, had two sons of fighting age. (One, Hillard Welch, would join the army and eventually serve as an infantryman in Italy.)

To oppose intervention against Germany and assistance to the beleaguered isle, Welch and 800,000 others joined the AFC. The AFC was the largest antiwar organization in the history of the United States. AFC leaders argued that involvement in World War II would introduce socialism into the United States and that Hitler actually was no threat to the American economy. If America's navy and air force remained preeminent, the Nazis would not encroach upon the Western Hemisphere, the AFC argued. Hitler was much more interested in securing land in eastern Europe and reaching a settlement with Britain than conquering the entire planet, the AFC argued. But Welch and other AFC members were being naive; Hitler wanted the world. And if the United States hunkered down, Hitler would get the world.

Though founded by R. Douglas Stuart, heir to the Quaker Oats Company fortune, and other Yale University law students, most members were midwesterners who opposed the encroaching power of the federal government. The AFC's national chair was Chicago-based Sears, Roebuck and Company board chair Robert E. Wood, a Republican. Gore Vidal and William F. Buckley Jr., who later became fierce adversaries, found common ground in the AFC. Publisher William H. Regnery, also a member of the GOP, supplied initial funding.

Senator Robert Taft, "Mr. Republican" himself, was a member, as was Hanford MacRider, American Legion national commander and a Republican. Also present were progressive isolationists such as Wisconsin's erstwhile governor Philip LaFollette, US senator Bennett Champ Clark from Missouri, pacifists, socialists, conservatives, and New Deal businesspeople. Even a young Harvard senior named Jack Kennedy, who was undoubtedly influenced by his father, sent the AFC a $100 check.

We do know that Welch backed Lindbergh just months before the Des Moines affair, insisting that his right to free speech was being violated. Welch claimed that Lindbergh "was tricked by Mayor LaGuardia out of radio time that had been allotted to him in New York City; and by such means that he did not even know the speech was not being made. He was, in fact, positively assured even at the end that it had been carried over the New York station. More specifically, and not subject to any controversy, he has just been denied the use of the normal hall for such purposes, in Philadelphia, on the grounds that his speeches attract Communists rather than Americans."[7]

Welch consistently associated with, was allied with, and remained loyal to associates, colleagues, or friends who had known anti-Semitic tendencies or were suspected of being sympathetic to Nazi Germany. This probably belied his mother's strong Baptist faith that the Bible was inerrant, and its word that loyalty, even the act of dying for a friend, was a great form of honor that Jesus taught. But it produced a myopia in Robert Welch.

As a Boston businessman making his fortune in the 1930s and 1940s, Welch became stuck in an older, darker time. He continued to revere Lindbergh even after the Des Moines speech.

Welch's chief role in the AFC was to drum up support in the South, where it was weakest. Engaging in rallies, scheduling speakers, and lobbying Congress, the AFC was a public relations program. Robert wrote an eviscerating letter to Frank O. Graham, attacking this president of the University of North Carolina, Robert's alma mater, for declaring "this is our war" and exaggerating support for American intervention. Welch attacked Graham for saying "we favor immediate aid to the allies, because the democracies, with all their injustices, frustration, and failures, give the world's people, including the German people, more hope of the opportunity to struggle for peace, freedom, democracy, and humane religion as the basis of them all." On September 27, 1940, Graham declared that by order of the trustees, the University of North Carolina was "offering its total resources to the nation for the defense of the freedom and democracy it was founded to serve."[8] Welch was incensed and told Graham: "not long ago in the course of a discussion in Birmingham Alabama your name came into the conversation. The comments were not laudatory. I remarked only: 'well, Frank Graham is at least sincere.' One of the ablest, most restrained, and most honorable businessmen of the South answered me: 'Sure, he's sincere, all right. He's just the most, gullible jackass in America.' This was harsh language. But I must admit the adjective had been well-earned."

Welch also told Graham that as he had traveled the country on candy business throughout 1940 and 1941, he was struck by the lack of support for intervention: "Within the past 12 months I have been in over 40 states in the union. Some 20 of them I have been in several times within the past six months. I know, as definitely as I am sitting here, that the people of this country in a ratio of least 2 to 1 do not want any part in Europe's war or Europe's power politics. If there was any effective way in which they could express themselves, they would show this to be true."[9]

Along with John T. Flynn, Garrett Garrett and Clarence Manion were other AFC members influencing Robert's ideas. Garrett, a journalist for the *Saturday Evening Post*, argued that New Deal "revolutionaries" had been influenced primarily from western Europe rather than

Soviet Russia. Roosevelt had surreptitiously attempted a "revolution within the form" and tried to convert a republic to a democracy with the New Deal. Garrett's most influential work was *The People's Pottage*, which Welch later included among his "One Dozen Candles," a book series that was "required reading" for John Birch Society members. Welch observed: "the Communist-inspired conversion of America, from a constitutional republic of self-reliant people into an unbridled democracy of handout-seeking whiners, was proceeding according to plan. And still is. *The People's Pottage* is the one book that tells this story best."[10]

Many in the AFC regarded Communism as far more dangerous to freedom than fascism, but anti-Semitism was a problem in the United States, especially in Catholic Boston, Welch's adopted hometown. Preoccupied with the danger of Communism, he, like many Boston businesspeople, failed to see anti-Semitism as a problem in his own backyard. Welch suffered from this blind spot for anti-Semitism for decades thereafter. Undoubtedly, his myopia was molded by coming of age in Boston in the 1930s and 1940s. During the 1930s, Father Charles Coughlin, Catholic priest and Detroit-based radioman, was a national figure. Thirty million Americans listened to his weekly radio address, testifying to anti-Semitism's national reach. He was adored by many Bostonians.[11] Coughlin was a vociferous anti-Semite, observing "when we get through with the Jews in America, they'll think the treatment they received in Germany was nothing."[12]

While Robert was dutifully peddling his brother's candy during World War II, Boston was supplying many members of the Christian Front, whose acolytes gathered in New York's Madison Square Garden in February 1939. A pro-Hitler rally took place there where Fritz Kuhn, the pernicious leader of the German American Bund, led 20,000 strong. In the cultural and financial epicenter of the United States, Kuhn delivered an intolerably un-American address while flanked by swastikas and speaking before a gargantuan portrait of George Washington. Attendees probably thought they were in Berlin during its darkest days. Kuhn was soon caught embezzling funds. Yet throughout World War II, "small pogroms," observed one New York Yiddish paper, occurred throughout Boston. Young Irish Catholic thugs beat Jews "almost daily." Meanwhile's Boston's mayor and the governor of Massachusetts ignored the beatings. Many Boston businesspeople might not have been beating Jews in the streets of Boston, but they were poisoning the discourse of the town with their anti-Semitism, calling Jews appalling epithets, within earshot or not.

Welch probably did not voice such epithets, at least publicly, as he worked closely with many in the Jewish community. Some Boston Jews were jobbers, or wholesalers, a new profession that was essential to the distribution of Robert's candy. Manufacturers like Robert needed to develop good relationships with jobbers, who delivered the manufacturer's products to retailers such as drugstores and newsstands.

Bostonians perused Henry Ford's *Dearborn Independent*, an anti-Semitic tract out of Michigan that covered nonsensical allegations of Jewish influence in print and politics. How did a Detroit-based newspaper become popular in Boston? Ford dealerships in Massachusetts, New York, and Iowa carried stacks of copies of the *Dearborn Independent*. Picking up their new car with that fresh new car smell, many new purchasers from Boston found a *Dearborn Independent* and its unmitigated hate in the passenger seat. Ford also published the *Protocols of the Elders of Zion*, a forged document proposing a global Jewish conspiracy, which, in fact, never existed. But that was beside the point. Many readers thought the global conspiracy was real, and the *Protocols* was often sold outside Catholic churches on Sundays before and after mass.[13]

More than any other member, however, Manion shaped Robert Welch's political education. From a working-class Catholic family in Henderson, Kentucky, Manion presaged the importance of Roman Catholics in the John Birch Society and, more generally, the conservative movement.[14] By the 1940s, Manion was the dean of Notre Dame Law School and an outspoken conservative leader. World War II brought Manion and Robert together. Robert found in Manion a lifetime friend, and the dean became one of the original members of the John Birch Society. Manion believed the war would foist upon the United States a completely different style of democracy—a European style of democracy.[15] "When a European speaks of 'democracy,'" Manion declared, "he generally means something that is entirely different from our traditional concept of democracy in the United States." Manion said that European democracy promised disorder, lack of tradition, egalitarianism, a dearth of reverence for time-honored values, and general social decadence.[16] According to Manion, European democracy was even more dangerous than Soviet Communism. The United States, Manion concluded, was not a democracy but a constitutional republic. In future years, Robert Welch and thousands of Birchers would declare that America was a "Republic . . . not a democracy. Let's keep it that way!"

Manion further feared that European values ran contrary to those of the Founding Fathers and would infuse America with decay. Americans believed, said Manion, that natural rights were given to them by God not from the state, which Europeans had held to be the case since the French Revolution. Involvement in European wars, accordingly, placed at risk America's preservation of natural law philosophy. With the French Revolution, Europeans, Manion said, "lost their dignity as men and assumed their man created status as 'nationals,'" substituting the "rights of nations" for the "rights of man." Consequently, violence would always engulf Europe. "When Europe subscribes as we subscribed to the self-evident truths of the Declaration of Independence, then Europeans will learn as Americans have learned, to live peaceably with one another"[17] Thus Manion saw war as corrupting Americans.

Manion also opposed intervention on the grounds of anti-statism. No friend of the New Deal, Manion saw in intervention "the trend towards consolidation and centralization in government." In the 1930s, he wrote for Catholic junior high school students an anti-statist civic textbook titled *Lessons in Liberty: A Study of American Government.* For Manion, big government was an unnecessary evil, "the pagan all-powerful state." Government must be based on "self-evident principles of God." For Manion, Communists inside the government were promoting intervention to increase the size of the state and pave the way for a Communist dictatorship.[18] War meant the consolidation of society and the centralization of government.

Along with big government, Manion's suspicions of big business explained his decision to join the AFC. He was convinced that big business, munitions makers, and other corporate masters of war were leading the parade. A man who represented the small businessperson, Manion argued that intervention served the interests of British bankers, manufacturers, and traders who were pro-Roosevelt. US participation in the European war also exclusively benefited the WASP establishment who ran both political parties.[19]

World War II was a catalyst for Welch's growing belief in conspiracies. As Robert spent time working for anti-interventionism in 1941, he became convinced that FDR was moving the country to war. "Perhaps the administration can maneuver into having its way without convincing us." He claimed that the interventionists were already enforcing loyalty in stifling the opposition: "The clamps are already being put on the free speech of those who do disagree with the war mongering policies." According to Welch, there was "immense subtle pressures" through "100 devious channels to quiet those would speak out."[20]

Welch was correct. According to Wayne S. Cole, the administration "did undertake anti-isolationist efforts." "The total effort by the Roosevelt administration," Cole said, "to defeat the isolationists was massive, many faceted, and effective."[21] It went further than the administration. John T. Flynn, the most outspoken isolationist columnist, was dropped from the *New Republic* in the spring of 1940 for his anti-interventionism. On May 20, 1941, when Roosevelt tapped New York City Mayor Fiorello H. LaGuardia to serve as director of the Office of Civilian Defense, he said he wanted to "offset the propaganda of the Wheelers, Nyes, Lindberghs, etc."

For Welch, the AFC was disappointing, but illuminating. It taught him something about the enemy. His experiences in the America First movement "convinced me personally that there's nothing so illiberal as the professional liberal." There is "nobody so intolerant of opposing convictions and those who hold them as the people who make a profession of ranting about intolerance." "There is nobody so anxious to regiment all other citizens with their own particular brand of straitjackets as the fellows who shout loudest that somebody else—Hitler, in this case—is trying to put a straitjacket on them."[22]

Consequently, anti-interventionism, at least in Europe, became a pillar for Welch in building the central tenets of his political philosophy. His opposition to intervention in Europe fueled his reaction against economic and social change. He blamed intervention repeatedly for problems that engulfed America in the coming decades.[23]

Waging a furious battle against the isolationists, Roosevelt secured reelection for an unprecedented third term in November 1940 and, in March 1941, convinced the Congress to pass the Lend Lease Act, allowing the provision of matériel to allies. But Hitler's invasion of the Soviet Union in June 1941 infused the AFC with a new enthusiasm. The invasion only deepened Robert's relationship with Manion, who astutely realized that after Hitler had renounced his pact with Stalin, the interventionists had been weakened. Manion, a fierce anti-Communist, argued that with Soviet Russia as an ally, the conflict was no longer a quest against totalitarianism. There was now no reason for Americans to enter because Russia's involvement decreased pressure on Britain. Moreover, Manion said, any American entry would just aid Soviet Russia. He favored allowing the two totalitarian menaces to fight it out, and Robert was in complete agreement.

America Firsters, especially Flynn, spent much of the 1930 and 1940s fending off attacks they were pro-fascist. That they were not reluctant to concede eastern Europe to Hitler and were open to appeasement with Nazi Germany made their rebuttals all the more challenging. That pro-Nazi organizations like the German American Bund and Father Coughlin's Christian Front supported America First did little to help its defense. While Flynn denounced such pro-fascist groups and declared that pro-fascist members were unwanted in his branch, other factions of America First were either not as aggressive in excluding pro-fascist elements or reluctant entirely. The upshot was a continued association of America First with pro-fascist sympathy and its continued reputation as a body that was unpatriotic and un-American.

By the fall of 1941, the interventionists still held that Hitler presented a fatal threat to liberal democracy, but the German leader—despite an unofficial war in the Atlantic—did not officially declare war on the Americans. On December 7, 1941, Japan bombed Pearl Harbor and sank half the American fleet. The following day, Roosevelt declared war on Japan, and Germany officially declared war on the United States.

After the attack on Pearl Harbor, rumors abounded that FDR engineered a "backdoor to war." Many right-wing anti-interventionists, among them Flynn and Welch, believed that a manipulative and conniving Roosevelt had staged a silent coup. Welch, a conspiracy theorist already, grew more conspiratorial.

In fact, the military had decoded communications from Japan, and America knew an attack was imminent, but government officials believed it would occur in Malaysia, Borneo, or the Philippines. General Walter Short and Admiral Husband Kimmell, the army and naval commanders in Hawaii, were alerted, but the message never indicated that an attack on Pearl Harbor was imminent. Rather than conspiring to enter the United States into the war, FDR had been outmaneuvered by Japan. Many on the Republican Right embraced a Pearl Harbor conspiracy, and most Republican readers of Robert R. McCormick's *Chicago Tribune* certainly did.

When the war began, Robert clamored for a Pacific First strategy. He was not alone. From the Midwest and the West, the cry could be heard from millions of Americans: "Get Japan first!" But Washington had already adopted the ABC-1 agreement to "get Germany first." Some who wanted quick revenge for the sneak attack were Pacific commanders and their Chinese allies. Welch had found little to complain about in Roosevelt's antebellum foreign policy in the Pacific, which saw China as the fulcrum in the East and Japan as a threat to peace in the region. Welch's own feelings about China would become all the more central to his worldview in the years after the war.[24]

7

Postwar Dreams and Delusions, 1946–1950

In the immediate postwar years, Robert Welch was drawn to the game of politics. He had been a Republican his entire life, but his party had not held the presidency since March 1933. As the Cold War heated up, Welch started thinking about getting into the political arena as a candidate. At the time, his ego told him he had a lot to offer. The voters would decide otherwise.

Welch was an introvert. He was not a back-slapping politician. That is likely why he felt an affinity to Robert Taft, another politician who did not enjoy the thrill of being out among the people. Personally, Welch remained far more interested in scholarly pursuits that precluded political activism. And he was doing well at work: in 1947 his peers had bestowed upon him the prestigious Kettle Award for candy manufacturer of the year—the candy industry's Oscar. Despite being reserved, Welch felt a sense of duty to his country. He felt an obligation to warn Americans of what he saw as the drift toward collectivism and tyranny. His duty became a nagging necessity. He centered his sights on the opinion leaders of the Greater Boston region and became a successful stump speaker for the issues that he cared about most.

Imagine him speaking. As he stumbled through his addresses, to his audience the introspective and aloof candyman must have appeared the exact opposite of the typical glib Massachusetts pol. He must have appeared the harried and absent-minded professor. He would tell his listeners of his busy schedule and his various responsibilities. The papers from the speech would fall from the rostrum to the floor. His persistent cough from all the cigars he loved to smoke would cause him to hack away without regard to the audience. That would produce phlegm. Then he would swallow the sputum, likely turning the stomachs of the attendees. The audience must have grown uneasy and queasy. Meanwhile Welch would ramble on. Every speech was typed out. He did not speak off the cuff. There were long, awkward pauses. He would grow pensive. He would ruminate. He often didn't connect. Sometimes he probably appeared to be on some other planet due to his distant cogitation. But he was so self-assured, he didn't care. Why was he so indifferent? Because when he delivered his speeches, he acted like he was delivering the secret answers to all the questions in the universe. All the keys to the kingdom. The stammering, the cough, the blizzard of papers—they were the bells and whistles—they didn't matter. The content was king. What came from his smoking typewriter was the real show. Welch always thought he was revealing something sacred—whatever that was.

Despite the catastrophe that people were watching in front of their very eyes, there was something endearing and composed and serene about this middle-aged candyman. How do we reconcile this serenity with a schedule that was hectic and a worldview that seems anything but relaxed?

Welch was an expert compartmentalizer. He could focus on a topic like a laser. But Welch could be fidgety on stage. He took his glasses off. Then put then back on. Then took them off again. But he was chipper even though the jowls on his face sagged as if some terrible tragedy had just befallen him. He was rarely in a frenzied state, although he did again like to point out to listeners how exhausted he was. He looked like he needed a good night's rest. He was serene because his conspiratorial worldview gave him an inner confidence that the way he understood and processed the world was correct. He was delivering the truth to the people—the stuff that would set them free. Trying to fit the pieces together like a good detective story, which he loved, and comprehending human events through a conspiratorial lens relaxed him. His loving family, his successful sons, and his adoring, growing followers who saw something in this strange mix of confidence and hand-wringing nervousness only bolstered Welch's tranquility. The folks back home in North Carolina—a lot of loving people—were all in his corner. And he loved all the attention.

His learning provided him serenity as well. He was proud of his library of 5,000 books, and his ego grew as his bookshelves did. There exists a photo of Welch standing relaxed but firm in front of his books. He looks ossified. But his face carries an unmistakable look of pride and satisfaction. He looks like an army general heading into some great battle with his library all behind him. He must have had a photographic memory because he knew by heart most of the words on the pages in all the books that were aligned behind him. The words were his soldiers, which he could call upon at a moment's notice. As his siblings assert, he possessed a confidence at an early age that he was always in the right. He never wavered. Ever.[1]

His first speech marking his turn toward political activism was with the League of Women Voters in Brookline, Massachusetts, on January 29, 1946. He was forty-six years old. The topic of the speech was whether the government ought to continue the practice of price controls and wartime rationing after the war ended. Robert solicited the invitation from the league, having read that a left-wing speaker in a previous address before the league had supported that idea. Robert penned a letter announcing his complete disagreement, included a $50 donation to the league, and concluded, "It's just too bad, that you don't have someone to present the other side. Why don't you?"[2]

The league had a policy of giving alternative positions a platform to present their views. Robert received an invitation to speak at the next meeting, and he accepted. But Robert was greatly disappointed to find out that he would not receive equal time. Another speaker, one Professor Warren of Amherst College, would first present his side in favor of the continuation of controls. Robert prepared carefully and was fully confident that after presenting his ten-point critique of price controls, he could crush his opponent's argument during the rebuttal period. According to Welch however, Warren enjoyed a full hour to present his argument, whereas Welch had only fifteen minutes to deliver his riposte. Robert had to hurry, but his speech was strong, and encapsulated familiar arguments from the libertarian intellectual playbook.

In "Against the Continuation of Price Controls," Robert made the case that government efforts to strengthen the economy by controlling it were counterproductive. Welch focused on how the administration of controls required a massive federal bureaucracy that devastated the taxpayer. He next rejected that price controls reduced inflation and argued that printing too much currency was its real cause. Robert argued that "the only force that will really hold prices down . . . of the things people wish to buy" is the purchaser. "We are going to have" plentiness "a great deal sooner if the breaks are taken off production," he added. He also observed that enforcing price controls was next to impossible because it was easy to get around them, such as by cheapening a product, which would be bad for the consumer. Another point was that government interventions in the economy dampened the individual spirit of competition and industry and encouraged Americans to rely on the federal government—a state of affairs that destroyed the pioneering spirit that made America great.[3]

The circumstances of the debate ultimately redounded to Welch's benefit. Many in attendance were initially favorably disposed toward Warren's viewpoint. But concluding that the process was fundamentally unfair to Welch, many wrote letters of protest to the League of Women Voters and expressed sympathy to Welch. We do not know whether he swayed any voters, but the brouhaha resulted in Welch being inundated with invitations to speak from other service clubs: Chambers of Commerce, Rotary clubs, and other organizations. To say he was in demand would be an understatement.

Throughout the 1940s, Welch sometimes perceived the rapid rise in collectivism in America but explained that natural historical processes, rather than conspiracy, accounted for this "anomaly." Throughout his life, Robert believed in the cycles of history, and despite embracing a conspiratorial view involving first a Communist cabal and subsequently the Illuminati, he believed civilizations continuously run the course of being victim of collectivist conspiracies followed by periods of freedom and rampant individualism in which a central authority is absent. The collectivists would then take over once again, followed by a continuation of the natural cycle of freedom to tyranny. Thus to call him a conspiracy theorist is reductionist, to some extent..[4]

Throughout his speeches prior to 1950, he argued that the natural laws that govern the rise and fall of nations tend to encourage societies to surrender to collectivism. Communism in the United States was a natural devolution that occurred because of the cycles of history. As historian Joyce Mao puts it, Welch saw collectivism as "a natural and perhaps predictable byproduct of degeneration."[5] Price controls and other forms of collectivism were symptoms of an advanced society that had grown soft and was in a state of decay just as the Babylonians and Assyrians and Romans had experienced: "Contrary to popular belief, price control is not a grand new idea, invented yesterday. There is nothing new about it at all. 3900 years ago in about 2000 BC, when the old Babylonian Empire had reached its apex and was already starting its process of disintegration, Hammurabi invoked a hard and fast price control as one of his measures to try to stave off chaos." "2500 years ago, in the sixth century B.C.," Welch added, "when the Assyrian Empire had gone to pieces, Nineveh itself was destroyed, and the remnants were being held together in a false burst of final glory that has become known as the neo-Babylonian Empire, Nebuchadnezzar used price control as one means" to give stability to an unstable society. "And, 1600 years ago, in the last decade of the third century A.D., the Roman Emperor Diocletian, facing the problems of economic decay, substituted a managed economy for law of supply and demand" and introduced price controls. "He distributed food to the port half the market price—don't think our food stamps are anything new—undertook extensive public works to busy the unemployed, and inaugurated a complete New Deal" with "rigid control of prices and wages." "We know a great deal about Diocletian's attempt to replace economic laws with governmental decrees," Welch went on, and they were a complete failure that marked a "dying civilization."[6]

Welch said it was only natural that western Europe was falling victim to collectivism because the problem could be traced back "into the fifth and six centuries A.D. when the Saxon chieftains in England and the ancestors of Charlemagne on the continent were carving for themselves feudal kingdoms out of the wreckage of that empire which Diocletian and Constantine had vainly tried to save." Yet America was different, for it "is an entirely new entity, still young and still with a glorious economic future ahead of it," whereas Europe was old and decrepit. "Our country today, and most of the people in it," Welch added "are in a mood to produce, rather than to spend all their energy in fighting over controls of and division of what is being produced." Because America was a young nation, he said, the grip of collectivism there was an "anomaly" and inconsistent with the natural laws of civilizations. This might not be convincing, but it does suggest that Welch was not always a conspiracy theorist.

At least in some instances prior to 1950, he explained the anomaly as a product of natural process rather than a conspiracy of nefarious men consciously seeking to introduce a Communist cancer into a healthy young nation. Gradually, however, the discourse of conspiracy entered his speeches until he held the belief that weakening and destroying the republic was a purposeful act on the part of a cabal of traitors. Detractors criticized Welch in later years for wasting too much time on conspiracy to the exclusion of addressing more potent challenges to collectivism, especially the libertarian argument that any form of it paved the way for totalitarianism—that is, a road to serfdom. This argument arose from the libertarian views of Friedrich Hayek and Ludwig von Mises, which Welch found to be blind to the coercive aspects of the collectivist conspiracy. Welch read all of Hayek's works but especially enjoyed *The Road to Serfdom*.

In that book, Hayek opined that state planning paved the way toward totalitarianism. A professor at the London School of Economics, Hayek lamented the growing embrace of centralized planning in western economies during World War II. Planning was misguided because the complexity of the ever-changing marketplace made it impossible for anyone to understand what was occurring at a given moment. Planning compromised individual freedom because it was impossible in a democratic system for planners to agree on goals. All decision-making responsibilities would fall to a small minority of the most unscrupulous and self-interested. This minority would prohibit equal treatment under the law and lead society down a slippery slope toward dictatorship. The only way to safeguard individual freedom was to unleash the "spontaneous forces of society" and embrace the free market and competition.[7]

Welch devoured Mises as well. Mises argued in his 1944 book *Bureaucracy* that the bureaucratic system of management—the antithesis of the profit system—was constraining creativity and contaminating both the public and private sectors in the United States. Even more uncompromising in his defense of the market than Hayek, Mises argued that only "under perfect capitalism, hitherto never and nowhere completely tried or achieved," could peace be sustained in the West.

His readings of Hayek and Mises were evident on September 27, 1946, when in a speech to the New England Conference of State Federations of Women's Clubs at Poland Springs, Maine, Welch introduced their argument that government subsidies resulted in an inevitable loss of freedom. As well as being inefficient and a waste of money, government subsidies allowed "individual bureaucrats to govern our lives by their own regulations and interpretations of regulations." "Letting every little Tom, Dick, and Harry who suddenly acquires the dignity and supposed respect—and at least the power—of a governmental job, become a law unto himself, is a stupid way to be a bunch of suckers."[8]

Yet Robert was no radical libertarian. He believed that government served an important function, protecting threats against property, freedom, and life. He challenged free-market radicals who resisted any government involvement. He also supported an enlightened monarchy over a representative government that feigned to have the interests of the people in mind but was actually corrupt. In 1946, Welch argued that big government was the source of man's social problems. "I am convinced America would be better off with a government of 300,000 officials and agents, every single one of them a thief, than a government of 3 million agents with every single one of them an honest, honorable public servant," he said. "For the first group would only steal from the American economic system; the second group would be bound in time to destroy it."[9]

In 1946, Robert traveled to Britain to study how socialism influenced the government. He set off with certain basic assumptions. He believed his country—first through the Square Deal, then the New Deal, and finally the Fair Deal—was following the exact same road to ruin as Britain, but trailed the mother country by a few years. He considered the trip an emergency. He needed to save his homeland and took on the role of crusader. By trying to predict what America would look like if it followed the British model of government control, Welch was playing the role of soothsayer. He thought that a careful appraisal of socialism in Britain could project what collectivism in America would look like in a decade. When he arrived home, he drafted a speech that he delivered more than 300 times without charge to civic, political, and social organizations. He presented a gruesome picture of what socialism had done to the standard of living in Britain. "The present English political picture as it looks to one American businessman," Welch said, was "stark and unadorned," and "there is no reason on earth why we should import, or let ourselves be infected by, such diseases of social old age as socialism and communism and other ideological cancers." These speeches also highlighted the continuing influence of Manion on his thought.[10]

Robert enjoyed delivering speeches, but he noticed a discouraging pattern: the audience nodded in assent, clapped enthusiastically, but returned to their daily routines, avoiding any further consideration of the topic. Robert concluded that to make a difference or to affect change, he needed to go into politics. He openly admitted that he did not want to, did not think he had the aptitude for the task, but declared, "I can't take what is happening any longer."[11]

Welch went into politics because for him, the Great Depression inaugurated a historical offensive on society. The New Deal represented a "collectivist" assault against freedom. Democratic "regimentation" under FDR was no less dangerous than the policies implemented in fascist Germany and Soviet Russia. Like other popular conservative writers of the postwar Right, Welch found an early hero in Robert Taft, first elected to the Senate from Ohio in 1938 and whose offensive against "New Deal socialism" sustained their resolve and earned their respect.

Taft was a remnant of a once hegemonic Republican Party. Despite a string of disastrous defeats between 1930 and 1936, midwestern Republicans of Taft's ilk remained steadfast to their fundamental principles. They became the core of the right-wing postwar Republicans. They were strong in the small towns of rural America; they were strong on Main Street USA; they found some of their strongest backers in outlying hubs of the Northeast—such as Worcester, Massachusetts. This retinue of hearty individualists, manufacturers, and writers plotted to return to power and the policies of the 1920s. Most rightists, including Taft and Welch, rejected any accommodation to the New Deal order and refused to adjust to "internationalist" foreign policies. Many wanted to roll back the damage inflicted by the New Deal and move American foreign policy away from Europe.

Robert was attracted to the desperation of being a Republican in this time. He liked being an underdog. At the start of the 1946 campaign, the Republican Party had suffered as the minority party for thirteen long years. FDR had been bad enough, but the ascension of Harry Truman, a product of the Missouri's Pendergast machine, to the presidency made it seem as though labor, liberals, and pinks were making a mad dash toward a socialist America at home and surrender overseas.[12]

Robert, an astute observer of the American scene, concluded that the Democratic Party was not fulfilling promises of peace. He saw opportunity. During the war, Americans looked forward to peace with deep yearning. They dreamed of buying new cars. They could purchase houses. Unemployment would drop. They wanted a return to normalcy. They wanted to get on with their lives after long years of sacrifice and fighting. They wanted the good life and the products that every American deserved: toasters, refrigerators, cigarettes, liquor, and a lot of red meat. The boys fought for it. They earned it. But a year after Japan's surrender aboard the *Missouri*, things were not turning out the way they had envisioned. Food was scarce. Housing was scarce too. Products were unavailable. The inflation rate was 20 percent. Strikes were ubiquitous.

Many Americans, Welch sensed, were tired of the New Deal. They were not even getting a Fair Deal. Many were tired of the Democratic Party. Robert Welch wanted to strike a blow against collectivism at home and tyranny abroad. Robert wanted to abolish the overweening Office of Price Administration. Robert wanted to set the economy free and allow it to work its magic. Robert was correct that the price ceilings were not keeping prices down but actually raising prices to the roof. Ranchers were not even releasing their stock with ceilings in effect, thus increasing prices because of the small supply. Ceilings on meat, he held correctly, produced rising prices on fish and chicken. Wage and price controls were not the wave of the future or the road to progress. They were the road to serfdom.

Robert Welch did not invent anti-Communism, nor was he among the earliest to practice it. But he came to believe that Communists existed at the highest levels of the American government and thought Communist infiltration was the greatest threat to the republic. The problem was this was not true.

A conspiracy theory of Communist subversion had some basis in reality at a certain time: the CIO was influenced by the CPUSA in the 1930s, for example. But by 1951, when Senator Joseph McCarthy declared a "conspiracy . . . so immense" at the highest levels of the federal government, and Welch echoed the charge in a series of books, speeches, letters, and pamphlets throughout the decade, the number of Soviet spies within the Truman and Eisenhower administrations was negligible and had little influence. Yet a cadre of columnists, politicians, and writers like Welch made many Americans believe that high-level officials like Dean Acheson, George Marshall, and even President Eisenhower were enemies of the state. Americans had ended their spy saga with the Communists by the 1940s, but they became convinced more than ever in the 1950s that subversion was real and the threat was enormous. The damages to civil liberties and lives would be incalculable.[13]

In the 1920s, the Soviet state established a massive and successful industrial espionage program and sent agents to infiltrate American businesses and steal intellectual property. By the 1930s, Soviet spies successfully infiltrated the federal government. Agents disguised as diplomats recruited a thriving network of American case officers who located and managed sources in federal agencies. Among those case officers was Whittaker Chambers, who ran an entire cell of Communists in the administration of Franklin Delano Roosevelt. Members of Chambers's cell included high-level diplomats like Harry Dexter White, who became assistant secretary of the Treasury, and Alger Hiss, a talented bureaucrat in the State Department.

Stalin, paranoid in the late 1930s, shut down the networks set up by his agents. Some of his best and brightest agents were picked up in America, shipped home to Moscow, charged with treason, and shot dead. Chambers and others were disillusioned by the purges, but the wartime alliance with the United States rekindled Soviet espionage in the federal government. The United States shared intelligence with the Soviets, though Stalin often did not reciprocate. Soviet spies knew about the Manhattan Project to build the atomic bomb, and the Soviets successfully tested their own atomic weapon in 1949, thanks to their spy network

The threat of Communism—or rather, the perception of that

threat—influenced Robert's decision to enter politics. Elizabeth Bentley, the "Red Spy Queen," piqued Robert's interest in July 1948 when she told the House Un-American Activities Committee (HUAC) that a Communist cell operated within the government. Bentley ran a wartime spy ring that collected intelligence from White. In November 1945, Bentley gave herself up to the FBI, but nothing happened. Robert believed the administration's failure to act proved that traitors circulated within the government, not that ineptitude or slipshod security procedures accounted for the inaction. Bentley's confessions inaugurated the great Red Scare of the 1940s and 1950s. She named dozens of Americans, including White, Hiss, and Franklin Roosevelt's special assistant Lauchlin Currie. Soviet officials shut down all spying operations in the United States, leaving their spies to do little but complain about anti-Soviet messaging in American movies and newspapers. Welch and other Americans did not—could not—know that the Soviet spies had been shut down, and he, like FBI Director J. Edgar Hoover and Senator McCarthy, believed that Bentley's ring was the tip of a massive conspiracy to undermine the republic. But the iceberg had already melted.

Welch, like millions of Americans in 1948, lived in a state of fear. Three years earlier, the world had changed when the United States used two nuclear bombs on Japan to end the war. Anywhere, anytime, an atomic bomb could destroy a whole city of civilians. It was a matter of time before another nation got an atomic weapon. All Americans were targets. Meanwhile the Truman Doctrine seemed like a declaration of war on the Soviet Union. In 1947, after Republican Senator Arthur Vandenburg advised him to "scare hell out of the American people," Truman gave a fire-breathing address calling for assistance to Turkey and Greece and declaring that "totalitarian regimes" wanted to end freedom as Americans knew it. It was time, Truman said, to choose "between alternative ways of life," and "it must be the policy of the United States to support free peoples."[14] International control of atomic energy failed. In 1948, atomic tests at Eniwetok Atoll confirmed more powerful bombs, more frightening weapons. The Soviet Union took over Czechoslovakia. West Berlin was blockaded by the Soviet Union. On July 1948, B-29s with nuclear weapons scrambled to

Britain in response. World war seemed imminent. Robert Welch was gravely concerned.

After Bentley's extraordinary testimony, Chambers told HUAC investigators he had even more information than she did. His testimony began on August 3, 1948. Chambers testified that Hiss was a Communist in the 1930s. While in the State Department, Hiss had helped organize the conferences that established the United Nations. Donald, Hiss's brother, was a partner at Covington and Burling, Dean Acheson's law firm. Draw the connections yourself. Hiss emphatically denied the charges and sued Chambers. But Chambers supplied evidence to HUAC that Hiss passed him State Department documents. In 1950, Hiss was indicted and convicted of perjury.[15]

The Hiss proceedings mesmerized Welch. For him, the Hiss case was a crucible that explained everything. Hiss had been convicted on account of espionage with the Soviet Union. Hiss had been a star in the Roosevelt administration and had a seat at the table in Yalta. He was a friend of Acheson, the secretary of state, who announced, whatever the outcome, "I do not intend to turn my back on Alger Hiss." Altogether, the Hiss case was an indictment of more than fifteen years of foreign policy under two Democratic administrations.[16] Already hot, Robert's blood ran hotter.[17]

The Hiss case gave Welch confidence that every antipathy he felt toward Communism since the Red Scare of 1919 was justified and convinced him that now was the time to run for public office. The Hiss case strengthened Robert's conviction that he was absolutely correct in adamantly assailing diplomatic recognition of the Soviet Union. The Hiss case resolved any doubt in Robert's mind about his opposition to intervention in World War II since it had now been proven that the Soviet Union had been the victors in the end. The Hiss case made rolling back the New Deal gains of the 1930s and restoring the classical liberalism of the 1920s a worthy cause for the 1950s. The country needed him, he thought, at this pivotal moment in its history.

8
The Candidate, 1950

Robert Welch decided to enter the arena of politics. But what would he run for? National politics was where the action was. And in national politics, Communism and Communists were everywhere.

In the fall of 1949, Mao Tse-tung and the Communists conquered mainland China. This was both a crisis for the Truman administration and a tremendous opportunity for Republican politicians. The Republican Right wanted a spokesman who was adept with the media and could capture the public's attention with continued assaults on the State Department and claims of Democratic treason. They found one in Senator Joseph McCarthy, who said the "loss" of China was due to the treason of Mao supporters in the State Department. In September 1949, Russia exploded its first nuclear bomb. Fear of war with the Soviets in 1948 morphed into outright panic.

McCarthy poured gasoline on the panic on February 1, 1950, by announcing that he had a list of 205 Communists working in the State Department. Welch completely agreed, and he felt fortified that a politician finally had the temerity to say so. Robert wished only that he had said it first. As McCarthy traveled the country over the next week, the number of Communists changed. On February 10 in Salt Lake City, the number was 57. In the Senate ten days later, the number was 81. The charges changed too. Perhaps the individuals were not "card-carrying" Communists. They were "loyalty risks" perhaps. They were perhaps "people with Communist connections." Perhaps.

Both McCarthy and later Welch relied on the information gathering of Alfred Kohlberg and his powerful anti-Communist network. McCarthy's allegations were secondhand, but the material appeared novel and solid because he supplied numbers and, perhaps, names. If anybody in Kohlberg's network hedged or offered qualifications, McCarthy did not. His explicit, sensational claims made front-page copy. Reporters echoed McCarthy's statements and supplied him with a constant stream of publicity.[1]

As Ellen Schrecker has observed, McCarthy was not an aberration or a peculiarity who appeared on the scene in the early 1950s and suffocated the air out of politics, held presidents hostage, and quickly exited the stage to allow for figures with a "sense of decency" to return. His ghost stalked the political landscape for decades thereafter in the form of new demagogues who rose to infamy. He also had many precursors who supplied material for his crusade and loyal connections who lent credibility to his unfounded aspersions. The forerunners provided a program and a lineup of targets as well. Still, he was his own man and a master manipulator for publicity. He wrote his own rules for the game and forced others to play by them.[2]

Robert Welch received a great emotional boost from McCarthy, who was a force in the 1950 campaign for many Republicans, giving thirty major speeches across fifteen states. McCarthy was making politics interesting again. It was warfare. It was mortal combat. It was hyperbole. And it was fun. Welch dreamed of joining him in the Senate.

Welch was not a complete newcomer to the political world. During World War II, he kept very busy serving on various boards. He belonged to the Office of Price Administration's advisory committee for the candy industry. He chaired the National Security Resources Board's candy industry committee. He served as chair, vice president, and member of the board of the Washington committee of the National Association of Manufacturers.[3] In 1946, he assisted Representative Robert Bradford in his successful campaign for governor of Massachusetts by establishing a large grassroots writing campaign. In 1948, Bradford persuaded Robert to serve as chair of the Republican Party Finance Committee. (Bradford lost that year, however.)

But even as Robert dreamed of being in the Senate fighting alongside McCarthy, or the archconservative California Republican William

Knowland, or the reactionary Indiana Republican William Jenner, he faced several problems. Massachusetts already had two Republican senators: Leverett Saltonstall and Henry Cabot Lodge. The House of Representatives was out, too, because the fifth district, where Robert lived, was already represented by the extremely popular Republican Edith Nourse Rogers, who was a fierce advocate for veterans. Congress was simply unavailable for Robert Welch, no matter his passion for foreign policy.

He looked to state politics and found an opening: lieutenant governor. Elected separately from the governor, the holder of the office of lieutenant governor would be in a grand position to run for governor in 1952. Robert Welch, candy manufacturer, took on four aspirants with considerable experience in politics—former state treasurer Laurence Curtis; Senate president Harris S. Richardson; former governor's councillor Warren G. Harris; and the mayor of Beverly, Daniel E. McLean.[4]

Robert distinguished himself with McCarthyite claims of collectivism in high places. He echoed John T. Flynn's *The Road Ahead*, which admonished the Right for preoccupying itself with Communism. The true dangers, as Flynn said and Welch echoed, were not Moscow but London, and "creeping socialism" rather than Communism. As Welch met voters on the campaign trail, he told them: "I am a conservative Republican and they can get a pretty good idea of where I stand from one fact: Calvin Coolidge was too 'liberal' for me."[5]

Welch's supporters were men like him, businessmen of small- and medium-sized firms, salesmen, professionals who had achieved monetary success. They were men of Main Street, not Wall Street. They hated FDR. They were not the corporate heads who had once made deals with "That Man in the White House." They loathed the New Deal, hated its overburdening regulations, its "alphabet soup" of programs that hindered the life of business. They saw in Truman's Fair Deal the same folly of federal encroachment. Nationwide, the collective wealth of such men exceeded that of all the corporations.[6]

Welch also had supporters in the working class. He and McCarthy both relished being tough fighters who dared say the things that others were afraid to say. Both men scored high among working-class folks whose own employment involved dirty but necessary tasks. Some men showered before work. McCarthy's and Welch's supporters showered after work. Politics, said McCarthy, was "a dirty, disagreeable job," like his boyhood chore of killing the skunks that invaded his family's chicken coop. He said neighbors refused to sit next to him afterward. Welch viewed politics the same way.[7] He remembered all the trips made back and forth to his candy plant while powdered in flour and weary from the long drive. That was dirty work too.

The *Boston Herald*'s astute political observer W. E. Mullins said "masters of political science" in Massachusetts called lieutenant governor and attorney general "the most valuable nominations on the Republican ticket this year." He added: "The optimism among Republicans that they will regain the office of Lieutenant Governor probably stems from the circumstance that only once in the past 35 years have they lost it in an election coming in between presidential elections." Some Republicans also reasoned that Democratic governor Dever faced "enormous problems" in the coming two years and "may be stoned out of office" for "building up a mountain of debt that can be scaled back only with the imposition of" high taxes. "It therefore will be vital to have an experienced and highly intelligent Republican in the lieutenant governorship as a means of having a good man in the watchtower," observed Mullins.[8] Experienced and intelligent, Welch must have thought. Well, that's me.

Welch was also very adept at promoting himself, though he could run the risk of appearing disingenuous. Sophistry was a fault of Welch, whose instincts as a salesmen were to frequently "gild the lily." He was shrewd, but sometimes folks caught on to his wiles. For example, with the primary more than eleven months away, he wrote to one newspaper: "Although publicity is, I have been told, always grist to any candidate's mill, it is not the purpose of this letter to seek any publicity in your columns at the present time." "In fact," Welch continued, "since I definitely shall have to build up support slowly and steadily, any excessive ballyhooing of my announcement might even be harmful." The newspaper was clearly not convinced that Welch was being sincere and observed, "we will endeavor to restrain ourselves on the subject." Welch was learning how to become a politician because he wanted to win. And he would do what it took to win. But he never thought himself above the law. Although he never did anything illegal or extralegal, he could connive as good salesman do and good politicians do.

Fifty-year-old Robert threw himself into the race with the energy of a man twenty years younger. His strategy in the state campaign differed greatly from McCarthy's or Knowland's in Washington. Whereas the central concern in Washington was the presence of Communists infiltrating the State Department, Welch focused on the incremental encroachment of socialism into the Massachusetts body politic and suggested that Massachusetts was a "guinea pig" for socialistic programs and initiatives. Avoiding contentious national issues—concerns that would inevitably turn off Massachusetts Republicans if they ever got whiff of his archconservative ideology—actually proved advantageous for him. Screaming about socialism was a lot less controversial than screaming about Communism.

The candidate received immeasurable support from his wife, Marian. She bolstered his confidence and self-worth, told him that he was on the right path, and committed herself as much as he did to stopping socialism in Massachusetts. Marian attended his speeches, took shorthand notes, and offered kind suggestions for improvement. She edited important letters to prominent officials and served as a trusted confidante. She did it because Robert believed that the crusade was just, and she followed and respected his decision out of duty and out of love.

Nothing indicates that Marian had concerns with Robert's preoccupation with fighting socialism some eighteen hours a day, seven days a week. While Robert was off giving speeches, Marian made curtains, slipcovers, and draperies for their home in Belmont. She did all the housework, cooked all the meals, and successfully raised their sons, Hillard and Robert III, who during this period were becoming highly accomplished young men. Marian made the shopping lists and went to the supermarket. She cleaned the home, vacuumed up the fur, and picked up the mess from the Welches' beloved shepherd collies—Patsy and Ajax—from many Belmont front lawns. Every morning, she pressed Robert's suits. She rose early, made the coffee, and cooked breakfast for her husband.[9] They made a great team.

Out on the road, Welch spoke before scores of social, business, and labor organizations throughout Massachusetts, two or three times a week, addressing contemporary issues from the perspective of a businessperson. He liked to say that he would climb on a soapbox to assail the evils of socialism when anybody would listen. Welch lamented that the United States was duplicating the English model. Massachusetts, he claimed, was being used as a "guinea pig" to introduce socialism throughout the country.[10]

England was not the only place overseas that Robert had traveled in recent years. In February 1948, he continued his study of socialism in western Europe, and in April 1949, he made a trip around the world stopping in eight Asiatic countries. His talk "Bird's Eye View of the World," which was based on his trip, consisted of anecdotes and observations of his experiences, the people he met, and the places he visited. But rather than an observation of other countries, it was a celebration of American supremacy, and sometimes highlighted the inferiority of the peoples and countries along his way. By 1950, he claimed to have traveled more than a million miles over the preceding twenty-five years. He crossed the continent twenty-two times, he proudly shared.[11] Welch believed for some strange reason that his status as a world traveler would benefit him in a race for lieutenant governor. But again, it was always about getting to the US Senate. That was his dream.

Robert had announced his candidacy for lieutenant governor before any other candidate, calling his platform a "bulwark against socialism." He delivered the antisocialist speech "A Businessman Looks at England" 300 times across Massachusetts. "Some of the approximately 25,000 controls in England today," Welch told a crowd in Attleboro, "are stupidly burdensome," introduce "red tape," and result in "wasted man-hours." The British socialist system created havoc on the economy, he told a crowd in Haverhill. "Nationalism of industry," Welch said, "handicapped and hurt British production." Food subsidies, social services, and price controls, Welch explained, "pulled everyone down to the lowest level instead of pulling the lower levels up and has meant an equal distribution of poverty for all." "The socialist government has done far more damage and more lasting damage to the English nation in five years than the war did in six," he told a Beverly audience. In Quincy, he told listeners that socialism produced "self-imposed obstacles" and a "terrific loss of incentive." He added: "taxes are so high on certain articles such as gas," "railroads, coal mines, steel, iron industries are all nationalized," and "patriotism has ceased to exist." A "general overall lack of ambition to do anything" prevailed. He admonished fellow citizens that Britain provided the American people an "excellent mirror" of what was to occur in their own country. "Nowhere in the country today must the challenge of collectivist planning be met more energetically than in Massachusetts," he concluded. But Welch explained with some reservations that things did not have to be that way: "No change of government can make very much difference. You just cannot unscramble eggs or put Humpty Dumpty back together again," but "we do not want in this country the feeling of bewilderment, frustration, and defeatism, in which the English people are forced to live today."[12]

Welch's campaign essentially applied John T. Flynn's "creeping socialism" thesis. The gradualist strategy of the Fabian Society was the project of American Socialists, Flynn argued. In Britain, the Fabian Socialists, in tandem with the Liberal Party and trade unions, established a welfare state. In the process, the Liberal Party saw its own demise and the ascension of the Labour Party and a socialist state. The same thing was happening in America, Flynn and Welch said, between the Democratic Party and the union movement, which were in cahoots with the Communist-dominated CIO. Thus, the danger rested not as much in Communism but in socialism. Flynn said that "the Cold War has had one significant" and detrimental "effect": "We have . . . been making war on the Communists," but, he warned, "if every Communist in America were rounded up and liquidated, the great menace to our form of social organization would be still among us."[13]

Welch opposed national health insurance and received much support from doctors who liked his strong stand against socialized medicine. His campaign finance committee included five physicians and dentists. Robert earned the support of E. S. Bagnell, the former president of the Massachusetts Medical Society, as well as Patrick T. Sullivan, the Society's vice president. Together, the two signed a letter sent to 7,000 Massachusetts physicians encouraging support for Welch. In March 1950, Welch delivered an address titled "A Businessman Looks at Medicine" while in "A Businessman Looks at Beacon Hill," he argued that socialized medicine was "a tool used by every dictator in his climb to power" and a "weapon first used by Bismarck for socializing the German people."

Business competitors also provided some enthusiasm for the Welch effort. One of Robert's competitors in the candy business sent out 250 personal letters. Robert also received the unqualified support of twenty-two other candy industry executives, who sent out a round-robin memorandum backing him. Welch also benefited from support from Lloyd B. Waring, a member of the Republican state committee—to the consternation of other candidates, who resented the committee's involvement.[14]

Austerity was another principle of his platform. The size of state government is "mushrooming" and "unnecessary." "We already have too much government in Washington without duplicating the whole confused mess in Boston." Correspondingly, we need a "drastic reduction of state taxation." "There isn't a business in America the size of our Massachusetts government," he said, "which could survive two annual reports with the waste of time, of materials, and of money in our state's operation of its affairs."[15] He called for a halt to new departments, a hiring freeze, salary cuts, and an end to the usurpation of towns' and cities' power by the state and federal governments. He attacked compensation programs for sick state employees. "Unlimited security," he railed, "was a soap bubble promise." Government cannot be a "perpetual Santa Claus."[16] Welch ran against public power and public proprietorship, assuming that private entities, in general, ran everything better than a public institution could.

Welch attacked the Dever administration for spending $394 million in 1950—"by far the costliest administration in the Commonwealth's history." Welch called the administration "spendthrift" and "socialistically inclined." During the closing days of the legislative session, Dever "rammed through" a controversial limited-access highways bill, and Welch attacked it. "This measure," Welch protested, put "the state into the roadside stand and gas station business along every highway in Massachusetts with Public Works Commissioner William P. Callahan, a Dever appointee, as virtual czar in charge."[17] He further castigated Dever for proposing "useless expenditures," such as a "snoop" commission on life's necessities and seventeen business agents for the Commonwealth's mental health institutions. Robert Welch wanted to run Massachusetts state government as a business.

But despite running for a state office, at times he appeared to be running against Washington. Again, securing a seat in the US Senate was never far from his mind. In "A Businessman Looks at Washington," Welch observed: "Washington is reaching its hands into your pockets and its fingers around your neck every time you buy a pack of cigarettes, take the children to a movie, send a telegram, or draw your paycheck." He added: "there are many tentacles of many different arms of this octopus reaching its slippery, crawling arms around our lives at the same time."[18] The answer to encroaching federal government control over our lives, he maintained, was rolling back the welfare state, introducing tax cuts, and establishing greater cooperation between management and labor to foster prosperity and build a better job market.

The national party did pay some attention to Welch. Speaking to 175 men and women of the women's Republican club of North Attleboro in May 1950, Welch was joined by the Republican House minority leader Joseph Martin. The pair tried to arouse the people to the dangers of socialism at the state and national levels. Martin assailed federal aid and condemned the Truman administration's efforts to destroy the incentive to work, save money, and sacrifice. "The administration was attempting and succeeding in its efforts to change the character of the American people through its waste in government spending," Welch added.[19]

Welch seethed with further fury against President Truman when on June 25, 1950, North Korea invaded South Korea, and Truman decided to repel the attack with American ground troops under the control of the United Nations. No American foreign policy should be decided by the UN, Welch believed. Welch was bewildered by the president's decision to obtain both the UN's denunciation of invasion and its approval for intervention.[20] Welch was mollified somewhat when Douglas MacArthur was chosen as commander in chief of the UN Command.

As primary day approached, the Welch campaigners felt very confident because their organization was better than that of any other candidate. Robert's advisors believed that he was well out in front of the field because he had thrown his hat in the ring early—in September 1949. He had crisscrossed the state. He delivered more than 200 speeches.

He garnered institutional support statewide, and his circle of followers established Welch for Lieutenant Governor Committees in at least half of the Bay State's 351 cities and towns. He had amassed an army of 8,000 men and women who were actively serving on more than 200 committees from across Massachusetts. He also received lots of publicity. By virtue of his enviable organizational structure, local papers gave lots of attention to the first-time candidate, flooding their readers with stories of Robert on the campaign trail.[21]

The turnout was large on Tuesday, September 19, and while the Old Guard elements backing Welch made an impressive showing, it was a day for the rank-and-file Republican voters, who cast their ballots overwhelmingly for former state treasurer Laurence Curtis. Welch's political organization did yeoman's work on election day, and Welch finished a very impressive second. He ran a remarkable race for a first-time candidate. Working full time at the James O. Welch Candy Company, Robert outpolled the president of the state senate. But the final vote count was 161,052 for Curtis and 59,238 for Welch.[22]

Welch's politics were too reactionary for Massachusetts. The victor knew that voters wanted liberal Republican leaders, and he ran as one, like Leverett Saltonstall and Henry Cabot Lodge Jr. But Welch put himself outside the mainstream at an early stage. He also faced a veteran problem, in that he was not one. Welch was fifty years old in 1950—too young for World War I and too old for World War II. Veterans had a decided electoral advantage over their opponents who did not serve, and injured veterans had even better shots. For instance, in 1946 a young navy veteran named John Fitzgerald Kennedy had secured a seat in the US Congress from Massachusetts by highlighting his heroics as a PT boat commander in the Pacific. Welch's victorious challenger had lost a leg as an aviator in World War I. In his campaign, Curtis highlighted his service as a department commander and national senior vice commander of the Disabled American Veterans. Politics was a popular profession for returning veterans of the Greatest Generation, and Welch hailed from an older generation who did not serve their country in war. In fact, Welch had railed against American involvement in the war effort. In that sense, he was on the wrong side of history, and his anti-interventionist stance in the great moral battle against the Nazi menace certainly did not assist his political aspirations, to say the least.

He chose poorly in the 1930s, aligned himself with the Old Right, and it may have come back to haunt him in seeking the office of lieutenant governor. Unlike Kennedy, who saved men in his PT boat crew, Welch was not able to make up for his mistake during WWII.

Despite Welch's loss, it was a Republican year, in part because of the situation in Korea. In the state legislature, Republicans gained 28 seats in the House and 5 in the Senate. In races for the US Senate, 3 of the primary victors were from the Republican Right. Democrats elected 126 to the House of Representatives, while the Republicans sent 196 outside the South. Republicans elected 18 senators, and the Democrats only 9 outside the South. Four McCarthyites joined the Senate: Maryland's John Marshall Butler, Herman Welker of Idaho, Everett Dirksen of Illinois, and Richard Nixon of California.[23] Nixon was a navy man himself, but his signature achievement in the Pacific largely consisted of winning hands of poker.

Only two days after Robert's defeat, he mailed a letter to all workers and contributors in which he observed optimistically: "I am happy about the whole thing. We made a fairly firm entry into the field of politics." He promised that there would be "other political campaigns to follow." This first unsuccessful campaign, "I have considered . . . as part of a broader educational campaign for more honesty in government, and more common sense in our economic thinking. So far as I am concerned, this crusade has just started." "I hope and believe that the 60,000 people who voted in this first campaign will become a solid core of support around which we can build a far stronger, more militant, and effective force of political strength and other campaigns to come."[24] Still processing the loss, which was a great jolt to his giant ego, the letter was perhaps an exercise in deluding himself. American politics is a "winner take all" sport, and, in reality, he did not "make a fairly firm entry into the field of politics."

Though naturally crestfallen by his loss, Robert continued to motivate his supporters. He likely intended to run for office in 1952. He wrote supporters on February 26, 1951, that the fight was not over; in fact, he planned to steam "all ahead full," though "it is too early to decide for what office, if any, I personally shall seek the nomination." He seemed to have caught a bad case of the political bug, whose only cure was victory at the polls. He broached the idea of establishing campaign committees. "In many communities," he said, "I have friends who wish to organize local Welch Campaign Committees. The 'Welch Campaign,' in this connection, would have a broader meaning, and these committees would have a broader purpose, than merely the promotion of the political candidacy of a particular man." He added: "The Welch Campaign would become—what I have intended it to be all along—a continuing movement of growing force for more honesty in government and more common sense in our economic thinking."[25]

He then solicited permission from the recipients to use their names on a committee of endorsers. He concluded: "I will add merely that, more important than my own time and money and strength required, is the sacrifice I am making of some considerable part of a promising business career, to fight for these things in which you and I believe, simply because somebody has to do so."[26]

The forerunner for the John Birch Society was hatched in Brockton, Massachusetts, on March 20, 1951. Seventy-five people attended the first meeting of the Welch Campaign Committee at the Brockton City Republican Committee Headquarters. Welch introduced them to his idea of establishing small groups throughout the state that would advance the principles of small government, fiscal solvency, and Americanist values. His speech sounded a helluva lot like the early stirrings of the John Birch Society, which would become the most successful anti-Communist organization in the country.

9

May God Forgive Us, 1951–1952

Losing an election turned Welch further toward conspiracy theory.

Richard Hofstadter wrote in his seminal essay "The Paranoid Style in American Politics": "the paranoid tendency is aroused by a confrontation of opposed interests which are . . . not susceptible to the normal political processes of bargain and compromise. The situation becomes worse when the representatives of a particular political interest—perhaps because of the very unrealistic and unrealizable nature of their demands—cannot make themselves felt in the political process." Since they have "no access to political bargaining or the making of decisions, they find their original conception of the world of power as omnipotent, sinister, and malicious fully confirmed." Robert was denied entry into the political process, the power to bargain and compromise, and embraced the paranoid style after his defeat for lieutenant governor. It was late in the campaign—on July 17, 1950—that Welch uttered the words "vast conspiracy" for the first time in his public career: "the forces on the socialist side amount to a vast conspiracy to change our political and economic system."[1]

When the wheels of the campaign came to a stop, Welch's exhausting schedule finally caught up to him. In a letter to his supporters the next year, Robert announced: "for the first time in my 51 years of hard work, I have recently become concerned seriously and justifiably about my health." Robert later called the collapse a "case of acute fatigue." One factor that may have contributed greatly to this was his relationship with his brother. Robert's budding political involvement was derailing his responsibilities at James's candy company and placing a great deal of stress on the brothers' relationship.[2]

While colleagues kept requesting his deeper political involvement, such as in the activities of the National Association of Manufacturers, at one point he needed to step back. On November 15, 1951, Welch notified members of the Brockton Welch Campaign Committee that he was dismantling the committee. He wrote: "Last spring, feeling so strongly the need for concerted action on the part of those of us who want to stop the insidious and increasing socialization of our country, I set out to organize a group of citizens' committees throughout Massachusetts for that purpose. . . . Shortly, thereafter personal circumstances arose which obliged me to withdraw from all political activities." He continued: "This was the hardest decision I have ever had to make. I still feel as strongly as ever about the necessity in the fight against socialism; I am still doing what little I can, on the sidelines, to encourage everybody who is in the fight; and I shall get back actively in it myself, assuming such responsibilities of leadership as my ability will permit, whenever circumstances will again enable me to do so."[3]

Welch was despondent, and not just over his loss. He was dejected by international events and found his "original conception of the world of power as omnipotent, sinister, and malicious fully confirmed." He felt surrounded. But his reaction was not to flee the battlefield. His reaction was to fight. He was not alone among the Right.

Many of the Right concluded that the Communist conspiracy was gaining in strength with every passing year. This was a period of incredible political passion, marked by name calling, character assassination, and cynical machinations. President Truman's approval rating was at 27 percent. While the Democratic Party was doing what it needed to do to hold onto the office, the Republicans were pursuing desperate measures to secure it. (Biographer William S. White called this period in Robert Taft's career his "sad, worst, period.") Both sides used exaggerations and accusations. For instance, on December 19, just as American troops pulled back in Korea, Truman committed to sending additional forces to Europe to bolster NATO; Taft and other Republicans wondered how both things could be happening. Why should socialist Britain get our boys when they recognized Red China and were trading with Mao? Why shouldn't we cut our military spending, guard against militarism and maintain freedom on the home front?[4]

Many of the reactionary Republicans making such claims were returning veterans who had fought the threat of Hitler and Tōjō. They had participated in a great cause to save freedom from tyranny; for them, fighting against the New Deal, the Fair Deal, and Communism was as central as defeating Hitler, beliefs that led some to extreme measures. They called New Dealers and Fair Dealers Communists and traitors, though that was often ridiculous. Many voters came to look upon Democrats as left-wing radicals who wanted to bring socialism to the United States in the form of minimum wage laws and social security.[5] The war against Hitler and Japan provided a template for foreign policy too. After Chinese troops interceded in the Korean conflict, they asked, Why not go after Communist China with America's full military might, even nuclear weapons? We had them. Why not use them? Everything should be on the table.

The fight over George Marshall's nomination as secretary of defense illustrates how tempers were flaring in Washington and how exaggeration and hyperbole were becoming part of political blood sport. It also demonstrates that Welch's later decision to call President Eisenhower a Communist was completely consistent with the tactics of other Republicans throughout the 1950s.

Right-wing Republicans first opposed the nomination on the grounds that existing law made only civilians eligible to serve as secretary of defense. Since Marshall was a general, he was ineligible. But the administration sought an exemption, and matters devolved quickly. Although right-wing Republicans had promised decorum, Indiana senator William E. Jenner assailed Marshall as a "front man for traitors" and apocalyptically announced that the "day of reckoning had come." "The Democratic Party," he said, edging into conspiracy theory, "has been captured from within and without, during these tragic years." It started under FDR, he said, with his "vicious propaganda of the 'four freedoms.'" It continued with FDR's attempts to "trick the American people into a war." Citing a popular belief of Far Right conspiracy theorists, Jenner attacked Marshall for his personal failure at Pearl Harbor.[6]

Jenner declared that Marshall committed too many sins, such as the plan to provide Russia lend lease, "selling out" China and Eastern Europe, and establishing his signature program, the Marshall Plan. If confirmed, Marshall would continue the treasonous activity of the Democratic Party. "General Marshall has been appointed as Secretary of Defense" for the purpose of "the vicious sell-out, not only of Chiang, not only of Formosa, which is vital to our security, but of the American GI's who are fighting and dying even now." "A deal," Jenner said "is in the making to sell China down the river and seat the Communist delegates in the United Nations." Jenner, Welch, and many on the Right lamented what they saw as Washington's halfhearted backing of Mao Tse-tung's foe Chiang Kai-shek, who in their account was "badgered, hamstrung, and abandoned."[7]

Taft listened to Jenner's extraordinary statement and then followed his lead, albeit omitting the assertions of treason: "The appointment of General Marshall," Taft said, is "confirming and approving the sympathetic attitude toward communism in the Far East which has dominated the Far Eastern Division of the State Department."[8] Setting the stage for McCarthy's attack on the army and Welch's attack on the former head of the army General Eisenhower, Jenner had called Marshall a traitor, and Taft did nothing to stop him, only dulling the dagger.

Jenner and Taft were not convincing. By a vote of forty-seven to twenty-one of the Senate, Marshall was granted the exemption. Yet some of the many, many important ideological allies of Robert Welch in the GOP were having their say.[9]

The world might be on fire, Welch thought in 1951, but at least the revered Douglas MacArthur was running things in Korea. Despite the conflict being officially a UN "police action," MacArthur took orders from Washington rather than the Security Council. Welch saw MacArthur as a contemporary George Washington. During the war, MacArthur's amphibious campaigns became the stuff of legend, and Robert treasured every story about the old warrior. So did an entire generation of American schoolchildren. His reconquest of the Philippines and his acceptance of Japan's surrender on the USS *Missouri* only grew the legend of Douglas MacArthur in the eyes of Robert Welch and many others.[10]

Robert thought his postwar command had also been stellar. Like a British viceroy of more halcyon days, MacArthur reconstructed and democratized Japan as Supreme Commander Allied Powers (SCAP). Robert was proud that MacArthur displayed a Western military bearing over Japan, and his influence was felt throughout the Pacific as the Commanding General, United States Army Far East, and as Commander in Chief, Far East, where his sturdy hand oversaw control of the American navy and air force.[11]

But Welch revered MacArthur for the general's stance on Formosa, or Taiwan. MacArthur believed that Taiwan was essential for American security because when the Philippines had been attacked in 1941, Japan's air force had used a base on Taiwan. MacArthur declared that the United States ought to use its navy to halt the Communist conquest of Taiwan. Even more important, the United States must remain resolute that the Nationalist government in Taiwan represented the true people of China, not Mao Tse-tung. MacArthur wanted to force Truman's commitment to Chiang Kai-shek. By defending Taiwan with the navy, Truman could not recognize the People's Republic, which would have ramifications at the United Nations. The United States could very well not favor the admission of the People's Republic to the UN if it did not recognize the government. Asia Firsters like MacArthur and Welch were so passionate that Republicans wholeheartedly favored plans to flood Taiwan with thousands of advisors from the United States—which probably would have led to a ground war in China.[12] Welch and MacArthur bequeathed the importance of Asia to contemporary Republican foreign policy.

Truman considered any plan to defend the island with the navy preposterous and far too dangerous. Meanwhile Truman continued to resist recognizing the People's Republic, and subsequent presidential administrations did as well until Jimmy Carter's.[13] Truman was being prudent because he saw a catastrophe coming.

Then, in April 1951, Harry Truman fired Douglas MacArthur. The decision dumbfounded Robert Welch, enough so that he had trouble sleeping. His "addiction to mathematics and logic," a contemporary said, "prompted him, with increasing insistence, to search out the causes of current problems," and MacArthur's firing presented an existential crisis for Robert. The contemporary explained Robert's train of thought:

> If *A, then B* was a logical sequence. It meant that if Situation A exists, then derivative Situation B must also exist. If all men die, then Jones will one day die. Well then, if America is the land of the brave and the free, why doesn't America pursue policies that enhance freedom and reward bravery? . . . We engaged in the military contest [in Korea] against a Communist force under the command of an American general whose skills and tenacity were unequaled. So? President Truman proceeded to win the war? No he proceeded to fire General MacArthur. The cordite in Robert Welch's mind burst into flames.[14]

We can't fathom today why Welch would suffer sleepless nights over MacArthur's firing. But many Americans did. "It is doubtful if there has ever been in this country so violent and spontaneous a discharge of political passion as that provoked by the president's dismissal of the General," observed Richard Rovere and Arthur M. Schlesinger Jr. "Certainly there has been nothing to match it since the Civil War." Until President Kennedy's assassination, the country would not receive such a shock to its system. "The citizen was on MacArthur's side. His private emotions have been deeply engaged," observed Rovere and Schlesinger.[15] Protests inundated the White House. George Gallup determined that voters backed MacArthur by 69 percent. Truman was booed at Griffith Stadium, a first since Herbert Hoover in 1932. Bumper stickers read "Oust President Truman." In Eastham, Massachusetts, and Oakland, California, among other spots, half-mast flags flew. Others flew the American flag upside down, a national distress signal. Citizens in San Gabriel, California, burned the president in effigy. Citizens in Ponca City, Oklahoma, burned Dean Acheson in effigy. Baltimore's Minute Women marched on the capital. A "Punch Harry in the Nose Club" was established in Denver. The recall was "a crime carried out in the dead of night," observed the *Daily Oklahoman*. The *New York Journal American* suggested that "maybe the State Department gave him some kind of mental or neural anodyne." Senator

McCarthy said that "bourbon and benedictine" had caused Truman's "treason in the White House" (this, despite McCarthy's own addiction to alcohol, which would kill him within a decade). Republicans in Congress wanted investigations of Truman's foreign policy. House Speaker Joseph Martin noted: "the question of possible impeachments were discussed."[16]

Republicans called for a major address by MacArthur before Congress, which he gave, observing: "Old soldiers never die. They just fade away." A New York tickertape parade in his honor brought out millions. In May and June, the Senate's Foreign Relations and Armed Services committees held hearings on the "Military Situation in the Far East." MacArthur then went on a "crusade," making speeches all over the country. He would deliver the keynote at the 1952 Republican National Convention.[17]

MacArthur's firing revolutionized Robert's thinking. "I did not enter the Massachusetts political campaign in 1950 as a battler against Communism," he said. "I was most concerned about the way we were following England" into socialism. "It was not until the firing of MacArthur . . . that I became convinced that the danger from the Communist conspiracy was far more important, urgent, and immediate than the parallel, interlocking, but far less rigidly organized efforts of the ADA and the ILO [Americans for Democratic Action and the International Labor Organization] and similar groups—always with Communist backing, to carry socialism in our country as far as possible by Fabian procedures."[18]

After the firing, many Republicans became convinced that high-profile individuals in the State Department were running the country according to Moscow, and Dean Acheson, Truman's secretary of state, was the chief toady of the Soviet Union. On June 14, 1951, McCarthy attacked Acheson and Marshall on the floor of the Senate. In a 60,000-word evisceration of Democratic foreign policy since 1939, McCarthy centered his attack around one question: how "since World War II the free world has been losing 100 million people per year to international communism." McCarthy said "the vast and complicated culture of the West is . . . in manifest decay." The West was failing, and Americanism and nationalism were retreating, he said. Acheson and Marshall headed a "conspiracy on a scale so immense as to dwarf any previous such venture in the history of man," McCarthy said. Truman was a "captive" of this conspiracy, and the firing of MacArthur, the old soldier defending the ramparts, a symptom of it. McCarthy then laid out the strategy of the cabal: "It is to abandon American interests in the Far East, surrender[] Formosa to the grasp of the United Nations strewn with our enemies," and "thrust the United States out of the Far East." McCarthy was speaking Robert Welch's language, and vice versa.

After attacking Marshall, McCarthy sank the knife deep into Acheson: "I have studied Acheson's public utterances sidewise, slantwise, hindwise, and frontwise; I have watched the demeanor of this glib, supercilious, and guilty man on the witness stand; I have reflected upon his career, and I come to only one conclusion: his primary loyalty in international affairs runs to the British labor government, his secondary allegiance is to the Kremlin, with none left over for the country of his birth."[19] McCarthy called Acheson a traitor.

Daily calls for Acheson's resignation because of his Asian policy became the norm for the Republican Right. They called Truman's foreign policy the Acheson-Hiss policy. Right-wing Senator Bridges had even delivered an address "Who is the Mastermind in the Department of State?" on the Senate floor in early 1950. Bridges observed, "We must find out the master spy, the servant of Russia who moves the puppets—the Hisses, . . . using them and using our State Department as he wills." "Who is he, Mr. President?" Bridges asked. Bridges then homed in on his target. "I suggest that Dean Acheson be thoroughly questioned by the committee."[20]

A stylish dandy, well educated, and well bred, Acheson was pinned by Republicans as the personification of the Anglophilic eastern establishment. "I watch his smart-aleck manner and his British clothes and that New Dealism, everlasting New Dealism, in everything he says and does, and I want to shout, Get out, Get out. You stand for everything that has been wrong with the United States for years," said Senator Hugh Butler of Nebraska.[21]

The firing of MacArthur and the subsequent Republican denunciations charged up Robert Welch. He awoke from his postelection doldrums with a new project and committed himself anew to speaking out about the cabal that threatened the republic. He was now a full-blown conspiracy theorist. If the Republican eastern establishment was going to exclude him from electoral politics, he thought, he would make his mark as a political commentator and conservative writer. He thought that his own construction of what really happened to MacArthur and how the Democrats lost China could bring more insight than anything that Jenner or McCarthy said.

Welch started doing his homework. He devoured the plentiful supply of right-wing books on Far East policy. He read Victor Lasky's *The Case Against Dean Acheson*. Later, in *May God Forgive Us,* Welch admitted to readers he plagiarized sections of Lasky's book because he found no room for improvement. Welch doubted any reprisal would be forthcoming because he said he and Lasky were "toilers in the same vineyard."[22]

During this period of intellectual inquiry, Alfred Kohlberg became an important confidant to Welch. Short, bald, and full of pep, Kohlberg had attended the University of California and had a lucrative career exporting textiles. The two became close friends. Unlike General Eisenhower, who scorned Jewish friendships, Welch formed many such friendships, although his relationship to Jews was extremely complicated and contradicting. Just prior to World War II, Kohlberg grossed approximately $1.5 million annually. He proudly backed Chiang Kai-shek and held fast to a belief in a Communist conspiracy dating back to 1928.[23] He worked indefatigably to bring the Nationalists to power in Asia, alongside other prominent Asia Firsters like Clare Boothe Luce, J. B. Powell, and publisher William Loeb.[24] His articles appeared in the Catholic *China Monthly: The Truth About China*. Kohlberg also contributed generously to conservative journals such as *Plain Talk* and *The Freeman,* to make sure Asia First ideas were represented there.[25] A faithful acolyte of Claire Chennault, Kohlberg wrote the crusty and frequently besotted military hero in 1945: "a voice like yours will be needed to straighten us out if we are not to abandon China to civil war and Communism."[26] Like Louis XIV's presumptuous claim "I am France," Kohlberg once boomed: "I am the China Lobby."

Robert kept reading. He devoured Arthur Bliss Lane's *I Saw Poland Betrayed* and echoed its central argument in *May God Forgive Us*. Bliss directed the Foreign Language Group Activities Section within the Ethnic Origins Division of the Republican National Committee and was central to forming strategy for the party in the Midwest. He argued that the Republicans could win over ethnic Democrats by repudiating the Yalta agreement and declaring unequivocal support for the policy of "liberation," or the emancipation of Eastern European countries from the grasp of Stalin. Many Polish and Irish Democrats would become Birchers.

His intellectual awakening became an odyssey. Welch was obsessed with the question of how long the conspiracy to destroy capitalism and establish Communism in the federal government had been sustained. When did it start? And where would it end? He concluded, for now, that it began under Woodrow Wilson and reached its climax with FDR's New Deal. He also became obsessed with determining exactly who were the top government officials who had been infiltrated by the Communists to bring about the loss of China and then the firing of MacArthur. He studied how deep the network of Communist agents penetrated the federal government and the institutions of the United States, whether the press, the mass media, the churches, or the schools.

No longer crestfallen, Robert went to work on a major speech, "Acheson and MacArthur," which he delivered at the second meeting of the Welch Campaign Committee, and then around the Boston area. He studied like a monk. His focus was laser-like. The speech summarized Jenner's broadsides and McCarthy's warnings and prognostications, and it suggested that the Truman administration was fraught with subversives. Reds were everywhere. "Acheson and MacArthur" said that treason within the federal government, not ineptitude, nor civilizational decay, explained the decline of the republic. The Communists were conquering from within. The traitors were prominent federal government appointees, recognizable to most Americans. Conspiracy in high places was leading America, the greatest experiment in human history, to an early grave. History moved quickly, Welch said. Treason did not take centuries, but a few years. Treason explained the loss of China and the rapid decline of the United States toward socialism after the war. Traitors tied the hands of MacArthur in the Far East and ensured his removal from the battlefield.

Obsessed with his topic, he continued to fiddle with the address. He often tinkered into the night. He delivered a revised version at the annual meeting of the New England Council of Young Republicans in

Portland, Maine. According to Welch's biographer, a certain Mr. Sawyer from Worcester, who had contributed to his campaign for lieutenant governor, learned that Welch was "naming names and criticizing specific people" and "wanted no part in it." Sawyer took Welch to task with a letter that attacked the speech and "scorched the envelope," as Welch said. Robert worked on weekends and holidays crafting an effective riposte to Sawyer. The candyman was obsessed with getting the story right. The response soon became a thirty-seven-page, single-spaced, typewritten letter, three onionskin copies of which he shared with interested friends. But then people began to talk of Welch's letter. Interest grew. The original three began to make their own copies of the letter. One businessman in the National Association of Manufacturers made 3,000 mimeographed copies, Welch claimed, and by December 1951, 30,000 copies of the letter were circulating. That letter laid the foundations for Welch's book *May God Forgive Us,* which he published in 1952.[27]

Robert contacted Henry Regnery, a conservative and publisher of William F. Buckley's *God and Man at Yale,* asking whether he was interested in publishing the letter. Welch wrote: "I have no interest in anything that could remotely be classified as 'vanity publishing' either in whole or in part. So I should like to have you consider the proposal strictly as a regular publishing venture, as I am sure you will. But it does seem worth pointing out, nevertheless, that one friend of mine, a prominent lawyer in New York City, has flatly offered to stand all the expense of duplicating and mailing this letter to the 17,000 members of the National Association of Manufacturers—of which I have the honor to be on the Board of Directors."[28]

Welch had lofty expectations for *May God Forgive Us*. The demure Regnery had been closing in on bankruptcy when he published *God and Man at Yale,* which became a bestseller. When Welch pitched Regnery, he bet him dinner that *May God Forgive Us* would sell twice as many books as Buckley's within the first twelve months.

Welch proved the master at marketing the tract. In a "stroke of political genius," historian Jonathan Schoenwald observed, Robert "bypass[ed] typical distribution channels" and founded the Welch Letter Mailing Committee, comprising five Massachusetts conservatives, who solicited sales. "Enlisting these," Schoenwald continued, "made the pamphlet's contents seem that much more revelatory."[29] Welch depended on friends, pulled in workers from his 1950 campaign, and drew on employees from his brother's candy company to distribute the book. This taught him that grassroots efforts involving committed people who believed in what they were doing were even more effective than campaigns backed by big money and reputation.

May God Forgive Us became very popular in the Midwest when the *Chicago Tribune* published four condensed installments. "We published one printing of 25,000, another of 110,000 and then two more of 25,000 each, 185,000 in all of the paper volumes," reported William Strube, Regnery's sales manager. "It seems the *Tribune*'s condensation is stimulating a big desire to read the whole volume," observed Elsie Adamson of Brentano's bookstore in Chicago. Guy Kendall of A. C. McClurg & Co. said only a few copies were left in his book department. Carl Kroch of Kroch's Bookstores completely sold out, as did Marshall Field's book department. Bertha Steen, the buyer for Chandler's bookstores in Evanston, Illinois, said: "one person bought 25 copies of the paper bound edition and another took 18."[30] At least in the Midwest, it seemed to be flying off bookshelves.

But Welch was confounded that *May God Forgive Us* did not sell more. For a man with an enormous ego, this made no sense. Did he think the book was being suppressed by some nefarious force? The historical record is not clear on this question, but this seemed to be where Welch was heading. He responded to Henry Regnery's assertions that there simply was not enough demand for the book by buying the remaining copies and selling them during Robert Taft's drive for the 1952 presidential nomination.[31] Robert's consternation that the book was not selling was not reasonable. The book sold very well for a first-time author. Welch not only benefited from his promotional and organizational prowess but gained a reputation in the conservative community as someone who wrote with vigor for the average reader about topics affecting their lives. As Schoenwald observed, "Welch soon became a player among conservatives in politics, publishing, and commerce."[32]

Despite Welch's newfound celebrity, at least in conservative circles, he included nothing altogether original in *May God Forgive Us*. An admixture of histrionics and conspiracy theory from right-wing politicians and authors, the book contained the provocative declaration:

"It is my utterly sincere belief that, through whatever puppets activate to exert their combined insidious pressures, MacArthur was fired by Stalin. He had to be removed."[33] *May God Forgive Us* cast a wide net and charged that MacArthur's firing was only one symptom of a deeper pathology that infected American life. Foreign policy was in the hands of the enemy ("Diplomacy is a wonderful thing if you own all the diplomats on one side and a sufficient number on the other"[34]), and the vast conspiracy engulfed Hollywood, print media, radio, and the State Department. Other symptoms of the conspiracy included the rise in government spending, foreign aid, the welfare state, and labor unions. Stalin engineered not only American foreign policy abroad but also collectivism at home. "Our enemies are the Communists. Our opponents are their allies, their dupes, and those who support them for whatever cause."[35] Welch linked the betrayal of Free China to not only Acheson and his malicious State Department but also collectivist forces fostering America's welfare state.

At Yalta, Stalin promised that Poland would have a representative government with free elections, but he flouted his promise. He promised free elections in Bulgaria and Romania, but broke his word here as well. Welch and the Right rejected Stalin's claims that his Eastern European satellites represented a "sphere of influence." Far from defensive, the Right held, they represented a practical application of the Communist dream of worldwide empire. Stalin also gained control over the railroads and essential Chinese industrial center of Manchuria and two vital seaports—Darien and Port Arthur. In his book, Welch concluded that these failures were due not to the stupidity of American officials; these countries were purposely given away by our diplomats, especially one. "Many men have spearheaded policies which were concocted of stupidity and treason in various degrees of combination," Robert wrote. "But one man has led all the rest, and that man is Dean Acheson." "He is an extremely left-wing socialist. The facts make clear that under his increasing sway over our State Department and our whole government, the traitors and dupes and allies have reached a terrifying position of influence and power."[36]

Why was it necessary to name names? The "Acheson clique" and the "devious game our State Department is playing" simply left no choice, he said. "When personalities as well as issues become of the very essence of a movement, and that movement seeks our total destruction, it is cowardice and not fair mindedness to skirt around the names of those who are used by the enemy." Indeed, "it is exactly this civilized tolerance," Welch wrote, "and the charity of our Christian outlook that the Communists are counting on."[37]

For Welch, the proof that Acheson was a traitor was the State Department's white paper of January 1950, advising US missions that Communist victory in Taiwan was inexorable. Acheson had authored that paper, which MacArthur leaked. Acheson said essentially the same thing in a January address to the National Press Club: China's northern provinces were coveted by the Soviet Union, and "we must not undertake to deflect from the Russians to ourselves the righteous anger, and the wrath, and the hatred of the Chinese people which must develop."[38]

His words—circuitous, ambiguous, practically indecipherable for the layperson—represented everything that Robert and the Republican Right hated about Acheson. He spoke in riddles, but his point that China was already lost to the Communists was appeasement, according to Welch. "The worst thing of all about the White Paper," Welch wrote, "was Mr. Acheson's complete recognition before the event of the Mao Communists as the conquerors." "Acheson has schemed and maneuvered in every way that he could to have us abandon Formosa."[39]

Welch completely rejected the white paper, Harry Truman's official account of China's loss. He wanted the Truman administration's unequivocal support—both militarily and economically—for Chiang's government in Taiwan as China's only legitimate government. Welch never considered that Chiang was corrupt and ineffective. Welch never considered the popular appeal of Mao's promises of reform to the poverty-stricken peasants of China. Instead, Welch blamed America's leaders for "allow[ing]" Stalin to secure Far Eastern land at Yalta and then abandoning Chiang when more American help would have stopped Mao "in his tracks."[40]

Welch's conclusions reflected the exaggerated belief in the capability of America at the dawn of the Cold War. It was the right and the capability of the United States to control human events, Welch believed. The actor Ronald Reagan shared the same alacrity for the potential of his country to make any change in the world it saw fit. Later, as president, Reagan said the United States could "begin the world again." This idea was not confined to the Right. A onetime PT boat commander turned congressman named John F. Kennedy embodied this belief in American exceptionalism and power. Standing coatless at his presidential inaugural, Kennedy confidently declared with staccato jabs into the cold Washington air: "Let every nation know, whether it wishes us well or ill, that we shall pay any price, bear any burden, meet any hardship, support any friend, oppose any foe, in order to assure the survival and the success of liberty."[41] Welch shared JFK's confidence in the power and the glory of his country.

Beyond calling Acheson a traitor, Welch had another bombshell: Stalin fired MacArthur. The premise behind this was that Stalin was behind the Korean conflict. "To put it bluntly, we would not have fought in Korea if Stalin had wished otherwise," wrote Welch. On this point, Welch was more right than he knew. Historians once thought that Stalin was surprised by the attack but now know that he likely approved it. Welch was on shakier ground when he wrote that Stalin "obviously wanted us to fight back in Korea," because Stalin gave the "greenlight" to Kim Il-Sung only because he believed the United States would not care whether North Korea attacked. There was reason for Stalin to believe this. The Americans ultimately did not fight in 1949 to save the Nationalists from losing the mainland of China. And Secretary of State Acheson observed that the American "defensive perimeter" did not apply to South Korea.[42]

But the Americans reacted to the attack as they did at Pearl Harbor. "We can't let the UN down," observed President Truman, who came to the defense of South Korea within hours of the attack.[43] Truman's response was nearly a failure as American and South Korean armies were bogged down in the peninsula's southeastern tip. But MacArthur staged a brilliant counterattack, landing at Inchon in September 1950, and the army soon occupied most of the Peninsula. The purpose of the war then changed to uniting the two Koreas. As MacArthur's forces neared China's border, hundreds of thousands of Chinese descended upon them, driving them back.

Welch believed Stalin was also behind this move: "We ignored the clearest repeated warnings of the forthcoming attack because he wanted us to until the very day he struck" with Chinese troops. Stalin "wanted a chance to test his jet planes and other engines of war and to 'blood' his Asiatic troops in battles with Western soldiery," Welch believed. But Welch overestimated how much control Communist leaders had over other Communist leaders. This was Mao's call, and he told his advisors "we should not fail to assist the Koreans."[44]

Two days after 300,000 Chinese attacked, MacArthur told Washington: we are in an "entirely new war." A "steady attrition leading to final destruction can reasonably be contemplated," he added. But MacArthur also publicly denounced the administration for restricting his supply lines. Washington responded by declaring that all statements to the press would now have to be cleared by the State and Defense Departments. Welch saw the hand of Stalin behind these moves as well.[45] And Stalin wasn't done. Even as the Chinese retreated, Truman abandoned the plan to unite Korea, which Welch determined was Stalin's design all along: "even then Stalin was sure enough of being master within our own house." "Whenever he thought it best, all he had to do was to consent to stop the war, on terms which would still be a disgrace to America."

MacArthur, Welch, and the China Lobby wanted to have it out with China. They saw the Korean War as full-blown Sino-American conflict. They wanted to take the fight to mainland China, use Chiang's troops, and go after Communist China with the full military might used against Hitler and Japan. If it meant nuclear war, it meant nuclear war.

Just as he saw the problem with Taiwan, Truman knew that the Korean conflict had to be limited or it would start World War III. Truman and Acheson also saw the Korean conflict as a trap. It would divide NATO allies and make it more difficult to deter Russian aggression in Eastern Europe. Truman was willing to settle on an armistice in Korea even if the conflict ended with a stalemate, which it did in July 1953.[46] MacArthur rejected the stalemate and smelled appeasement and conspiracy. So did Welch.

In *May God Forgive Us,* Welch knit a tapestry of conspiracy. He revealed that seemingly unconnected occurrences were part of a plot that only he was sniffing out. He looked for events that buttressed his conclusion that high-level traitors were offering their country to the Communists.

First there was the story of US ambassador to China Patrick J. Hurley, Chiang Kai-shek's favored US special representative in China. In February 1945, while Hurley was in Washington, Chargé d'affaires George Atcheson issued a policy draft recommending the United States arm the Communists—which would pressure Chiang to work with them. Hurley went ballistic, perceiving an effort to undercut his role, and demanded that any foreign service officers involved in the affair be reassigned. They were. But by late 1945, Hurley's effort to secure a coalition government in China on nationalist terms had not worked. But when Russian troops entered Manchuria, Chinese Communists followed closely behind and snatched up Japanese arms and supplies. The United States then decided to extend military and economic assistance to Chiang, but only if he cooperated in negotiating with the Communists. Hurley again went into a rage. He resigned his post, later writing: "the professional foreign service men sided with the Chinese Communist armed party and the imperialist bloc of nations whose policy it was to keep China divided against herself. Our professional diplomats continuously advised the Communists that my efforts in preventing the collapse of the Nationalist Government did not represent the policy of the United States. These same professionals openly advised the Communist armed party to decline unification of the Chinese Communist Army with the Nationalist Army unless the Chinese Communists were given control."[47] Hurley's comments became a key piece of Robert's conspiracy theory explaining how American perfidy accounted for China's loss. Kohlberg had been suspecting as much since 1943. In truth, some China hands leaned toward Mao, but they were low-level characters who couldn't make any difference. But Welch thought the little people were the keys to the whole puzzle. And a few bad apples, even at the bottom, could rotten the whole barrel.

According to Welch, another piece in the puzzle of the China "loss" was the *Amerasia* case. In June 1945, the Federal Bureau of Investigation arrested foreign service officers John Stewart Service and Emmanuel Larsen in the offices of *Amerasia*, a left-wing publication that specialized in Far Eastern affairs. The FBI also arrested naval intelligence officer Lieutenant Andrew Roth, along with *Amerasia*'s editors Phillip Jaffe and Kate Mitchell, and journalist Mark Gayn. The FBI found numerous classified documents concerning China in *Amerasia*'s offices;

those arrested were charged first with conspiracy to violate the espionage act. Yet, since the FBI found no transfer of the documents to a foreign government, the charge was altered to conspiracy to steal government documents—a lesser violation. Jaffe and Larsen pled guilty and paid light fines. For Welch, this showed that cabals in high places helped China go Communist.[48]

The Wedemeyer affair supplied Welch's red-hot brain with even more evidence that high-level Democratic officials deliberately lost China. Albert C. Wedemeyer was a China hawk whom Truman sent to assess conditions there. In September 1947, he advised sending 10,000 American officers and noncommissioned officers to China to train Chiang's forces. Because of widespread corruption throughout Chiang's regime, Wedemeyer also recommended a five-year economic program, overseen by competent American advisors who would administer the funds.[49]

But then George Marshall suppressed the report, an action that became more fodder for Welch's charges of conspiracy and betrayal. Wedemeyer said on his deathbed, decades later: "had munitions been given in appropriate quantities to mainland China in 1947–48, and had Manchuria and Korea been temporarily placed under the aegis of the U.N., the spread of Communism might never have occurred in the Far East." Herbert Hoover was incensed by the muzzling of the Wedemeyer report, too, writing Wedemeyer: "the last chance to save China was when your report of 1947 was suppressed and its recommendations repudiated."[50] Hoover's conclusions suggested that belief in conspiracy and cover-up was not limited to the fringe but was becoming mainstream in the Republican Party.

The untimely retirement of Claire Chennault from the military also grated on Robert. Chennault was fifty-four years old and suffering from chronic loss of hearing due to exposure to the din of aircraft engines, but "it has been suggested," the *Philadelphia Record* observed, "Chennault is too sympathetic with Chang Kai-shek's wish to have Chinese troops rather than have Americans bear the brunt of the fight against the Japs." Despite the fact that the hearing-impaired Chennault was looking forward to retirement, Welch was unable or unwilling to consider the evidence and constructed a reality in which invidious forces wanted to silence Chennault. As with Hurley's statement and the *Amerasia* case, here Welch used a huge brush and drew a sweeping conclusion that a darker, more hidden motive was at play.[51]

Welch searched for more information that corroborated his suspicion of treason, finding it in the Institute of Pacific Relations (IPR). Henry Luce was a magnanimous benefactor to the IPR, which was committed to increasing mutual understanding among Asian nations and peoples.[52] Echoing Kohlberg, Welch's main thrust was that Communists had infiltrated the IPR, which now served as the propaganda arm against the Nationalists. In addition, Welch claimed the IPR was rife with Communist members of the State Department. For Kohlberg, Frederick Vanderbilt Field, the secretary of the American Council within the IPR from 1934 to 1940, sympathized with the Communists; he also had helped found *Amerasia*. For Welch and Kohlberg, the IPR ran the State Department, and anybody with IPR connections, especially Asian scholars Owen Lattimore, William Lockwood, and T. A. Bisson, had Communist affiliations. The IPR received much of its funding from the Carnegie Corporation, the Rockefeller Foundation, and large American companies, all of which became suspect. The assertions were powerful, and Luce decided on their basis to sever financial ties with the IPR.[53]

Like a patchwork quilt, in *May God Forgive Us*, Welch sewed together Whittaker Chambers's contacts with Alger Hiss and Harry Dexter White, the atom spies, and Elizabeth Bentley's ring. He saw George Marshall and Dean Acheson and other high-level Truman administration officials as un-American and traitorous. Truman himself received Welch's arrows for failing to recognize White's treason: "after the FBI had insisted [to Truman] that Harry Dexter White was a Communist spy, he promoted White to a more influential position." "I do not think Harry Truman is a Communist or sympathetic with Russian imperial ambitions. He is, I do think, a callous politician with few scruples about the means used to achieve a political end." Although Acheson received the most venom from Welch's pen, Marshall caught his share as Welch charged him with following Acheson, abandoning the courage of his convictions, and succumbing to the point that he became responsible as well for losing China.[54]

Robert was not the only American who believed that the Kremlin was running a master conspiracy. John Foster Dulles, Eisenhower's secretary of state, and J. Edgar Hoover, director of the FBI, were making the same case. Presidents Truman and Eisenhower halfheartedly believed it too. They were wrong, but it became a postwar American axiom that the Kremlin called all the shots when it came to Communism. In the Cold War, saying anything less might raise the suspicion that you sympathized with the Reds. And this was true not only for Korea. By 1953, the Huks were resisting the government in the Philippines. Insurgents were battling the British in Malaysia. And the Vietminh were making great headway against the French in Vietnam.[55] In all instances, high-level American officials overestimated the reach of the Kremlin.

In *May God Forgive Us,* Welch painted too simplistic a portrait of events. His arguments exaggerated the situation, but compared to the nonsensical hyperbole that McCarthy was spewing, *May God Forgive Us* made Welch appear a scholar and a statesman, at least in the eyes of the Right.

That said, for one, there was no doubt the atomic spy ring was real, but its impact is still debatable. After all, the bulk of the Soviet spy network had left America by the 1950s. From a certain perspective, the real "secret" given away by the Americans occurred at Hiroshima, and that was that an atomic bomb could be developed at all. Similarly, although there were American diplomats favorably disposed to Mao, whether they had any impact is still open to debate.[56]

Truman, though certainly following a Europe First policy, can't be accused of ignoring Asia. Nine billion dollars in Marshall Plan aid went there. Truman prioritized Europe because he feared, as had happened after World War I, that Europe would succumb to totalitarianism—Communistic, fascistic, or otherwise—if aid were not generous.

Acheson and the men who ran the State Department were loyal Americans. They were all Cold Warriors. They loved their country, and if any of them suffered from ineptitude or incompetence, it was not conscious or because they were playing for the other side. Marshall, one of the most honorable public servants of the twentieth century, was not a traitor. If any man in business or politics or the professions was a patriot, it was Marshall, and any aspersion against his character was ludicrous. Truman had sent Marshall to China to mediate between Mao and Chiang, but the project was completely futile from the start because Marshall announced that any amount of aid to Chiang would be ineffective; his opponents irresponsibly charged treason rather than an acquiescence to the inevitable.[57] Welch's suggestion that America back Chiang Kai-shek, the Nationalist Party, and Formosa to the hilt, to the exclusion of Europe, was myopic and looked past the fact that sending money to Chiang was throwing money down the drain. Most Americans agreed with Truman in 1950.

Welch's view of Yalta was misguided. The Soviet Union was attacked twice in the twentieth century over Eastern Europe. Stalin was right to be suspicious, and friendly governments next door sought to maintain the security of the Soviet Union. Establishing an Eastern and Central European sphere of influence was never a secret that Stalin held in his vest. Throughout World War II, he always made clear that safeguarding the Soviet western border was one his primary objectives. In truth, Yalta contained Stalin's ambitions because the Russian leader might have established much wider control over China and Eastern Europe. His strong Red Army forces were deeply ensconced in China and Eastern Europe when the guns of war went silent. Any liberation campaign by the allies was quixotic, dangerous, and inane.

Also, the Truman administration was not soft on Communism. In 1946, it kicked the Soviet Union out of Iran. In 1947, it aided the Greek government extensively and expensively to halt Communism. In 1948, it carried out the Berlin Airlift and established the Marshall Plan. The administration participated in forming NATO in 1949 and fought the North Korean Communists in 1950. Truman, Acheson, and Marshall pursued these policies under the Truman Doctrine, which committed the United States to resisting Communist penetration anywhere. Meanwhile, it was Truman's Justice Department that jailed Hiss. His attorney general actively fought Communism with a comprehensive list identifying Communist front organizations, and an executive order naming subversives in government. Far from a pusillanimous enabler of Communists, Truman was seen by many liberals as a dangerous provocateur who would prolong the Cold War and a testy belligerent whose foreign policy was unnecessarily aggressive. Some of them said the untested and pugnacious Truman took far too many risks, challenged the Soviets when compromise was a safer course, and took a hardline approach that endangered the peace and prosperity of the entire world. Liberals saw the president as a reactionary who lost course, jettisoned the New Deal, and started a witch hunt for Communists. Any claim of treason by the leadership of the Truman White House was a distorted judgment, however popular it became.[58]

Truman—not Stalin—fired MacArthur, and for good reason. The seeds of MacArthur's firing were sown long before. He seemed to misunderstand that Truman was the commander in chief, and he had gone rogue before. On July 31, 1950, MacArthur visited Taiwan and publicly voiced more American assistance to the Nationalists than anything Truman was willing to grant. Truman sent Averill Harriman to Tokyo to make it abundantly clear to MacArthur that Chiang wanted war between the United States and China—something that Truman did not want. MacArthur later insisted that he be allowed to push north, leaving open the possibility of fully invading China and using nuclear weapons. Truman resisted; he still did not want war with China. Then, on March 24, 1951, MacArthur went rogue again with his own offer to the North Korean commander of a cease-fire conference. MacArthur was conducting foreign policy, which was Truman's job. The straw that broke the camel's back came when the House Republican minority leader called for a "second Asiatic front" and MacArthur publicly voiced his support.[59]

With all that said, Welch was sincere. He was far less the roguish charlatan of McCarthy, who narcissistically clamored for media attention. Welch truly believed that the MacArthur's firing was a grave threat to America. He truly believed that the people leading American foreign policy were playing on the other side. Welch believed that the greatest threat to America came from its own government rather than the Soviet Union. Welch believed Communists were taking over the American government. Welch saw socialism in the persisting programs of the New Deal, and he saw in socialism the road to serfdom, dictatorship, and one-world government. By this logic, New Dealers were inescapably pro-Communist. It was a wrong argument, but many Republicans—McCarthy, Jenner, Bridges, even Nixon—embraced the same notion that the New Deal weakened American sovereignty at home and abroad. It explained why many went to extremes and exaggerated the threat of their political opponents. The statements of right-wing Republicans spurred on Robert's own penchant to see conspiracy in high places. Everybody seemed to be saying it. Why not me, Welch must have thought.

10

There's Just Something about Ike, 1952

A strong wind from the Right blew between 1948 and 1952, and Robert Welch was among the right-wing Republicans turning the country's political sails in that direction. A great delayed reaction to the New Deal had occurred after 1948. Foreign policy shifted from Europe to Asia and the "loss" of China. Truman's stalemate in Korea, the Soviets' discovery of the bomb, the continued questions over the failure to back Chiang, the myriad espionage headlines, and Republican support from Eastern European ethnics who once voted Democratic redounded to the benefit of Republicans by 1952. The Right said that the country was growing tired of Roosevelt and Truman's desecration of "true" liberalism. The reaction came late but, at least, Republicans thought, it came.

Communism in government was another important driver for the Republican Right, and Joe McCarthy was its primary figure. Fueled by his daylong consumption of alcohol that eventually destroyed his liver, ruined his political career, and ended his life, the sweaty senator had few qualms about destroying lives if it benefited his personal political ambitions. McCarthy and the Republican Right had embraced the notion that the Democratic Party was a Trojan horse of Communism or socialism. That theory held that since the Communist Party twice enjoyed a "popular front" period in the Democratic Party, it continued to do so well into the 1950s. McCarthy and others said the Reds were dominating the Democratic Party. Others did not go so far and observed only that Marx said that socialism was the first step on the road to Communism. "Twenty years of treason," McCarthy said, necessitated an immediate expulsion from the federal bureaucracy of Communists or anybody having socialist tendencies.[1]

As Robert looked out over this political landscape in 1952, he deemed it time to fulfill his promise of running again for political office. But the seat was a much more modest one: he ran for school committee in Belmont, Massachusetts, where he lived. He won this time, served a three-year term, and declined to run for reelection. It was the last time Robert Welch would hold elective office at the local, state, or federal level.

But Welch remained engaged in national politics. As a proud Republican, he looked forward to the 1952 presidential election. "I think the Republican Party is the one practical instrumentality which offers any chance of a return in this country to more honesty and sanity in government and more common sense in our economic thinking."[2] Welch eagerly anticipated a Republican nominee beholden not to Wall Street but to Main Street, one who saw that the welfare state threatened the latter more than the former. He wanted a Republican president who would roll back the New Deal. He wanted a president who would curtail big government. He wanted a president from the Midwest who would disrupt the alliance between the Democratic Party and ethnic minorities abandoned by Roosevelt and Truman. He wanted a president who would promote fiscal conservatism and tax reform and believed that government benefited when business was happy. He wanted a president who would put an end to the Europe First foreign policy. He wanted a president who would avoid entangling "police actions" like Korea and other recent unprecedented interventions. He wanted a president who would bring American troops home from Europe as soon as possible. He wanted a president who would reject "collective security" and oppose NATO, which provoked war. Europeans should fight Europeans, if that be their lot. Altruistic foreign policy—the stuff of Henry Luce and his dreams of an American century—was the folly of the Eastern establishment.[3] He wanted a president who believed that the story of America was one of individual opportunity through faith, persistence, and freedom, that the success of the country depended on maintaining the rugged individualism of the frontier, that the twentieth-century ascendancy of the executive branch was a great tragedy, that the aggrandizing power of the presidency and its bureaucracies threatened America's libertarian ethos, that all individual liberty rested on economic liberty, and that a handout state would destroy what made America great.

For Robert, that president would be Robert Taft.

Robert wrote: "Taft has undisputed qualifications for the presidency which our country needs more desperately today than at any time in the past 87 years. He is able, honest, intelligent, just, and straightforward." Welch also regarded Taft as the most formidable vote getter of his day. Taft was reelected easily to the Senate from Ohio in 1950 by a 400,000-vote margin.

Taft would drain the Washington swamp, Welch said. "We need Taft, and no lesser man in experience or courage to clean up Washington. For 20 years our government has been growing like some wild and smothering vine. It has become overreaching in size, destructive in its greediness, strangling in its power. Hidden beneath the thick leaves and tendrils of that vine, there is now a 20-year accumulation of unhealthy muck. To trim this vine back to its proper size, to lead in the light of day on the foul mass underneath, Taft offers a leadership we cannot afford to do without."[4]

When Welch became a candidate for delegate to the 1952 Republican convention, he pledged his support for Taft. Robert, along with another Taft-pledged candidate, Ralph Bonnell, the former chair of the Republican state committee, ran against Congressman Christian Herter, who was running for governor and supporting Dwight Eisenhower for president.[5]

Robert was lucky enough to personally campaign with Taft in eastern Massachusetts, spending an entire day in the back of an automobile with the Ohio senator. Bald with rimless glasses and vested business suits, Taft looked the midwestern lawyer that he was. Son of President William Howard Taft, he had followed his father into public service. An introvert, he was not a baby kisser and hated the usual routines of most politicians. Welch concluded that Taft lacked a sense of humor. Welch needed ribald jokes and teasing to ease his anxieties. Taft, ever the staunch workhorse, did not.

Welch had spun a story about a Mr. Goldstein, who boasted in his local barbershop about his trip to Europe. "Goldstein," Welch told Taft, "claimed to have visited personally with the Prime Minister of England, the president of France, and naturally, the Pope as well. Needless to say, Goldstein could speak Italian fluently as a result of his vast experience in the construction industry. And the Pope found this visitor so interesting that he rang for his car, chauffeur and foot man—and he and Goldstein drove through Rome with the top down while continuing their conversation. As they did so, throngs of people surged forward for a better view and many of them began to cheer wildly. 'What were they saying?' asked Goldstein's barber. Goldstein replied nonchalantly, 'well, most of them were saying "who's that driving with Goldstein?"'" Welch timed the joke to coincide with their arrival at the James O. Welch candy manufacturing plant, where Taft was to be greeted by employees. Welch concluded: "Don't be surprised, Senator, if you hear people on the sidewalk say, 'who's that riding with Bob Welch?'" It was corny and classic Robert Welch, but he often had too impressive an appraisal of his own jokes, which often fell flat. Welch was also stroking his own ego, making it known to the midwesterner that he was big man in Cambridge. Welch expected Taft to be in stitches, but the Ohio senator only smiled politely.[6] The entire strange episode highlighted that a narcissistic megalomania was another aspect of Robert's complicated personality. It is little wonder that Taft failed to laugh. While spending the day with a leading contender to be president of the United States, Welch made their arrival at his brother's company exclusively about himself. Taft probably felt a yearning to be back in his native Ohio.

But Taft and Welch were soulmates in ideology, if not style. Taft regarded the New Deal and the Fair Deal as wasteful and increasingly dictatorial.[7] "If Mr. Roosevelt is not a Communist today," Taft said in 1936, "he is bound to become one." The intellectual Taft had a capacity for battle and rhetorical hyperbole that made him seem reactionary to some. He was a protégé of Herbert Hoover and followed the social Darwinism of his father's day. His message was the same as Friedrich Hayek's and John T. Flynn's: the final tragic result of liberalism was living in a socialistic country.

Robert adored Taft's position toward eastern internationalists, his nemeses. Taft thought the eastern establishment was coming close to imperialism in its avarice to corner both foreign markets and midwestern ones. He condemned the establishment's mimicry of Europe's backward social welfare programs. Taft loathed the monopolies and economic concentration of the East. He considered them dangerous to capitalism and contrary to the entrepreneurial spirit. Indeed, his father had busted more trusts than even his predecessor, Theodore Roosevelt.

Taft never forgot the little company on Main Street and rued that easterners were preoccupied with Wall Street. Taft saw his Taft-Hartley Labor Relations Act as his signature legislative achievement of the post-war. The act protected small-business owners on Main Street because it allowed states to prohibit the union shop. He also sought massive cuts to welfare and social spending. Taft assailed Truman's continuation of FDR's big government and welfare state programs, and savaged the inflation that ticked up in the late 1940s as the price of disrespecting the entrepreneurial spirit and work ethic. To a Cambridge candy maker who pedaled his wares from Springfield to Lynn to New Bedford, Taft made sense. At his core, Taft believed that the expansion of the public sector threatened capitalism.[8]

Welch also loved Taft's stance on foreign policy, which criticized Democratic liberalism as exacerbating the Communist threat. Like Welch, Taft hated European politics and believed that America's priorities rested in the Pacific and the Western Hemisphere. Taft viewed the Soviet Union and international Communism as insidious evils and saw the international and interventionist policies of Roosevelt and Truman as convenient excuses to aggrandize the liberal welfare state. Welch endorsed Taft's 1951 book *A Foreign Policy for Americans*, which supported liberation. Taft's vision of liberation did not involve American ground troops; it instead was a propaganda war, or "an underground war of infiltration in Iron Curtain countries," as Taft put it. Taft advocated what he called the "policy of the freehand"—a pro-German, anti-Communist "flexible response" for the 1950s.[9]

Both men had opposed aid to the countries that had resisted fascism at the onset of World War II. Supplying aid to Britain, Taft had said, would mean intervention "to save the British Empire." American involvement would also mean huge deficits, massive spending, conscription, price controls, and a more powerful bureaucratic state. He opposed aid to the Soviet Union when Hitler invaded as well, saying, "The victory of communism in the world would be far more dangerous to the United States than the victory of fascism." Taft hated war more than fascism too. "War is worse than a German victory," he said in 1940. America must remain a fortress of solitude, Taft said, and be ready to go it alone.[10]

The same was true after the war. In 1951, Taft said "Russia is far more a threat to the security of the United States than Hitler or Germany ever was." Though softening in his initial opposition to the Marshall Plan and the Truman Doctrine, Taft was consistent in his ire for NATO. "I do not think this moral leadership ideal justifies our engaging in any preventive war, or going to the defense of one country against another, or getting ourselves into a vulnerable fiscal and economic position at home which may invite war."[11] Yet on Asia, Taft was open to intervention and shared with Welch and John Birch a missionary impulse for the Chinese anti-Communists. After Mao's victory and Chiang Kai-shek's flight to the island of Taiwan, Taft wanted to defend the island with the American navy. Taft also ultimately backed intervention in the Korean War, but he faulted the "bungling and inconsistent foreign policy of the administration."

For Robert Welch, Robert Taft was another gateway to the idea that the Democrats not only were soft on Communism abroad but also conspired to aid the enemy more consciously. Taft, as Alonzo Hamby put it, "helped lay the groundwork for the ultimate anti-Communist flight from reality—McCarthyism." After all, when Chiang and the Nationalists fled to Taiwan, Taft said that the Truman State Department was "guided by a left-wing group who have obviously wanted to get rid of Chiang and were willing at least to turn China over to the Communists for that purpose."[12]

On March 31, 1952, Welch bought airtime for twenty-five broadcasts on Boston radio station WBZ to support Taft's candidacy for president. The first was five minutes long and the last thirty minutes. The broadcasts, which Robert delivered himself, lamented the growth of socialism in America, censured the malfeasance of the Truman administration, pilloried national health insurance schemes, and savaged how welfare was ruining the entrepreneurial spirit in the United States. Additional broadcasts knocked government's involvement in the electrical industry, the printing and publishing businesses, and the regulation of the lending industry. His messages also denounced the Marshall Plan, the United Nations Relief and Rehabilitation Administration, and the proliferation of the federal payroll during the Truman administration. Each broadcast culminated with an unequivocal endorsement of Robert Taft as the only politician able to restore the country to greatness, turn back the tide of socialism and Communism, and put America's interests before those of other nations.

Taft swept the 1952 primaries in the Midwest, winning in Illinois, Ohio, Nebraska, Wisconsin, and South Dakota. But Dwight David Eisenhower was about to enter the race. Welch was perhaps so confident that Taft was destined to win the nomination in 1952 that on April 28 he wrote the following speech, attacking Eisenhower.

> I have been disturbed even more by reports of extreme left-wing support for General Eisenhower everywhere. Some of the letters on this subject, which have come to me from all parts of the country, would disturb you, too. I have had no opportunity to verify the accuracy of these reports, and I would neither mention them nor be so worried about them except for a specific experience of my own. . . . [T]here has been only one occasion when I have been able to face an opposing speaker in Belmont, . . . my opponent for Eisenhower and myself for Senator Taft. . . . The opposing speaker made some statements which were subtle enough and insidious enough to cause me to look him up. And I found this man, whom the Eisenhower forces sent right into my hometown to speak against me, had been a close associate and an official associate of Alger Hiss, Harriet Lucy Moore, Frederick Vanderbilt Field, and others of their ilk. He did not claim to be Republican, but an Independent in politics. He was certainly strange support for a candidate for the Republican nomination for the presidency. You cannot help generalizing from the particular. If hundreds of us are each given an apple out of the same barrel, and I find my apple is bad, and received dozens of letters from friends claiming that they got bad apples too, I cannot help worrying about the proportion of bad apples that was in the barrel. . . .
>
> As Republicans, with the goal of restoring decency and economy to our government and some common sense to our economic thinking, we are supposed to be fighting the socialists and the sympathizers with Communism, not to be getting in bed with them. To see them getting in bed with us, or with one of our leading candidates, calls for some sober thought.[13]

Welch never delivered this speech, but the aspersion foreshadowed an important subsequent letter, which called Eisenhower a Communist. Eisenhower was a vigorous sixty-two-year-old with intense blue eyes and an amiable nature. His smile was beguiling. His wide grin exuded warmth. He also happened to be the victor of the war in Europe. He had been MacArthur's chief of staff in the Philippines in the 1930s, but his career skyrocketed as a strategist in the War Plans Division. His career reached its apogee as commanding general, European Theater of Operations, under Army Chief of Staff George Marshall. On D-Day, Eisenhower gained a reputation for decisive action and unparalleled success. He embodied authority and discipline, but needed to keep his temper under wraps. He was a masterful politician who knew how Washington worked and the most prepared individual ever to assume the office of the presidency. He was calculating and ruthless. And his reason for running was personal: Taft needed to be stopped.

When Eisenhower had been supreme Allied commander under NATO in Europe, he worried deeply about Taft's hesitancy toward NATO and blanched at the thought of seeing him in the Oval Office. Meeting with Taft during the debate over sending American troops to Europe convinced Ike that he may be an indispensable man in 1952: Taft's NATO policy risked the postwar peace. The United States had just fought a war to establish collective security, but Taft did not believe in collective security. Senator Lodge had the same opinion of Taft and spoke with Ike of the need to block Taft. Governor Dewey came on board, and convened in New York an "initial advisory group." Lodge was appointed campaign manager. Suddenly, Ike was running for president.[14]

Welch did not think Eisenhower could win the nomination. Dominating the Republican Party were midwestern and western power brokers of the Old Guard who voted against NATO and opposed the Marshall Plan. Eisenhower's support came from the East, which had sold the United States down the river at Yalta and lost China. The Old Guard would never back a liberal president of Columbia University, which Ike had also been, solidifying his position with eastern elites. Welch thought the Old Guard would never swallow a "Democratic general" who befriended New York and Boston banking and corporate leaders, and palled around with rich liberals. For sure, Ike was also from the Midwest, but the eastern establishment elites of finance, communications, and corporate business loved him. They appreciated Ike's penchant for efficiency, contempt for crass politicians, skill for compromise, and aptitude with the media. But he was untested in the political arena.

The issues of the day gave Welch confidence in Taft. The midterm elections of 1942, 1944, 1950 demonstrated forcefully that the American people were preoccupied with China, spies in government, and the growth of the state—issues that Taft had led the way on. The party regulars backed Taft. Black Republicans in the South were in his corner. The *Los Angeles Times*, the McCormick papers, the *Wall Street Journal*, the *Omaha World Herald* all backed Taft too.[15]

But Eisenhower began mollifying the Old Guard. He opposed centralized government, criticized corruption in the federal bureaucracy, and bemoaned the loss of China and the secrecy of Yalta. "If we had been less trusting," Eisenhower said, "if we had been less soft and weak, there would probably have been no war in Korea!" It was sweet music to the Old Guard. Polls showed that Ike was the favorite among the rank-and-file, but he also polled well among Democrats. Eisenhower won primaries in New Hampshire, Pennsylvania, New Jersey, Massachusetts, Oregon, and Minnesota.[16]

Eisenhower played his most important card and made his most successful appeal to the Old Guard with his use of John Foster Dulles and support for liberation in Eastern Europe. Dulles, his presumptive nominee for secretary of state, wrote an article called "A Policy of Boldness," which approved the Truman containment policies, including NATO, the Berlin Airlift, and Korea, but declared that containment did not go far enough. It was too defensive and put the United States on the road to the "twin evils of militarism and bankruptcy" and catered to Europe. "Those who think only of Western Europe and of making it 'impregnable'—without regard to the Near, Middle, and Far East and Africa—are just as blind as those who think only of the United States and making it 'impregnable.' Policies that do not defend freedom in Asia are fatally defective." Eisenhower was giving Asia Firsters what they wanted to hear. The United States, Dulles said, needed to take the "political offensive" and establish "freedom programs" for "captive nations" subdued by Communism. Nothing less than a "great new

Declaration of Independence" for Eastern Europe was required, he said. Dulles's masterful volley was everything the Old Guard needed.[17]

Ike also displayed his unalloyed ruthlessness. On the eve of the convention, when Taft had 530 delegates and Eisenhower 427, Taft had the southern delegations locked down, just as his father had in 1912 against Theodore Roosevelt. Then Lodge, just as *his* father had, demonstrated his mastery of parliamentary procedure. Lodge was a steamroller, intimidating undecided delegates and successfully challenging the credentials of Taft delegations from Texas, Georgia, and Louisiana.

Eisenhower got the nomination on the first ballot.

Looking back, Taft blamed the media and "the power of New York financial interests," which was anti-Semitic-adjacent, for his loss. But Welch suggested that the Communists were behind the Eisenhower candidacy from the start. Something was not quite right about Eisenhower, thought Robert. He heard reports of Communist influences in Ike's camp.[18] But in the end, Welch supported Eisenhower, albeit reluctantly, writing:

> The feeling is very strong among millions of Americans that Tweedledee [Adlai] Stevenson and Tweedledum Eisenhower are both Truman stooges, going through the motions of fighting each other without any real issues to fight over. I hope that this gloom is exaggerated, and that Eisenhower will prove to be more alert to, and effective against, the Communist menace than many of his detractors now expect. And I also hope that he will be elected, as at least the best of a bad bargain, and because his election will naturally sweep along with it a number of Republican congressmen and senators who will give some additional reinforcement of common sense to our government.[19]

...

The Taft candidacy energized the Right, including Welch, and forced Eisenhower to select a vice presidential candidate who was acceptable to the Right wing of the party. Richard Milhouse Nixon, US senator from California, fit many of the requirements. He was from the West, for geographic balance. He was young, balancing Eisenhower's grandfatherly mien. Nixon had proven himself a notorious Red hunter, first winning election to the Senate in 1950 by claiming that Helen Gahagan Douglas was "pink down to her underwear," and then effectively questioning the loyalty of Alger Hiss. Nixon's credentials as a fierce and reasonable, albeit ruthless, anti-Communist earned him the respect of his seniors. Nixon gave the right-wing anti-Communists committed to liberation—the philosophically pliable doctrine that fastened more ethnic voters to the Republican Party—one of their own at the seat of power.[20]

The doctrine of liberation that Eisenhower downplayed but Nixon played well and with avidity throughout his tenure as vice president seemed to run contrary to the laissez-faire principles of the Republican Right. Zealous anti-Communists with appetites for liberation fostered adventurism in Republican foreign policy and a temptation for revanchist wars against Communist regimes that had usurped power in China, Spain, and elsewhere. The reactionary regimes of Franco in Spain and Chiang Kai-shek in China certainly seemed to contrast starkly with the Republican Right's supposed belief in unfettered capitalism. But the main strategy of liberation was to attract more ethnic voters to the GOP.

And Nixon did. Eisenhower had often dampened the promise of counterrevolution through liberation, cautioning that it was a moral commitment rather than a military solution that could bring on World War III. Nixon, however, worked to avoid being pinned down on the moral parameters of liberation. He thus became a more attractive member of the ticket for Eastern European émigrés and others who appreciated the liberation doctrine and Nixon's vociferous anti-Communism. In essence, Nixon was not as averse as Eisenhower was in bringing the world to the brink of World War III, and that willingness paid dividends. Speaking on Pulaski Day, Nixon repudiated the Yalta agreements to the delight of Polish voters. Eisenhower did the same.

In October, in a speech recognizing the anniversary of the Hungarian war of independence's finale—Martyr's Day—the general mentioned that Republicans supported liberation by "peaceful means." The Republican national committee even got into the act. "Liberation Rallies" were planned. "Liberation Weeks" were organized. Committees of Crusades to Lift the Iron Curtain opened "Liberation Centers." The Foreign Language Groups section of the national committee blanketed urban ethnic communities with propaganda and turned out copy in the foreign press. The blitz to attract Eastern European ethnic groups—who later became some of the biggest followers of Robert Welch and his John Birch Society—was on in 1952. And it appeared to pay off. Democrats historically garnered 70 percent of the Polish American vote; in 1952, Democrats received only 50 percent of it.[21]

Democrats called Republican efforts to secure ethnic votes a cynical ploy. They cited the 1952 passage, over Truman's veto, of the Immigration and Naturalization Act. Otherwise known as the McCarran-Walter Act, the nativist law brazenly discriminated against Eastern Europeans by continuing the national origins quota system. Republicans had backed the measure overwhelmingly in both the House and Senate.

In September, the two former Republican rivals—Taft and Eisenhower—met in New York City. Eisenhower acquiesced to keeping the Taft-Hartley Act, supporting constitutional limitations on the powers of the presidency, and cutting federal expenditures.[22] His party was united, with the exception of MacArthur, who held out. The revelation that Nixon had a secret fund provided the campaign its sole crisis. When Nixon went on television and explained the fund had never been used for personal enrichment or gain, Welch became only more convinced that Nixon was a slippery politician who could not be trusted. Welch likely favored Nixon's replacement with the more conservative William Knowland.[23]

Joseph McCarthy loyally supported Eisenhower in 1952. (In a nationally televised address that Clint W. Murchison and Sears Roebuck's Robert E. Wood bankrolled, McCarthy called Democratic nominee Stevenson Alger instead of Adlai.) McCarthy made strong cases for electing right-wing candidates of Robert's own ilk, and they won: William Purtell in Connecticut bested the incumbent liberal Democrat Senator William Benton. In Arizona, Barry Goldwater defeated the Democratic Senate majority leader Ernest McFarland. McCarthy's fingerprints were all over both victories. But Ike did not give McCarthy any credit whatsoever. And that deeply bothered Robert Welch.

11

A Republican Looks at His President, 1953–1954

Robert Welch was happy with Ike's first moves in 1953. Personnel is policy, and Welch cheered the appointments of such midwestern industrialists as General Motors's Charles E. Wilson for secretary of defense and the M. A. Hanna Company's George Humphrey, a Cleveland fixture, for secretary of the treasury.[1] Ezra Taft Benson, a farm cooperative agent, staunch Taft Republican, and Mormon Church leader, also received approval from Welch as secretary of agriculture. Benson later became active in the John Birch Society. Though chagrined by the appointment of the anti-Taft-Hartley Martin Durkin of the plumbers union as secretary of labor, Welch had less than eight months to suffer before Durkin resigned. Welch and the Republican Right were happy with the appointment of Arthur W. Bradford, an Asia Firster, as chair of the Joint Chiefs of Staff.[2] To the delight of Welch, Eisenhower was listening to Main Street rather than Wall Street, and following what Taft would have done. Or so it seemed.

Welch was buoyed also by the ascendance of Old Guard leadership in Congress in 1953. Taft became majority leader in the Senate, and some called him the "Prime Minister" of the administration. Moderates took a backseat. Styles Bridges and Eugene Milliken chaired Appropriations and Finance, while William Knowland, a personal favorite of Robert's, was appointed chair of the Republican Policy Committee.[3]

Welch *was* dismayed by the nomination of Charles E. Bohlen for ambassador to the Soviet Union. "Bohlen was a protégé of Acheson, and another close friend of Alger Hiss. Even at the hearings on his confirmation, he still brazenly supported the Tehran, Yalta, and Potsdam conferences and agreements, in each of which he had participated."[4] In Bohlen's appointment, Welch observed, "Eisenhower was edging Communist sympathizers, right out of the old Acheson-Hiss coterie, into every position of importance that he dared."[5] Bohlen made a fantastic target for McCarthy and the Right. He spent his career in the foreign service, and he was at Yalta. Although not a Communist, Bohlen was likely a homosexual, and that was dangerous to be in 1953. Eisenhower defended him vehemently: "I have known Mr. Bohlen for some years. I was once, at least, a guest in his home, and with his very charming family. . . . He is the best qualified man." After Eisenhower even made the case that Bohlen golfed with him, Bohlen's nomination was saved by Taft, over the protest of Robert Welch.[6]

Still, in the early days of the Eisenhower administration, Robert felt the country was on the right track. Eisenhower removed wage and price controls, which always irked Welch, who felt deeply burdened by them in the candy industry.[7] Welch argued that the controls did not work and that ending them would increase productivity and lower inflation, or even eliminate it entirely. He thought that the controls hindered the growth of the economy and limited revenue.[8]

But larger questions remained for Welch too. How susceptible would the new regime become to the reaction—how far would the shift to the right go? Would Eisenhower try to roll back the New Deal, or would he allow it to remain ensconced in American life? An even more pressing question was whether the United States would remain internationalist in the 1950s or return to the isolationism of the 1920s. Robert hoped Ike would roll back the New Deal, break from Democratic supranational organizations, and more strongly commit to the Pacific.

After the encouraging first months, Welch's position on the Eisenhower presidency soured from domestic policy to foreign policy. Eisenhower took positions that affirmed Welch's original fears. About halfway through the president's first term, Welch was fairly certain that Eisenhower was following what Moscow wanted him to do.

Welch was gravely disappointed with Eisenhower's domestic policy, which continued to expand the scope of government. During his presidency, Eisenhower adopted liberal programs to build a strong Republican majority. The popular New Deal and Fair Deal programs remained as vital features of American life.[9] In fact, social welfare programs expanded: Eisenhower created the Department of Health, Education, and Welfare; increased the minimum wage; added more Social Security benefits; established a meager healthcare scheme for indigent seniors; and passed the National Defense Education Act. Welch wanted a reversal of the New Deal social legislation. Eisenhower did otherwise.[10]

But Eisenhower had good reasons for following a middle-of-the-road strategy. He realized, unlike Robert Welch, that the social contract forged during the Great Depression was here to stay because the American people wanted it. "Should any political party attempt to abolish Social Security, unemployment insurance, and eliminate labor and farm programs," wrote Eisenhower to his brother Edgar in late 1954, "you would not hear of that party again in our political history."[11]

Robert appreciated the president's early commitment to balancing the budget, but Eisenhower's first fiscal-year budget grew to a whopping size. Eisenhower brought down expenditures by fiscal year 1955, though. But Welch failed to notice that the president was able to slow the growth rate of the enormous military buildup under Truman. Also unnoticed by Welch was Eisenhower's support among southern conservatives for transferring offshore oil field control from the federal government to the states. Welch never admitted that Eisenhower attempted to reduce "creeping socialism" by curbing the power of the Tennessee Valley Authority public utility and backing private power companies to the hilt.

Welch never acknowledged that Eisenhower was an ally of his on immigration. In 1954, under Operation Wetback, Eisenhower rounded up 1 million Mexicans who had journeyed across the Rio Grande and sent them back to Mexico.[12] Welch also failed to notice that Eisenhower reversed the New Deal's tribal preservation policies. Eisenhower actually wanted to eliminate the tribes' rights as legal entities, though he did not succeed.

Welch wanted cuts to foreign aid, but foreign aid was keeping many countries out of the Communist camp. Federal aid, especially economic assistance to Third World countries, was central to winning the Cold War, providing political stability, and establishing sustainable democracies. As Eisenhower said, "unless we can put things in the hands of people who are starving to death, we can never lick Communism."[13]

Robert wanted victory in Korea, but that did not happen. The administration actually shifted to the right on Korea, although Welch did not see it that way. Eisenhower had promised to "go to Korea," and he did for three days in December 1952. But he did not endorse General MacArthur's idea of a nuclear ultimatum. Whether such a threat could have ended the conflict is uncertain, but Welch viewed it as a missed opportunity. Seven months after the Korean trip, the United States signed an armistice that ended the fighting, which had raged for three years; ended 30,000 American lives and likely a million Chinese, South Korean, and North Korean lives; cost tens of billions of dollars; and only restored the stalemate. Welch blamed Eisenhower for the loss of Korea: "it has been a well-nourished impression that the deliberate failure of our forces to fight the Korean War to win it . . . is solely attributable to the Truman administration. This is simply not true," stated Welch. "After Eisenhower's election, the Communist influence was even more decisive," he said. As little as three to four months after Eisenhower's inauguration, Welch argued, the United States could have won. Robert based his argument on a speech by General James A. Van Fleet, the commander of the Eighth Army, who declared "victory was denied us," "we had the enemy on the run," and "we should have won."[14]

But Eisenhower had rejected any offensive maneuver that involved American ground troops because there was just no stomach for driving the Chinese back across the Yalu River or for any unification campaign that might start World War III. For Eisenhower, a stalemate was the best course of action.[15] Welch thought that the failure to take the offensive was tantamount to defeat. But unconditional surrender of the sort seen in 1945 was now impossible under the specter of nuclear weapons. Unlimited war was simply unwinnable and impossible in the atomic age.[16]

Robert disagreed with Eisenhower over the Bricker amendment, which would have required Senate approval for treaties or executive agreements. Robert favored it because he hated the United Nations, which he feared would introduce its worldview in the United States through the executive branch. Many southern conservatives feared that segregation was imperiled because of the UN's commitment to human rights. The American Medical Association warned that commitment was going to bring about socialized medicine.[17] For Welch, the failure to provide a legislative check on the presidency could mean "socialism by treaty," the adoption of the UN social philosophy, or worse. The likely "path of procedure by which the Communists might eventually take over the United States," Welch said, "would follow the course of inducing gradual surrender of American sovereignty, piece by piece and step-by-step to" the UN. "Eventually, a world-wide police state, absolutely and brutally governed from the Kremlin would become a viable and accomplished fact," he continued. But Eisenhower attacked the Bricker amendment with derision: "Bricker seems determined to save the country from Eleanor Roosevelt," he said, and the Constitution was being destroyed "brick by brick by Bricker." Eisenhower made a strong case that the amendment restricted presidential power. Welch excoriated Eisenhower for using "every ounce of the power and prestige of his office and every measure of personal cajolery by himself as president" to defeat the amendment, which fell one vote short of the necessary two-thirds majority in the Senate in 1954.[18]

But John Bricker's amendment was backed by forty out of forty-seven Republican senators, and it had the backing of the Veterans of Foreign Wars, the American Medical Association, the American Legion, the Daughters of the American Revolution, and the US Chamber of Commerce. It also had the support of Clarence Manion, who was fired from President Eisenhower's commission on federal-state relations for that reason. His termination helped open the way for the McCarthyite Right to embrace Welch's interpretation that Eisenhower might be a Communist at heart.

But the real problem was that the Bricker amendment made literally no sense, declaring "a treaty shall become effective as internal law in the United States only through legislation which would be valid in the absence of the treaty." It was legalistic gobbledygook. Eisenhower put it best: "Bricker was an addition to the Constitution that said you could not violate the Constitution. How silly!" Its supporters said that it would prevent more Yaltas, but that argument was absurd because the details in Yalta did not have an impact within the United States. Moreover, the Bricker amendment would not have applied then because FDR was exercising his wartime powers as commander in chief.[19]

The Bricker amendment was not the only policy from the Right that challenged the administration. Eisenhower initially acquiesced to right-wing pressure to "unleash" Chiang Kai-shek by removing the Seventh Fleet from the Formosa Strait. The change was largely symbolic, but Welch—even further to the Right than the Right—saw Eisenhower's actions as a "cease-fire" and a victory for the Communists. He portrayed Eisenhower's course as "one of the most costly and disastrous intentional fumbles of his playing career." The "cease-fire," Welch said, was a "morale-shattering repudiation of Chiang Kai-shek's official position and of everything our alliance with him was supposed to mean." "If the United States had deliberately dropped a hostile bomb on Chiang-kai-shek's government buildings in Taipei, we could not have done more damage to the whole anti-Communist cause throughout Southeast Asia."[20] Eisenhower's internationalism consistently drew Welch's ire.

Similarly, John Foster Dulles's selection as secretary of state was a complete disaster for Welch. Dulles was committed to foreign aid and NATO, which he and Eisenhower saw as the basis for American defense in Europe. Dulles's propensity for internationalism and collective security was what Welch feared the most. To be sure, Welch, along with many of the Old Guard, cheered the "New Look's" reduction in military expenditures, its emphasis on the Strategic Air Command, its savings, or its "more bang for the buck," and they appreciated its resemblance to Republican doctrines of the 1920s, but soon grew weary of Eisenhower's adventurism. The most important business was putting the country first, and Welch thought Ike was putting the world first.[21]

While the Right generally found satisfactory the administration's buildup of anti-Communist ground forces in Formosa and Korea, Welch was leery about the growing troop presence in West Germany. Eisenhower redeployed ground troops within the United States as a "strategic mobile reserve," explaining that it would offer "more basic security at less cost" and allow for rapid increase in the size of the army if a crisis arose. Welch opposed this approach because he worried about the rise of a national security state, feared the growth of a police state, and had legitimate concerns about any unintended consequences.[22]

Perhaps worst of all for Welch, in 1953, Eisenhower jettisoned his campaign's repudiation of Yalta as well as his liberation pledge. Instead, the administration merely assailed Russia for not living up to the Yalta agreements—the very position of the Democratic Party. But with Stalin's death in February 1953, the administration abandoned even this approach. By 1956, Welch lamented accurately that Eisenhower had done nothing to liberate Eastern Europe. He concluded that Eisenhower's attendance at the Geneva Summit in 1955 demonstrated that America had decided that Russian occupation of Eastern Europe was a foregone conclusion.[23]

But there was a good reason for Eisenhower to keep America's word at Yalta even if Stalin did not. If the United States abandoned Yalta's commitments, so would the rest of the world. Yalta provided American occupation rights in West Berlin. If the United States said Yalta was invalid, the Russians would do the same, and American protests against Russian occupation in Eastern European satellites would even be weaker. The United States would lose the moral high ground.[24]

Eisenhower showed his unwillingness to liberate in June 1953, when East German workers protested against their regime, and the United States was silent. The Soviet Army crushed the revolt. This stand-down was unacceptable, said Welch: "When the East Germans rose against their Communist Masters, on June 17, 1953, their courage could easily have started a rollback of the Iron Curtain that would have continued until the whole world was free." "And we stood by . . . passively," Welch lamented, "while these anti-Communists were slaughtered by the thousands." Welch continued, turning conspiratorial: "This writer has received reports, which he believes, as follows: That in anticipation of help from us, leaders of the revolt tipped off secret agents of our government in advance" and "the Russians were informed by Washington of what was brewing."[25]

Eisenhower's policy toward Vietnam also perturbed Welch. As early as 1953, the Right was calling for more militancy there, and Robert was joining the parade. Like the administration, Welch saw the conflict from the perspective of the domino theory, the Cold War, and Communist pressure from Beijing and Moscow. It was not a civil war, Welch believed. His view ran contrary to reality. But so did the views of nearly everybody else making American policy in Vietnam.

Throughout the world, nationalist movements were trying to overthrow French colonial rule. As the magnetic Vietnamese leader Ho Chi Minh became more Communist and the United States grew more anti-Communist, Americans had increasing difficulty recognizing a social revolution for what it was. Moreover, the United States was financing 75 percent of France's colonial conflict in Vietnam by 1954. When Ho Chi Minh and the Vietminh surrounded the fortress of Dien Bien Phu in March, however, Eisenhower was reluctant to provide the airstrikes the French requested, on the basis that French soldiers would be killed as well. Wary of being pulled into another Asian war by the Right, Eisenhower set conditions for using ground forces and established the caveat that any military operation must be approved by Congress. The president was ahead of his time on Vietnam.

The public grew tense when Vice President Nixon declared "off the record" that ground forces might have to be used in Vietnam anyway. Ho Chi Minh's guerrilla nationalists had won the battle of Dien Bien Phu, and the Geneva Accords halved Vietnam at the 17th parallel, with the United States' agreement. The Right, including Senator Knowland and Robert Welch, eviscerated the administration for participating at Geneva at all. And their voices did not go unheeded. When Chou Enlai reached out his hand to John Foster Dulles, the secretary of state did not shake it. And US aircraft carriers with nuclear weapons coursed frosty paths off the coast of Indochina throughout the conference. The administration considered, but Eisenhower rejected, an amphibious landing at Haiphong. US ground forces would then march on Hanoi, but General Matthew Ridgway realized—quite presciently—that Vietnam involved more logistic and political nightmares than Korea.[26]

Welch was apoplectic about the outcome at Geneva: "While we gave the appearance of not knowing . . . what the Geneva conference was all about, the Communists were aiming at the very definite and important goal. This was to hand their agent, Ho Chi Minh, the better half of Vietnam." Welch continued: "During that same spring of 1954, . . . while Eisenhower was doing absolutely nothing towards relieving the fortress of Dienbienphu, he nevertheless went out of his way to explain gravely that Indochina must not be allowed to fall to the Communists, because if it did," other nations would topple. "I will not be a party to any agreement that makes anybody a slave," Eisenhower said. Welch responded: "only three weeks later with his [Ike's] full blessing, a top official of our government sat in, without protest, at the establishment of another ignominious truce, this one making very unwilling slaves out of 13 million Vietnamese."[27]

There is no indication that Welch at the time saw Vietnam as a "phony war," as he put it later, with both sides being run by the Communists. Welch wanted an American air strike on Dien Bien Phu, greater American involvement, and unification of the country. But in 1954 Americans wanted the French to fight for themselves. In the partition, the Americans got the best deal they could, given that the Vietminh wanted the whole of the country. With the exception of a nuclear strike, which would have been a pyrrhic victory at best, the United States could not stop the impetus of the Vietminh. Eisenhower was facing reality. The United States had just fought the Korean War to a stalemate and was tired of war. How could the American people endorse a conflict for a French colony only a short time after Korea?[28]

Robert also said Eisenhower was not doing enough about internal security. "Eisenhower as President has initiated and sparked a continuing, unhesitating, and highly successful effort to prevent any real exposure of Communists high up in government, and to minimize the exposure of Communists in the lower echelons—of either the Truman Administration or its own."[29] Welch said Ike had permitted thousands of Communists, pinks, and homosexuals to serve in government—with dire impacts throughout the country. "Since Eisenhower became President, practically all of the known termites have come out of their holes and begun going boldly about their business again. Communist sympathies and even actual pro-Communist subversive activities are daily made more respectable, not only by our government, but by our labor unions" and "our great universities."[30]

On this subject and others, Senator Joe McCarthy continued to divide the GOP. Welch viewed him as a national treasure while some moderates declared him a national disgrace. Ike loathed McCarthy, but some moderates, Henry Cabot Lodge being one, saw his usefulness. McCarthy and Eisenhower kept their distance, and barely tolerated each other. Welch wanted Eisenhower to be as aggressive and ruthless as McCarthy in dismissing Communists from the government. But Eisenhower would not. For example, while Welch and McCarthy wanted to completely eliminate foreign trade with Communist countries, Eisenhower believed that "there is no instrument in the hands of diplomacy that is quite as powerful as trade." Trade with Iron Curtain countries kept them in the American camp, he said. "The last thing you can do is to force all these [satellites] to depend on Moscow for the rest of their lives." Trade gives you "something pulling their interest your way," Eisenhower observed.[31]

Eisenhower's tolerant approach toward the holdings of Communist books in America's overseas libraries also perturbed Welch—ironically because Welch loved books and had 5,000 in his personal library. Welch also believed in "knowing your enemy" and was known as one of the most dedicated anti-Communist readers of Communist propaganda. Roy Cohn and David Schine investigated the Voice of America's overseas libraries and discovered books by 418 Communists and fellow travelers. Dulles reacted by banning all Communist authors and publications containing material by Communists. In addition, 830 employees of the Voice of America were fired and books were burned. McCarthy wanted to go even further and determine who ordered the books. On June 14, 1953, Eisenhower assailed McCarthy at Dartmouth's commencement: "Don't join the book-burners. Don't think you are going to conceal faults by concealing evidence that they ever existed. Don't be afraid to go in your library and read every book, as long as that document does not offend your ideas of decency. That should be the only censorship." Most knew it to be a rebuke to McCarthy.[32]

In another effort to repudiate McCarthy, if not his politics, Eisenhower eliminated the Truman administration's departmental panels and loyalty review boards and put in place a new loyalty/security program replete with security boards and officers for reviews. Eisenhower broadened the criterion for removal by encompassing not only politics but also ostensibly any form of malfeasance or infraction or "deviance," including homosexuality. This may also have been a rebuke of McCarthy because rumors abounded that Cohn, Schine, and even McCarthy were homosexuals—which Cohn, at least, was.[33]

Eisenhower shifted the burden of proof onto the employee who needed to demonstrate that failure to retain his service was not in the interest of national security. Peacetime espionage became a capital offense. Penalties were stiffened for harboring fugitives. To compel testimony, immunity was given to witnesses. Eisenhower wanted more stringent perjury laws and greater use of wiretapping, but Congress balked. Persons who advocated government overthrow lost citizenship rights. Though Eisenhower removed 2,200 individuals under the new program, including the "China hands" of the State Department, and J. Robert Oppenheimer, the principal overseer of the atomic bomb's development, Welch remained critical: "the Executive Department of government . . . has become, to a large extent, an active agency for the promotion of Communist aims," he said. "Alger Hiss expounding at Princeton, Robert Oppenheimer lecturing at Harvard," Welch said, "are but symptoms of a spreading, deepening Communist influence throughout our national life."[34]

On January 23, 16,500 State Department employees received a letter demanding their "positive loyalty" to the administration. Then Dulles appointed Donold B. Lourie of the Quaker Oats Company to clean house there. Soon, two dozen FBI agents started rooting out individuals in the State Department. In less than a month, 21 were fired for homosexuality. 306 employees were fired without so much as a hearing. But McCarthy was still not happy, and neither was Robert Welch: nothing the administration did for internal security was good enough. Meanwhile, morale plummeted at the State Department, and some of its best people on Asia were removed, just as events in Vietnam heated up.[35] Personnel is policy, which carries consequences.

Eisenhower even engaged in "McCarthyism" himself on at least one occasion: the Harry Dexter White affair. According to Welch, Eisenhower was "emphatic and heavy-handed in stopping the exposures by his own Attorney General, Herbert Brownell of Communist activities under Truman," but nothing could be further from the truth. Brownell exposed the Truman administration for approving the appointment of Harry Dexter White as the International Monetary Fund's executive director, even though the FBI was investigating White as a suspected Russian agent. Eisenhower was trying to out-McCarthy McCarthy by approving the release of the information and claiming the mantle of Communist hunter. But Eisenhower's strategy backfired. The affair unintentionally proved quite a boon for McCarthy. His approval rating soared to 50 percent, and McCarthy relished the need to deny he would be a presidential candidate in 1956.

By September 1953, McCarthy had reached his zenith. In October, he charged that Fort Monmouth's Army Signal Corps was a haven for Communists. Then, in early 1954, McCarthy highlighted the case of a "pink" army dentist, Irving Peress, who was quietly promoted and given an honorable discharge after his Communist sympathies came to light. McCarthy and Welch demanded to know who promoted Peress. The promotion was likely an administrative blunder, but McCarthy and Welch saw more nefarious motives at play. McCarthy fingered Brigadier General Ralph Zwicker, who he said had "the brains of a five-year" and was "not fit to wear the uniform." Zwicker, Welch claimed, "lied under oath to protect the Communists above him." In fact, Zwicker was not only opposed to the promotion of Peress but supported his firing. When McCarthy wanted Zwicker to testify before the House Un-American Activities Committee, Eisenhower realized that a strong statement establishing executive privilege was needed. On March 2, 1954, Eisenhower requested from the Department of Justice a legal brief on the president's power to keep subordinates from testifying. It was the beginning of Eisenhower's sweeping declaration of executive privilege. It was also the beginning of Joe McCarthy's great fall.[36]

In May 1954, as Welch said, "Eisenhower quietly clamped a dictatorial embargo on the supply of any information by government departments to investigating committees." Eisenhower declared that executive departments were not to disclose "conversations, communications, and documents" concerning why and how policies had been established "because it is essential to efficient and effective administration that employees of the Executive Branch be in a position to be completely candid with each other on official matters." In the history of the American presidency, Eisenhower's statement was the most definitive and all-encompassing on executive privilege.[37] The president was even more emphatic to his subordinates: "anyone who testifies as to the advice he gave me won't be working for me that night. . . . I will not allow people around me to be subpoenaed and you might as well know it now." McCarthy called it an "iron curtain." It was "the first time I've seen the executive branch of government take the fifth amendment," he declared. But the Wisconsin senator admitted, "I must submit that I am somewhat at a loss as to know what to do at this moment."

The sweeping declaration of executive privilege was what angered Robert the most about Eisenhower's presidency. The declaration, Welch believed, "stymie[d] McCarthy's investigation, at a crucial period, for nine months." Welch lamented that "this was long enough to prevent any revelation of where the trail of treason actually led" and to "ensure that McCarthy's investigations could finally be stopped altogether by a Democratic Congress." Eisenhower's claim of executive privilege, said Welch, was a "blocking method which the Communists had devised."[38]

Two months earlier, in March, the national broadcasts of Edward R. Murrow's *See It Now* program had damaged McCarthy by letting the senator speak for himself. Vermont Republican senator Ralph Flanders observed in the Senate that McCarthy was "doing his best to shatter the party whose label he wears." That same week, the army charged that McCarthy tried to gain preferential treatment for Schine. But McCarthy counterattacked, making forty-six charges against the army. Hearings conducted to establish the facts were televised and juxtaposed a belligerent and crass McCarthy with the astute and gentlemanly army counsel, Joseph L. Welch. The curtain was about to fall on the Wisconsin senator.[39]

McCarthy's star faded. He suffered sinus headaches and acute stomach pain. He was drinking heavily. The political center abandoned him, but the Republican Right and some Catholic Democrats stayed by his side. So did Robert Welch. Of the Army-McCarthy hearings, Welch concluded, "the whole factitious proceeding was cooked up inside the White House."[40] Senator Flanders moved to censure McCarthy, and in December 1954, the Senate condemned McCarthy, sixty-seven to twenty-two. "All of the artificial storm and fury," Welch wrote, "from which you might have thought—and were supposed to think—that McCarthy had committed every crime in the book from arson to treason, eventually boiled down to the question of a censure motion against McCarthy for language and methods supposedly unbecoming of a senator." Welch denounced Flanders as a "badly confused" man "whose language and methods have frequently been worse than anything of which McCarthy was ever accused." For Welch, McCarthy's censure was tragic; he could no longer be a standard bearer of the fledgling conservative movement that he, William Buckley, and others were building.[41]

McCarthy's censure derailed the momentum of the Right. Welch wondered where all the heroes had gone. First MacArthur. Fired. Then Taft. Dead of cancer in 1953. Now McCarthy. Censured. Robert hoped that Senators Knowland of California and Jenner of Indiana could fill the void, but none had any of the eloquence of a MacArthur, the mental acuity of a Taft, or a sense for the dramatic of a McCarthy. (Eisenhower wrote of Knowland in his diary, "there seems to be no final answer to the question 'How stupid can you get?'") Senator Barry Goldwater of Arizona was colorful and charismatic but not yet ready to lead a national movement. McCarthy's activities may have killed opportunities for hundreds, assassinated characters, and destroyed lives, but he did get the dirty jobs done, thought Robert.[42]

Months earlier on May 17, Welch suffered the torment of the Supreme Court's landmark decision in *Brown v. Board of Education* that segregation was unconstitutional. Communists were behind it, he said: "the storm over integration. . . . has been brought on by the Communists. . . . Among their objectives are riots and promotion of interracial distrust and bitterness, a reopening of old animosities between North and South, the creation of 'civil rights' programs and organizations which can attract gullible do-gooders and then serve many other Communist purposes."[43] Welch denied that he carried even one iota of hatred toward the Black race, but he had grown up in the South, in a society that derided the achievements and speech patterns of African Americans. He did, too, both as a youngster and as an adult. "His specialty is the Southern-oriented joke, obviously a holdover from his boyhood in North Carolina," noted a contemporary of Robert's. "He is at his best when he is able to exchange Negro dialect jokes with any Negro members of the Society that may be present."[44] Welch strongly believed any improvement in racial relations needed to start locally. Coercion would not work. A law, or court decision, would create a conflict between the federal and state governments, and derail any potential improvement in racial amity. And Welch believed that things were already improving between Blacks and Whites.

Although no frothing at the mouth racist, Welch associated with segregationists, incorrectly believed that integration was a Communist conspiracy, and was stunted on the subject of civil rights. Welch failed to see that Blacks needed greater progress on civil rights in school desegregation whether through legislative, executive, or judicial action. Welch undermined the cause of civil rights and, as a White male and a leading businessman in postwar America, failed miserably to tame the lesser angels of human nature. Like his chief nemesis, Dwight David Eisenhower, Welch failed to exert leadership when the country needed great change in the condition and opportunities for African Americans. Welch failed because he was stuck in the nineteenth century. Further, he invigorated racists and segregationists when he later placed billboards calling for Earl Warren's impeachment on the side of highways, when less fallible men may have championed the greatest chief justice of the twentieth century, particularly for changing the nature of America for the good with his visionary decision in *Brown v. Board of Education*. Welch failed miserably when he did not support Eisenhower's advocacy of sending troops into Little Rock in 1957, and erroneously saw the event through the conspiratorial lens of Communist subversion into the United States. Welch inhibited progress on civil rights, whether denigrating or questioning the courage of Dr. Martin Luther King, who was certainly no Communist but an imperfect titan who brought love and compassion in a time when the country needed it most. But Welch's greatest failure probably was his willingness and participation in provoking a greater, more violent White southern resistance, when his instinct—instilled from his Baptist youth—was to love thy neighbor, but more importantly thine enemies.

Like many entitled White males of his generation, Welch unabashedly and unashamedly imitated the dialects of African Americans, whether in their presence or not. His intention cannot be explained away as a cultural anachronism, and it most certainly left any Blacks who witnessed it feeling slighted, angry, or both. At the very least, it failed to uphold the credo that "all men are created equal." As somebody who revered the wisdom of the Founding Fathers, Welch should have expected more from himself, especially having grown up in a diverse southern world. In Welch's world, where systemic racism and institutionalized prejudice were omnipotent and ubiquitous, such mimicry was not morally neutral. It suggests at least a certain lack of empathy as well as a failure to recognize Blacks' full humanity. A more compassionate man would have seen the damage such mimicry can do.

The question of whether Welch personally harbored racialist views is not really the issue. The heart of the matter is that Welch bolstered the forces of massive White resistance, whether mocking a Black man in public, attending the States Rights National Convention in 1956, or simply standing on the wrong side of history yelling stop when history needed a grand push forward. Like his peers—William F. Buckley, Barry Goldwater, and George Wallace, among others—he was complicit or at least manipulative in his attempts to seem race neutral, declaring that things were already improving between Blacks and Whites.

In general, Robert was deeply disappointed with the early years of the Eisenhower presidency, as were many members of the Old Guard. But most Americans liked their president and continued to support his middle-of-the-road policies. Even McCarthy did not attack Eisenhower directly. That attack would come from Robert Welch himself and inaugurate the controversy that made the John Birch Society infamous.

12

The Saga of John Birch, 1954

In 1954, the Right faced an intellectual vacuum, and Robert Welch was thinking hard about how he could fill it. It was not the most opportune moment to lead a reactionary phalanx against eastern moderates. Eisenhower was pursuing many of the policies of the previous two administrations, and the American people seemed happy about it. Times had changed, and not to the benefit of the Republican Right. There were no more Alger Hisses to attack. China was lost. Stalin had recently died, weakening the argument for a monolithic conspiracy run by Moscow. Under Khrushchev, international tensions seemed to be relaxing. Even conservative journals were in freefall. The *American Mercury* and the *Freeman* were becoming politically unacceptable, and many contributors resigned. Morale plummeted on the staff of the *Freeman*, and it became, as William F. Buckley called it, "staid and academic." The year was similar but even worse for the *American Mercury*, whose new owner, Russell Maguire, started publishing vicious anti-Semitic articles.[1] The Republican Right was a shell of itself, and was dominated, at least on the organizational level, by neo-isolationist and anti-Semitic remnants such as the Congress of Freedom and Gerald L. K. Smith's Nationalist Christian Crusade.

But Welch saw opportunity in 1954. He tried to fill the vacuum by writing frenziedly throughout 1954. Writing relaxed him and provided catharsis from the burdens of the Eisenhower administration's failures.[2] He was working on what he considered his most important work, *The Life of John Birch*. It was Robert's second book published by

Henry Regnery, and he had even greater expectations for it than for *May God Forgive Us*. (In the interim, Regnery had refused to publish Welch's novel about a civilization of ants enslaved by an encroaching state.) As he approached Regnery, Welch was confident that, despite all of Eisenhower's shortcomings, his victory "highlighted a definite turn back from the left, which will make it easier for the soundly factual books which you publish to obtain a wider readership."[3]

Welch's profound confidence in his writerly success was grounded in his faith in the American people. If the American people were told the truth in print, Welch believed, they would purchase the books, elect the right leaders, and solve any crisis. Specifically, when folks heard the story of Birch, all would become right with the world again. Welch displayed the same confidence years later when Eisenhower invited Khrushchev to the United States for a summit meeting. At a meeting for Clarence Manion's Americans for Goldwater Committee, Welch posited, incorrectly, that the Republican base would secure Goldwater's presidential nomination in 1960 if Goldwater simply assailed the summit invitation with vigor.

The new narrative that Welch peddled was a conspiratorial thesis addressing who lost China, and at the center of it was John Birch. For Welch, Birch offered the evidence of a massive conspiracy and cover-up centered on the loss of China and treason by high-level American officials. Welch wrote that Birch was the "first casualty of the Cold War."

John Birch was a Baptist missionary killed by the Chinese Communists ten days after the end of World War II. Born to missionary parents in India, Birch was a disciple of J. Frank Norris, an anti-Communist fundamentalist who directed congregations in Detroit and Fort Worth. Through his weekly newsletter, *The Fundamentalist*, Norris assailed religious modernism and encouraged missionary activity, especially in China. Norris wanted to bring China southern religion, southern honor, and rugged masculinity.[4] As the historian Barry Hankins writes, for Norris, "modernism, communism and New Dealism were merely three names for the same threat to American political institutions and Christian orthodoxy."[5] For Norris, the interdenominational Federal Council of Churches was dangerous and "financed by one of the most subversive aggregations of socialists, Communists, and other radicals in the United States."[6] In John Birch, Norris found a young man who exuded Americanism, valor, and commitment to sharing the good news with the Communist heathens. But most of all, perhaps, he found someone willing to fight for his faith.

Welch saw a younger version of himself in John Birch, as they came from similar circumstances. They were both from the South. (Birch grew up in Macon, Georgia.) Both were raised by fundamentalist Baptists with the strain of premillennial dispensationalism, which proposed that the Bible foretold the end of the world. Welch strayed from his religious fundamentalism. Birch did not. Both could run hot. Both had absolutist temperaments. Both believed adamantly that their view of the world was more important and veracious than that of others. Both shared a zealous belief that America's role in China was ordained by God. Birch was often apocalyptic and may have believed that sinful humans would inevitably fail in converting Asia. But that didn't stop him. Jesus would solve everything in the end. Welch completely agreed.[7]

At seventeen, Birch began Mercer University in Macon, where he and twelve other students soon charged six members of the faculty with teaching religious modernism. After hearing a J. Frank Norris speech in 1939 on developments in the Far East, Birch left the event with "China on his heart." He enrolled in Norris's Fundamental Baptist Bible Institute, which trained missionaries to spread fundamentalism. A quick study, he learned Mandarin and was among the institute's first graduates, bound to China aboard a freighter within a year. He embraced Norris's message of the need to save souls from atheistic Communism not only in China, but also in lands contiguous to the Central Kingdom. "There is war, starvation, disease, sin, idolatry, superstition, suffering, and death on every side, but our Savior keeps saving souls, answering prayers and giving joy in the midst of sorrow," said Birch.[8]

Arriving to teach at a boys' school in Hangzhou, Zhejiang Province, Birch entered a war zone. The Japanese controlled the coastal cities, while the Communists and Nationalists fought over the interior. Artillery awakened him from many unrestful slumbers. Despite his precarious situation, Birch compared his fellow missionaries to New Testament saints. He wrote of curing a young child of fever, exorcising a demon from a possessed woman, and observing a miraculous escape by another missionary.[9] Birch cared deeply about the Chinese people's plight and hoped that through "all this suffering may bring multitudes of Chinese to Christ." On one occasion, he wrote of the Japanese refusing to open the gate to the city of Hangchow. Birch prayed and "the Lord heard the prayer and the Japanese officer changed his mind and so we entered the city."[10] Birch was a soldier for Jesus Christ.

Writing to friends in 1941, John observed that "the Christians" at one of his congregations "have just finished their first church building . . . in the midst of fighting, burning, looting, and all the other horrors of war, along with all sorts of persecutions from the unbelievers." Although eventually directed to leave China by the State Department, Birch persevered, blended in, mastered a local dialect, subsisted off "bamboo shoots and the cheapest red rice," and became even more ardent in bringing Jesus Christ to the Chinese villagers. The holy spirit was alive in China, thought Birch. Jesus was nearby.

By 1942, Birch knew that the Japanese needed to be defeated before China could be converted to Christianity. He volunteered for the American Military Mission to China and asked to become a chaplain. By chance he encountered Jimmy Doolittle and his band of Tokyo Raiders when they ditched their B-25s near Quzhou, after bombing Japan's main island of Honshu. After spotting a bearded white man, one of the airmen cried out: "Well, Jesus Christ!" Birch retorted, "That's an actually good name, but I am not he." According to Birch's biographer, Terry Lautz, the young missionary played a "useful but limited" role in ferrying the Tokyo Raiders to safety.

Critically, Doolittle introduced Birch to Claire Chennault, the commander of the China Air Task Force, formerly the Flying Tigers. Popularized by the 1942 film *The Flying Tigers* starring John Wayne, the cohort comprised 300 men personally recruited by Chennault. "Most of them had problems" and "were escaping something," observed Lautz. "They drank Bols gin, morning, noon, and night." Profane Chennault made great copy, and his wizened leathery visage appeared on the covers of *Time* and *Life*. Chennault adored airplanes, hunting ducks, and playing poker. He also loved John Birch like a son. While Chennault was hard drinking and Birch abstemious, they shared many qualities; like Welch would, Chennault saw a younger version of himself in the strong-willed, adventurous, and very intense, even zealous, young man. They shared a deep love of the Chinese people. They were both outspoken mavericks, audacious, and loyal to the death for causes they considered worthy. For their time, they were both what they called "a man's man."[11] After some lobbying by Chennault, Birch received the Legion of Merit award, and Chennault praised the young hero for doing more "than any other man to win the war against Japan in China." Birch's work became known to Madame Chiang Kai-shek, herself a daughter of a Methodist missionary and a child of Macon, Georgia. "He is the finest young man that ever came to us, and please send us some more," she said.[12]

Like Chennault, prescient Birch was an Asia Firster, musing in April 1944 that the Far East would "play a rising part in the affairs of the postwar world—a world that should be more ripe for the gospel than ever before." "As for my own future activities," Birch propounded, "as soon as this war ends in victory and I can make a trip home, and if God leads, I should like to push westward, possibly in an effort to storm the mountainous Buddhist Citadel of Tibet, or else to move through Lanchow to little-reached Chinese Turkistan and some day to load with the Word of God and itinerant native preachers the camel caravans and eventual airships of Continental Asia!" But postwar "activities" would not be in store for John Birch in this life.[13] After atomic bombs leveled Hiroshima and Nagasaki and Japan finally surrendered, Birch, who was proficient with radios, reading maps, and negotiating difficult terrain, was sent on a final intelligence-gathering mission in Jiangsu Province. On August 25, 1945, Birch encountered Chinese Communist soldiers and was ordered to disarm. Never one to back down, Birch refused, and was shot dead. The soldiers mutilated his face "beyond recognition with a bayonet or knife."[14] A Chinese Nationalist soldier with him survived and shared the tale.

Welch had always intended to write a hagiography of Birch, for he thought him a saint. "In writing a *Life of John Birch*," Welch said, "I can not only do justice to a great American, and put him in the same category with Nathan Hale, where he belongs, but at the same time can point out that patriotism and love of country and honesty and decency and courage still mean something, and are worth the devotion of one's life; even in a world now so badly confused by the lone infiltration of Communist doctrine and beastliness."[15]

Although the region was fraught with problems for missionaries, Welch presented Birch as a victim of two conspiracies. The first was calculated murder by the Chinese Communist Party. The second was the cover-up by the craven State Department, which Welch alleged sought to keep the sellout of China under wraps. The deep state was complicit, said Welch. Had Birch lived, wrote Welch, the world would be very different now. Chiang would have defeated Mao. China would be a democratic republic. Welch believed that every American needed to know Birch's story; the survival of Western civilization was all that was at stake.[16]

Robert Welch was not the first conservative to allege that machinations and treason in high places were involved in the assassination of John Birch. While Joseph McCarthy was digging up State Department malfeasance and treason, William Knowland was the first to tell the tale of Birch's demise as a cover-up by the State Department. Knowland said that Birch died before he could warn the world about how satanic China under the Chinese Communist Party was. As he lay dying, his last words were: "It doesn't make very much difference what happens to me. It is important my country find out whether or not these people—the Communists—are going to be friends or enemies. If they are determined to be our enemies, my country needs to find out now."[17] Knowland implied that powerful forces inside the American government wanted to silence Birch's very explicit answer: the Chinese Communists were indeed enemies.

Knowland may have told the tale first, but Welch made Birch famous. Welch presented Birch as a martyr who could change the world. In life, Birch was stubborn, defiant, and snappy. But Welch portrayed the young man as not unlike Jesus Christ himself. Welch's messianic Birch was a doubtless believer with immaculate virtue and almost superhuman virility and vitality.[18] Abstemious, he avoided alcohol, but did not judge the habits or other vices of others. Indefatigable with limitless energy, he saved souls with his missionary activity and rescued bodies—both Japanese and American—with his courage and unique physical gifts. Intellectually gifted, mentally acute, he learned Mandarin so quickly and spoke with such felicity that Chinese friends thought him a native. Resourceful and adept with technology and military equipment, he engineered a bathtub out of a downed fuselage and repaired radios with consummate skill and ease.[19] Welch suggested that both heavenly grace and the circumstances of his upbringing—his fundamentalist parents and the austerity and asceticism of the Great Depression years—accounted for his singular gifts. Welch's account looked at Birch's premillennialism and hopeful expectation for Christ's return. Birch was a martyr, but also a prophet of bad times ahead before the second coming—just as fundamentalist eschatology holds. "[This] war," Birch wrote, "and the ensuing federations will set the world stage . . . [for] the rise of the Anti-Christ." Clarence Manion believed that Welch's martyrology was a grand success: "your book describes not the life but the death of John Birch and the menacing threat of death to all of the Godly goodness for which [he] lived and died."[20]

Welch was not the only figure who made messianic parallels about the tragic young man. Welch included Birch's friends, one of whom wrote John's mother: "You gave us your beloved son for the restoration of the democracy of the world." The friend compared John's mother to Jesus's mother Mary. Welch finished the book with language echoing the Catholic Eucharistic prayer. "With his death and in his death the battle lines were drawn, in a struggle from which either Communism or Christian-style civilization must emerge with one completely triumphant and the other completely destroyed."[21] One of Welch's purposes in writing about the life of John Birch was to warn Christians of Red China's threat to their religion. Red China wanted to root out Christianity: "How bitterly they hate Asiatic Christians, and the influence of the Christianity of John Birch and other missionaries among the Asiatics, is revealed by the recent report within."[22] *The Life of John Birch* made sense for many devoutly Christian conservatives. There was a reason why William F. Buckley, one of the most prolific and gifted writers of the twentieth century, wrote that Welch was "the author of two of the finest pamphlets this country has read in a decade," meaning *May God Forgive Us* and *The Life of John Birch*.[23]

The Life of John Birch betrayed Robert Welch's incessant belief in the unbeatable potency of muscular masculinity. The virtuous white male, finding faith and family and blessed with a selfless desire to share the word of God with the benighted foreigner, would commit to the fight to "save our civilization" from the Communist heathens who wanted nothing more than to become our masters. John Wayne,

Ronald Reagan, and other silver-screen icons played the role all the time in the movies of the 1950s. Welch's construction of Birch as an example of immaculate masculine virtue set up his next argument: Americans never heard of this stellar young man because the State Department's deep state covered up Birch's attempt to warn us of Communist China's perfidy.[24]

The Life of John Birch cited no sources, although Welch assured readers that "previously unpublished sources" were his best evidence. Those sources were letters to and from John Birch's parents, who already had concluded that foul play was involved in their son's untimely death. The government's initial report, which attributed Birch's death to stray bullets that hit him while en route to Suchow, along the Lunghai Railway, accounted for his mother Ethel's suspicion. She learned what really happened from nongovernmental sources and, in 1949, was successful in getting the record corrected. Even before Robert Welch, Ethel Birch thought John a martyr for Christianity. She wrote a friend: "had the conclusion of World War II been handled differently, and America had been alerted to what Russia via Chinese Communists was attempting our leaders would not have driven democracy out of China." "John's death," she said, "could have been the means of changing the whole picture in the Orient," and Communism in the East would have been stopped. The American people would never have let Communism come to China. They would have fought. For John Birch. For democracy.

The State Department, however, had plenty of reasons to hide the details of Birch's death in August 1945 when Chinese-American relations were precarious at best. The fact is there was no deep state lurking in the bowels of the State Department. China was suffering the civil war between Nationalists and Communists, but the United States was technically an ally to both, and it was hardly interested in straining either relationship. A tragedy such as a soldier's death was sadly a minor detail in the larger game. General Albert C. Wedemeyer wrote to George Birch, John's father, promising him he had "talked personally to Mao's tse-Tung and Chou-En-lai . . . and received assurances that there would never be a recurrence" of what happened to John. But few Americans, then or even today, would be willing to take the word of Mao Tse-tung or Chou En-lai as proof positive.

But Welch never considered the pragmatic diplomatic explanation. He wrote to Wedemeyer: "The Pentagon knew what had happened to John Birch and how he had been killed. . . . But somebody there with sufficient influence was determined that the American people should not know."[25] Rather than seeing a less sinister explanation, Welch again saw a conspiracy and cover-up.

13

Adventures in the Far East, 1954–1955

In December 1954, Welch took a car ride to Irvington-on-Hudson, New York with Howard Pew, the president of Sun Oil Company, and two other men. They had all attended a National Association of Manufacturers meeting in New York City and were en route to lunch with Leonard Read, who established the Foundation for Economic Education. "The conversation became quite serious," Welch said. He later described the entire conversation, which would have implications for the fate of American conservatism, even into the twenty-first century:

> I expressed my concern over what appeared to me to have been the doublecrossing by Mr. Eisenhower, in the Congressional elections just finished, of a number of conservative Republican candidates for both the Senate and the House. . . .
>
> This surprised one of my listeners so much that, when I began to bring out parts of Eisenhower's earlier record which made such a view possible, this friend asked me if I would be willing to put my comments in the form of a memorandum which he could study. I agreed. And on my return to Boston I wrote him a letter of some 9000 words. . . .
>
> This was the beginning of *The Politician*. I sent carbon copies of this letter to each of the other friends. And one or two of them immediately wanted additional copies sent to other friends. It was quite a while before I could have a new typing of the letter made, and in the meantime I had added a considerable amount to it.

> The demand in this process continued until, some three years later, the letter had evolved into over 200 pages reproduced by offset and collated with a plastic link binding. I still considered it a private unfinished manuscript for limited confidential distribution, but a study which might sometime be further expanded, modified, and probably moderated for formal publication.[1]

The original letter that he wrote Pew in 1954 began the biggest controversy in the life of Robert Welch and in the history of the John Birch Society: that Welch called President Eisenhower a Communist. We have the original letter now for the very first time because of the generosity of a confidential source. Welch denied that he ever said this because, as he put it, he was writing to a close circle of friends and did not think the matter would go any further. (It may be hard to picture this today, when private electronic messages are routinely hacked.) Furthermore, Welch even hedged his conclusions in the initial letter to Pew, writing: "There will be no undertaking to document anything, nor even to attempt to prove anything." Welch continued: "I shall merely set forth a number of observations which . . . have the cumulative effect of supporting the frightful surmise that I expressed" in the car.[2] As late as 1958, when Welch distributed copies to interested friends, he included the following caveat: "this document started as a letter to a friend and the whole manuscript has still been written in the same spirit."[3]

That core "surmise" was that Eisenhower "could be an actual Communist agent, a disciplined member of the Communist Party who has been acting on orders from the Communist Party for at least 15 years." But after his dramatic "surmise," Welch drew back: "Any one of the facts, events, and developments, which are the bases of these observations, could have any number of perfectly satisfactory explanations," but taken as a whole, they suggest that Eisenhower is "an actual Communist agent." Then circumspection and paranoia crept in: Keep "this letter in strictest confidence. In fact, I would appreciate it if, without making any copy of this letter, you would return this original to me. For it is entirely possible that Communists might break into your home or [your] office."[4]

Or was it paranoia? Was he on to something, or at least had good reason to be suspicious given what American leaders were telling the people? During the Cold War, many Americans imagined Communism and Communists as more powerful than they were. Was Robert Welch just another victim of a misunderstanding about how impotent the Communist Party was in 1954? During the period of the popular fronts during the 1930s, his caution would make perfect sense. But the CPUSA by 1954 was a shell of the organization of the 1930s. But Welch, just like millions of other Americans, didn't and couldn't know that. Are we to judge him harshly for misunderstanding something in a time fraught with Cold War anxiety, McCarthyism, and allegations of treason in high places?

In this seminal 1954 letter, Welch proceeded to list the facts, events, and developments that made him surmise that Eisenhower was a Red, including Ike's "incredibly good press," cover-up of Communism in government, opposition to the Bricker amendment, socialist policies, position as a "protégé to George Marshall,"[5] refusal to unleash Patton at the end of World War II, and allowance of Communist books in the State Department libraries overseas, among other evidence.[6]

The basic assumption was that America had unlimited power at the advent of the Cold War: because the United States possessed unrestricted influence in the postwar world, only treason within the government could explain the contemporary difficulties the country was having. After the letter became *The Politician* in 1963, Welch wrote in the introduction that it was "not possible to lose so much ground, so rapidly to an enemy so inferior by chance or by stupidity." As D. J. Mulloy astutely observed, McCarthy made the same case seven years earlier: "How can we account for our present situation unless we believe that men high in this government are concerting to deliver us to disaster?" It must be the result of "a conspiracy on a scale so immense as to dwarf any previous such venture in the history of man."[7]

Welch continued to revise the letter and include recent developments to support his central arguments. By 1958, the book manuscript exceeded 300 pages. The private letter reached scores of conservatives over the next few years. Revilo Oliver, a classics professor, outspoken racist, and anti-Semite, observed that "every man present" at the original December 1958 John Birch Society meeting in Indianapolis had read the letter and believed Welch's conclusion. Oliver suggested that the letter be required reading for membership in the JBS. He estimated that Welch had distributed "something like a thousand copies" by the time of the Indianapolis meeting.[8]

But other conservatives who read the letter were not as enthusiastic to embrace Welch's conclusions. Reactions to the letter ranged "from wholehearted acceptance to mild skepticism to outright disbelief," as the historian Jonathan Schoenwald put it. Detroit banker B. E. Hutchinson received his manuscript and "agree[d] completely." Howard Kershner, businessman and newspaper editor from Dodge City, was not "convinced that he [Ike] is a member of the Communists." "It is more inertia and ignorance than intentional wrongdoing. Other people who intend wrong are making his decisions for him."[9] Stuart Thompson from Seattle resigned from the John Birch Society when he received a copy. "The book frightened me, and not for the reason it was intended."[10] Even his allies disagreed on whether Eisenhower was a conscious or unconscious agent of the conspiracy. They generally agreed that Eisenhower was a New Dealer and had abandoned "rollback," whether in domestic or foreign affairs, for diplomacy and coexistence with Communism. They argued, however, that the letter constituted a public relations problem that could hurt their movement.[11]

Alfred Kohlberg had cheered *May God Forgive Us* but did not have the same reaction to Welch's views on Eisenhower. Welch had not proven his case, Kohlberg wrote, "except by implication, which is not good enough in so serious a matter." Kohlberg thought Welch should keep his view about Eisenhower's true ideology to himself. The president, Kohlberg believed, was not a Communist but "a smart cookie when it comes to ingratiating himself with people, but . . . essentially ignorant, uninformed, and lazy." Welch replied: "I thoroughly agree that my approach to the public which is through my speeches and the magazine, has to be entirely different." But, he added, "I did not really intend to prove anything." The letter was not "intended for publication, or even wide distribution."[12] And yet, Welch saw no need to keep any of his views to himself. For the last twenty years, Welch said, he had been "laying out the facts to speak for themselves," letting readers reach their own conclusions, "and during that time we have been going straight down the road to Communism, at an even faster pace."[13]

Welch continued to send out his controversial letter to conservative admirers, but with admonitions. When conservatives asked for it, he sent it registered mail. He told recipients that the "Eisenhower letter" was to be considered "on loan, in confidence, for your eyes only, and to be lent to no one while it is in your possession; to be returned within 30 days."[14] When Welch received the book back from the borrower, he gave it to Jack McManus, his righthand man, who burned it. Welch trusted these men to keep its content to themselves.

Welch's star was rising in the 1950s. When William F. Buckley was raising funds for his fledgling and floundering *National Review*, he solicited Robert Welch, who purchased $1,000 in privately issued stock. Welch pledged another $1,000 to *National Review* two years later. Buckley considered Welch one of the most widely known and revered conservative figures in the United States, and he responded with absolute delight to Welch's benefaction. It seemed to be the beginning of a wonderful friendship.

Both agreed that despite whatever personal liabilities McCarthy possessed, the damage of Communism would be much worse. Both believed in defending the objective of the McCarthy crusade and stopping Communists wherever they set foot. Robert and William both believed that the cause of McCarthyism kept pressure on President Eisenhower to eliminate security risks, both Communists and those policymakers who aided and abetted Communism. Both believed that individuals like Owen Lattimore and John Stewart Service, who wanted to find some form of peaceful coexistence with the Communist Chinese, should be fired. Both thought the Communist Party ought to be outlawed and wanted more government loyalty tests implemented. Both attacked Republicans for abandoning McCarthy after the 1954 Army-McCarthy hearings. Despite McCarthy's decline into isolation, alcoholism, and infamy, in 1955 Welch appeared in public with the senator in Boston. Both Buckley and Welch agreed that more conservative publications were necessary to balance what they viewed as a press biased to liberals.[15]

But the cracks in the friendship were apparent if one looked close enough. Unlike Welch, Buckley never believed that domestic Communists, as opposed to foreign ones, were a greater threat to America's survival. Buckley also saw as problematic to the conservative movement Welch's view that the government was run by Communists. Buckley feared that it made the Right appear to be cracking up. But they remained friends between 1954 and 1957, when Welch implored Buckley to understand that Eisenhower was "on the other side."[16] Buckley received from Welch a typewritten copy of *The Politician*, read it, and disagreed with its "hypotheses." He thought them "curiously—almost pathetically optimistic." Things will "possibly" get worse when Eisenhower is no longer president, declared Buckley. Welch told Buckley that he was the only person who read the letter and "completely disagreed."[17] The disagreement would dissolve into a feud.

As his name in the conservative movement became more prominent, Robert started to broaden his horizons. International travel, often with his wife, became a priority. He enjoyed visiting exotic lands, but his purpose was to study Communism and bolster the efforts of anti-Communist leaders. In the summer of 1955, he made an odyssey to the Far East. He had neither a title, nor credentials, only his reputation as an anti-Communist. In Tokyo, "all I really had time for . . . was a call at the Chinese Embassy." His writings had sparked a friendship with the Free China ambassador, Doctor Wellington Koo, who allowed Welch to be "most cordially received by the justly famous Dr. Hollington Tong, Chinese Ambassador to Japan." As Welch said, "he invited me to have dinner at his home when I should be back in Tokyo the following week" and "presented me with flatteringly inscribed copies of both of his own two books, DATELINE CHINA and the LIFE OF CHIANG KAI-SHEK."

Robert then traveled to Seoul and stayed at the Bando Hotel for four days. There, he wrote a four-page letter to President Syngman Rhee and asked to meet. Rhee was a maverick who was trying to unify his country. Rhee had told Eisenhower in 1953 that any armistice that left Chinese armies in North Korea was simply unacceptable. If America signed such an armistice, he promised to invade North Korea. Eisenhower was rightfully horrified. "Such action," Ike told Rhee, "could only result in disaster for your country." Rhee was still upset by the terms that ended the Korean War. Robert was upset too. Both wanted victory, rather than an armistice, even in 1955.[18]

The time of Welch's visit was a very busy one for Rhee, as Welch noted. "Saturday was the final day of the ultimatum Syngman Rhee had given the Czech and Polish Communist spies . . . to get out of the country. Sunday is the one day of rest which Dr. Rhee takes from his many problems. Monday was Korean Independence Day, celebrating both the delivery of the country from the Japanese on August 15, 1945, and the formal establishment of the Republic of Korea on August 15, 1948. And I was to leave Korea Tuesday morning."[19] Amazingly, Robert was able to meet the South Korean president. The two hit it off immediately. They both marched to the beat of their own drum. "I had a long and interesting talk and visit with Dr. Rhee on Saturday morning; we have become very good friends, and he has asked me to keep regularly in touch with him." Robert was not exaggerating. He was given a tour of the ancient royal palace and grounds, "including a trip through the secret gardens"—a site unavailable to the public. On Independence Day, Rhee made a speech to 10,000 South Korean uniformed soldiers in a Seoul stadium. He was flanked by diplomats and South Korean government officials—and Robert Welch, who sat on the reviewing dais a few places from Rhee.

Robert wrote home to his mother in excitement: "the whole place, the political and economic situation, and even the details of my visit here, are all incredible. What our government has been doing to Syngman Rhee and the South Koreans is, in many ways even worse than I knew or surmised. The Communists, the Japanese, and our government, between them, have got this grand old man and his people caught in a pocket more completely frustrating than any I have ever seen before."[20]

"Please convey," Rhee wrote to Robert when he arrived home, "to the board of directors of the National Association of Manufacturers . . . my greetings from one who also believes unwaveringly in individual freedom and individual responsibility in all human activities, and one who hopes in time to see a system of free competitive enterprise create a rising standard of living for our people, as it has done so successfully among yours." Please tell, Rhee asked Robert, "these great leaders of American free enterprise, that not only all of our work but all of theirs; all of their savings, all that they have built in the past and all that they hope to build in the future . . . will be destroyed in only a few more years unless the Communist conspiracy is destroyed first." "Do your best," Rhee implored Robert, "to have even the doubters among your associates see the unchanging purposes of the Communists as clearly as you and I see them, and these friends can then help mightily to save not only my country and your country but our civilization itself." The two men continued to have contact for many years. Rhee wrote to Welch in March 1956: "I did not know we had such a staunch ally and champion as you in America." "We are fully aware that the Communists will come down any day and destroy us," but "we are not afraid, trusting in God and hoping that the American people will be awakened in time to save their nation and the rest of the world."[21]

After visiting Seoul, Robert flew back to Tokyo, where "Ambassador Tong's car and secretary called for me." Robert dined at the embassy along with twenty-four other guests including the older brother of the Dalai Lama of Tibet. "This older brother, himself only 33 years old, and looking very much like a prosperous young American business executive, was very much in the news at the time, as having just come out of 2 ½ years of hiding from the Communists."[22] Then Robert flew to Taiwan. He was met by "a representative of both the Foreign Office and the Ministry of Information." He was escorted "painlessly through customs and all other formalities" and was "given hospitality and cooperation, at every turn, which could not have been exceeded." The government "made reservations for me at both the Grand Hotel and the Friends of China Club, so that I could take my choice." "I selected the Friends of China Club in order to be 'in the middle of things,' and I stayed in the middle of 'em for seven days." The Ministry of Information even assigned him a personal interpreter, a guide, and a chauffeured car. He learned that *May God Forgive Us* had been translated and published in Chinese. Robert was feted and treated like a dignitary, and South Koreans learned of his visit in their major dailies. He was a celebrity in South Korea, he thought. It was a very good week for his ego and self-confidence, and it convinced him that he probably was more influential than he thought he was in his own country.

Throughout the week in Taiwan, Robert met or interviewed Chiang Kai-shek, Madame Chiang, Vice President Chen Cheng, Prime Minister O. K. Yui, Defense Minister Yu Ta-wei, the commanders-in-chief of the army, navy, and air force, and other high officials of the Nationalist government. Robert absolutely adored Chiang Kai-shek: "The Good Lord himself would, I am sure, have been severely reprimanded for causing me to be thirty seconds late to that appointment" to meet Chiang. "Having been an admirer of Chiang kai-shek for a long time, I saw little in Formosa to decrease that admiration and much to strengthen it." "While I am well aware that you cannot learn anything about a foreign country in a one-week visit, or about a dynamic leader from talking to him for half an hour, you can thus make what you do learn about them from other sources mean far more because of this personal contact. And I felt that my seven days on Taiwan, though quite crowded, were well spent." Both men wanted to liberate those in thrall to the Communists, and both said liberation was proving to be a scam. Peace was not achieved in Korea, they said, because millions of North Koreans were still in chains.

As he met with Chiang and his wife in their mountainside home above Taipei, Robert worried that the Chinese Communists would replace the Nationalist Chinese seat on the UN Security Council. But the worries were unfounded. Eisenhower wanted to keep Red China out of the UN and would not recognize the Communist Chinese government.[23] Still, Welch told Chiang that the American government was helping the Communists. Chiang wished only that more Americans saw things Welch's way, but he was happy that one man at least was as zealously anti-Communist as he.

Throughout his summertime sojourn, which also included jaunts to Hong Kong and the Philippines, Welch was highly critical of the administration. But today these criticisms must be weighed against the efforts of Eisenhower and his administration that Welch did not and could not know about. In many cases, Eisenhower was under enormous pressure from his advisors for a more belligerent response to world events, but he decided on caution over aggression. In 1954 alone, the State Department, the National Security Council, and the Joint Chiefs of Staff argued for intervention five times; in each case, they recommended the use of nuclear weapons. We now know that Eisenhower expanded covert operations against suspected Communists throughout his presidency and overthrew popularly elected governments in Guatemala and Iran. Eisenhower's Taiwan policy did not lead to Communist attacks. The Eisenhower years were a time of peace. But Robert Welch did not concur.[24]

14

Arrivals and Departures, 1955–1958

No high officials from the American government greeted Robert Welch at Logan Airport when he arrived back in Boston on September 3, 1955. He disembarked the plane, and nobody recognized him but his wife. No notices of his impending arrival appeared in the newspapers. His name was no longer in the marquee lights. He was just a fifty-five-year-old white-haired businessman. He knew that upon his return, "during the first few weeks after I get back to Boston I am going to be completely overwhelmed with work." He wrote a single-spaced seven-page "brief report" on his trip to the Far East "before plunging into the work ahead." The world was on fire, he thought, while I made candy.[1]

Although he may have felt despondent upon arriving at Logan, he soon brushed off such melancholy. The Far East trip had emboldened Robert. His ego grew, and he felt like a young man again. He threw himself into the work of the National Association of Manufacturers, his principal professional outlet. As Rhee alluded, Robert became a prominent figure in the leadership of the National Association of Manufacturers, or NAM, in the 1950s. He also served on numerous civic and business associations in the 1950s, knew the other men on them, and was aware of what those men wanted to hear. As in the 1930s and 1940s, he was on the go every day, sometimes twenty hours a day. He made speeches, he wrote letters, he attended conventions. He knew what to say as well as how to say it. Robert was high energy, and his pace frenetic.

The National Association of Manufacturers was formed in 1895 to advocate for high tariffs on imports. In part, the brainchild and product of William McKinley and Mark Hanna who needed the support of manufacturing to defeat William Jennings Bryan in 1896, NAM focused on small- and medium-sized southern manufacturers. By the 1920s, NAM had reversed course and abandoned tariffs, turning its ire against labor unions and their fight for higher wages and better working conditions.[2]

By 1944, NAM had set its sights on fighting a "war of ideas and opinions" to free private industry from governmental controls. Welch and other members wanted to demonstrate that industry leaders—far more than federal bureaucrats—knew the correct path to "more jobs, higher living standards, and greater security." NAM leaders recognized that business suffered from a poor image on account of the Great Depression, when industry ignored the economic plight of the people and "government—and government only— . . . volunteered to take decisive action."[3] A NAM memorandum observed that without a "conscious decision by the public to reestablish an economy of freedom and individual initiative, public opinion will allow government controls to be extended indefinitely." America, the memo warned, would be sent "down the same road of collectivism that is being taken by almost every other civilized nation." To showcase that industry "operates as much in the public interest as the private interest," NAM invigorated its public relations arm, the National Industrial Information Committee, chaired by J. Howard Pew. Pew's team highlighted that business in the postwar years needed to be a "sincere sponsor and the most reliable protagonist of social progress."

But "social progress" is in the eye of the beholder. NAM encouraged employers to check union progress on collective bargaining and demand an end to postwar pricing controls and production controls—most of which were lifted in 1946. Welch held a variety of positions in NAM during this time, helping it pile up postwar victories. Robert was especially active in NAM concerning education issues. Rejecting Felix Frankfurter's assertions that tension between employer and employee were inevitable, Welch believed employers, not unions, were the true friends of workers. With Welch working behind the scenes and using his golden pen for shaping public opinion, NAM filled national newspapers with its message that the boss was not a figure to be feared but loved. In 1947, NAM ads appeared in 265 papers, and pamphlets and leaflets appeared in the millions. *Industry on Parade,* a $1.5 million radio show arrived in 1950, with its own singers and full-time debaters, broadcasting to wives in new homes and commuters in new cars. There were even NAM comic books with Hitler, Stalin, Mussolini, and Marx appearing in colored ink as the antagonists of business.[4] Altogether, NAM built an identity rooted in personal responsibility, faith, patriotism, and freedom. A 1952 NAM memorandum "Building a Better America," expounded: "A better America must include a growing support of religion and high moral principles based on religious convictions. It can only come from unwavering faith—from dedication to the belief that God, in creating man meant him to retain his individual dignity all through life, with freedom from regimentation and exploitation by government or any group."[5]

Welch's work with NAM changed him. His "activities," his brother observed, and his "association on equal terms with so many big businessmen and leaders of American industry, had obviously given [Robert] an assurance that [he] had not had before." Robert had aspirations to lead NAM, but his position at the James O. Welch Company precluded any run for the presidency, which was typically held by a president or board chair of the individual's own company—an unwritten rule Robert endorsed. "Despite this principle," Robert told James, "there has been a heck of a discussion or even argument going on within the NAM board for the past three years about making me president." Two past chairmen of the NAM nominating committees stated in open meetings that Robert Welch should be the president. One member even offered to make Robert the head of his subsidiary company to secure him the presidency of NAM.

Robert's life had changed: His sons were grown and through college. His wife "had enough to live on." "A job," Robert said, "except for providing for my wife and sons when necessary, never had meant anything to me personally." He continued: "I have only one life to live and that life is far too short and too much of an adventure, for me to spend it as what our socialist friends call a 'wage-slave.'" Indeed, Welch concluded that he "didn't have to have this job" anymore.[6] Take this job and shove it? Welch pondered that question.

And yet, Welch said, "If I was going to give up the opportunity and security and perquisites and pleasant associations of the James O. Welch Company," he sought to do something "with the rest of my life that I've long wanted to do." Robert wanted "to devote it to writing and speaking," but he had larger political ambitions. "I intend to run for Congress, from the fifth Congressional District, or for the Senate to succeed Kennedy in 1958." (Such aspirations attest to Welch's delusions of grandeur and surging megalomania, given that Kennedy would win more than 73 percent of the Massachusetts voters in 1958, against his Republican challenger Vincent Celeste, before beginning his quest for the presidency.) He said he wanted "all of my writing and speechmaking . . . to have some bearing on these plans." He was in demand as a speaker. "I am turning down right now opportunities to speak, with fees attached, which would . . . provide me at least a living," he reported.

There were also other reasons for Robert's exit from the James O. Welch Company. Robert admitted feeling perturbed and undervalued by his brother. Robert loved his brother dearly, and their relations in the future remained amiable, but it was time to part ways as businessmen. While he told his brother that he had the "friendliest feeling towards yourself, a tremendous lasting loyalty to the James O. Welch Company, and a sense of sincere and great appreciation for the sum total of my treatment as a member of the business family over the past 20 years," "two considerations" had "considerable bearing on my final decision to resign." According to Robert, six years before, James made a remark "in a completely offhand manner, out in the parking lot as we were both getting into our respective cars to go home," that "changed my whole outlook towards my place and future in the company." Apparently James said Robert "had been extremely fortunate during the war years; through being in sales," there were "no problems or worries."

Robert proceeded to describe to James everything he had done during the war years for the company. He said that "as the juggernaut of regimentation began to gather steam, he secured the gas and tires for our cars" "from puny bureaucrats going drunk with sudden power over businessmen they had always envied." He faced their "sneers and the hostile skepticism" and "stood in long lines to get to them and put up with being pushed around . . . to get the ration coupons we had to have." Welch observed that he secured sugar during years of rationing and was responsible for the growth of the company by securing what he called the Hamill memorandum. Robert recalled that he "sat literally for hours on benches outside the railing of that huge barnlike accumulation of desks and bureaucrats which constituted the rationing office in Boston, again waiting for some fellow whom, a few months before, I would not have given a job at $20 a week." According to Welch he found Hamill, a rationing clerk who "was not exactly hostile to business," and developed an arrangement: "I could get him to do almost anything I could persuade him was fair and he had the power to do." Robert prepared a long memo, "not asking for anything but setting forth the reasons why we felt we had the legal right under the regulations to do what was proposed, stating that we were going to do it, and asking for his routine approval on behalf of the rationing authority." Robert secured Hamill's signature on the document, which he considered "the greatest 'sale' I had ever achieved." The memo gave the James O. Welch Candy Company an enormous advantage over its competitors during the war years. It may have helped Robert win the prestigious Kettle Award in 1947—the candy industry's Oscar.

As Robert explained, this memo authorized the company "instead of waiting two, three, and sometimes six months for the different post exchanges to issue checks for the sugar covered by our certifications of individual shipments, to treat the sugar thus due us as 'sugar accounts receivable,' and borrow against it the full-time at once." In other words, "we did not have to wait for the sugar to make more candy," which was in high demand from military bases. The memo was a "bombshell" and made Robert a legend in the candy business. "The Hamill Memorandum had been a tremendous factor in our intermediate growth," Welch explained.

James's remark in the parking lot "almost knocked me off my feet," remembered Robert, but there was more. Robert also resented that his brother and boss never acknowledged his role in procuring and retaining factory help during the war years. "It was I, not you" Robert wrote, who "went off on cold and slippery winter nights to appear before draft boards in Cohasset or East Cambridge or West Lynn to try to save some needed worker from the draft or to get his induction deferred."

Robert was also bothered that his remuneration dwindled over time, despite what he saw as a "firm arrangement for me to have 10%

of the gross income of the company before taxes, on top of my salary." Initially, Robert did not rebel against the reduction because he "certainly felt willing to trade off my 'interest' or equity for the opportunity to take some of my time and energy for other purposes." But then James reduced the profit-sharing agreement to 5 percent. Then to 3 percent. And then to 2 ½ percent. Robert had taught James the candy business, how to make candy, and created or inspired with his constant tinkering legendary confections loved by children even today. The Sugar Daddy. Sugar Babies. Juniors Mints. And now Robert had quit. But although James and Robert parted ways, they remained close. After everything was said and done, they *were* brothers, and the feud was forgotten over Christmas dinners and Thanksgiving feasts. They had squabbled since Stockton, and a little misunderstanding was not going to break their bond.[7] They both loved each other too much to hold a grudge and realized their rivalry made them better teammates, as well as very affluent men.

In his retirement from James O. Welch, Robert wrote letters, gave speeches, wrote articles. He wanted to awaken the American people to the great tragedy that was unfolding in front of them. As Jonathan Schoenwald wrote, Welch's 1956 speech before the Economic Club of Detroit, "What is Happening to America Abroad," demonstrated that "Welch's analysis of American foreign policy . . . was inspired as much by what was not happening as what was."[8] Welch asked why so many countries had fallen to Communism in the ten years after World War II. In looking at Europe, Asia, and Latin America, he observed, "our defensive strength and proportion to the force of a known enemy, our moral leadership throughout the world, and our very security itself have toppled from great heights into a sticky morass where the footing grows less solid every day." It was not only Communist advances, he argued, that led to the loss, but loss of American will. It was the moral resignation of American leaders who gave into defeat. Such "defeats" were traitorous, craven betrayals that gave confidence to the enemy.

As the 1950s passed, Welch grew more confident and proud of his expertise in foreign policy. He was not very interested in domestic policy or civil rights. He believed he had greater expertise than fellow anti-Communists because of his globetrotting. He knew most of the leading American anti-Communists, and his correspondence with them was voluminous. He was a voracious reader of the "anti-Communist books and objective histories," as he put it. He read the literature of Communism—the seminal texts, the monthlies, the periodicals. "It is to the presentation by the Communists themselves," he said, "that the serious student of history of the conspiracy goes to learn of their progress and plans." He openly admitted that he had a "fairly sensitive and accurate nose" for anti-Communism. J. B. Matthews, the former McCarthy staffer and "dean" of the anti-Communist Right, vouched for Robert's prominence in the movement.[9]

At the heart of Welch's worldview was the belief that if the American people knew the truth of the wickedness done by their leaders, aiding the enemy in Moscow and Beijing, they would rise up and take power. That populist vision birthed the Birch Society. Welch's worldview was similar to that of nonconspiracy theorists of the liberal middle class. Many critics of the Right from Arthur Schlesinger to Daniel Bell to Richard Hofstadter had taken it for granted that middle-class democracy was increasingly the norm. Welch embraced this vision of republican democracy, concluding that countries that failed to develop it were obviously being corrupted by politicians since the people were by definition incorruptible. It was a recipe that was Lyndon Johnson's undoing in Vietnam and George W. Bush's in Afghanistan and Iraq.

Welch believed that it was possible to resist the influence of Moscow and Beijing, despite their strength, and America needed to seize the moment and help other countries do so. Like many middle-class critics, he shared the postwar belief in seemingly unlimited American capability; if a country fell to Communist aggression, it must have been the result of American policymaker's action or inaction. Many shared this underlying worldview. From Woodrow Wilson's administration to the New Frontier to the early years of the Great Society, many American leaders and their followers concluded that republican democracy was the highest point of the Enlightenment and the correct course for all civilizations around the world. Welch, typically, went further: he believed that countries wanted to be like us, follow our example, and if they didn't, it was our fault. For policymakers who understood all that America was doing to introduce democracy around the world, Welch's conclusion was an insult, an abomination, and wrong. For policymakers who realized that America was already maybe doing too much around the globe—from assassinations in Iran, South Vietnam, and Guatemala to covert wars—Welch's vision was downright dangerous. But like Welch, many Americans could reject the claim that the United States was doing its best, and they became some of Welch's strongest followers.[10]

Ironically, Welch left the James O. Welch Company to become a full-time proselytizer for the despondent Right at a moment when things were going great for most Americans. An entire generation had never had it so good, due not to the austerity programs that the Old Guard favored but the administration's Keynesian economics. Eisenhower spent federal moneys throughout the recession sparked by the Korean War, expanded Social Security, raised the minimum wage, and secured unemployment compensation for 4 million more workers. There was no inflation, but the economy was soaring. Americans were buying everything—cars, washing machines, and homes.[11] The prosperity that Americans enjoyed between approximately 1950 and 1970 were the seeds of great changes: the civil rights movement, the feminist movement, the consumer movement, and the LGBTQ movement. Everybody wanted a slice of the pie. Since everybody was getting theirs, why shouldn't I get a slice too?

Americans enjoyed both prosperity and peace. The boys had come home from Korea. A war over Taiwan and a war in Vietnam had been delayed, at least for the time being. Since he had no use for pacific language that lulled people into a false sense of security, Robert Welch was incensed when on June 20, Dwight Eisenhower gave an address on the tenth anniversary of the United Nations and said "the summer of 1955, like that one in 1945, is another season of high hope for the world. There again stirs in the hearts of men a renewed devotion to the work for the elimination of war."[12]

Robert realized that Americans liked Ike, but he simply did not think Eisenhower was the center-right leader they dreamed of. Welch thought Americans would like a true conservative and a true conservative magazine even more. Having read Albert Jay Nock's work, he knew that a conservative movement was always more successful when it was part of a remnant, a vestige of treasured things that mattered but lost. With a magazine that could apply pressure on the "ins" and supply hope for the "outs," Robert would matter again, just as he had when conservative thought leaders and newspapermen wrote fondly about *May God Forgive Us*. He would matter again just as he had in Taiwan. He would be feted again. He would be loved.

Thus, in 1956, Welch started a small monthly magazine, *One Man's Opinion*, which evolved into the principal organ of the John Birch Society, *American Opinion*. In soliciting donations for the fledgling magazine, Robert cautioned: "I do not make as strong a 'pitch' for the magazine as might otherwise be possible. I have accentuated the casualness or 'on-the-side' appearance of the project." A subscription cost $5 for six issues. Subscribers never knew when each issue would arrive. When Welch found the time, he said, the subscribers would get their issue, but there was no set schedule for the release. In the inaugural issue, he assured readers that "in case I drop dead . . . as I have occasionally been advised to do, or I am shot by a Communist, or meet with some convenient accident," prepaid subscriptions would be refunded. His ego was getting the best of him again when he wrote of the prospect of assassination attempts. He wrote six issues in 1956 and six more in 1957. The debut issue was thirty-six pages long. Although printed from copy written on an IBM electric typewriter and printed relatively cheaply, the product was professional looking.

Each issue was approximately thirty pages and contained a biographical essay on a political leader Welch respected, an article about a contemporary issue, or an article by an author selected by Welch himself. *One Man's Opinion* was peppered with humor and poetry— two of Welch's favorite topics. Some of Welch's most revered public officials—Ohio governor Frank Lausche, Chiang Kai-shek, Syngman Rhee—all received friendly portrayals in the magazine. Article authors included General Albert C. Wedemeyer, Medford Evans, and Polish leader Stanislaw Mikolajczyk.[13] But Welch wrote most of the magazine himself—though he joked, "As to committing myself to writing some 18,000 words per month for the rest of my life, I am not so foolish."

In his articles, Robert de-emphasized his enormous vocabulary and muscular prose. He wrote simply for average Americans sweating in factories, tilling their fields, and running their businesses. While William F. Buckley's *National Review* appealed to conservative elites, Welch's products appealed to the grassroots. Welch was never shooting for the thought leaders, and proudly shunned the intelligentsia and the establishment. Where *National Review* was witty, biting, sarcastic, and haughty, Welch was down to earth. "ONE MAN'S OPINION," he said, was "largely a consolidation of what I am already writing to friends all over the world who are foolish enough to ask me questions."[14]

Robert drew no salary and, he said, the venture involved "none of the editors, assistants, circulation, managers, and other expensive staff which usually break any small magazine." Robert calculated that he could "put it in the black with as few as 2000 subscriptions," which he thought would "come from friends who believe so strongly in what I stand for and am trying to do that they will buy bulk subscriptions, each to be sent to some educator or business or professional man of my own selection." Whether it would succeed, he said, "depended largely on how well I write it and what I have to say"—though, he said optimistically, "Capital for the magazine, if and to the extent that I need it, seems to be available." He tried out the proposal on four friends—two within NAM and two outside it—three of whom responded. One, not a rich man, agreed to put up $1,000 but wished he could put up $5,000. Another, an affluent man, agreed to put in "part of" the $25,000 Robert had suggested. Another thought the magazine was bound to be a success but thought Robert should put "energy, as a crusader for the conservative cause, more effectively in other ways." Robert concluded: "I can get one hundred thousand dollars to back up the magazine if I try at all hard to do so." He carefully chose the title and plan of the magazine. "After I get it on its feet, the One Man's part of the title and contents will gradually grow smaller; the title will finally become just "Opinion; and I can have as many editors or contributors as I want or the magazine can afford." He continued: "but it will remain a voice of conservatism, common sense, and steadfast adherence to basic principles." Writing with characteristic schmaltzy, awkward, but endearing corniness, Robert declared "if the project causes my vanity to show like 4 inches of petticoat at the bottom of a gingham dress, it can't be helped."[15]

In addition to persuading friends and colleagues in NAM to contribute seed money, Welch successfully solicited initial funding from the midwestern isolationists associated with Colonel McCormick and his *Chicago Tribune*, as well as from right-wing Texas millionaires who had funded McCarthy. A smattering of money came from the

Northeast, where Robert had an excellent reputation as a businessman. Money also came in from successful eastern and midwestern ethnic Catholics who felt frustrated with Stalin's control of Eastern Europe and who zealously supported "rolling back" Communism in those countries.

One Man's Opinion launched in February 1956; by the beginning of 1957, it had 5,000 subscribers across the country. Robert had not yet resigned from the James O. Welch Candy Company at this time, and he was chairing the upcoming National Confectioners' Association Annual Convention in Boston. But he began disengaging from his daily responsibilities. The inaugural issue warned the reader that Robert Welch was becoming a free man now and this "one-man now-and-then magazine" would be published his way: "WHATEVER I wish . . . WHENEVER I wish," and "HOWEVER I wish."[16]

In June 1956, Welch formally resigned from the James O. Welch Company, effective January 1, 1957. Robert secured from his brother one-third of his final salary to continue serving on the company's executive committee, attend monthly meetings, and provide counsel. At the end of 1956, Welch paid a year's rent in advance for a new office in the front corner of a new brick building at 385 Concord Avenue in Belmont, where he completed much of the work for *One Man's Opinion*. It soon became the early headquarters of the John Birch Society.[17] With the part-time assistance of Miss Lovett, his longtime secretary at James O. Welch, Robert was now in business for himself.

Of most consequence in the first issue of *One Man's Opinion* was Welch's prediction of how a Communist takeover in the United States might occur. "There are three strategic plans on which the Communists are counting separately or in some combination or sequence." "The first of these plans" depended on disguising Communism as "just another political party" and "seiz[ing] power by a peaceful coup d'état." The second was "the combination of internal civil war and the application of external military force in support of the Soviet side of that war." The third, which would likely occur if appropriate action were not taken, involved "inducing gradual surrender of American sovereignty, piece by piece and step-by-step, to an international organization like the United Nations, while simultaneously and equally gradually getting complete working control of that organization."[18]

All of the early issues showcased Robert's developing penchant for conspiracy theory. When in 1956 the Hungarians engaged in a general uprising against the Russians, Eisenhower refused to provide aid; Khrushchev proceeded to quash the uprising.[19] Welch was not surprised. "VICE PRESIDENT Nixon says that the Hungarian revolt dealt the Soviet empire a mortal blow from which it cannot recover," observed Welch in the February-March 1957 issue. But "we believe that precisely the opposite is true," wrote Welch. The Hungarian uprising was not the twilight of the Communists, but the Soviet Union wanted the United States to think it was so that the country would lower its guard down at a crucial moment of danger. The general uprising by the Hungarians, Welch concluded, was itself the work of Moscow. Moscow wanted to bring the anti-Communists into the open and dispense with them, he said.[20]

Welch was incorrect. The demonstrations in Hungary were expected but not a plot by Russia. In the spring of 1956, the liberation of the satellites seemed at least to become a possibility because Khrushchev had repudiated Stalin for crimes against his own people and seemed to suggest a lessening of Communist control over its satellites. American officials began predicting some form of demonstration in Hungary. Radio Free Europe and Voice of America were both encouraging a revolt, and the Central Intelligence Agency had established resistance cells to foment such an uprising.[21]

Welch's November 1956 exposé in *One Man's Opinion* said the same thing was occurring in Poland. Riots had occurred in Poznan, and many American commentators saw this as signaling the decline of Communist influence. Welch argued that such commentary was dangerous because it was simply wishful thinking. Any decline of Communist influence, Welch argued, was exactly what the Communists wanted the American people to see. "The whole revolt is a phony," Welch said, "and as carefully stage-managed to achieve beguiling realism, as was the break between Stalin and Tito in 1948. The . . . true purpose of the riots was securing more aid for Communist Poland, convincing the West that communism was on its last legs, and securing the entry of red China into the United Nations."[22]

The fiasco in the Suez Canal made Robert only more confident that weakening American sovereignty and strengthening the United

Nations were the real objectives of American foreign policy. For Welch, the Suez crisis laid bare important evidence that American policymakers were purposely trying to cede their own autonomy to the United Nations and thereby make the fall to Soviet dictatorship come about more swiftly. Again, Welch saw the entire episode through the conspiratorial lens. President Nasser of Egypt wanted to build a large dam on the Nile for power and irrigation, and began to confide in the Communist camp for assistance. When Nasser nationalized the Suez Canal, the French, British, and Israelis responded with force without notifying the United States. America's allies assumed that Eisenhower would supply their scant oil reserves with enough oil to survive the crisis, but Eisenhower, livid about having been in the dark, determined to let them "boil in their own oil." Britain and French forces withdrew and the United Nations, for the first time in its history, picked up the slack—a fateful outcome that Robert Welch said was the plan all along.[23]

The only problem with this theory was the agency of the British, French, and the Israelis. There indeed was a plot, but it was entered into by Britain, France, and Israel, not the Kremlin. Moreover, the poorly planned cabal seemed a last-gasp venture of nineteenth-century colonialism. Eisenhower did not believe the Soviet Union was behind it but wondered whether Churchill perhaps was; the president noted, "this action is in the mid Victorian-style."[24]

What really irked Robert about the Suez crisis was that it turned out to be a great moment for the United Nations. Small nations were elated that the United States backed Egypt over the colonial powers and were ecstatic that Eisenhower declared that such powers uphold the primacy of the United Nations. The United States had upheld the rule of law and sought a just peace—to Robert's disgust. Worse, Eisenhower said that "the United Nations was essential because global war is now unthinkable." Welch heartily disagreed but had no input on the matter.[25] His soapbox was only *One Man's Opinion.*

Welch did pay attention to some domestic matters. An escalation in Black demands for civil rights and stirrings of a southern backlash occurred in 1956. In February, four southern state legislatures declared *Brown v. Board of Education* null and void in their jurisdictions. In March, 101 southern congressmen signed and passed the notorious manifesto seeking to abolish *Brown.* Meanwhile Martin Luther King Jr.

was heading a bus boycott in Montgomery, Alabama. Homes were bombed. Churches were set afire. Blacks were shot. Montgomery's police were arresting civil rights activists and not sparing the rod.[26] Welch saw the struggle for civil rights as the work of the Communists. Eisenhower was not ready to go there yet, but he did think that Communists would take advantage of the civil unrest. J. Edgar Hoover said the same thing. In a twenty-four-page memorandum, Hoover blamed both sides: extremists in both the NAACP and the White citizens councils were stoking the flames and responsible for the violence. The "both sides are to blame" argument would be invoked by President Trump in Charlottesville, Virginia, in 2017. Trump, like Hoover and Welch, was deeply concerned with how Communists would infiltrate the movement and cause more social disorder.

Welch worried about another civil war. He saw northerners as pressuring the South on the issue just as they had one hundred years earlier. Welch insisted that coercion through law was a terrible mistake and would make the problem only worse. Racial progress would be set back by coercion; progress had to be made through moral persuasion, state by state.[27]

In September 1956, Welch published "A Letter to the South" in *One Man's Opinion*. He wrote "we had come to believe it to be inevitable, and desirable, that formal segregation would eventually be abandoned everywhere in the South," but "a voluntary and incomplete segregation in purely social activities, resulting from the rights of any man, white or colored, to have friends of his own choosing, and from the tendency of those with like interests and friends in common to associate together." Welch realized that many of his readers would disagree with this. Welch conceded that the conditions of Blacks were "far-from-equal." But "the gap between the positions of colored man and white man has been getting perceptibly narrower." In fact, Welch declared "the material standard of living of the average American Negro" was higher than that of the "average Englishman." Welch said that *Brown* had turned the progress toward "voluntary segregation" back a generation. It was not the fault of "the ordinary colored people of the South." "They were easily . . . misled by clever agitators as you would be if you were in their position." Welch turned to the Bible: "They know not what they do; and if there was ever a time and place when patience and charity and a huge reservoir of deep good will were needed, it is in the South today." Fault rested "squarely on the shoulders of the Communists" who fostered the "rising racial bitterness." That animosity was "the finest grist the Communists have yet been able to obtain for their American mill."[28]

Welch remained silent on the matter of "how far and how fast" desegregation should come about, but he warned against the perils of "direct resistance." "Our friends in the South write us that they will not be forced; that nothing will force them to immediate desegregation, short of civil war. And what we are trying to tell you, what this whole letter is really about, is the very real danger of this extreme result; of a civil war that would engulf the South and spread through race riots and other Communistic-fomented disorders into a chaotic terror over our whole nation." That is what the Communists wanted, he said. All their civil wars in China, Spain, Vietnam, and Yugoslavia "always begin as localized clashes, over some such principle as 'agrarian reform' or 'abolition of tyranny.'" This time, Welch said, "the phrase is 'civil rights.'" No longer, he said, can we say "it can't happen here." "It is happening here, right now. In Mississippi and South Carolina, and all over a fourth of our country the Communists have already entered—incipiently, insidiously, patiently, farsightedly, deceptively—onto the last stage, the physical fighting stage, of their three-pronged strategy for making the US a group of provinces ruled by Moscow."

Welch's letter was deeply flawed because he failed to realize that the civil rights movement genuinely represented the cause of his Black fellow citizens to further their lot in a society defined by institutional racism. Welch understood the civil rights cause as exclusively the work of the Communist conspiracy and indicated his limited ability to empathize with causes having little to do with his own White privilege. When it came to civil rights, he was stunted, in a bygone world, at a time when the world was changing. He became blind to others' plight because he grew too preoccupied with the danger of encroaching federal power over states' rights.

Welch welcomed Black members into the John Birch Society, although there were few; remarkably, there were exclusively African American chapters in the integrated North. Even Seymour Martin Lipset and Earl Raab admitted that "the Society itself did not consciously attempt to build a mass appeal around" an "emergent nativism directed against Negroes." The sociologist Sara Diamond found that unlike the Liberty Lobby, the Society "did not officially peddle theories of racial biological determinism" to oppose civil rights. To be sure, some Birchers were racists, and Welch fired unrepentant ones, along with anti-Semites, from the organization. Some may argue that although the Society came of age at the time of the civil rights movement, the Society was not a response to it. The fights against Communism and liberalism, they say, were the chief reasons for the existence of *One Man's Opinion* and, soon, the John Birch Society.[29]

Such defenses are wrongheaded and indefensible as well. As we shall see, Welch doubted the reality of police brutality. He put the civil rights movement under the umbrella of a vast Communist conspiracy, a ridiculous argument. Pushing racists and anti-Semites out of the John Birch Society was done slowly and incompetently. The nefarious never should have been there in the first place. *American Opinion,* like Buckley's *National Review,* featured horrid racists advocating backward policies that would have turned back the clock on the civil rights movement and its desperately needed Second Reconstruction.

Welch would never have considered himself a racist—but that misses the point; neither did D. W. Griffith, who made *Birth of a Nation*; Leander Perez, who led the Dixiecrat movement along with Strom Thurmond; or William F. Buckley, who called the Thirteenth, Fourteenth, and Fifteenth Amendments mere "inorganic accretions" tacked on after the Civil War. Even as Welch did not endorse racists, racists endorsed the John Birch Society. The Reverend Carey Daniel of the White Citizens Council of Dallas lavished the John Birch Society with generous praise: "God bless all John Birchers. Please say that the White Citizens Council is backing them 100%. I am thinking of joining."[30]

The above said, Welch's collaborations with African American John Birch Society members highlighted Welch's failure to go in a different direction when the spirit of times required him to, as his nemesis William F. Buckley belatedly seems to have. It is tragic because Welch grew up relatively unprivileged in a community where African Americans were a majority—something you just can't say about Buckley, or about Eisenhower, another of his lifetime enemies. Unlike Welch, his nemeses never viewed upfront the strain, pain, stress lines, and trauma on the faces of his African American brothers and sisters. Welch had the advantage over his isolated contemporaries because he saw that trauma and should have known better. Yet Welch turned away from recognizing the full humanity of his Black neighbors, making his story more tragic than theirs.

Coming up in 1956 was the next presidential election. In September 1955 President Eisenhower had suffered a moderate heart attack, which made most assume that a reelection campaign was out of the question. Who would be the nominee in 1956? Welch wanted William Knowland because of the California senator's strong support for Taiwan and Chiang Kai-shek, and he used the pages of *One Man's Opinion* to promote Knowland as a standard bearer for the conservative movement. The magazine was chock-full of addresses by the senator and promotional pieces portraying him as "a man for all seasons." Knowland, Welch argued, had the character and the judgment to replace Eisenhower in 1956. His preoccupation with Knowland highlights that many on the Right were looking for a conservative star after Taft's death in 1953 and McCarthy's collapse. A few of Welch's letters in the early 1950s attested to his belief that Welch himself could be that leader. But his promotion of others evidenced that Welch had concluded that, at least as a politician, his time had passed.[31]

Knowland, Robert boasted, was willing to speak out about "the mess our country was making in the Far East." "After the intensive and extensive smears he has faced as the 'senator from Formosa,'" Welch wrote, Knowland "is not likely to become too upset by anything they can think up in the future." Tapped by Robert Taft as his successor as majority leader, Knowland "is very much like the bridge player who was told by all the experts how miserably he was playing his hand, but who came up with a grand slam." Knowland, Welch dreamed, "may eventually come up with 'The Grand Slam' in the great game of American politics." As was often the case, Welch grew conspiratorial: Knowland will "save the Republican Party" from the "'planned destruction' of which we think it now stands."[32]

But although Knowland was the publisher of the *Oakland Tribune*, he did not possess the influence and political skill of Taft. He had trouble corralling the intractable Right wing of which he was a member. Knowland's mind, observed the ever-astute Harry McPherson, "had a single trajectory—flat—and at point-blank range. His integrity was that of a bull, admirable in its way, but unsuited for political leadership. He was entirely predictable, and permitted more skillful men to tie him (and thus his party) in inflexibly fixed positions."[33]

Welch never saw Knowland's faults, whom after McCarthy he saw as the heir apparent of the conservative movement. "A man of tremendous personality and vitality," Welch gushed, Knowland was "a political leader of unquestioned stature, patriotism, and respect for American principles." "You always know exactly where he stands," Welch added. Knowland opposed giving American jets to Yugoslavia's Tito, whom Welch considered a pawn of the Kremlin despite his split with the Russians. Knowland opposed granting loans to the Communist government of Poland and opposed Red China's admission to the United Nations. "Dame fortune smiled on" Knowland, Welch wrote. Knowland possessed a combination of attractive "appearance," "a brilliant and well-balanced mind," "impeachable character," and an "industriousness that ease never weakens," wrote Welch reverently. For Welch, Knowland "stands out like a states-man-lion surrounded by an army of politician sheep." "He has the courage to be himself, and to stand by his convictions."[34]

But Knowland was unavailable or unwilling to challenge the popular president, who did run for reelection after all. While some conservatives such as Buckley announced tepid support for Eisenhower in 1956, Robert Welch was not among them. Neither was Clarence Manion, the former dean of Notre Dame Law School and the author of the 1950 book *Key to Peace*. Manion admired Welch's approach to foreign policy and shared his Asia First stance. The two developed a deep friendship in the 1950s and dreamed of fusing the remnants of Taft's midwestern conservatism with the segregationist Dixiecrats of the South. They came to believe that T. Coleman Andrews, a former tax official in the Eisenhower administration, who now supported the abolition of the income tax, might bridge the gap between the two groups. (Andrews went down to defeat on the States Rights ticket.) In 1954, Manion and Andrews founded For America, a successor to the America First Committee that opposed "adventurism," "internationalism," and "interventionism." For America members worried that the Korean conflict was a bad precedent, and more generally, they opposed "so-called preventive wars or police actions" that sent "our American boys to fight all over the world, without the consent of Congress." For America was Patrick Buchanan's style of American populist politics for the 1950s.

For America coincided with Manion's inaugural radio broadcast, the *Manion Forum*, which Welch listened to religiously. Welch also joined Manion, Alfred Kohlberg, and Generals Chennault and Wedemeyer in establishing the Committee of Endorsers, which similarly assailed adventurism. Other members were George Schuyler, John Dos Passos, Freda Utley, and James Fifield. Taking out a full-page advertisement in the *New York Times*, the Committee of Endorsers affirmed: "In a Republic, all policy must be a function of public consent," and "independent sovereignty" depended on "minimum standards of law and equity." Communism presented the world's "greatest present obstacle" to peace, and while the committee did not advocate "preventive war," it declared: "we will not shrink from war if the Kremlin forces us to choose between conflict and surrender to Communist slavery."[35] Opposed to collective security and supranational organizations, the committee believed that "the independent sovereignty of the United States must forever remain the ultimate objective of American foreign policy." But "Communist Dictatorship" threatened that sovereignty, and "our aim must be to neutralize, isolate, reduce, and eventually eliminate Communist Power." American foreign policymakers must therefore "wage unremitting psychological warfare against Communist regimes," expel Communist-member states from the United Nations, and "exterminate the Communist conspiracy in the United States."[36]

For Welch, a dangerous symptom of the conspiracy was the cause of peace. The Soviet Union's pacific rhetoric and inauthentic proposals to disarm its nuclear weapons masked its satanic ambitions. For Welch, those who protested American military might favored the goals of Lenin. Consequently, Eisenhower's willingness to participate in nuclear disarmament talks at the 1955 Geneva Summit earned Welch's ire.[37]

Welch also served on the board of the Foundation for Economic Education, or FEE, which espoused the virtues of libertarianism and was a veritable media empire. Factory workers on their cigarette and coffee breaks perused the pamphlet *31 Cents*, which reminded them how much out of every dollar Uncle Sam claimed for taxes. High schools received free reactionary textbooks that extolled the virtues of the free market, and 1950s youngsters read *The First Leftists* before their sock hops and record parties. *The Freeman*, FEE's flagship magazine, was sent by zealous business owners on their own dime to employees, retailers, and jobbers.

Ever the workhorse, Welch thrived in numerous leadership roles, and from 1950 to 1959 he served on the NAM board of directors and was regional vice president for three of those years. He chaired the NAM educational committee. Welch's experiences there and with FEE helped make him an organizational genius. His passion was effusive and his energy was seemingly limitless. He rearranged office furniture between writing articles and still worked eighteen-hour days. But he now walked with a cane. He napped for fifteen-minute intervals on old sofas at his Belmont headquarters and caught his winks in the backs of automobiles on his way to the next convention or speech. Lack of sleep was detrimental to his nerves, and he appeared even more fidgety on the dais. Welch's awkward nervous energy was more noticeable, and his stilted delivery was often commented upon. Years of writing letters into the wee hours were starting to take their toll. But he considered himself a soldier in the war and knew that rest was not a luxury for a man in the trenches.[38] His mind grew myopic and ever more conspiratorial. He believed that Sputnik was a hoax. The real threat of the Soviet Union was inside the United States, Welch said, not outside. Welch and Birchers, observed Clare Boothe Luce, "refuse to believe that sheer stupidity and ignorance of history have an enormous amount to do with our foreign policy and that the increasing secularization of a pluralistic society naturally favors the Left."[39]

The terrain was always shifting. By 1957, the Cold War's battlegrounds were in Latin America, Africa, and the Middle East more than in Europe, Taiwan, and Korea. Welch believed that the United States should discourage the independent rise of the Third World. He also believed that because the French and British ran things efficiently in Algeria and Rhodesia, the colonial powers should have American support. Welch thought the people of Algeria had neither the education nor the training to lead their nation effectively.[40]

Latin Americans were increasingly unhappy with Uncle Sam's meager record of generosity to South America and Central America. But they also grew frustrated by American support of bloody dictatorships, such as the corrupt Fulgencio Batista in Cuba. As early as 1958, Robert Welch was certain that Batista's nemesis, Fidel Castro, who promised social justice, economic reform, open elections, as well as free tuition, was a Communist. "To consider Castro as anything else but an agent of the Kremlin seems to us to demand mental gymnastics beyond the call of duty," said Welch. But the State Department, while wrong, was still unsure. Christian Herter, who took over as secretary of state after the death of John Foster Dulles, wrote on December 23, 1958: "the Communists are utilizing the Castro movement to some extent, but there is insufficient evidence on which to base a charge that the rebels are Communist-dominated." But on New Year's Day 1959, Castro entered Havana, and Batista fled the country. Welch turned out to be completely correct. Castro began executing Batista's backers, and he legalized the Communist Party. Attacks on the United States ensued. Welch said Castro's actions revealed his Communism: "tying prisoners together, having them transported to a trench previously dug, lining them up alongside the trench, shooting them, and pushing them in, to be burned forthwith in one mass grave, has also been a well-known Communist trademark for many years," and Castro was following the same troubling method. Communists in Korea, Welch noted, had done the same thing.[41] But in February 1959, the CIA director Allen Dulles denied that Castro was a Communist, even though Castro had postponed elections he had promised, expropriated American properties, and redistributed land in Cuba. But after the United States cut off imports of Cuban sugar, Castro confiscated more American property and drew closer to the Kremlin. Washington finally cut diplomatic relations with Cuba in 1961.[42] At least on the issue of Cuba, whatever else, call Welch prescient.

Welch came to see Castro's rise to power as a result of Eisenhower's treason. "The delivery of Cuba into Communist hands and eventual conversion . . . into the Communist spearhead for subjugating all the Americas" started when Eisenhower cut off the supply of arms to Batista. Meanwhile, Castro, "by transparent subterfuge," was able "to get all the arms" from the United States. In 1959, Welch wrote conspiratorially, that government officials had used "American support, American prestige, American money and American good will to build up Castro and get him solidly established." At the same time, Castro established his "subservience to Moscow and actual enmity for the United States" and laid "the groundwork for the next stage in this Communist advance." Welch held that just as US officials had abandoned Chiang Kai-shek and China, they had done the same to Batista and helped aid Castro's ascendancy.

Welch's interpretation of events in Cuba fit a tendency that would grow stronger. As he aged, more events fit Welch's conspiratorial worldview. He viewed the world increasingly with suspicion and hypervigilance. For him, all events seemed to fit together.[43]

He had continued to dream of becoming a player in national politics. But after flirting with running against Leverett Saltonstall in 1957, and apparently conceding that Kennedy was unbeatable in 1958, Welch abandoned electoral politics. He concluded the Communists were achieving world domination not at the ballot box but by usurping control of institutions. Rather than running candidates for public office, his strategy was to establish his own institution of anti-Communist zealots. He would raise an army of grassroots men and women who believed that a conspiracy existed to end American sovereignty and imprison America in a Communist nightmare. The John Birch Society was about to be born.

15

The Indy Eleven, 1957–1959

"We are living in America today in such a fool's paradise as the people of China lived in 20 years ago, as the people of Czechoslovakia lived in a dozen years ago, as the people of North Korea lived in five years ago, and as the people of Iraq lived in only yesterday." Lenin announced his three-tier plan for world conquest: "First, we will take Eastern Europe, then the masses of Asia, then we will encircle that last bastion of capitalism, the United States of America; we shall not have to attack; it will fall like overripe fruit into our hands."

Thus Robert Welch began the first meeting of the John Birch Society. He probably got the spurious Lenin quote from J. Howard Pew, his good friend and president of Sun Oil, who thought that Welch was doing something McCarthy had never done.[1] "Personally, I think the country needs one-hundred McCarthys," said Pew, because McCarthy had not gone far enough. McCarthy failed in part because he did not possess a salesman's instincts. And in exclusively targeting Communists in government, he did not educate Americans about "the process by which Communism is effected"—incrementally implemented through socialistic programs like the New Deal, the Fair Deal, and Eisenhower's Modern Republicanism. Welch, Pew averred, by educating the American people, was more important than McCarthy. He regarded Welch as a last best hope whose record as a businessman gave him legitimacy and whose record as a salesman could convince Americans to roll back the New Deal and turn public opinion against the liberal consensus that had dominated since the 1930s.[2]

Pew was not alone. The eleven men who gathered in the Indianapolis home of Marguerite Dice, the national vice chair of the Minute Women of the United States, to hear Welch's founding manifesto were true believers too. The affair was religious in tone. Drawing on his lapsed Southern Baptism, Welch said his new society needed "true fundamentalists" with "unshakable confidence in absolutes, in external principles and truths, in a world of increasing relativity and transitoriness." Christianity itself had devolved to "a so-called social gospel . . . in fact indistinguishable from advocacy of the welfare state socialist politicians."[3]

He told them "we are losing a Cold War in which our freedom, our country, and our very existence are at stake. And while we don't seem to know we are losing this war, you can be sure the Communists do." Americans had not won in Korea. Ho Chi Minh won the battle of Dien Bien Phu. The Soviets had trampled the Hungarian uprising under the tracks of their tanks. America's Vanguard TV-3 satellite made lift-off, rose four feet, and crashed on the launchpad. Meanwhile Sputnik I and Sputnik II gave credence to Soviet premier Khrushchev's statement that the Soviet Union would "bury" the West.

"The first great break for the Communist conspiracy," he told the men, was FDR's recognition of the Soviet Union in 1933. The second big break was World War II, which was "largely brought on through the world wide diplomatic conniving of Stalin's agents." During the war, Stalin "swallowed up" Lithuania, Estonia, Latvia, and Poland. The end of World War II, Welch said, saw Stalin's further acquisition of Hungary, Romania, Bulgaria, Yugoslavia, Czechoslovakia, and East Germany. At Yalta, said Welch, "Roosevelt and Churchill gave Stalin many countries which were not theirs to give." Asia was next. In 1948, they established "their government" in North Korea. In the ensuing war they killed 5,000 "boys from your hometown and mine." They took the "better half" of Indochina. In China in 1949, "we deliberately turned over rule of China's 400 million people to Stalin's stooge."[4]

But it would not be enough to halt the spread of Communism, decrease the size of the national debt, or enervate the welfare state: civilization itself was in its death throes. Welch believed his country was facing a demonic menace trained as a terrorist, practiced as a great manipulator, and set to eradicate everything Welch and Western civilization cherished: property, liberty, and life as we know it. This was a truly apocalyptic war, with the fate of civilization in the balance. The Communists, he said, knew no end of depravity. During the Spanish Civil War, Welch alleged, they murdered "over 4000 priests" and raped "more than that many nuns." Communists "herded priests and their congregations into churches, set the churches on fire, and burned the Christians and their buildings together."[5]

Welch chose to deliver this jeremiad in Indiana's capital city because it was relatively centrally located to the homes of many of the eleven men in attendance. They had heard Welch's speeches before, had read his books, and respected his business acumen. They had subscribed to *One Man's Opinion*. Many even liked his candy. They were committed enough to take two weekdays to hear Welch talk on an unspecified subject. These very powerful and busy men owned large companies. They had responsibilities for their employees and their shareholders. But they had concluded that Welch had a more important thing to say—whatever it was. They trusted him because he had done this before. His political career and promulgation of his books to businesspeople nationwide showed he knew how to get the word out and mobilize people without relying on the national media.

The men were William J. Grede, a former NAM president and president of a Milwaukee foundry; Laurence E. Baker, a retired army colonel, former aide to Douglas MacArthur, and at the time of the meeting a lawyer living in Wellesley, Massachusetts; T. Coleman Andrews, the former IRS commissioner whose views had evolved to oppose the income tax; Ernest G. Swigert, another former president of NAM and founder of Portland's Hyster Corporation, which manufactured heavy equipment; W. B. McMillan, the president of the Hussman Refrigerator Company of St. Louis; Fred Koch, another NAM leader who was president of Rock Island Oil and Refinery Company, which later became Koch industries; Revilo P. Oliver, a classics professor at the University of Illinois; Louis Ruthenbury, the erstwhile board chair of Evansville, Indiana's Servel Corporation; William R. Kent, a Milwaukee businessman; Fitzhugh Scott, the president of a Milwaukee architectural firm; and Robert Stoddard, chair of the *Worcester Telegram and Gazette*.

These eleven conservative businessmen had long believed that socialism threatened the body politic. Some of their ideas about economics, collectivization, and Western culture were defined by the anti-Communism of their time.[6] Lenin's vision to seize the world, they believed, was to be achieved by means of the growth of the federal government, along with institutional, cultural, and economic subjugation. Concerns over national security connected directly to cultural and economic concerns. This coterie believed that though the Communists were perpetrating violence and chaos, common sense and smaller government could break the liberal consensus and produce a better world. The men were loyal to Robert Welch and revered his felicity with words and articulation of a conspiracy that was not only nefarious but convoluted. Most believed his assertion that the Communists controlled or were on the verge of controlling Algeria, Egypt, Lebanon, Libya, Morocco, and Tunisia. "For all practical purposes, Finland, Norway, Iceland were controlled by Moscow too," Welch said. The Communists "complete[ly] controlled" Bolivia, British Guyana, and Venezuela.[7]

To be sure, the attendees had their share of disagreements. These men were used to getting things their way. They had large egos and strong personalities. Although together they agreed to form the John Birch Society National Council, consensus was a rarity and the atmosphere was contentious for years. They crossed swords over Welch's insistence that the "educational" purpose of the John Birch Society made it important to refrain from direct partisan political activity.[8] Some wanted to champion individual candidates; others saw the ideas and ideology as too cerebral. Others wanted a greater presence of religion and God in JBS publications, while Welch, despite his fundamentalist call to action, strayed into more secular themes.

What maintained a semblance of comity and kept discord to a minimum, at least during the early years when loyalty to the "educational" project seemed paramount, was the collective belief that a conspiracy to subvert the sovereignty of the United States was afoot; traitors inside the government had abetted these forces of darkness in the past; and current national leaders in the halls of power were committing treason. They also shared a truism: a distinct American philosophy of governance was long ago sanctioned by the Founding Fathers and embodied what their enemies wanted to destroy. More than any other reason, this belief that the enemy sought the annihilation of everything

America stood for since its founding explained their remarkable commitment to Welch's vision. This cause gave these men reason enough to consider their lives worth living, as much as or perhaps more than did their families or companies. The very fate of America, which Western civilization depended on, was at stake.

Across December 8 and 9, 1958, Robert spoke for a total of seventeen hours at the Dice residence. Welch offered ten predictions for the future. He predicted "greatly expanded government spending . . . for foreign aid" and "every conceivable means of getting rid of ever larger sums of American money as wastefully as possible." Welch predicted higher taxes, unbalanced budgets, "wild inflation" of American currency, "government control of prices, wages, and materials," "greatly increased socialistic controls," and "centralization of power in Washington." But he also predicted more federal control over the education system and a "constant hammering into the American consciousness of the horror of modern warfare." Whatever else, call him prescient.

Welch also drew corollaries between the abandonment of unfettered capitalism and the international Communist movement. Here Welch addressed issues that stir the populism of America both today and in his own time: illegal immigration, the elimination of national borders, and the dissolution of national sovereignty. "Right under our noses," he thundered, "the Communists are gradually carrying out their plan of grand strategy . . . to so change the economic and political structure of the United States that it can be comfortably merged with Soviet Russia in a one world socialist government." What ripened the fruit, Welch announced, was incremental growth brought about by higher taxes, the opening of our borders, the federal usurpation of public education, foreign aid, foreign wars, domestic spending and its accompanying inflation, and price controls to staunch the inflation.

Robert also explained how the John Birch Society would function. Critically, it was not a secret society, like the Ku Klux Klan; it was, rather, an anonymous society. The distinction eluded some critics. Ironically, there were aspects of the Society that mirrored the tactics the Communists had pursued in the 1930s. It would use organized fronts to spearhead political causes. It would lead letter-writing campaigns. With monthly bulletins, members would inform headquarters of local chapter activity throughout the nation—in the spirit of the colonial

Committees of Correspondence. Early joiners were urged to read conservative books and dedicate time in their local libraries to study the Communist conspiracy. At weekly chapter meetings, members would watch anti-Communist films. They would hear lectures. They would discuss the contents of the monthly bulletin. At home, in the barbershop, at the hair salon, or in the bait shop, they could read and share the JBS magazine *American Opinion*. All these endeavors would be done under the banner of Americanism, which Welch defined "as the very antithesis of socialism and communism with a little c." "The true americanist," Welch proclaimed, "believes that the individual should retain the freedom to make his own bargains with life, and the responsibility for the results of that bargain."[9]

After returning home from Indianapolis, Robert gave in January 1959 the same address to approximately seventy friends and supporters in Greater Boston. Many joined the Society's first six chapters, all based in Massachusetts. Among the first chapter leaders was Belmont's Dr. N. E. Adamson, a rising young surgeon. During World War II, Adamson was a US Army medical officer and was called back into service in Korea. Adamson was convinced to join the Society when his wife Anne, a nurse, heard one of Welch's speeches. Anne thought Robert sounded a lot like her husband. Like Robert, Adamson was deeply disturbed by MacArthur's removal and then McCarthy's censure. Anne was hooked and thought her husband would be as well. She told her husband, "he lives right here in Belmont. You've got to meet him." Eventually, Adamson and Robert grew very close, with Adamson becoming not only the youngest member of the Society's National Council but Welch's protégé.[10]

After establishing John Birch Society chapters throughout Massachusetts, Welch hit the road to deliver the founding speech throughout the country. He gave the same address eighty times over the next three years—a period when the JBS grew exponentially. In the first months of 1959, meetings were scheduled in Milwaukee, Boca Raton, and twice in New York City. The Milwaukee meeting was "the most rewarding experience of my life," observed Harry L. Bradley of the Allen-Bradley Company. Chapters were started in Florida, Illinois, and Michigan. Then Welch traveled to California. There, upward of 2,000 men and women cheered him on. By 1959, the Society's monthly bulletin, written entirely by Welch, was being received by chapter leaders and members. The Birch Society was alive.

The Society grew fast and had great strength in California, Texas, and other Sunbelt states, with mostly white, middle-class members. It soon had chapters throughout the country and was the first truly feasible national anti-Communist organization. And yet, it never did achieve more than 100,000 members, and its financial statement in Massachusetts reported only 24,000 members nationwide. The Birch Society was a nonpartisan organization, so it did not participate in political campaigns, but its members were very active in national, state, and local politics.[11] Birchers became involved in efforts to impeach Chief Justice Earl Warren and withdraw the United States from the United Nations. But even while members cared about similar issues, some had different objectives for the Society. This became a common headache for Welch, who then had to decide whether the member belonged in the Society. Sometimes the problem solved itself when the member resigned, but sometimes it didn't. One high-profile and emblematic case came from Robert's association with T. Coleman Andrews. For Andrews, civil rights was a symptom of a much larger problem, with which he was obsessed. "Blood is going to flow before the integration question is settled," Andrews said. Welch was not willing to concede that, and neither would have John Birch. For Welch, being "a party, even unwittingly, to anything that would be done in the name of a man who would've been unalterably opposed to violence of the sort that I fear that we are apt to face sooner or later" was a real concern.[12]

The first full year of the JBS was very busy. Chapter leaders in February 1959 got a box of books; Welch instructed them to read at least one per month. The chapter leaders received their first monthly *Bulletin* in March. The *Bulletin* was initially 5 to 12 pages and was printed with a spirit duplicator—a technique resembling mimeographing. The *Bulletin* was soon reaching 30 pages each month, and sometimes there were whoppers of up to 146 pages. By the late 1960s, Welch had filed more than 1 million words in all the bulletins. Each *Bulletin* began with a short quotation from a poem. ("Hear ye not the hum of mighty workings"). Then Welch offered a pessimistic commentary on world events and laid out the JBS agenda for the month. His initial *Bulletin* included a printed message from him protesting high taxes in Massachusetts.

Summoning the spirit of the 1773 Boston Tea Party, Welch told chapter leaders to get their members to attach a teabag to Welch's carefully prepared message and send it to the governor.

The March 1959 *Bulletin* encouraged members to sign up new recruits, much as the Sons of Liberty had done in colonial Boston. Members were asked to subscribe to conservative periodicals like *Human Events*, *National Review*, the *Dan Smoot Report*, and *American Opinion*. Welch worked to get conservative magazines on airplanes and trains. "After we get *Human Events* on the planes, we can try to do the same for *National Review*."[13] The April *Bulletin* included a postcard protesting foreign aid as unconstitutional. Welch also disclosed that month that department stores throughout the nation were stocking subversively secular UN holiday propaganda instead of traditional "Merry Christmas" decorations. Department stores, Welch alleged, wanted to take Christ out of Christmas. He asked members to send to all department stores a copy of "There Goes Christmas," which had already appeared in *American Opinion*. A few months later, Robert declared that many department store officials would be continuing with their Christmas decorations because of the hard work of the John Birch Society, and despite the opposition of the United Nations. But the battle for Christmas—just one early battle in the culture wars—would continue.[14]

Robert was working constantly. When he was not crashing at the office, he rose quietly at dawn, so as to not wake his wife. Robert put on his suit, which Marian had laid out the night before. He perused the morning papers—the *New York Times*, the *Wall Street Journal*, the *Boston Globe*, the *Washington Post*, and the *Chicago Tribune*—and made clippings, often jotting notes on the margins. He was a very fast reader and corrected the prose in his head as he read. He also devoured the Communist press, including the *Daily Worker*. After all, he wanted to get inside the head of the enemy. Robert wolfed down breakfast—often eggs, toast, and coffee—unless he was so hot to get to the office that he didn't want to eat.

His life was hectic. Meetings and interviews were plentiful. When not reading or writing, he was listening to his staff, directing them, calling the shots because the buck stopped on the founder's desk. Robert worked his staff hard, but he drove himself even harder. He was meticulous about details. He gave exact instructions on how to frame letters, how to address the controversy or crisis of the moment. His lunches were usually working lunches—simple sandwiches and coffee. He would surround himself with aides and talk of the crusade and of his life, peppering the stories with off-color jokes, sharp insight into the world situation, and informal banter. He often worked late, doing a lot of his writing between 10:00 p.m. and 4:00 a.m. He would dash off letters to the editor to correct a point. He hated criticism of himself and of the Society, and gave as good as he got. He was naturally thin-skinned, and sensitive, but developed a thicker skin by his fifties. If he spent the night on the office couch, in the morning he would slip on a fresh shirt, shave, and get back to work. Food was unimportant to him, just sustenance to fight the Communist conspiracy, but his favorite meal was Pig Knuckles at Jacob Wirth's restaurant in Boston. He ate anything that Marian cooked and thanked her profusely for it. He did not overeat and maintained his weight of 175 pounds on his 5′10″ frame for most of his adult life, perhaps through nervous energy. His slight paunch was noticeable only because some men wore their pants higher in the mid-twentieth century. He was not a heavy drinker, but he enjoyed Manhattans. He did overindulge in cigars.[15]

Robert had few hobbies. He had given up chess in the 1940s because his work at James O. Welch did not provide enough time for it. Robert did not play cards but did enjoy golf, though his son observed that he was horrendous at it. He loved mathematics and enjoyed solving difficult equations during vacations. He calculated that he dedicated at least two years of his life to trying to solve Fermat's Theorem; he filled multiple notebooks with his efforts. His library was enormous, and he loved reading, especially detective stories at the end of a long day. He saw the world like the good detective novel: a solvable riddle with good guys and bad guys. The answers were simple but involved study, and the enigma fit a familiar pattern. He was not a simple man by any means—quite the opposite—but he was a grounded man who was completely happy with himself. He liked to be Robert Welch.

Who were his staffers, and why did they all work so hard for him? They had time for church on Sundays, and then it was back to the office to finish a memorandum or put the finishing touches on a letter. Many had fought in World War II because freedom was on the line, and they had sacrificed everything—their bodies, their time, their spirit. This crusade against Communism was an even more important one. Mao and Stalin were even more evil than Hitler.

By his side was Marian, who was an excellent editor, extremely intelligent, and completely loyal—completely in awe of him, devoted to his every need, and convinced, like the other members of his staff, that he was a genius. She was a phenomenal typist and stenographer, and a true believer. She helped him develop the plain-spoken prose of the John Birch Society *Bulletin* and criticized his prose if it was too cryptic. Although Robert was not an easygoing boss, Marian enjoyed being in his presence, and he appreciated both her beauty and deep intelligence. They were a perfect husband-wife team, pushing each other to greater heights, although Robert made greater demands on her than she did him.[16]

Robert had great respect for women, whom he believed had unique talents that no man possessed. He was comfortable around women, though secretaries at the James O. Welch Company were terribly afraid of him at first. He was cantankerous and had a bad temper, until he warmed up to them. Women were not close friends, nor should they be, he believed. The primary roles for women, Robert thought, as most men of his generation did, were as child-bearing mothers, doting wives, and meticulous secretaries. Though long surrounded by attractive young ebullient secretaries, no evidence suggests he harbored any lustful passion for anybody except his wife. He had but one love throughout all his days: Marian. He was not interested in infidelity, nor fleeting sexual gratification, because he was preoccupied with the romantic love that still burned for Marian. They read poetry together and stared into each other's eyes. There is a picture of the two from 1956, the year that Robert began publishing *One Man's Opinion,* that captured how much he revered his spouse. The two are at a table in their basement study. Robert is slumped, with pencil and notebook in hand, jotting down what Marian has to say. In this moment, Robert is the secretary. He looks perfectly content, admiring, attentive, meek, a schoolboy, a puppy. He appears spellbound by what she has to say or moonstruck by how she looks. He was the rare man of his time who genuflected to his wife's intellectual capacities.

He displayed the same level of respect for the talents of two other women in his life. Miss Lovett, who had been his secretary at James O. Welch, had stayed with him. She was effective, blessed with an eagle-eye, and intelligent, and she had Robert's complete confidence. She could identify what he needed even before he did. She was better than he in excising the latent anti-Semitism and racism that permeated some of the articles by Westbrook Pegler and Revilo Oliver. With red pen in hand, she removed many statements that would have embarrassed the Society.

One of the Society's first big campaigns was against negotiating with the Russians. Welch had long considered them near-satanic liars. On October 4, 1957, the Soviet Union had shocked the world by launching into orbit a 184-pound satellite, Sputnik I. That November, the Soviets dispirited millions of Americans by launching the 1120-pound Sputnik II with a dog in it.[17] But Welch never believed that the Soviets had a space program at all; he thought both incidents hoaxes. Welch concluded that the Soviets either stole the technology from Americans or treasonous conspirators in the United States launched the satellites for them. Either way, the real enemy, Welch wrote in "An Open Letter to Khrushchev" in March 1958, was not "your military strength or ours" but "our internal security against treason."[18] In the April 1958 issue of *American Opinion,* Robert openly dismissed claims of Soviet scientific successes and missile superiority. "We are to take for granted that, just as a by-product of building your sputniks, you have or will have a battery of intercontinental missiles ready to pinpoint Times Square, the Boston State House, and Capitol Hill as targets from five-thousand miles away. Pfui! We don't claim your grapes are sour, comrade Khrushchev. Knowing what an inveterate liar you are, we don't believe they even exist."[19]

The sputniks were real, but Welch was more right than he or the American people knew. Through the intelligence gathered from the U-2 flights, Eisenhower knew that Soviet missile technology and its nuclear weapon stockpile were far inferior to the United States. The Soviet R-7 intercontinental missile launched Sputnik I and Sputnik II, but it was not able to carry a nuclear warhead until July 1959. As late as February 1960, the Soviet Union had only four operational R-7s.[20]

Still, Eisenhower increased military spending in the last half of his second term and bolstered false Democratic claims of a "missile gap" that helped Kennedy win the White House.

Welch was suspicious not only of the sputniks but of Khrushchev's hold on power, calling the Russian premier a "front-man." Welch did write that Khrushchev was responsible for brutal crimes, including the starvation of one million Ukrainians in the 1930s and the 1956 attack on Hungarian freedom fighters, but the real head of state, he alleged, was Georgi Malenkov.[21] "You have created a blanket of twisted information, misleading slants, subtle propaganda, and brazen falsehoods between the American people and any clear view of your activities," Welch lectured Khrushchev. The "unseen tentacles" of the Communist conspiracy were controlling the "media of mass communication in the United States," but the American people had "one, all powerful weapon," which was knowledge of the truth. Truth was "the only thing in all the world today that you and your cohorts fear." Welch told Khrushchev to call off the Communist conspiracy and focus "energy and cleverness into raising" the Russian living standards. Otherwise the "truth-seeking" Americans would have to end the conspiracy for him—"something you fear more than all of our hydrogen bombs and NATO alliances."[22]

To Welch's horror, in August 1959, President Eisenhower invited Nikita Khrushchev to become the first Soviet premier to visit the United States. Earlier that year, the John Birch Society had launched the Committee Against Summit Entanglements (CASE), which attempted to halt any summit meeting with Khrushchev. CASE was likely inspired by the Committee for One Million, which opposed the admission of China to the United Nations. One of the Committee for One Million's biggest supporters was Alfred Kohlberg, who wrote CASE's slogan, which anticipated and disparaged any invitation from Khrushchev to Eisenhower to visit the Soviet Union: "Please, Mr. President, Don't Go."[23]

Welch thought that any formal sit down between Eisenhower and Khrushchev would give confidence to the Communists and dispirit their opposition. CASE announced that "to negotiate is to surrender"; Eisenhower was playing Khrushchev's game if he traveled to Moscow to negotiate with a ruthless dictator. Khrushchev had an "utter lack of conscience," and it would constitute "a crime against humanity" and a "propaganda triumph" if Khrushchev walked on American soil as an "honored guest." Petitions from the Society urging Eisenhower to rescind the offer appeared in the *New York Times*, the *Chicago Tribune*, the *Wall Street Journal*, and other papers. CASE sent Eisenhower an open letter, which showcased how "Killer Khrushchev" came to power "over piles of corpses," as Gene Lyons said.

Welch solicited thousands of dollars for CASE from his affluent friends. With Welch serving as chair, the executive committee of CASE included Fred Koch, the father of the Koch brothers; Clarence Manion; Revilo Oliver; and Thomas Anderson. CASE's members included libertarian economist Ludwig von Mises, William F. Buckley, and Barry Goldwater. Buckley had even reached out to Welch (through Oliver) and inquired why he had not been asked to join CASE earlier. Despite *National Review*'s initial criticism of the JBS, Buckley became a member of CASE's national board and piggybacked on Welch's idea, selling "Khrushchev Not Welcome Here" bumper stickers. On September 17, 1959, the day Khrushchev addressed the UN in New York, Buckley held a protest rally at Carnegie Hall and warned that he would dye the Hudson River red when the Soviet premier arrived. Others protested with hunger strikes and flew American flags upside down—the international symbol of distress.[24]

By June 1959, the Society was continuing its splendid growth. Welch announced that eight new chapters had opened in New York City alone. The July *Bulletin* emphasized that Welch's stemwinding tours were swelling the size of JBS membership. It also asked members to send a letter of support to Jacques Soustelle, then leading the anti-Communist resistance in the French colony of Algeria. In the August issue, Welch included a letter from Soustelle, which thanked Welch and assured readers that Algeria was a ground zero for the Communist plans for world domination. The August issue also promoted the sale of the *Blue Book*—a transcript of Welch's two-day Indianapolis speech. Welch said the JBS was working on a film of the speech to go along with a tape recording of it.[25]

In late 1959, the Society was busy establishing its institutional structure. When the Society turned one year old in December, Welch proudly reported that the organization had "seven full-time coordinators," and "five volunteer coordinators." The Society was operating in fifteen states, with twenty-five home chapter members, but, observed Welch, "we have barely scratched the surface in building the John Birch Society." Throughout the country, Welch was hiring fully paid field coordinators who would cover a particular geographical area, establishing chapters and recruiting members. Soon, Welch had named coordinators in Florida, Illinois, Massachusetts, Michigan, New York, Tennessee, and Texas.[26]

Thomas N. Hill was hired as the Texas coordinator. Originally from Gloucester, Massachusetts, Hill was finishing his education at Southern Methodist University in Dallas. Welch described Hill as having a "60-year old brain in his 30-year old body." The Massachusetts native was soon tapped to come to Belmont, where he became Robert's "right hand" for twenty-five years. Hill was cautious, but too much so. But he had early successes. Among Hill's early victories was securing from Welch a statement on his religious beliefs, which helped grow membership since prospective members were often very religious. In "the Roemer letter," so named because a pastor of that name got the first one, Welch said, "I have tried all my life . . . to be a good Christian. But I am not a fundamentalist." "I do not ask anybody to follow, or even to accept, my specific religious views. My concern is with morality and purpose, based on those eternal truths on which we can all agree. It is nobody else's business what my exact shades of religious belief may be, so long as I am giving my life to preserving his right to believe exactly what he wishes."

The letter enabled many who held strong religious views to conclude that working with JBS members who did not share those views would not compromise their principles. San Diego's Tim LaHaye, a fundamentalist Baptist of a premillennial bent, joined the John Birch Society, probably because of Hill, and made an "exception" to his rule as a man devoted to his brand of faith not to join ecumenically anti-Communist organizations. LaHaye even appeared in a film that encouraged evangelical Christians to join the JBS.[27] Hill, at least, had a good start.

As the JBS grew in strength, so did its conspiratorial mindset. The December 1959 *Bulletin* highlighted the mysterious deaths of anti-

Communists, including the fatal car crash of Manning Johnson, the African American JBS member whose book *Color, Communism, and Common Sense* was later published by the Society. Welch also wrote of the story of Paul Bang-Jensen, the Danish diplomat who refused to give to the UN names of anti-Communists involved in the unsuccessful 1956 uprising in Hungary. After Bang-Jensen refused to be an informer, his body was found in a New York park and his death ruled a suicide. Welch also found suspicious the deaths of Robert Taft and Joseph McCarthy. The December *Bulletin* also contained a direct blast against fluoride in the American water supply. Welch urged Americans to oppose it on the basis that its health impact was largely unknown and that it established a bad precedent for inserting other additives in the water supply.[28]

The February 1960 *Bulletin* announced the establishment of the Society's twenty-five-man National Council. Welch described the council's purpose as providing "advice and guidance" and selecting a "successor to myself as head of the John Birch Society, if and when any accident, 'suicide' or anything sufficiently fatal is arranged for me by the Communists—or I simply die in bed of old age and a cantankerous disposition." Nine men who attended the first meeting in Indianapolis—Andrews, Bunker, Grede, Koch, McMillan, Oliver, Ruthenbury, Stoddard, and Swigert—were the leaders of the initial council. The other original fifteen were Dr. N. E. Adamson, Tom Anderson, John Beatty, Spruille Braden, Ralph Davis, Slobodan Draskovich, A. G. Heinsohn, Dr. Granville Knight, Alfred Kohlberg, Clarence Manion, Frank Masland, Adolphe Menjou, Cola Parker, James Simpson, and Lieut. Gen. Charles B. Stone.[29] Welch drew from the National Council a five-man Executive Committee, below which was the director of field activities, the coordinators, section leaders, chapter leaders, and rank-and-file members, twenty per chapter. While Welch himself was not subject to removal or even election, he could remove the council at his discretion.[30]

Welch's conspiratorialism kicked into a new gear when, on May 1, 1960, the Soviets shot down a U-2 spy plane.[31] Eisenhower denied knowledge of the affair until Khrushchev announced to the world that the pilot, Francis Gary Powers, was alive but in Soviet custody. A summit scheduled for two weeks later largely failed, but Welch dismissed as nonsense the claim that the crash was the reason why. Rather, Welch took full credit for the summit's doom and highlighted the work of CASE. In the May 1960 *Bulletin,* Welch suggested the U-2 crash was a cover story and that the plane had been "deliberately flown into Russian territory at [that] particular time" for Moscow to shoot it out of the sky. Welch continued his conspiratorial screed. "Few things could be basically more absurd—and laughable—than Khrushchev's swelling his veins in anger and going through his bombastic gestures over so trivial an incident," Welch said. "With Soviet spies and agents crawling out of the woodwork all over the United States, Khrushchev's corny gesticulations over this ethereal Lone Ranger would've been an excellent performance by the mimic in a burlesque show." CASE's letters that "flooded the White House," along with the assistance "by the agents of the Kremlin," were what really stopped the summit from being a success for Moscow, at least according to Welch.[32] If not for CASE, Eisenhower would have gone to Moscow and signed a disarmament scheme with the Soviet leader. At least Welch thought.

Khrushchev actually saw things partly as Welch did. He believed that CIA director Allen Dulles sought to sabotage the summit and prevent better relations between the USSR and the United States.[33] Khrushchev was wrong about Dulles's complicity, but not about the result. After the crash, relations between the Soviets and Americans turned icy. During Eisenhower's last eight months in office, the president ignored Khrushchev and the Soviet Union. President Kennedy was left with the tense relations, which he exacerbated with the ill-fated invasion at the Bay of Pigs.[34]

16

Revelations, 1959–1960

On July 11, 1960, Robert Welch's compulsive mailing of the Eisenhower letter—which had never abated—finally backfired when the Christian Anti-Communism Crusade's Fred Schwarz revealed its existence. In Glenview, Illinois, before a crowd of more than 200, Schwarz asked John Birch Society council member Stillwell Conner whether Welch called Eisenhower a Communist. Conner replied he didn't know what Schwarz was talking about. But then Fred Vignola started reading his copy of the letter and the jig was up.[1]

The story of this exchange appeared in the *Chicago Daily News* on July 25.[2] Jack Mabley called out Welch for "dictatorial" bearing, but portrayed JBS members as "well-meaning, conscientious men and women." Mabley's criticism of Welch's alleged autocratic behavior while handing a pass to the rank-and-file became a trend in future years among JBS's critics. Mabley also assailed Welch for his supposedly anti-democratic tendencies—another common critique among JBS watchers. In two more articles, Mabley called the JBS "ultraconservatives," that while it was "not a secret society in the normal sense of the word," it tried to "avoid publicity." Mabley said those following Welch "should know the thinking of the man to whom they are pledging their energies and loyalty." Welch had a "dim view of democracy," alleged Mabley, who called the JBS authoritarian and dictatorial and members' acceptance of Welch's leadership "unquestioning." Mabley managed to obtain a copy of the "302-page black paperbound book," otherwise known as the "Eisenhower letter," which was "intended for secret distribution only to the leaders of the society." Mabley disclosed that this "fantastic" document contained the lines: "while I too think that Milton Eisenhower is a Communist, and has been for 30 years, this opinion is based largely on general circumstances of his conduct. But my firm belief that Dwight Eisenhower is a dedicated, conscious agent of the Communist conspiracy is based on an accumulation of detailed evidence so extensive and so palpable that it seems to me to put this conviction beyond any reasonable doubt." Mabley wrote that Welch also accused Secretary of State John Foster Dulles, CIA director Allen Dulles, and Chief Justice Earl Warren of being Communists.[3] Mabley's revelations were repeated in subsequent articles in the *Chicago Sun-Times*, the *Milwaukee Journal*, and the *Boston Herald*.

Welch argued that the whole hullabaloo made the Society stronger. The JBS was "rapidly gaining stature" and the bad coverage were the "growing pains" on the road to maturity. "The total net effect" of Mabley's aspersions, Welch said, was infinitesimal. Only three brand-new members had asked that their membership be "held in abeyance until they could find out what was what." Mabley was an opportunist, Welch alleged, "whose only real purpose may have been to make his column exciting," for which Robert conceded him "a certain measure of success." But, he warned, this "vicious attack . . . is undoubtedly only the forerunner of many more, of many times, to come." Welch predicted correctly: the onslaught of 1961 would be much more intense than the squabble of 1960.

Publicly, Welch blamed the February 1961 edition of the San Francisco–based Communist newspaper *People World's* for exposing the letter, but privately Fred Schwarz got the worst of it and received an angry nine-page missive from Welch.[4] An Australian émigré, Schwarz had established the Christian Anti-Communism Crusade. An indefatigable lecturer and seminar organizer, Schwarz was also the author of *You Can Trust the Communists (to be Communists)*. Schwarz was not a conspiracy theorist but was attracted to Welch because he cheered the establishment of local groups to attack Communism.

Historian Colin Reynolds suggests that Herbert Philbrick may have been the man who sent Mabley *The Politician*. A former member of the Communist Party USA and an FBI spy, Philbrick's life inspired the popular TV series *I Led Three Lives* and the radio show *I Was a*

Communist for the FBI. Throughout the 1950s, Philbrick told his story at Schwarz's school of anti-Communism. Philbrick consistently donated to the John Birch Society, and served as a member of the home chapter. But he was the consummate double agent. He exaggerated his devotion to the John Birch Society despite warning friends that the organization endangered American ideals. According to Philbrick, the JBS had a "cloak and dagger atmosphere," and Welch's obsession with members not questioning his decisions was "a great deal similar to the appeal made by Adolf Hitler." Whether or not Philbrick sent Mabley the book, he was no friend of Welch's.[5]

After this exposure, the John Birch Society faced a storm of controversy for the first half of the 1960s. But Welch made it abundantly clear to members that they did not need to be concerned with the association of the JBS with *The Politician.* "Since at least two-thirds of our Chapter Leaders had never even heard of *The Politician,*" any "attempted tying of the Society to the manuscript . . . is entirely unsupported by the facts." The manuscript was not even a book, argued Welch, and "still of the nature of a long letter to a friend." It had never been published, and there were no plans to publish it. But Welch never distanced himself too much from its contents, and he defended its conclusions. While members, he said, "do not like the word *treason* in these pages, [they] must remember that the most effective weapon the Communists have had for 40 years has always been treason in other governments." "By far the most important model of that weapon for 25 years has been the treason in our government."[6]

Throughout the broader American conservative movement, though, leaders did become concerned about Welch's "private letter." In 1959 and 1960, few knew about it. But Welch had sent it to hundreds, if not thousands, of conservatives over the years. Establishment conservatives such as William F. Buckley, far more discerning than most, distanced himself from the Society, fearing that the letter, and broader exposure of the John Birch Society, would make it more difficult to elect a conservative president in 1964.

Buckley felt threatened, and with good reason. The editorial board of *American Opinion* included a *National Review* editor, Willi Schlamm, and a *National Review* writer, Medford Evans. The primary financial backer of the *National Review* was Roger Milliken, a JBS member. The

Birch Society's National Council was filled with folks closely associated with *National Review*, including Spruile Braden, Clarence Manion, Adolphe Menjou, and Revilo Oliver. Buckley knew it was impossible to separate the network of the JBS from *National Review*—but he had to. One risked being a cancer on the other.

So in 1959, Buckley attacked Welch and the Society, though not individual members. Buckley could not countenance Welch's view from the 1958 manuscript that Eisenhower was a Communist and that the government was run by Communists. The April 1959 *National Review* mocked *American Opinion*'s claim that the censoring of *Doctor Zhivago* was simply a trick by Moscow to get the West to embrace an anti-capitalist novel. *National Review* also ridiculed the John Birch Society's rejection of a split between Tito and Stalin. Both assertions were part of a problematic theme running through the JBS, observed Gene Lyons in the *National Review*: "Certainly there are elements of deception . . . in all manifestations of Communist internal troubles. But to write them off as propaganda devices . . . is to concede to the Communist world a monolithic perfection, a super human cleverness, which does not and could not exist outside a fiction *1984*. Those who see Communism in such Sophoclean terms might as well give up the fight, since the odds against mere mortals would be too steep to overcome." Buckley wrote Welch to tell him he was printing the critical essay and that he agreed with it. "Probably a little friendly controversy among ourselves every now and then is not too bad an idea," he wrote. "I shall not mind in the least your publishing Gene Lyons' criticism," Welch responded.

Only Welch did mind. He found "one or two aspects of that [article] annoying." The article, he said, "consisted of holding up to complete and sarcastic ridicule a theme to which we had given careful and considered argument, and which we still believe future history will prove us to have been entirely correct." Medford Evans did not like it either and wrote Buckley: "My view on the subject is that *National Review* should refrain from making any criticism of other conservative periodicals except in the one case when we earnestly feel that a spokesman for conservatism has made a grievous error." Buckley had decided to become the surgeon, but was now realizing how difficult it was to cut out the cancer.[7]

Paranoia was ubiquitous and omnipresent in the early 1960s. Americans feared that war could erupt at a moment's notice. They ducked and covered in public schools. They unquestionably supported the arms race. They built bunkers to shelter themselves. They popped sedatives, or "mommy's little helpers," to assuage their anxiety. With the Republican Party turning more liberal, the reactionary John Birch Society filled a need for tens of thousands of people. It made complete sense that thousands of women became members of the Society. In *The Feminine Mystique,* Betty Friedan, a suburban housewife, had written of bored homemakers suffering from a "problem that has no name." The John Birch Society solved the problem of ennui. One woman who joined the Society said, "I just don't have time for anything. I'm fighting communism three nights a week."[8]

In many communities, the JBS was an organization available every night of the week. And despite Buckley's efforts, it remained a force in the conservative movement. For many, the Birch Society was fun. Whether they were practical or had fantastical objectives—and many members concluded they were quixotic—many Birchers sincerely loved participating in activities with their peers. Some found solace. Some found a reason to live. Many found love. Robert and Marian Welch were not the only husband-wife duo fighting Communism in the JBS.[9]

One popular Society program during this period was the distribution and showing of the film *Communism on the Map*. JBS members had held "literally thousands of showings" of the film by April 1961. The film was a product of Harding College, a Church of Christ College in Searcy, Arkansas, but JBS members had assisted in the production. The film carried the theme that socialism and Communism were one and the same. There were two reasons for this conclusion, the film said. First, history demonstrated the "kinship" between the two, and socialism was a common precursor to Communism. Welch had foreshadowed the merger between the United States and the USSR, but the film went further. "Wherever communism can't take over by fomenting internal revolt, the Reds seek to establish so-called democratic socialist governments which they can infiltrate and gradually turn into totalitarian nations ruled by Moscow."

"Take over from within," would occur, the film observed, and the basic strategy would be to sow conflict between groups. In "nation after nation," Communists "set Chinese against Chinese, Koreans against Koreans, Indonesians against their own people, Cubans against Cubans, and so on." The rank-and-file of the John Birch Society delivered the message of *Communism on the Map*. Regular men and women were the grassroots warriors who spread the message.

Battling the enemy was captivating. It involved elements of fun, and mystery, and danger. When chapters reached twenty-four members, they split to avoid detection. Make sure to keep that reel of JBS film to hide detection from Communists, warned the chapter leaders. Put the *Blue Book* in a safe place in case some unfriendly neighbor stopped to "borrow sugar." Make sure to maintain the anonymity of members. The Communists love to gather lists of names and "out" folks fighting for freedom. Keep quiet and don't divulge what went on in Tuesday night's meeting. It might hurt the cause.

The peril, suspicion, and secrecy were attractive features of the hunt. It was primal to a certain extent. Men and women had been telling ghost stories around campfires for thousands of years. And the story that Birchers told—that the Communists were infiltrating American society and JBS chapter meetings—was echoed by the director of the FBI and the attorney general. Government officials reported that Communists surrounded Americans. They didn't, but folks listened to their leaders in the early 1960s. And leaders told them that Soviet spies were among them, maybe right next door, maybe at work, maybe in their own homes. The paranoia went down the line from every state house, to every schoolhouse, to every movie house, even to private homes.

In May 1960, Communists in San Francisco led by the longshoreman Archie Brown tried to abolish the House Un-American Activities Committee (HUAC). JBS members relished the opportunity to get the word out about this atrocity. They got the HUAC-produced film *Operation Abolition* into the hands of as many real Americans as possible.[10] Members established reading rooms with like-minded folks. They distributed copies of Fred Koch's *A Businessman Looks at Communism*. They wrote letters to John Wayne or, as Robert Welch called him, "one of the few great actors of our times who was also a Great American."[11] Welch requested that they commend "the Duke" for his grand work on *The Alamo*, which embodied the frontier spirit, and his cherished Americanism. Welch warned that ours is a "Republic not a democracy"—a JBS maxim. Birchers also encouraged movie houses to showcase the patriotic film and boycott Stanley Kubrick's dodgy *Spartacus*. What's more, just as the martyr Joe McCarthy had done, members campaigned against the sale of slave labor products—like Polish hams, Czechoslovakian nails, Yugoslavian caps.[12]

There was also the battle for Christmas, which Welch continued to wage. It was one front in the war against Christianity, and Americans needed to win lest the Communists eradicate the right to embrace the Christ child. The Communists were not only assailing the right to practice one's faith, they were after the Second Amendment. As early as the 1950s, Welch was a forceful advocate of gun rights and foreshadowed the NRA's later stands: "there has been a continued and increasing drive in this country for many years to have legislation passed requiring the registration of all privately owned firearms," and "the real purpose of such enforced registration, of course, would be to make ultimate seizure of such firearms by the government both easier and more complete." He continued: "as the Communists get ever nearer to taking us over or to making more explicit the takeover so insidiously acquired and as preparations proceed for the gradual introduction of police state control over our population, the pressure for this firearm legislation grows stronger." And yet, he promised, "no dictator—tyrant can long rule any people, previously accustomed to freedom, where private firearms are plentiful among its citizenry."[13]

One of the central projects of the JBS—to impeach Chief Justice Earl Warren—was pursued not exclusively because Warren had overseen *Brown v. Board of Education*. To be sure, Welch called that decision "the most brazen and flagrant usurpation of power that has been seen in any major court in the whole Anglo-American system of jurisprudence in 300 years" and relayed that "there have been credible reports that he was made Chief Justice . . . to assure that this decision came off according to schedule." But the JBS's *Blue Book*, its primary foundational document, did not emphasize civil rights, observing only that the Kremlin was using the issue to embroil the nation in civil war.[14]

Rather, the drive to impeach Warren was both an effort to give members something, however futile, to accomplish and a response to a whole host of things that, according to Welch, Warren had done to protect Communists in government and turn the country into a democracy instead of a republic. Welch believed that Warren belonged to a larger conspiracy to aggrandize the federal government and eliminate "all remaining vestiges of State's Rights." "It is that residual hard-core of local government and regional rights, that ready framework for resistance to a monolithic dictatorship in Washington, that the Communists must destroy." Welch urged that "the impeachment of Earl Warren would dramatize and crystallize the whole basic question of whether the United States remains the United States, or becomes gradually transformed into a province of the worldwide Soviet system."[15]

Welch cited the decisions in *Pennsylvania v. Nelson* (1956), *Konigsberg v. State Bar* (1957), *Watkins v. United States* (1957), and *Sweezy v. New Hampshire* (1957) to justify Warren's immediate impeachment. *Pennsylvania v. Nelson* upheld a state court decision reversing the conviction of an American Communist Party member who advocated overthrowing the government. *Konigsberg v. State Bar* allowed Rafael Konigsberg to join the California Bar Association despite taking the Fifth Amendment when asked whether he was a member of the Communist Party. Handed down on June 17, 1957, a date that anti-Communists would thereafter call "Red Monday," both *Watkins* and *Sweezy* curbed the power of legislative bodies to ask individuals about their past political associations. Both decisions highlighted that the Court was moving away from the hysteria of the McCarthy era.

Welch was hardly alone in wanting to impeach Warren. After *Pennsylvania v. Nelson,* the *National Review* wondered why the Kremlin "need[ed] a fifth column in the United States so long as the Supreme Court is determined to be so helpful." After "Red Monday," President Eisenhower said that appointing Warren was the "biggest damn fool thing I ever did."[16] Strom Thurmond had called for Warren's impeachment. Rosalie Gordon's popular *Nine Men Against America: The Supreme Court and Its Attack on American Liberties,* published in 1958, also inspired Robert's call for Warren's removal. The JBS reprinted *Nine Men Against America* and sent the book to chapter leaders and subscribers to *American Opinion.* If "we could get 1 million Americans to read" *Nine Men Against America,* Welch said in July 1961, "Warren's impeachment . . . would follow as shortly and swiftly as children dash for an open box of candy." Welch urged members to write many letters to their US legislators "in restrained language" with "sound reason" calling for Warren's removal. He also called for members to form "Impeach Warren Committees" and urged other organizations to get behind the effort. Once again, Welch believed that if the American people had access to the truth, they would solve their problems.

In August 1961, Welch introduced a new front in the campaign to impeach Warren with an essay-writing contest for undergraduates. The prize money was $2,500. The winner was Eddie Rose, who, while not a member of the JBS, said he shared "98% of their views." But by June 1962, Robert knew that impeachment was a long shot and relegated the campaign to a "long-range priority." Still, "Impeach Earl Warren" JBS signs appeared on cars, roadside billboards, barns, and boats. In 1963, Roman Catholic priest Francis Fenton was censured by the Bridgeport, Connecticut, diocese for encouraging the impeachment of Warren to his parishioners.[17] And certainly the Left used the JBS's campaign against Warren, along with the "Eisenhower letter," to portray the Society as unreasonable, dangerous, and extremist.

17
Goldwater in '60, 1960

At the close of the Eisenhower years, Robert Welch's mind turned to the 1960 presidential election. He dreaded the thought of Richard Nixon in the White House. Nixon was the consummate fake politician, thought Welch. For one, Welch never considered Nixon a conservative, despite his anti-Communist credentials from the Hiss case. Nixon was an opportunist and "one of the ablest, shrewdest, most disingenuous, and slipperiest politicians that ever showed up on the American scene." In Welch's view, Nixon wasn't "committed to anything other than the career of Richard Nixon."[1] Robert never forgave Nixon for the corrupt bargain that he believed was struck in 1952 when he and Eisenhower promised Earl Warren the position of chief justice of the Supreme Court in return for support from the California delegation at the Republican convention. As far as Welch was concerned, Nixon was instrumental in destroying Robert Taft's bid for the presidency.

Meanwhile Nixon's primary competitor for the Republican presidential nomination, Nelson Rockefeller, personified for Welch and Clarence Manion everything that was corrupt and wrong about the eastern establishment. An internationalist, a globalist who backed Wall Street over Main Street, Rockefeller was given everything in life, never had to run his own business, or worry about paying his loans. Heck, he probably never had any debts in his life. In an effort to keep Nixon or Rockefeller from succeeding Eisenhower, Robert began working to establish a conservative third party.

In October 1959, Robert Welch, William F. Buckley, Dallas radio host Dan Smoot, the New Orleans–based publisher of the *Independent American* Kent Courtney, *Farm and Ranch* magazine publisher Tom Anderson, secretary of the States' Rights Party of Louisiana Medford Evans, Dallas rancher and historian J. Evetts Haley, former Utah governor J. Bracken Lee, Revilo Oliver, and 1,000 other conservatives representing thirty-four states met in Chicago's Morrison Hotel at the "New Party Rally." They intended to launch a third party as a national amalgam of the States' Rights Party in Louisiana, the Conservative Party in New Jersey, and other third parties. It would pick up where T. Coleman Andrews left off in 1956 and attempt to get on the ballot in thirty states in 1960. They believed the Republican and Democratic parties had merged their platforms and principles, and no longer had clear-cut differences. "Changing from Eisenhower to Rockefeller, Nixon, Symington or Kennedy," Tom Anderson said, "is like leaving the diaper on the baby and just changing the pin." "There's no difference between the old parties—people haven't been given a choice," said Courtney.[2]

The "New Party Rally" convened panels, heard a stemwinder from Buckley, and held an evening session featuring Smoot and somebody named Robert Lee. They passed measures favoring the repeal of the personal income tax, curbing the Supreme Court, eliminating foreign aid, protecting states' rights, abolishing Social Security, passing the Bricker amendment, outlawing the Communist Party, and giving the United States' seat in the United Nations to Red China.[3] J. Bracken Lee provocatively announced his support for a preventive war with the Soviet Union. "Let's get the war over with, like we did with Hitler."[4]

Barry Goldwater caught their eye as a potential nominee in 1960 if he would leave the GOP, but Goldwater rejected the appeal. Other possible nominees included Strom Thurmond, William Jenner, and Dan Smoot.[5] After J. Bracken Lee mentioned a Jenner-Thurmond ticket, Clarence Manion, Welch's friend and JBS council member, said "personally, nothing would please me more." Manion, like Welch, came to embrace the language and politics of states' rights with more alacrity by the 1960s, even while anti-Communism drove his politics. Other rally attendees wanted Arkansas governor Orval Faubus, who opposed integration at Little Rock in 1957, but Manion preferred the idea of a revolt in the Democratic Party led by South Carolina's governor Ernest

Hollings. Manion saw civil rights as a growing problem for Democrats in the South and spotted an opportunity to divide the party. Hollings wanted nothing to do with it.

Despite the participation of Welch and Buckley, the "New Party Rally" effort was a bust. Manion thought that it just repeated the regional problem of the 1956 T. Coleman Andrews campaign, which had garnered only a small percentage of the popular vote. Much of the "New Party Rally" support came from the South, and few midwesterners were present. But Manion was happy about this because it meant that Goldwater, though a long shot, was still a possibility in 1960. Manion saw dreams walking. Manion was always ambivalent about establishing a third party as the best move for conservatives and ultimately decided that working within the Republican Party was the better choice. In 1959, he founded the Draft Goldwater organization. He still expected the effort to fail, but Manion held onto a dream scenario that a conservative third party behind Goldwater, a bevy of new conservative activists, and an unnamed southern Democrat as vice president would lead the Right into the White House on election day.

Manion was a fascinating paradox: a stubborn realist who could be quixotic. His "politics were largely anticorporate in sentiment and Roman Catholic in orientation," observed historian Donald Critchlow.[6] Manion attended St. Mary's in Henderson, Kentucky, and then Catholic University in Washington, DC; by 1941 he was the dean of the University of Notre Dame in Indiana. Manion had rejected FDR's efforts to intervene in World War II because he distrusted the Wasps who led both parties, opposed "bigness" in both government and business, and abhorred regimentation. Manion was emblematic of the important Catholics who were joining the John Birch Society and committing to the conservative movement. Half of the JBS's members were Catholics, estimated Welch. Joe McCarthy had inspired a whole generation of conservative Catholics to embrace anti-Communism, making the John Birch Society a natural home for them. "Our activities," Welch said, "have constituted primarily a continuation of the effort begun by Joe McCarthy. But with one vital difference. McCarthy had no grassroots organization for implementing his arguments or extending his reach. And without such permanently organized popular support he and his whole effort could be, and were, completely destroyed."[7] Welch went to his grave convinced that if the John Birch Society had been around in 1954, McCarthy would never have been censured and would have succeeded.

Manion promised to protect the "little fellow in business and politics," lamented the rise of the "militant old-fashioned individualists" on Wall Street, and savaged "the pagan all-powerful" state. For Manion, the "self-evident principles of God" were the basis of government. When man mistakenly arrived at the conclusion that God was not "the masthead of every properly constituted political system," Communism and fascism became inevitable.

Robert Welch, Barry Goldwater, and Clarence Manion believed in many of the same principles. Goldwater wanted to roll back Communism. He wanted to end trade with the Eastern Bloc, and stop trade with the Soviet Union. He opposed foreign aid and supported right-to-work laws. He advocated a first-strike nuclear policy, opposed arms-control agreements, wanted to abolish the income tax, rescind official recognition of Russia, blockade Cuba before the Cuban missile crisis, and end the Vietnam War with tactical nuclear weapons. For sure, Goldwater never said Sputnik was a hoax, knew the difference between a Communist and a liberal Democrat, and never called Eisenhower a Communist, but his worldview reflected that of many in the John Birch Society.[8] Despite the contemporary tendency to see Goldwater as a temperate figure, he was a man of the radical Right.

Welch admired Goldwater, even though he was a politician, writing of him in the *Blue Book*: "Barry Goldwater has political know-how and the painstaking genius to use that know-how with regard to infinite details. He is a superb political organizer, and inspires deep and lasting loyalty. He is absolutely sound in his Americanism, has the political and moral courage to stand by his Americanist principles, and in my opinion can be trusted to stand by them until hell freezes over. I'd love to see him president of the United States, and maybe some day we shall."[9]

Manion and Welch agreed on Goldwater and much else, but rifts between the two began to show. Whereas Manion was completely committed to Goldwater as a candidate, Welch saw his role in the conservative movement not for the promotion of candidates for public office but the edification of the American people about the perfidious conspiracy. That is why Manion was perturbed when Welch allegedly used Manion's Draft Goldwater Committee to recruit members into the John Birch Society. Manion was not the only conservative to be offended by Welch's attempt to benefit from the Draft Goldwater movement.[10]

Manion successfully convinced Goldwater that Americans needed an introduction to the conservative philosophy that Goldwater personified. If that happened, Manion saw Goldwater as having the best chance to bridge the chasm between the midwestern Republicans and the southern Democrats who embraced states' rights and opposed civil rights. Manion sought a writer who could introduce Goldwater to a larger segment of the American public and found L. Brent Bozell, William F. Buckley's brother-in-law, and arranged for him to ghostwrite Goldwater's *The Conscience of a Conservative*. Manion published and distributed the book through Victor Publishing, a nonprofit he established. Appearing in March 1960, the little book became a bestseller. Welch was impressed, saying that "the *Conscience of a Conservative* pulls no punches and is a very forceful presentation of the Americanist point of view."[11]

For many Americans, *The Conscience of a Conservative* was an introduction to American conservatism. According to it, conservatism buttressed "the dignity of the individual human being" and was "at odds with dictators who ruled by terror and equally those gentler collectivists who ask our permission to play God with the human race."[12] America needed to win the Cold War, and victory could not be achieved if America continued to lavish the world with foreign aid and provide Americans expensive domestic programs. Austerity and sacrifice at home, and a belligerent foreign policy abroad were necessary, Goldwater said. America's military needed to be second to none, argued Goldwater, because the "Communists' aim is to conquer the world."

As John Kennedy and Richard Nixon barnstormed across the United States in pursuit of the presidency, *The Conscience of a Conservative* captured the imaginations of millions with its implicit argument that Eisenhower's foreign policy and domestic policy were giant failures. Goldwater echoed some of the themes Welch had broached in *The Politician*. The book attacked Ike for supporting foreign trade, backing a nuclear testing ban, and backing a summit with Khrushchev.

It assailed Eisenhower's expansion of Social Security. It challenged Eisenhower's willingness to tolerate federal programs to build highways, clear slums, and reform education policies that belonged in the jurisdiction of the states.

Manion led the charge, but other prominent members of the John Birch Society were very active in the Goldwater movement. While JBS council member and lifelong Democrat Tom Anderson said, "I'd rather have Strom Thurmond any day of the week," he campaigned across the country for the Arizona senator and referred to himself as a member of the "Goldwater branch of the Republican Party." As far as he was concerned, Goldwater was the real deal. So believed Robert Welch, who wrote a generous profile of the "Fighter from Phoenix" as early as the March 1958 *American Opinion*. Robert thus took some credit for Goldwater's rise to fame.[13]

Committed to his educational mission, Robert never mandated that members should back Goldwater in 1960 but announced as early as March that he would. "We are," Welch said, "aware that some of our most influential members are convinced today that, under all of the circumstances that now prevail, it is their best course to support Richard Nixon for the Republican nomination." Robert continued: "There is nothing wrong with so deciding" because "the John Birch Society merely wants each of its members to use his or her own best judgment in such matters. But there is also nothing wrong with my stating that, as an individual American citizen, I have been a supporter of Goldwater for the presidency since years before the Society was founded, and that—being careful not to commit the Society in any way—I personally shall continue that support."[14]

Welch appreciated Goldwater's willingness to stand up to the Soviet Union, and he celebrated Goldwater's March 15 speech in the Senate urging American withdrawal of diplomatic recognition from the Soviet Union. "This was reported in some newspapers," Welch wrote, "but the conspiracy of silence against Goldwater is so strong that you may not even have heard about it." Welch urged members to write to the senator announcing their approbation: "Let's show Senator Goldwater that there is indeed, a very 'substantial body' of such opinion. Let's flood him with letters of approval, and get all of our friends we can to increase the flood."[15]

The John Birch Society may have been "wild about Barry," but Barry did not reciprocate toward Robert. For him, the Eisenhower controversy had been bad news. Goldwater actively lobbied leaders of the JBS council to cut their ties with Welch. "Remove Bob Welch and the Society cannot be attacked," Goldwater told Robert Love, a council member. The man who would yell "extremism in the defense of liberty is no vice" in 1964 was not in the early years of the decade about to allow himself to be surrounded by folks considered extremist.

Despite the efforts of Manion, it was all for nothing. Goldwater had made it openly clear that under no circumstances would he be a candidate in 1960. Goldwater endorsed Nixon. But at the Republican National Convention, Nixon compromised with Rockefeller on the civil rights plank of the platform. Goldwater called Nixon's compromise the GOP's Munich. Conservatives remained hopeful that Goldwater would challenge Nixon for the nomination. Goldwater allowed his name to be placed before the delegates. He then withdrew it, and demonstrations erupted on the floor. "We had our chance," Goldwater told the delegates. "Let's grow up conservatives. If we want to take this party back—and I think we can someday, let's get to work."

Nixon lost to Kennedy, but Manion's work had made Goldwater the front runner for 1964. Manion provided an effective syndicated radio program to maintain conservative hopes that a Goldwater nomination remained a possibility in the future. His programs reached millions of conservatives during the brief thousand days of Kennedy, and together with the John Birch Society, Manion dampened the dreams of Camelot. But Welch was crestfallen and felt that Goldwater had let conservatives down. L. Brent Bozell had murmured "that son of a bitch" when Goldwater gave his "grow up" line, and Welch was equally indignant. He was certain that "members of the John Birch Society throughout the nation were responsible for about one third of the Goldwater 'boom' and Barry let them down by not fighting hard enough for the nomination" in 1960.[16]

Robert wrote, "the conscience of our conservative and the exigent danger of our country, should have led Goldwater to take a bolder course." "It is my personal opinion that Goldwater failed to realize the size, and especially the earnestness of the following throughout the country that supplied his strength." Welch dreamed of an alternative speech: "Suppose Goldwater had said . . . : 'every single thing we conservative Republicans asked for, to justify our continued loyalty to the Party, has been denied us. In the surrender by Nixon to Rockefeller, . . . we have been completely ignored. There no longer being any place for conservative Americans within the Republican Party, therefore, anymore than within the Democratic Party, the time has come when the conservatives of both parties must unite to save our country from socialist stagnation and Communist tyranny. For those who wish to stand on American principles with me, the American Party is now in existence, as of this minute, with a membership of one. We have no other course.'" Welch continued: "That statement would've electrified the nation." "By Goldwater's own statesmanship over many years, by the intensive and uniting work of tens of thousands of patriotic Americans, and by the gradually developed concatenation of circumstances, there had been created for him a rendezvous with history which it was a tragedy for him not to keep."[17]

But Welch viewed the 1960 election as a battle between two puppets. John F. Kennedy was the "longtime stooge" of United Auto Workers Union head Walter Reuther, and Richard Nixon was simply Nelson Rockefeller's "newly acquired stooge." The election would decide merely whether Rockefeller or Reuther would "be the boss of the United States under a one-world international socialist government." "We have no clear grasp of what is going on," Welch lamented, "or how near we are to the end of American independence."[18]

Despite Eisenhower's impending departure, one month before the election, Welch issued a strong condemnation of him and developed a new conspiracy theory: "It is entirely possible that the Soviets might be planning to have President Eisenhower elected the first president of the United Nations, shortly after he ceases to be President of what is now referred to in so many parts of the world—with far more sadness than humor—as the most important Soviet satellite." "If Mr. Eisenhower could," Welch continued, "to the great acclaim and satisfaction of the American people be made the first 'World President,' and if he could then be traveling or golfing most of the time . . . then the advisors and assistants by whom he would be surrounded could carry out in his name . . . practically every" policy "their Communist bosses desired," and the United States could be pulled into a "one-world super government." Welch added: "it is at least possible that this whole maneuver 'is in the works.'"[19]

FIGURE 1 Welch was fiercely proud of his library of 5,000 books. He must have had a photographic memory. He knew by heart most of the words on the pages in the books behind him. The words were his soldiers. He could call upon them at a moment's notice.

FIGURE 2 Robert Welch wielding his most powerful weapon: his pen.

FIGURE 3 Senators Joe McCarthy and Robert Taft—two of Robert Welch's favorite politicians—shake hands. Welch worked hard for Taft in 1952, but the US senator from Ohio lost the Republican nomination to Dwight D. Eisenhower. Welch believed the election was rigged for Eisenhower. Senator McCarthy attacked Secretary of State Dean Acheson and former Army Chief of Staff George Marshall as part of "a conspiracy on a scale so immense so as to dwarf any previous such venture in the history of man." McCarthy's attacks on the US Army set the stage for Robert Welch to declare that "beyond any reasonable doubt," President Dwight Eisenhower, the former head of the US Army, was "a dedicated, conscious agent of the Communist conspiracy."

FIGURE 4 Harry Truman flanked by Secretary of Defense George Marshall, on the president's right, and Secretary of State Dean Acheson, on his left. In *May God Forgive Us,* Robert Welch denounced Marshall and Acheson and other high-level Truman administration officials as un-American traitors for "losing China" to the Communists.

FIGURE 5 Robert Welch saw Douglas MacArthur as a contemporary George Washington. In April 1951, President Harry Truman fired MacArthur, and for good reason: MacArthur did not understand that President Truman was his boss and commander in chief. The decision dumbfounded Welch, who had trouble sleeping. In 1951, Welch wrote *May God Forgive Us*, concluding that General MacArthur had been fired by Joseph Stalin, the premier of the Soviet Union.

FIGURE 6 Former president Dwight Eisenhower walks with GOP congressmen in 1961. One month before the 1960 presidential election, Welch issued a new conspiracy theory about Eisenhower: "It is entirely possible that the Soviets might be planning to have President Eisenhower elected the first president of the United Nations, shortly after he ceases to be President of what is now referred to in so many parts of the world—with far more sadness than humor—as the most important Soviet satellite." To the immediate right of Eisenhower is John Rousselot. After losing his congressional seat in 1962, Rousselot became the JBS's public relations director and was tasked with selling Welch's book *The Politician*, a slightly watered-down version of the infamous private letter calling Eisenhower a "dedicated, conscious agent of the communist conspiracy."

FIGURE 7 In the early 1950s, William F. Buckley wrote that Robert Welch was "the author of two of the finest pamphlets this country has read in a decade," meaning *May God Forgive Us* and *The Life of John Birch*. Buckley eventually concluded that Welch's conspiratorial style was bad for the conservative movement and tried to drive him out of it. Buckley failed. Welch was never excommunicated by Buckley, and Welch's conspiratorial style of politics remains powerful to this day.

FIGURE 8 At a John Birch Society meeting in 1961, members pledge allegiance to the flag of the United States.

FIGURE 9 Alan Stang convinced Robert Welch to mount a strong campaign that the civil rights movement was controlled by the Communists. In 1965, the John Birch Society published Stang's book *It's Very Simple: The True Story of Civil Rights*. In 1968, Welch proposed that the Communists killed Martin Luther King because he was more valuable to them as a dead martyr than a live human being.

FIGURE 10 A member of the John Birch Society shows her support for the Vietnam War in New York City in 1967. In the mid-1960s, Robert Welch believed Vietnam to be a "phony war," in which both sides were being run from the Kremlin. By 1967, Welch called for victory in Vietnam.

FIGURE 11 The John Birch Society continued to be a strong force in the 1970s. At a JBS meeting in 1970, members pledge their allegiance.

FIGURE 12 Many “hardhats,” or White working-class men in the construction industry, found a home in the John Birch Society in the 1970s. This attendee of the JBS’s 1972 New England Rally for God, Family, and Country held at Boston’s Statler Hilton Hotel proudly displays his provocative pin: “Sock it to ’em Spiro,” referencing President Nixon’s combative vice president, Spiro Agnew.

FIGURE 13 A young man peeks above John Birch Society literature at the New England Rally for God, Family, and Country in 1972. JBS's book publishing division, Western Islands Press, doubled in reach and size in the 1970s. The books were very popular among the Far Right and sold well. JBS books were hawked at booths at county fairs and business conventions. One book, *Teddy Bare,* about Ted Kennedy and Chappaquiddick, made the *New York Times* bestseller list for three months.

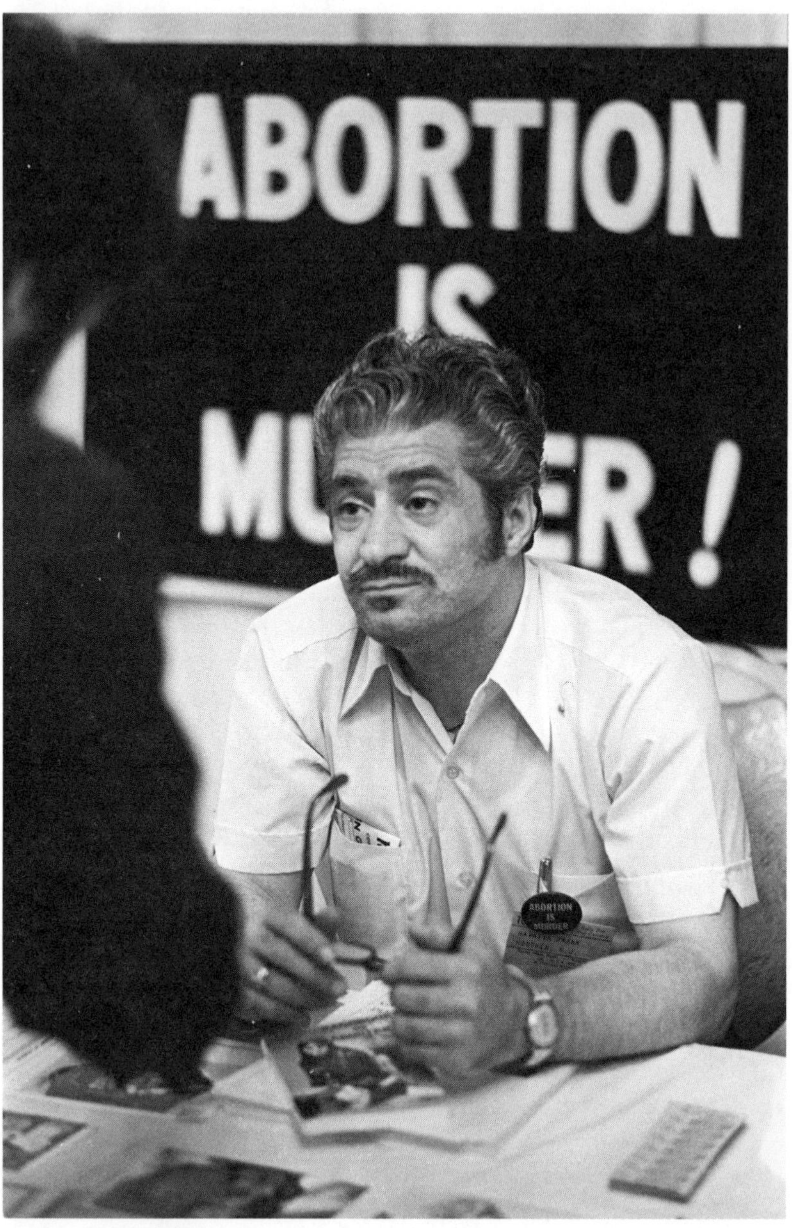

FIGURE 14 An anti-abortion attendee at the John Birch Society's 1972 New England Rally for God, Family, and Country. In the 1970s, the JBS established ad hoc committees. These committees helped bridge the gap between capitalist libertarians who wanted smaller government, lower taxes, and less regulation and the social conservatives concerned with societal transformations in gender rights, the liberalization of sexuality and pornography, and civil rights reforms. In this way, the JBS constructed the scaffolding of what became new conservative coalitions. Issues that preoccupied these ad hoc groups in the 1970s included abortion, the Equal Rights Amendment, homosexuality, the United Nations, sex education, and tax reform.

FIGURE 15 Captivated spectators appear at the JBS's 1972 New England Rally for God, Family, and Country, held at the Statler Hilton Hotel, Park Square, Boston.

18

Staccato Jabs, 1961–1962

Welch worried about the incoming Kennedy administration. Kennedy was wet behind the ears, green, untested. More important, Welch and other conservatives abhorred Kennedy and his policies, which would send the country down the road to serfdom. Kennedy's support for senior health insurance, civil rights, federal expansion into public education would further the socialization of the country. Whereas Kennedy saw the long-standing legacy of racial prejudice and inequities as the cause of the growing civil rights movement, Welch saw the unrest as nothing more than Communism at work.[1] Kennedy, who enjoyed foreign policy more than domestic affairs, advocated the New Frontier in part to mollify the civil rights movement with job training, education, and work opportunities.[2] Critics like Welch criticized Kennedy's plans to "socialize medicine," expand the role of the state, and restrict the freedom of business.

Despondent, Robert proclaimed that president-elect "Kennedy has received no mandate for establishing any more of a welfare state than we already have." Welch continued: "we want no 'bipartisan honeymoon' of liberals having everything their own way" as Franklin Roosevelt did.[3] He also attacked Kennedy's early appointees: "Almost to a man they are visibly in favor of a one world socialist government and will do everything they can to bring it about." Robert wrote in January 1961 "that the new administration far more openly than any that have preceded it, will be working for the same things—most of the same things—as the international Communists." "Whether the intention be defined as treason," Robert added, "the results will include the total surrender of the independence of the United States" and the triumph of the Communists.[4]

John Birch Society council member Tom Anderson also loathed the young upstart in the White House. "Our menace is not the Big Red Army from without, but the Big Pink Enemy within. Our menace is the KKK—Kennedy, Kennedy, and Kennedy," he observed.[5] Republicans and southern Democrats in Congress not only rejected Kennedy's domestic policy but attacked his foreign policy too. Kennedy thought that the Third World was attracted to Communism because of its widespread poverty and other social causes; Welch and other conservatives regarded this as nonsense.[6] Welch and many on the Right decried the administration's increasing affinity for the language of peace and JFK's frequent calls for nuclear disarmament to ease tensions with the Soviet Union. Barry Goldwater and John Tower, among a host of conservative Republican politicians and retired generals, admonished JFK's early mistakes at the Bay of Pigs and his less than aggressive response to the Soviet buildup of nuclear weapons in Cuba.[7]

The Right was perturbed that the American public found the boyish, shaky commander in chief to be magnetic, intelligent, and persuasive. They assailed what they saw as blatant manipulation and management of the media, reminiscent of the Roosevelt administration. While rumors swirled in Washington and Georgetown cocktail parties of Kennedy's infidelities and health problems, the Right questioned Kennedy's character on a different front. "I'm for Jack Kennedy showing less profile and more courage," said the quotable Tom Anderson, "and the other super-rich-by-inheritance, built-in-guilt-complex do-gooders should share their own wealth and not mine."[8]

Meanwhile Kennedy and others on the Left were deeply concerned by the growth of the John Birch Society and the broader conservative movement. Kennedy worried that political activism on the Right was making it more difficult to ease tensions with the Soviet Union, among other problems. The mainstream press also became preoccupied with the influence of ultraconservatives. In the *New York Times Magazine*, Alan Barth, a liberal professor, wrote that conservatives were "in a rage to destroy." The Right's "darling," Barry Goldwater, Barth wrote, would soon have to "choose between the support of the Right and the support of real Republicans who will not care to forsake the traditions of their party for a forlorn kind of fascism." Throughout the Kennedy years, the Left held that the Right was racist, anti-Semitic, and prone to fascism. In the *Nation*, Fred Cook observed: the "Radical Right was not the face of fascism as we have known it in Europe. But unmistakably it is a face bearing the marks of a sickness that could develop into fascism."

By contrast, Daniel Bell's *The Radical Right* identified what he called the Ultra Right as not really anti-Communists but beleaguered pariahs whose isolation was due in large part to having no real contemporary purpose. Welch and other "Ultras" were attacking "modernity." According to Bell, people on the Right like Welch tended to be part of an older generation of executives and managers from small-town America who had become dislocated from modern society and suffered from their loss of status. Needless to say, Robert Welch did not feel dislocated or low in status. He had a successful marriage and a fine home in a pleasant suburb, actively participated in his community and professional organizations, and enjoyed his adoring children and grandchildren. Welch never suffered status envy, at least as measured by the fortune in his bank account. *Danger on the Right* by Arnold Forster and Benjamin Epstein was even more pointed in its appraisal: Welch was authoritarian and a danger to democracy, despite his decentralized management style and commitment to bringing democracy to China just as Douglas MacArthur did in Japan.[9]

Now it is true that Welch could be brusque and had an affinity for polemics and apocalyptic discourse. His tendency to make extravagant and hyperbolic statements was evident throughout the pages of the *Blue Book* and the JBS's *Bulletin*. For instance, he observed in the *Blue Book* that his fellow citizens had "only a few more years before the country in which you live will become four separate provinces in a worldwide Communist domination ruled by police state methods from the Kremlin."[10]

And it is true that Welch employed what some might consider "Communist methods" to vanquish the conspiracy.[11] He told members to infiltrate PTAs. He established front groups. He justified this strategy by pointing out that his merciless opponent would do absolutely anything to achieve world domination. If the JBS was going to defeat the Communist conspiracy, how couldn't the most successful anti-Communist organization in the world use the same tactics if need be?

And it is true that Welch often exercised nineteenth-century views in the twentieth century. Although he often called his wife the ablest Bircher, and he envisioned women not only as members but directors of chapters, in truth the most essential leadership roles were given to corporate men like himself. Class, wealth, and occupational status were all factors in the Birch Society's hierarchical structure, as well as in Robert's worldview.[12]

It wasn't only in politics that Welch saw the Red threat. In the early 1960s, Welch and many on the Right worried that the popular culture was making Americans become soft and unwilling to fight. Some in the Society suggested that the Soviets had produced novels and films depicting nuclear holocaust such as Nevil Shute's *On the Beach*, Peter Bryant's *Two Hours to Doom*, and Stanley Kubrick's *Dr. Strangelove*. Welch understood these portrayals of the Cold War as propaganda aimed at turning Americans against the prospect of what might be a necessary nuclear war. He held that their true purpose was to weaken the United States by convincing the public that peaceful coexistence with the Soviet Union was not only possible but the only way to survive. Welch argued that only an aggressive and belligerent posture from all Americans would deter the Soviet Union from a nuclear first strike. Doomsday was a liberal illusion of the Kennedy White House wonks and their Communist masters, said Welch.[13]

Despite liberal claims, Welch believed Soviet Premier Nikita Khrushchev was as bent on world domination as Stalin. Welch doubted the sincerity of Khrushchev's supposed repudiation of Stalin in 1956 and concluded that Lenin's plan to bury the West was alive and well. Arms control was a Communist ploy, argued Welch. The wily Khrushchev would never commit his country to a treaty in earnest; he merely sought to convince Americans to put down their arms. John Birch Society members devoured books like Fred Schwarz's *You Can Trust the Communists (to be Communists)* and Robert Morris's *Disarmament: Weapon of Conquest*. Welch found Morris's conspiratorial worldview to be convincing and sincere.

Billy James Hargis, Robert Morris, Edwin Walker, and US Representative John Rousselot participated in the same anti-Communist, anti–civil rights, and anti-nuclear disarmament crusades. Probably the most eloquent spokesmen of anybody in the John Birch Society, Rousselot shared Morris's opposition to disarmament. President Kennedy wanted a nuclear test ban treaty for the atmosphere, but at Hargis's 1962 Christian Crusade in Tulsa, Rousselot claimed JFK wanted "total and complete disarmament." While the congressman was unwilling to call the president's advisors—special assistant Arthur Schlesinger Jr. and national security advisor Walt Rostow—Communists, he accused them of "show[ing] bad judgment, to say the least." The "un-American," "best and brightest" of the New Frontier, Rousselot said, were brainwashing and "mentally condition[ing] the populace to forsake Americanism and adopt Leftist politics that would ultimately destroy American sovereignty."[14]

Rousselot presented the fascinating worldview of the John Birch Society that day in Tulsa. He said that after Khrushchev met with Eisenhower in September 1959, full disarmament was placed on the table, and Khrushchev even brought the "Soviet Plan for World Disarmament" to the United Nations. Nuclear weapons would go first, Rousselot maintained. Then US forces would be placed under UN control. Finally, "law and order" would be left up to a "small police force." The Communists, the congressman continued, would create chaos in America, which would be engulfed by "extensive agitation." Students and other troublemakers, who allegedly sought disarmament but really wanted one-world government, would riot. And then one morning, the United States would be gone, merged with Russia. Rousselot said that this was neither a fictional account nor a horror movie: it was happening before Americans' very eyes. Moreover, it wasn't even a secret. Rousselot said that a few months after an important disarmament meeting in Crimea, the State Department published and disseminated *Freedom from War*. Then the UN convened, and the American delegation offered its three-phase plan "for General and Complete Disarmament in a Peaceful World." First, came an abatement in the armed forces of the United States and USSR, then the establishment of a permanent UN peace force, and finally the destruction of all nuclear weapons, "except for those of agreed types and quantities to be used by the UN peace force." The plan, according to its authors, he said, sought to establish a "free, secure and, peaceful world of independent states adhering to common standards of justice and international conduct and subjecting the use of force to the rule of law."[15]

Dan Smoot sounded a similar alarm in *The Invisible Government*, warning that the Council on Foreign Relations sought to hand over control of the US nuclear arsenal to a UN police force, leading to the United States' merger with the Soviet Union. When the Soviets expressed interest in nuclear disarmament, the purpose was never pacific; they sought to cause turmoil within the United States, leading ultimately to the loss of American sovereignty.

This nonsense, of course, was all a product of selective reading. While President Kennedy had made many overtures that nuclear weapons were far more dangerous than he realized when entering the office of the presidency, especially after the nearly catastrophic outcome of the Cuban missile crisis, there was never a blueprint for unilateral or bilateral disarmament by the United States. The UN document did exist, but Rousselot, Smoot, and Morris ignored that it specifically referenced the continued existence of "independent states" and focused instead on the consequences of a permanent UN peace force. Rousselot claimed that the US program and "the one that Mr. Khrushchev gave in 1959" are "are almost identical." The congressman's strategy was the one employed by Smoot: ignore one crucial fact and emphasize another that helps your argument. Rousselot was not calling anybody a Communist, but he was alleging that American officials were following the policy of the Soviet Union.[16]

Robert Welch worried not only about American traitors taking orders from Moscow but also about the opponent ninety miles away in Cuba. Fidel Castro's rise to power provided absolute proof that the Communists were intent on establishing a world government in the Western Hemisphere. As Cuba became ground zero for the Cold War, Welch took great pride in his 1958 prediction that Castro was a Communist. Welch was not the only JBS member who made accurate predictions about Cuba. Even before Kennedy defeated Nixon, Phyllis Schlafly, whom Welch called a "very loyal member of the John Birch Society," argued that the Soviet Union would attempt to place missiles in Cuba. Welch implored the president not to give "up our naval base at Guantánamo or our exclusive authority over the Panama Canal."

The "developments in the Caribbean are horrible, frightening and of terrific importance," he added. Welch was convinced that Castro had grander designs for "revolution across Latin America." Invasions by Communist forces have been attempted since 1958 against Panama, Nicaragua, and other Latin American countries, he said, with the assault always "launched from Cuban soil under Castro's direction with direct support from" Romulo Betancourt's government of Venezuela. Welch claimed Castro wanted "to take over the whole Caribbean, and then all of Central America, as rapidly as possible."[17]

Castro's nationalization of two US utility companies, as well as Cuba's sugar industry, were all that Americans needed to know of his intentions, Welch warned. Welch also condemned foreign aid to Castro in 1960: "The sending of one quarter of $1 million to our arch enemy Castro, for military aid—which our government has done right within the past three months—is still plain unadulterated treason to the United States." "We want every congressman and senator fully to realize that Fidel Castro is a vicious, dangerous, clear enemy of the United States."[18]

In 1960, the United States did impose an economic embargo of Cuba, and diplomatic relations ceased. Also, the Eisenhower administration authorized assassination attempts to remove Castro. Senator Kennedy made Cuba a central issue in his presidential campaign, attacking the administration for allowing a "Communist satellite" as close as "eight minutes by jet." After winning, Kennedy gave the green light to invade the island and overthrow Castro. Despite having grave reservations about the plan's viability, the young president concluded mistakenly that discontent for Castro was strong enough that the amphibious landing of CIA-trained Cuban exiles would foment a more general uprising. The Bay of Pigs invasion was a complete disaster; 10 percent of the 1,453 exiles were killed, and 1,189 were captured.[19]

Welch had wanted the invasion, but then eviscerated Kennedy for his "insurrectionary fiasco." "The venality of our government in cooperating with, condoning, or even permitting any such humiliation of the American nation and people is almost beyond belief, even in these days when the unbelievable occurs every hour on the hour." Castro had "emerged far stronger than ever, not only having put down a revolt, but as the Communist David who had defeated the great capitalist Goliath." Welch later concluded that the botched invasion was not botched at all. It was "planned to happen . . . from the very inception of the whole scheme." Because traitorous US government officials wanted to safeguard Castro, the Cuban leader was "able to count on the full cooperation of Washington at every turn."[20]

In a press conference about the Bay of Pigs on April 21, 1961, Kennedy rebutted the allegations of the John Birch Society that internal subversion had much to do with the invasion's failure. Kennedy said the JBS was not wrestling "with the real problems which are created by the Communist advance around the world." Later, he said the JBS was misdirected in seeking "solutions and safety in a complicated and dangerous world." The real problems were external not internal, Kennedy said, and it was tragic that some people peddled such nonsense.[21]

Welch did not think Kennedy was good for America, but he was great for the Society. The month following Kennedy's victory over Nixon, Welch celebrated the recent growth of the Society. "So far we have been doubling in size approximately once every four months. There have been one or two periods, such as the early part of 1960, when our numbers increased 100% in three months." Welch was optimistic about the prospects of further growth. "I do think that for the next year, and perhaps two, it is possible and practicable for us to double our size every six months or twice a year."[22]

But as the Society continued to grow throughout 1961, Robert felt beleaguered by the news media. "Having used the period of 1951–1956 to destroy Joe McCarthy," he later said, the media "set out exactly 10 years later with several times as much force, falsehood and determination to destroy the Society," at the bidding of their Communist masters. Welch called articles shredding the JBS and the Right "brazenly distorted," "maliciously libelous," and the work of the "AFL-CIO national battery of house organs."[23]

The second "attack" on the Birch Society began in January 1961 in California with an investigation by Hans Engh in the *Santa Barbara News-Press*. JBS membership in Santa Barbara County numbered in the hundreds. The rumors about Welch, Engh wrote, were "flying." His investigation regurgitated many of Jack Mabley's accusations, but Engh also accurately reminded readers that Welch encouraged Birchers to take over local PTAs. The following month, the paper added editorials that opined that democracy was as endangered by "extremists on the right as extremists on the left." The grand republic could not sustain "secret or semi-secret political organizations," which had "no place" in America. "Democracy," Engh wrote, "suffers when fear of communism leads to irresponsible, unsubstantiated charges of treason or evil connivance against our political, religious, educational or cultural leaders." "Americans needed to keep our balance in what we do."[24] Engh did not mention Joe McCarthy, but he did not need to.

In March, the *Los Angeles Times* took up the charge. Publisher Otis Chandler editorialized that Welch mistakenly held to the "treacherous fallacy that an honorable or noble objective justifies any means to achieve it." The problem with the Birchers, Chandler believed, was that they embraced the very "techniques and the rules of conspiracy to fight Communists in Communist fashion." Thus, the JBS weakened "the very strong case for conservatism," which the *Times* "believes implicitly in." "The *Times* does not believe that the argument for conservatism can be won . . . by smearing as enemies and traitors those with whom we sometimes disagree." The *Times* interpreted the JBS's aggressive letter-writing campaigns to mean the organization could not be dismissed as "tiresome" or a "comic-opera joke."[25]

The *Los Angeles Times* articles coincided with another vilification in *Time* magazine and an equally compelling and denunciatory assessment by North Dakota Republican senator Milton Young. *Time* magazine's "The Americanists" falsely alleged that the Society met in cells, rather than chapters, and its members followed the "hard-boiled dictatorial direction of one man." *Time* concluded that the entire objective of the John Birch Society council was to elect a leader in case Welch were assassinated. The magazine presented Welch as brooking no dissension within his ranks. Despite the assertion of actor Adolphe Menjou, diplomat Spruille Braden, and Clarence Manion that Robert was primarily interested in the fight for freedom, *Time* pointed out Welch's contempt for those who dissented from his views. To be sure, Welch's organization was hierarchical, but probably no more so than most corporate governing structures in mid-twentieth-century America. Welch fully admitted that he was in charge of the John Birch Society and did not tolerate disrespect or insubordination, but in truth he spent more time than he should have infighting with subordinates and trying to convince them to follow his lead. What's more, Welch's efforts at achieving consensus were often unsuccessful—like that of many American corporate heads. He had to tolerate dissension within the ranks because there was so much of it.

Time magazine went so far as to say that the John Birch Society was "barely a goose-step away from the formation of goon squads"—even though it had demonstrated no inclination toward violence. It also suggested that the organization was fascistic, saying that "Welch's 'Mein Kampf' is a masterpiece of invective called The Politician." The anti-Semitic characterization skirted libel but stuck.[26] Such characterizations ramped up in late 1961. FDR's youngest son, John Aspinwall Roosevelt, called the JBS an "un-American organization with incipient Hitler-like tendencies." Milton Young, who was becoming the chief critic of the JBS in Congress, said Welch "is aping Hitler and using the tactics Hitler used on his road to power." In June 1961, Mike Newberry released a forty-seven-page pamphlet, "The Fascist Revival: The Inside Story of the John Birch Society." Newberry highlighted the influence of big businesspeople on the JBS and referred to Welch as the "Fuhrer" throughout. He also pointed out that Hitler once used anti-Communism as well to defeat his enemies. "By blacklisting, persecuting, and jailing 'Communists,' the legal precedent and political foundation is [*sic*] established for the destruction of the liberties and rights of the whole people and the path to fascism is cleared of its first obstacle-democracy," observed Newberry. In an exposé in 1962, the *Saturday Evening Post* included a photo of Robert Welch juxtaposed next to the American Nazi Party's George Lincoln Rockwell. Welch was outraged, saying he admonished John Birch Society members that any association with anti-Semitism or racism was simply intolerable.

Even President Kennedy subtly compared Birchers to Nazis. "There have always been those fringes of our society who have sought to escape their own responsibility by finding a simple solution, an appealing slogan, or a convenient scapegoat," said the president on November 18. "They look suspiciously at their neighbors and their leaders. They call for 'a man on horseback' because they do not trust the people. . . . They equate the Democratic Party with the welfare state, the welfare state with socialism and socialism with communism. They object quite rightly to politics' intruding on the military—but they are anxious for the military to engage in politics."[27]

Welch blanched at the assertion that he or his organization was anti-Semitic. In April 1961, Welch called the charges of anti-Semitism "a dangerous weapon" that his nemeses were recklessly using to discredit him. Throughout his life, Welch said, I "probably had more good friends of the Jewish faith than any other Gentile in America." "I am just about as anti-Semitic as Willi Schlamm." Schlamm was a Jewish journalist who had helped found *National Review* and by this time was writing articles on foreign policy for *American Opinion*. Welch observed that he had Jewish friends and colleagues like Alfred Kohlberg, for whom he was a protégé.[28] What's more, his son, Hillard, had served in the US Army in Europe during World War II, fighting Hitler and all he stood for.[29]

The attacks on Welch as an anti-Semite had been ignited in part by his criticism of the anti-defamation league of B'nai B'rith, though Welch insisted that any such criticism was no more anti-Semitic than any disparagement of the Methodist Federation for Social Action was anti-Christian. Welch may have believed that, but he had little control over anti-Semitic statements by individual members of the Society, even when he denounced them.

Slobodan Draskovich was a problem for Welch throughout the early 1960s. Draskovich, a council member, had written an article in the *American Opinion* calling the United States' involvement in World War II against the Nazis a profound mistake. This extremely unpopular position reeked of anti-Semitism or at least a lack of patriotism. Though Draskovich had actually fought against the Nazis, he seemed to suggest that the United States had lost the war because the Soviet Union grew more powerful after it. The US war effort, he said, had only fostered Communism.[30]

Then there were Welch's own words in the Eisenhower letter, which continued to draw attention. In trying to find fault with Eisenhower, Welch became preoccupied with atrocities perpetuated on the Nazis and the German people by Eisenhower—a position some called callous and others anti-Semitic. For instance, Welch called Eisenhower the true author of the "Morgenthau Plan," which, as Welch put it, tried to convert "Germany into a goat pasture—so that it could never stand as a bulwark against the eventual Russian march across Europe." (Treasury Secretary Henry Morgenthau had indeed suggested permanently deindustrializing Germany after the war.) Welch also attacked Eisenhower for unfair treatment of Germans at the Nuremberg trials, where he participated "in the planning that brought them about, and in the gathering of the completely one-sided evidence on which they were based." It was too early for any sympathy toward Germany given its instigation of the war and the Holocaust. These writings served as grist for the mills for the charge that Robert Welch was anti-Semitic.[31]

Less grounded in Welch's writings were the charges that he sympathized with or propagated the *Protocols of the Elders of Zion*, one of the most notorious lies ever published. With its ludicrous, feverish, and grossly inaccurate fears of plots by Jews to seize control of the world economy and the print media, that anti-Semitic conspiracy theory resembled Welch's type of anti-Communist conspiracy theory. As blatant anti-Semitic rhetoric became less common by the 1950s, but still latent, the *Protocols* hindered the efforts of many anti-Communist activists, who were often chagrined to be associated with the *Protocols*. William F. Buckley noted this when he wrote Welch to lament that Welch was "cooperat[ing]" with Russell Maguire, the editor of *American Mercury*, who was prone to using the *Protocols* in his editorials. Buckley called Maguire "a considerable liability to the conservative cause."

Welch's own conspiratorial view of the origins of the *Protocols* posited that Lenin, or one of his followers, wrote them to discredit anti-Communist organizations like the John Birch Society. According to Welch, the *Protocols* "had been written to lay out the program which the Communists were to follow for the next two generations, but in such a manner that a large part of the blame would be misdirected onto others." By 1962, Welch was observing the "extensive, emphatic, and almost violent spread of anti-Semitic theories" and concluding that Communists were planting anti-Semites within the conservative movement—especially the John Birch Society—as agents-provocateurs and delegitimizing the movement by these means.[32]

In fact, Welch continued to give a blind eye to strident anti-Semites of the Old Right and continued to allow them to publish their screeds in the pages of *American Opinion* into the 1960s. He maintained correspondence with them at least into the 1960s as well. Even if we credit him for removing Oliver and others of his ilk from the John Birch Society, that misses the point: the fact that they were allowed in from the beginning demonstrates that Welch tolerated individuals who held abhorrent views about Jews and Judaism.

His blind spot developed in the 1930s but continued well into the 1960s, as Welch corresponded and associated with Maguire of the *American Mercury*, which was growing more anti-Semitic. Thus Welch and the Society were, as historian D. J. Mulloy observed, a "kind of bridge between the Old Right [of the 1930s,] of the 1940s, and the 1950s"—including the McCarthyite Right—and the New Right of the 1970s and 1980s, but Welch was never able to completely traverse the bridge from the anti-Semitism of the Old Right to the supposed philo-Semitism of the New Right.[33]

As a salesman, and a good one, Welch harbored an incessant need to please in his epistles. Being one to "gild the lily," or convince the reader with a touch of sophistry, he was prone to occasional duplicity and probably did not even know his own mind in some instances, as he kept up with his blizzard of correspondences often into the wee hours of the morning when he was far from fresh. Writing to the notoriously anti-Semitic Verne Kaub in February 1961, Welch noted his "respect and confidence and friendship for yourself." While Robert acknowledged that he and Kaub "do not see exactly eye to eye on some matters"—he was specifically referencing Jews—he wrote, "it is my very deep rooted intention to try to work on just as friendly terms as I possibly can with every good patriot in this country who is honestly and truly opposed to the Communist advance and willing to stand up and fight against that advance, despite whatever other characteristics any such person might have with which I would not be in sympathy." Here, Welch at least belied he was infallible, but also divulged his weakness for working with less than honorable men. Then he circled back with a caveat: "(Provided, of course, there is nothing dishonorable in either the character or the actions to be considered.)" Here he was being too clever by half. Welch continued: "Which is why I was perfectly willing to keep working with Russell Maguire and letting him reprint my material—for which Bill Buckley kept jumping all over me—even though Maguire certainly had some characteristics (having nothing to do with the Jews or anti-Semitism or any related matter in any respect) of which neither you nor I could possible [*sic*] approve." Here Welch was being facetious and employing more sophistry, but he was admitting that he would work with dishonorable men.[34]

In the same letter, Welch divulged to Kaub that he had asked Merwin Hart, another anti-Semite, to join his Committee on Endorsers. Hart accepted "despite the fact—and this is in the strictest confidence, between you and myself—I personally have been jumped on twice, the second time quite emphatically, by the ADL [Anti-Defamation League], or at least by one of its representatives, for my association with and support by Merwin Hart." Hart was on Welch's Committee Against Summit Entanglements and was a chapter leader of the John Birch Society. "But Merwin Hart is a man, like yourself, of solid conscience and great honor," Welch told Kaub.[35]

On the other hand, Welch commendably drew a hard line in the sand with Gerald L. K. Smith, probably the most ignominious former Hitlerite, publisher of the *Cross and the Flag*, advocate of Christian nationalism, and 1944 presidential candidate. "We must never be governed by aliens. We must keep control of our money and our blood," Smith once rather reprehensively declared.[36] Smith went too far for Welch, who excommunicated him.

Smith, Welch confessed to Kaub, "might not really be on our side."[37] In other words, Welch feared Smith was working with the Communists to paint the whole conservative movement as anti-Semitic. Smith was a Neutralizer, according to Welch. Welch continued to Kaub: "I decided that I wanted absolutely nothing to do with" Smith, "now or later, for reasons which at least cast doubt in my own mind as to his intentions."[38] In the final letter to Smith from Welch, their relationship was terminated, as Welch made it abundantly clear that Smith's position on Jews was to blame for the falling out. "In this fight against the Communist conspiracy, Mr. Smith, it is not possible for us to cooperate with you," Welch said, "because of a basic disagreement between us as to the main source of the strength of the conspiracy."[39] Welch saw the Communists as the primary source, whereas Smith saw Jews as the main figures. Welch explained to Smith that he had studied the matter closely for years and knew what he was talking about: "I believe that I have probably read everything that you have, on the subject at issue, from the earliest disclosures of the Protocols of Zion, through Henry Ford's 'International Jew,' through the writings of Robert H. Williams and Conde McGinley and a great many—including some of the leading writers in French and Spanish on the same subject—and I simply come out with a different conclusion."[40]

What was that conclusion? As was always the case with Welch, the answer was complicated and involved a peculiar conspiracy theory. He told Smith in his last letter that "I am, as I have said many times, fighting the Communists, and nobody else." But then Welch qualified this point. At some point, in traversing the bridge from Old Right to New Right, Welch got stuck. He refused to abandon his conviction that Jews played a secondary role in the conspiracy or that they were the ones who started such an unfounded conspiracy in the first place, a dangerous prevarication. Indeed, as he tried to meander his way over this invisible bridge, Welch fell back.

"In 1900 or 1905," Welch observed, "at the time of the first Russian revolution which was led by Trotsky, or in 1917, or even up to until the middle 1920s, the Communist conspiracy was largely a child or at least a ward of the Zionist conspiracy. And for that reason Jews were preponderant in the top levels of the communist hierarchy. But it seems equally clear to me that by 1937 or 1938, when Stalin had finally succeeded in taking into his own hands all of the reins of Communist power stretching out all over the world, the child had quite largely outgrown the parent—as so often happens in the case of organizations as well as individuals. There followed a period when the Zionist conspiracy and the Communist conspiracy undoubtedly worked closely together, each one hoping and counting on 'using' the other, and coming out on top. But it seems equally clear to me that today—and that this has been completely true for at least the past 15 years—the communist conspiracy has now absorbed into itself so many other leaders and elements, and has so outgrown the Zionist conspiracy, that it completely dominates the picture and that that the Zionist conspiracy has itself become merely one of the tools of the top Communist command."[41]

The fight, Welch wrote, was against the Communist conspiracy, "which threatens ever more imminently to enslave America along with the rest of the world." "I am certainly not willing to let myself be distracted, by Communist guile and propaganda, and red herrings cleverly disguised, and led even further into a blind alley where I am futilely fighting strawmen set up for me, or at the very best one expendable detachment of the conspirators."[42]

"I am utterly unwilling," Welch said, "to accept the thinking of those who assume that practically all Jews are Communists and vice versa. Nothing could be more ridiculous" as "I know or have known personally and well such Jews as Alfred Kohlberg and William Schlamm and many others who have sacrificed more and shown more personal courage in fighting the Communist conspiracy than an awful lot of my anti-Communist Gentile friends." The Communists have "put so much heavier invisible pressure on Jews who oppose them, than in the case of other segments of our population, that the Jews who really fight them—as Morris Ryskind does, for instance—deserves much more credit probably than do you and I," Welch told a colleague.

Welch then summed up his position. "Blaming the whole Communist conspiracy today, or in the past decade, on the Jews is an extremely dangerous over-simplification of our problem," "exactly what the Communists want us to do," and "I simply cannot go along with it." But then he finished the epistle with an appalling stereotype. "The fact still remains that the vast majority of the ordinary Jews in this country are simply being led by the nose."[43]

For all that, Robert Welch was no fascist, and efforts to portray Birchers as inherently fascistic were unfair. The JBS included anti-Semitic members such as Revilo Oliver, but Welch purged them before they could have any philosophical impact, albeit Welch was egregious in the slowness of their removal. That they were present in the first place reveals his myopia and inability to purge his affinity for the Old Right.

Welch was no Nazi. Unlike the Nazis, Welch did not believe in the perfectibility of man or state. Having grown up as a Baptist fundamentalist, he believed wholeheartedly in original sin and the fallibility of the individual, a trait he obviously had. His own public presence was evidence of that. He was a poor public speaker, who droned on in his monotone, snorting repeatedly because of a sinus condition. He shuffled his papers. His nervous energy did little to inspire and engage an audience. Some of his followers—even some of the folks on the JBS council—wished that he would resign. He had difficulty controlling leaders of the National Council, much less rank-and-file members. Hitler wanted to harness the economy to further a national goal—an economic prescription completely at odds with Robert's goals. He wanted to make the economy as free as a bucking young stallion. To be sure, Welch was suspicious of democracy and fiercely anti-Communist—traits loosely associated with fascism—but so were most Americans in 1961.[44]

In fact, Robert Welch was a dreamer, not an autocrat manager. He was in fact very hands-off. Too much so. Welch saw himself as an eccentric philosopher who was smarter than everybody else surrounding him—and who liked to be told that. Of course, he really was that smart, but he should not have needed to hear it from his employees. As a result, when he should have been seeking out folks who were skilled at managing people and personalities, Welch sometimes hired sycophants and yes-men.

William F. Buckley was neither a yes-man nor sycophant, and his criticism of Welch and his society was about to reach a new level. The timing of Buckley's assault on the JBS suggested that it was motivated as much by politics as by actual ideological difference. Buckley was extremely sensitive about being called anti-Semitic.[45] He feared that the entire conservative movement might be painted with that brush when *Time* used it on the JBS. Buckley worried not only that Welch would become the face of the conservative movement but also that Welch and his ilk would take a fundamentalist turn and bring the rest of the movement with them.

William Rusher worried about the same thing. He wrote Buckley: "my own hunch is that we are in the early stages of a conservative trend which is going to grow and harden and quite possibly get out of hand as the scope and pace of the free world's collapse becomes apparent to the American people and desire for a scapegoat takes hold." Here Rusher was being prescient by decades—far from myopic. But Rusher also cautioned Buckley against attacking the JBS. Rusher wanted an organizational alternative to the JBS that preferred the *National Review*'s flavor of conservatism. "I rather suspect" that your attack on Welch, Rusher hypothesized, "is based rather more on your impatience with an organization of conservatives that is not obediently following our lead, rather than upon a conviction that all of these people are irretrievably tainted." Here Rusher suggested that Buckley was perhaps less concerned about the sake of the conservative movement's future success than he claimed to be. Frank Meyer also warned Buckley: "some of the solidest conservatives in the country are members of the John Birch Society, and we should act in such a way as to alienate them no more than is strictly necessary from a moral, political, or tactical point of view."[46]

Buckley listened and decided to attack Welch's conspiratorial philosophy rather than assailing the JBS itself. He wrote an article in which he genuflected to Welch, saying "I have always admired his [Robert's] personal courage and devotion to the cause," but distinguished between the conspiratorial analysis of events in *American Opinion* and the "different analysis of the cause of our difficulty" contained "in every issue of *National Review*." Buckley also observed that many John Birch Society members did not hold Welch's perspective that the US government was under "effective control" by Communists. "I myself have never met a single member who declared himself in agreement with certain of Mr. Welch's conclusions," observed Buckley. "If Mr. Welch is right," he said, it's time "to leave the typewriter, the lectern, and the radio microphone, and look instead to one's rifles." Welch wrote Buckley, expressing that he found the article "both objectively fair and subjectively honorable."

But Welch's other responses to the great "smear" of 1961 were not so measured. He continued to deny that he called Eisenhower a "card-carrying Communist." He reiterated that the evidence taken as a whole created a suspicious pattern and led him to conclude that, "beyond any reasonable doubt," Eisenhower was "a dedicated, conscious agent of the Communist conspiracy." But "reasonable doubt" was too clever by half; he was not lying, but he was being too cute.

Welch's second defense was to encourage investigations into the JBS. He said neither he nor it had anything to hide. He distributed a list of the National Council's members and explained its functions to quash suspicions that the council ran a secret society. Further, he began sending the JBS's monthly bulletin to not only "the few individual newspapers which had specifically requested us to do so," but to popular daily and weekly newspapers. Welch got what he asked for. The liberal Democratic governor of California Edmund G. "Pat" Brown asked

Attorney General Stanley Mosk to investigate the Society, and the California Senate held hearings in June 1961. Five full-time investigators explored allegations of racism and anti-Semitism in the Society. Welch welcomed the inquiry and wanted members to testify on the record. "Unlike our Communist enemies," Welch assured the chair of the Un-American Activities Subcommittee, "none of our members will take the Fifth Amendment." He looked forward to getting his message out. (Welch also urged an inquiry into the Birch Society by Congress and asked James Eastland, the chair of the Senate Internal Security Subcommittee, to open one because of "the charges now being so widely circulated about us, some of which are extreme distortions of fact and many of which are sheer fabrications.")

In the end, California's Un-American Activities Subcommittee found no evidence that the JBS was a "secret, fascist, subversive, un-American, anti-Semitic organization." Welch concluded that the "total investigation was very thorough" and "the result was a complete clearance of the society on racism, secrecy and all other charges." According to Welch, the subcommittee found the "society to be an open, honorable, and patriotic educational organization." But this investigation failed to "put on a blanket over the battle axes" of our enemies.[47]

The media exposure drew to the surface congressional members who were also Birchers. California Representative Edgar Hiestand identified his membership, and the following day, he "outed" fellow Republican Congressman John Rousselot. Rousselot vigorously defended Welch and Society. The JBS, he said, "is basically made up of individual study groups in which the members read about and discuss communism in an effort to understand fully the menace it presents to America." Members "write friends and public officials and discuss thinking on political issues."[48]

In addition, and despite evidence to the contrary, Welch identified the Kremlin as being behind the "smear campaign." Welch became convinced that the "whole official Communist press in Moscow set the pace and led the way for the first few years" and were joined by "their tools within the *New York Times*, *Life*, *Newsweek*, and all of the other 'Liberal' media in America." "They must have made *Pravda* blush with shame over being outdone in dirty tactics by another member of the same team," he added.[49] Welch said "the smear campaigns against us increase in size, numbers, and viciousness." In the March 1961 *Bulletin,* Welch admonished members "not to believe anything you hear about us or our policies or views until it has been unmistakably confirmed by" the JBS Belmont office because a "present-all-out attack" was underway.[50] Before too long, Welch held that a secret "directive from Moscow" issued in December 1960 established that "destruction" of such anti-Communist groups as the JBS were a priority for 1961.[51]

Many critics mocked Welch for being far too paranoid. They portrayed Welch as a control freak and his headquarters as a centralized fascist machine. While not true, this narrative reached its zenith in popular culture with Bob Dylan's folk song "Talkin' John Birch Paranoid Blues." Recorded in early 1962 and intended as a satire on the Society, the song was ostensibly narrated by a Bircher who was convinced the Reds were everywhere. Under the bed. Under the table. In the government. In his toilet bowl. In his sink. In his glove compartment. The narrator refers to Betsy Ross as a Communist and declares "we all agree with Hitler's views." He called Jefferson, Lincoln, FDR, and Eisenhower Communist spies. For him, the only true American was George Lincoln Rockwell. By the end of the tune, the narrator is investigating himself.

Amid the various attacks in the media, many of the John Birch Society council members worried about the fallout. Most did not abandon support for the Society. But more and more thought that *The Politician* had to be repudiated. In March 1961, Leo Reardon, the erstwhile business manager to Clarence Manion, drafted a response for Welch to issue to an unforgiving press: "I am quite sure the former president is not, nor ever was, a member of the Communist Party," Manion told Welch to concede.[52] Manion hoped that Welch would say Ike unintentionally helped the Communists—that is, he lacked a sufficient knowledge of Communism to be one. But Welch would not follow Manion's advice. Welch was stubborn. He was proud. He was not a politician, or at least he was a poor one. He was unwilling to backtrack, despite the consequences, on a matter that he thought central to the problem of the day. The entire purpose of *The Politician,* Welch thought, was to show that Eisenhower was not ignorant of what he was doing. Welch felt that he would be lying if he did. So he didn't do it.[53]

Another strategy was tried to bottle the acid and stop the bleeding. In May 1961, Welch appeared on NBC's *Meet the Press* with Lawrence Spivak, where Manion thought he would settle the matter, and the crisis would abate. But it was a failure, a missed opportunity. Welch made no effort to control the crisis. He just reiterated that he had never intended to publish his conclusions or prove anything in *The Politician*. No author, he said, should be held accountable for statements written in unpublished drafts, despite that it had been sent to thousands of individuals. When asked by Spivak whether he wrote that Eisenhower was "a dedicated, conscious agent of the Communist conspiracy," Welch merely replied: "I never had that opinion and I do not have it now with any such assurance or firmness that I would ever state it in public, and I never have."[54] That type of too-cute language made him squirm when he heard it from Dean Acheson. Welch did not make things worse, but he surely did not make them better.

Welch found solace when Manion assured him in September 1961 that he would forever be a soldier to the cause of the John Birch Society. But Manion was still nervous. "Nobody who is anybody," a Manion colleague lamented, "will now join the John Birch Society." But Manion was a friend to Welch and a true believer in the cause: "I believe in its objectives and I am convinced that [its] continuous growth, strengths, and prestige . . . are necessary."

Manion did wonder aloud to Welch whether "a new face" was needed to lead what he considered the only organization that could save the United States. He recommended that Welch "gracefully retire into the editorial room." A more magnetic personality who had not become a lightning rod, Manion believed, was now needed to lead the John Birch Society.[55]

19
Succession? 1961–1962

Who would lead the John Birch Society after Robert Welch? As far as Welch was concerned, no one. There were potential successors, whom he respected, but the idea that any one of them might head the JBS came from those who feared Welch was harming his own cause. What made them interesting as candidates was not so much their own qualities but how they illuminated Welch's shortcomings.

John Rousselot was considered the heir apparent throughout the 1960s. After losing his congressional seat in 1962 after seven terms, Rousselot became the national public relations director for the Society. He was considered a Birch "moderate" who rejected Welch's perspective on Eisenhower's ideology and ably served as the "Number 2" in "Bircher West," a colonial building in San Marino, California. A Christian Scientist, Rousselot was an effective fundraiser and collected approximately $900,000 over the 1960s.

Another conservative who arguably possessed the gravitas and ideological consistency to fill Welch's shoes was Dan Smoot, the ruggedly handsome, Dallas-based, silver-tongued broadcaster who had been a G-man with the FBI between 1942 and 1951. Unlike Rousselot, Smoot believed in the Eisenhower conspiracy. He published the weekly *Dan Smoot Report* from the late 1950s to 1971 and starred in the television show of the same name. In a May 1961 broadcast, Smoot observed that the controversy over Welch actually derived from the Society's campaign to impeach Earl Warren, which Smoot had long backed as well.[1]

Smoot was a reactionary thinker whose worldview embraced belief in a conspiracy that went far beyond Communists simply leading a cabal. Anti-Communist conspiracy theory had long charged that the real origins of the conspiracy originated from the Bolshevik revolution, and its greatest threat came from Moscow. Smoot argued that its true inception was inside the United States, where government leaders were the real conspirators. A secret American government, Smoot said, was the biggest threat to the world. Smoot had a deep impact on Welch's evolving conspiratorial vision and that of many on the radical Right.

Smoot's contribution was transformative. At the 1961 Symposium on Freedom in Los Angeles, Smoot argued that the real purpose of Cold War politics was to contain rather than defeat Communism, and the Council on Foreign Relations, or CFR, was the body behind containment. The CFR was established by Edward Mandell "Colonel" House, the primary advisor to President Woodrow Wilson. Smoot found that the Rockefeller Foundation had been funding the CFR since 1927, and CFR members were passionate interventionists during World War II. Smoot argued that CFR members wanted a "one world socialist system" and sought "the same aim as that of international Communism." The CFR, Smoot continued, was Washington's "invisible government," and sought to "condition the American people" to "embrace socialist aims." Smoot alleged a momentous and nefarious meeting with drastic implications for American foreign policy had occurred on May 12, 1961, when "prominent Soviet and American citizens" met to address nuclear disarmament in the Crimean peninsula. The meeting, he said, was sanctioned by the State Department and arranged by the CFR. Smoot was absolutely convinced that the Soviets could not be trusted to any diplomatic promise much less on any matter concerning nuclear disarmament.

Smoot expounded on his theory in his 1962 book *The Invisible Government,* a seminal book for all conspiracy theorists but especially those aligned with the notion of an all-controlling deep establishment. The book took a deep dive into the secret history of the Council on Foreign Relations, and alleged its influence on the Institute of Pacific Relations and other institutions that allegedly were tied to Communist subversion. Smoot argued that House yearned for "a socialist dictatorship of the proletariat" like that "which now exists in the Soviet Union" a full four years before the Bolshevik revolution. House had therefore established the CFR in frustration after the United States had followed the will of the people in neglecting to sign the Treaty of Versailles and join the League of Nations after World War I. people. According to Smoot, House realized that the United States "could not become a province in a one-world socialist system unless" the American "economy was first socialized," which it was through the two wars, the New Deal, the Fair Deal, and "modern Republicanism." Through this socialization—which was well under way—a secret cabal of planners within the government intended to "merge" the political, economic, social, even cultural systems of the Soviet Union and the United States.

These wild claims echoed other conspiracists' theories. But Smoot revolutionized anti-Communist conspiracy theory by no longer presenting the merger as a Communist plot. Rather, Smoot said, a nefarious band of globalists and internationalists, long active on the American scene, were striking at the very heart of American sovereignty through the CFR. Smoot's contribution was an important development in American conspiracy theory not only in the twentieth century but, as it turned out, in the twenty-first. *The Invisible Government* was the first anti-Communist conspiracy theory that targeted politically connected globalists without actually calling them Communists. It came at an important time because Americans were no longer completely buying into the idea of a monolithic Communist conspiracy, though they were seeing conspiracies play out in their daily lives.[2] Smoot reinvigorated conspiracy for an age when conspiracies seemed to be everywhere.

Robert devoured the idea of an anti-anti-Communist conspiracy, and he came to adopt it in his own writing. Robert designated *The Invisible Government* as one of his "One Dozen Candles," books that he claimed were revolutionary in the development of the JBS worldview. Welch was realizing—partly because of his declaration that Dwight Eisenhower played an active role in the Communist cabal—that the standard warnings of a monolithic Communist conspiracy involving government figures were falling on deaf ears. They had played out their usefulness and actually seemed to be creating a long-standing public relations disaster. Welch therefore tried conspiracy another way and broadened it. He eventually abandoned mentioning Communism as the overarching menace and replaced it with a cabal that was pro-establishment, internationalist, or globalist, traceable back to the Illuminati.[3]

In embracing Smoot's peculiar angle, Welch not only invigorated conspiracy theory but augured, in some sense, the Right's "colorblind" strategy against liberalism—an effective gamechanger for conservatives in the 1970s. Similarly, Welch's embrace of Smoot's unique angle of conspiracy theory foreshadowed how Catholic and evangelical conservatives lay aside their theological differences, adopted a "cobelligerency" strategy in the interest of defeating liberals, and organized the Christian Right in the 1970s.

But even as Welch furthered his political education through authors like Smoot, he believed he faced "direct blows and undermining tactics" from the "henchmen" of the conspiracy: the politicians. On the whole, public officials were finding that ridicule and mockery were more effective weapons than formal investigations to diminish the influence of the Society. As early as his first press conference as attorney general, Robert Kennedy used what historian D. J. Mulloy called the "art of mockery" to deal a blow to the JBS. Kennedy said that while he had never met any Birchers, the JBS was "ridiculous," "in the area of being humorous," and contributed nothing "to the fight against communism." California's attorney general Stanley Mosk used mockery as well when he issued his finding on the JBS on July 7, 1961: "The cadre of the John Birch society seems to be formed primarily of wealthy businessmen, retired military officers and little old ladies in tennis shoes." "They seek, by fair means or foul, to force the rest of us to follow their example. They are pathetic." "Wherever [Welch] makes his speeches, he loses rather than gains public support."[4]

But the Kennedy administration abandoned its mockery in the face of the strange case of General Edwin Walker. During his first months in office, President Kennedy had to deal with the consequences of a 1956 army report that concluded some American soldiers captured by North Korea had been easily "brainwashed" because they lacked a sufficient understanding of Communism and the values of their own country. The report resulted in a 1958 National Security Council directive requiring military officers to educate their troops about the nature of the Communist enemy.[5] The result was right-wing seminars full of retired and active military personnel, held on military bases "in almost every area of the country." They were headlined by speakers who viewed the international Communist threat as ancillary to the internal enemy and lambasted the president's domestic agenda, in Senator J. William Fulbright's words, "as steps towards Communism."[6] Fulbright gave voice to a growing and disturbing phenomenon: "If the military is infected with [the] virus of rightwing radicalism, the danger is worthy of attention," he observed. In April 1961, Charles de Gaulle faced an attempted coup d'état from retired generals who opposed de Gaulle's Algerian policies; Fulbright wanted to avoid the "ultimate danger" of a similar scenario in the United States.

Along with his aides, including brother Robert, Arthur Schlesinger Jr., and Myer Feldman, the president worried that political activism on the Right and the military's deepening involvement in political affairs was making it more difficult to ease tensions with the Soviet Union.[7] To counter these developments, the administration went to battle with some of the nation's most archconservative military brass. General Edwin Walker became one of its primary targets.

Robert Welch was the best-known figure in the John Birch Society. General Edwin Walker was its most controversial. Kennedy wanted to make an example of him. After assuming command in 1959 of the Twenty-Fourth Division in Germany, Walker implemented the 1958 National Security Council order by setting up a "Pro-Blue" program. Walker's troops were told to read Welch's *Life of John Birch* and literature from the militant Christian anti-Communists Edgar Bundy, Billy James Hargis, and George Benson. *Overseas Weekly* (a salacious magazine for troops often appearing alongside *Stars and Stripes*) accused Walker of attempting to recruit soldiers for the John Birch Society. The magazine also accused Walker of calling Harry Truman, Dean Acheson, and Eleanor Roosevelt pinks. On April 17, Walker was relieved of command, and President Kennedy would investigate the whole matter.[8] On June 12, the army, with JFK's approval, "admonished" Walker for committing "injudicious actions" and attacking top men and calling Eleanor Roosevelt "definitely pink." Walker's "Pro-Blue" program came to an end by order of the White House.[9]

Like a figure from the New Testament, Walker became a martyr. He was also compared to Douglas MacArthur, and Kennedy's "muzzling" of the new hero echoed Truman's silencing of MacArthur, that "old soldier" who, as he put it, would never die, but fade away.[10] The Right's new citizen soldier was now seen as a man that the country could rally around. He looked and seemed at the time like another MacArthur—an "American Caesar." Handsome in his uniform. His medals were emblazoned across his broad chest. Walker's removal provided the Right the evidence they needed to conclude there were traitors in Washington, or at least the federal government was responsible for a massive dereliction of duty.[11] The Right concluded that responses to Communism, under Kennedy's and prior administrations, were either morally indefensible or traitorous. Kennedy had committed the worst sin possible: passivity could account for the loss of China and the stalemate in Korea, but the persecution of a dedicated patriot who was rallying his division against Communism was inexcusable.[12] Many on the Right turned to nostalgia and talked of Walker's heroics: leading commandos on nighttime raids against the Germans in Italy during World War II, taking part in some of the bloodiest fighting in Korea.[13]

When Walker resigned from the army in the fall of 1961, he traded in his fatigues for a black suit and white Stetson. His public appearances, starting with his resignation statement, made it clear that he possessed none of MacArthur's eloquence or flair for the dramatic. He was certainly not the Moses who would lead conservatives out of exile. Walker moved to Dallas. He eulogized about states' rights and fleshed out his racially charged vision of America.

In the fall of 1961, with the Walker case still at the forefront and allegations of fascism against the JBS becoming more common, the administration began to take a more aggressive approach toward the JBS and the Right in general. Rather than mocking the Society, Robert Kennedy asked Walter P. and Victor G. Reuther of the United Automobile Workers and civil rights lawyer Joseph L. Rauh to write a memo on how to handle the John Birch Society and the radical Right. The contents of the memo were leaked soon after RFK received it on December 16, 1961. It centered primarily on the JBS, but also addressed Schwarz's Christian Anti-Communism Crusade and Hargis's Christian Crusade, and stated the radical Right was "better organized than at any time in recent history" and was "growing in strength." Referring to Walker and like-minded generals, the memo noted that their "infiltration of the Armed Services adds in [a] new dimension to the seriousness with which they must be viewed." The memo suggested the administration showed too much "tolerance" for right-wing views; it urged Robert McNamara to begin firing generals "who lost confidence in democracy and who feel that the danger to our country is treason at home rather than the strength of the international Communist movement abroad." The memo also urged "deliberate administration policies and programs to contain the radical Right from further expansion" and "reduce it to its historic role of the impotent lunatic fringe." Attorney general RFK should add right-wing extremists to a "subversive list." The FBI should infiltrate right-wing groups. The IRS should investigate their tax-exempt status. The FCC should revoke their licenses. Yet the memo also encouraged the president to dampen his anti-Communist rhetoric, which stoked charges of "treason, traitors, and treachery." The Kennedy brothers, the memo implored, should not be "dramatiz[ing] the domestic Communist issue." President Kennedy followed the advice, deploying the IRS against the JBS, the Christian Crusade, and other right-wing organizations. The JBS saw in the memo evidence that the administration was soft on Communism.[14]

The Reuther memorandum notwithstanding, the conservative movement was on fire in 1961, largely because of external developments. Kennedy had failed miserably at the Bay of Pigs. (*American Opinion* declared that Kennedy purposely fell on his sword for the Kremlin to speed up the inexorable merger with the Soviet Union.) In Vienna in June, Kennedy was outmatched by Khrushchev. Also that month, John Tower, a conservative Republican won an election to replace Lyndon Johnson, who had taken office as Kennedy's vice president, in the Senate. In August, the Soviets built a wall to separate East and West Berlin. The John Birch Society continued to gain new members.

But the conservative movement faced factional warfare, especially between the cohorts more aligned with William F. Buckley and those attached to Robert Welch, although such factions often blurred. Conflicts within the Young Americans for Freedom prompted Buckley to issue a stronger attack on the John Birch Society. Scott Stanley was both a member of the John Birch Society and the board of directors of the Young Americans for Freedom. A magnificent orator, the bright young Stanley became managing editor of *American Opinion* in October 1962. At YAF, Stanley competed with Doug Caddy, who was trying to pull the organization in the direction of the New York governor Nelson Rockefeller's brand of liberal Republicanism by calling Stanley's group the "*National Review* faction." *National Review*'s Lee Edwards observed, "We were beginning to get into the real world of national politics, dealing with people like John Tower and Barry Goldwater and others. It was just obvious that we couldn't carry around baggage from the John Birch Society."

The New York Conservative Party, which later nominated and was responsible for electing James Buckley—William's brother—to the US Senate, also had a Birch problem, as William saw it. Mainstream New York Republicans were attempting to discredit the Conservative Party by associating it with the JBS. This was a great embarrassment to Bill Buckley because he saw the Conservative Party as his baby and wanted it linked to his own brand of "reasonable" conservatism. Deciding to "dig in on the subject," Buckley and *National Review* prepared for a much stronger attack on the JBS in 1962.[15]

20

"Where Were You in '62?," 1962

By 1962, William F. Buckley had decided to run the John Birch Society out of the conservative movement. For decades he seemed to be successful, but he was not. Only after Buckley's death in 2008 and Donald Trump's victory in 2016 did his utter failure become clear. Robert Welch was never excommunicated from the conservative movement.

Beyond the exposure of Welch's Eisenhower letter, with which he disagreed, Buckley also became frustrated with Welch's other unsubstantiated statements. Buckley bemoaned Welch's suggestion in a speech in Stamford, Connecticut, "that the government of the United States is under operative control of the Communist Party of the United States."[1]

Buckley and other conservatives met with Barry Goldwater, whom Buckley regarded as *National Review*'s "most prominent constituent," at the Breakers Hotel in Palm Beach to convince the Arizona senator that the JBS was a "menace" for conservatism. Buckley wanted Goldwater to publicly disassociate himself from the Society, just as the *National Review* had. Russell Kirk, who attended the meeting, told Goldwater, "Eisenhower isn't a Communist. He is a golfer." Goldwater agreed that there were "kooks" in the Society, but there were also "nice guys." He made no commitments at the meeting but promised to think about it.

Soon thereafter, Goldwater wrote Buckley to say he would like to see either the JBS disband or Welch resign. The letter provided what Buckley had been looking for. In various commentaries over the coming months, Buckley said Welch was "divert[ing] militant conservative action to irrelevance and ineffectuality."[2] "There are, as we say, great things that need doing, the winning of a national election, the reeducation of the governing class. John Birch chapters can do much to forward those aims, but only as they dissipate the fog of confusion that issues from Mr. Welch's smoking typewriter. Mr. Welch has revived in many men the spirit of patriotism, and that same spirit calls now for rejecting, out of a love of truth and country, his false counsels."[3] Welch was "damaging the cause of anti-communism" because he persisted in distorting and even refused to make the important distinction between Communists and anti-Communist liberals. "There are bounds to the dictum, Anyone on the right is my ally." Buckley had declared war on Welch and the JBS.[4] Buckley would win many battles, but Welch won the war.

Time magazine and the *Washington Post* cheered Buckley's stand. US senator John Tower from Texas called it "a courageous and responsible analysis." Other conservatives joined Buckley in ostracizing Welch, such as Walter Judd, the Minnesota congressman; Fred Schwarz, the anti-Communist spokesman; and radioman Fulton Lewis Jr.[5] Russell Kirk also encouraged Welch to resign in the Catholic weekly *America* because the JBS founder had "done more to injure the cause of respectable conservatism than to act effectively against communism." But congressman John Rousselot came to Welch's defense. Rousselot had "obvious and pointed disagreements" with Welch, especially his conclusion that Eisenhower was a Communist, but the California congressman was standing by the Founder.

Welch then disclosed in the February 1962 *JBS Bulletin* that some members of the JBS's executive committee had suggested in June 1961 that he step aside for the good of the Society's image. Welch said he gave the idea a "full airing" at a September National Council meeting, and the idea had been tabled. The suggestion that the JBS was "monolithic" and that he possessed a "martyr complex" was nonsense, Welch avowed. Welch never considered himself an "indispensable man," but he was not resigning as the leader and chief spokesman of the JBS. Resignation "would be nothing less than a betrayal . . . of the well understood compact between our members and myself." Welch was not about to be derailed from his mission and "beguiled into abandoning such a dedicated body of the finest and most purposeful people on earth." The Founder was not going anywhere.[6]

But Welch felt hurt and betrayed by a friend. He did not see Buckley's attempted "excommunication" coming. But Welch did not counterattack Buckley, at least not yet. He did respond in *American Opinion*: "Let us repeat: we care about fighting the Communists—and nobody else! To avoid adding fuel to all of the friction among the anti-Communist forces, we shall even refrain from defending ourselves against the slings and arrows of the Right."[7] Roger Milliken, *National Review*'s chief financier and JBS member, was very upset with Buckley's effort to ostracize Welch. Buckley suffered a "wrenching" conversation with Milliken, but he never indicated any remorse for eviscerating somebody who had generously given to *National Review* when it was nothing but an idea.

Buckley's attacks were scarring, and Welch masked his sensitivity and hurt behind his muscular prose. In the March *Bulletin* article "A Fable for Conservatives," Welch wrote of a certain "publisher B," who began "to pull a few of the props out from under the Liberal Establishment" before becoming preoccupied with the question of extremism. B's new concern, Welch asserted, served "Communist purposes." Welch finished by declaring that he wanted "peace in the conservative family." This seemed true, at least in the case of Russell Kirk, whom Welch had excused for getting "lost" upon leaving the ivory tower to traverse "rough terrain marked Conspiratoria." Welch told JBS members "to keep right on buying, distributing, and recommending" Kirk's books. Welch also acted generously when it came to *National Review* by continuing to praise it. But Welch offered one dig, observing that *National Review* "appeal[ed] to the academic world," which had "tremendous value to the conservative cause." Welch observed that there was "basic and completely honest disagreement between some of our critics and ourselves, as to be what might be called this whole conspiratorial theory and explanation of the Communist advance." But Welch concluded that history proved time and time again that the JBS version of reality was the "correct one."[8]

Buckley's attacks on his former benefactor established his credibility as a member of the "responsible right," despite the fact that Buckley's statements on race and Africa and decolonialism were far more incendiary and racist than anything that Welch had ever said. They suggest that the concept of a "responsible right" was a delusion itself. According to Buckley, the Fourteenth and Fifteenth Amendments were "inorganic accretions" tacked onto the Constitution by the "victors-at-war by force" to punish the South and make African Americans the equals of white men.[9] Buckley also said atrocious things about colonialism, on one occasion averring that Africans would be ready for self-government "when they stop eating each other." The mainstream media looked the other way when the erudite and eloquent Buckley made the provocative anti-democratic suggestion that states should disenfranchise the uneducated of all races and suggested in *Why the South Must Prevail* (1957) that "the white community is so entitled" to take measures "to prevail, politically, and culturally" because "for the time being, it is the advanced race." Buckley said ugly, really mean-spirited things that made some want to sock him in his "god-damned face"—and that would never have come out of Robert Welch's mouth. Welch was an eccentric, a conspiracy theorist who said zany things, but he had sincerity. As ludicrous as it sounded, Welch really believed that the Communists were controlling anti-colonial Africans and the civil rights movement, but he offered those opinions without the venom that Buckley spewed.[10] At least for the time being. Welch did consider Buckley a hypocrite and soon developed a great dislike of him. Welch, born on a farm, relished attacking silver-spooned Buckley for his inherited fortune and for never having to sweat for his supper one day of his life. By the 1970s, Welch declared it his "unshakable opinion" that Buckley "has been part of the Conspiracy since his days at Yale."[11] By the 1970s, Welch's appraisal of Buckley was the same as that of Willmoore Kendall, who had been Buckley's mentor and friend: "the Buckleys consume people as a furnace consumes coal."

Welch also panned Buckley for his love of the limelight. John Judis wrote that Buckley was becoming a "celebrity" and "less tolerant of the Far Right and more tolerant of liberals." Newly christened by the establishment, Buckley moved to the Upper East Side, attended swanky ballroom parties adorned in masks, and zoomed into his office on his Honda scooter. Buckley was excellent television, an elegant raconteur on his long-running *Firing Line*, as well as a guest on mainstream news programs that featured public intellectuals such as Joan Didion, Gore Vidal, Norman Mailer, and Ayn Rand. He was still young, blessed with a razor-sharp wit, vivacious, and iconoclastic, and although he wore his Catholicism on his sleeve, his eyes maintained a glimmer of the Irish mischief that hinted he was up to something. Buckley had become the establishment, and everything Welch fought against.

The television camera was not as kind to Robert. He was a pallid, droopy-eyed, cigar-chomping older gentleman with protruding ears and various cowlicks. He seemed to have a chronic case of bedhead. Encumbered by his heavy cane and rumpled dark suits, his delivery was stilted. Welch looked like Mr. Magoo and often had the temperament of Oscar the Grouch on a good day. Buckley, a member of the Greatest Generation, looked and sailed like a right-wing Kennedy. Robert was a nineteenth-century man, and it looked like his time had passed. He seemed the "superfluous man," as Albert Jay Nock wrote. He seemed better suited to sitting in the audience on Lawrence Welk. But the twenty-first century would embrace his version of conservatism.

And yet: the "ostracization thesis"—the argument that Buckley successfully drummed Welch out of the conservative movement—that Buckley promoted for decades, has been greatly exaggerated. That is in part due to Buckley being one of the most prolific writers and most protective chroniclers of the story of movement conservatism throughout his lifetime. It is also due to the movement's "rampant factionalism," with Welch situated on the fringe of what came to be called the "respectable right." The truth is Welch and the JBS played crucial roles in the conservative ascendancy after Buckley's supposed excommunication.[12] There are reasons why Welch's significance in movement conservatism has been downplayed. Some excellent conservative historians, Patrick Allitt and George Nash, among others, have never really considered Welch a conservative. They have embraced Nash's model, which identified conservatism as three separate strands of libertarianism, social conservatism, and anti-Communism—which has the effect of ignoring conservatives preoccupied with apocalyptic fantasies, overheated rhetoric, conspiracy theories, and other aspects of what Kim Phillips-Fein called the "baroque strangeness" of the Far Right.[13]

In addition, Buckley and many historians underestimated Welch's support. It is very difficult to imagine this today, but most Birchers and many Americans subscribed to Welch's vision of an imminent takeover by the Soviet Union. People believed Welch because the government and other leaders were also telling them it was about to occur. In 1961, Attorney General Robert Kennedy made the false remark that "Communist espionage here in this country is more active than it has ever been." In October 1963, after the bombings, the march, Bull Connor's hoses, and his brother's address that called the principle of civil rights as "old as the scriptures," Kennedy ordered J. Edgar Hoover to tap Martin Luther King's phone lines because he suspected that King had Communist associates. James Jesus Angleton, the CIA counterintelligence chief, announced a KGB "Master Plan" in which all Soviet defectors to the United States were actually KGB double agents." Angleton said a second Kremlin existed within the real Kremlin. George Meany, the president of the AFL-CIO, told his members that they were an important bulwark against Communism. In Czechoslovakia, Meany said, the Communists had focused their first efforts on getting control of the unions. Once they had, "within seven days, they controlled the country." It could happen here, thought many Americans. Welch was saying that it was happening here. He was easy to believe, and the reports of his excommunication were greatly exaggerated.[14] In fact, he was never excommunicated at all.

In the election year of 1962, the JBS was becoming an issue in partisan politics. In California, one of the epicenters of the JBS because of strong support in Orange County and Los Angeles, Richard Nixon had decided to take on the popular and affable Democratic governor Edmund "Pat" Brown. In Welch's view, "Nixon, on orders of Nelson Rockefeller, was obliged to run for governor of California even though he knew he did not have a chance in the world of being elected."[15] Yet in 1960, Nixon had carried the state by 38,000, and polls showed him beating Brown by a ratio of five to three. But Brown enjoyed a booming economy and knew the issues that Californians cared about—roads, schools, and water. Moreover, the Republican Party was badly split between moderates and ultraconservatives, while Democratic registration was soaring.

The presence of the JBS was a real challenge for Nixon. Two California legislators were members along with several members of the state assembly. One of them was Nixon's opponent in the Republican gubernatorial primary, Joe Shell, a salty, honest JBS member and party leader. Reporters encouraged Nixon to pick a fight against the Birchers, and he did. In a March meeting before the Republican state assembly, Nixon said that he knew "how to fight communism and how not to fight it." "No greater disservice can be done to the effort of combatting Communism than to demagogue and overstate the case."[16] Nixon asked the assembly to "repudiate once and for all Robert Welch and those who accept his leadership and viewpoints." He then wrote to Eisenhower: "this statement of mine will undoubtedly cost some financial support and probably a few votes as well but in the end I think it is vitally important that the Republican Party not carry the anchor of the reactionary right into our campaign this Fall." He beat Shell in the primary but alienated so many Birchers, who stayed home on the day of the general election, that he lost to Brown.[17]

The Nixon campaign showed Welch beset, beleaguered, and at his worst. Robert felt besieged from all angles. He claimed that Nixon, "on orders from Nelson Rockefeller," had "tried to strengthen his position" as part of the conspiracy "by devoting practically his whole campaign to damaging the John Birch society." "Radicals in the California Democratic Party," "extreme gerrymandering of [California's] congressional districts," and "plentiful malodorous assistance from Walter Reuther's COPE" combined to defeat two Bircher California congressmen, Eck Hiestand and John Rousselot.[18] For the rest of his days, Welch blamed Nixon for losing those seats. And it wasn't just California; in Michigan, George Romney called Birchers "purveyors of hate."

In October 1962, just before the elections, the world came as close as it has ever come to nuclear war. The Bay of Pigs had pushed the Soviets and the Cubans closer together. Aerial photographs from an American U-2 spy plane revealed that the Soviets were installing armed nuclear missiles in Cuba. President Kennedy resisted the advice of his generals to strike the launching sites. Instead, he established a naval quarantine and demanded that Khrushchev remove the missiles. Kennedy and Khrushchev were eyeball to eyeball, as Dean Rusk put it, for two tense weeks when it appeared the fate of the planet hung in the balance. Khrushchev blinked. On October 28, Russia agreed to remove its missiles, and United States promised never to invade the island. Quietly, Kennedy agreed to remove American Jupiter missiles from Turkey, which were already in the process of being decommissioned. It was a tremendous victory for Kennedy, who held his ground, but an absolute debacle for Khrushchev, who soon became an "unperson" in his country as hardliners in the Kremlin assumed power and pursued a more aggressive military expansion.[19]

In California, Nixon, embracing a Bircher ethos, became convinced that Kennedy's hatred of him sealed his loss. The "Cuban thing" kept us "from getting our message through," Nixon said. As usual Welch was equally conspiratorial, again intuiting a classic inside job. The crisis was a "grandstand ploy, carefully timed . . . to help elect favorites of the Administration and to defeat Conservatives." Welch and Nixon were in complete agreement in 1962. Learning of Kennedy's guarantee not to invade Cuba in exchange for Khrushchev's "worthless promise," he saw the outcome as on par with Eisenhower's betrayals of Chiang Kai-shek. What really perturbed Welch, however, was that Kennedy responded in the face of a Soviet nuclear threat, which Welch deemed illusory. For Welch, the Soviets neither had the temerity nor the capacity to launch viable nuclear weapons—an absolutely incorrect and dangerous presumption. He believed they always used internal invasion rather than military exercises to conquer anybody. The Cuban missile crisis was "an even greater victory for Castro and Khrushchev than the Bay of Pigs," he said. Most historians disagree.[20]

Just before the missiles of October, General Edwin Walker came back from the dead, as it were. His ascension was in part because of the Kennedy administration's new willingness to take on the Right after the release of the Reuther memorandum. The proximate cause was the attempt of James Meredith, an air force veteran, to become the first African American to enroll at the University of Mississippi. The situation initially seemed to be under control, as President Kennedy and his brother negotiated secretly with Governor Ross Barnett. Meredith was to enroll on October 1. But on September 30, 2,000 protesters arrived on campus, yelling "Go to hell, JFK" and hurling rocks and bricks at the federal marshals. Walker, ever the troglodyte, acted like it was 1862, presenting the showdown as not a battle against integration but a conflict between federal power and states' rights—a common cover for racist endeavors in the South. He went on the radio to tell his followers: "Bring your flags, your tents and skillets! It's time!" A riot ensued, and two people died and 375 were injured, including 160 US marshals. The Justice Department claimed that Walker instigated the rioting. Walker was arrested and sent, at the behest of Robert Kennedy, for psychiatric observation. One Texan called Walker's institutionalization "unlawful reconstruction number two."[21]

Walker had been acting strangely throughout the summer and spring of 1962. His zealotry and obsession with conspiracy theories verged on paranoia. He defended Welch's assertion that Eisenhower was a Communist.[22] He began to channel Joe McCarthy and held up what he termed a State Department "blueprint" that supposedly placed American military personnel and weapons under the control of the United Nations. The executive branch and the Supreme Court had been "captured," he said, and the plan now was to "UN-ize" the American soldier. Another time, in a letter to President Kennedy, Walker ridiculed him for "idle talk and rocking chair action" and asked him to give the state of Texas authority over its national guard in light of the "government's release of all state and national sovereignty under [the president's] announced program to place all armed forces and weapons under the United Nations."[23]

Walker continued his erratic behavior before the Senate Preparedness Investigating Subcommittee. His performance was unintelligible.[24] Walker said that "high-ranking US government officials" were part of a "hidden control apparatus" in the grasp of the international Communist conspiracy. Walker, the *Washington Post* observed, was "an exceedingly poor spokesman for the radical right." One reporter said, "Walker might be trouble but he won't be. By the grace of God, he is the worst speaker in the United States."[25]

Welch saw the events in Mississippi as an invasion, but he nevertheless urged restraint: "the more hectic the excitement and confusion, the more clever the provocations of the Left to tempt us to rashness, the more need there is for us to remain resolute but calm."[26] He said that the invasion of Mississippi was a "veritable trap" for "Conservative and Constitutionalist Americans." Walker had fallen into the trap, but the John Birch Society needed to be "loyal to our friends . . . [e]ven when we think they have made mistakes." Welch believed that Walker's incarceration was a "fantastic persecution, obviously intended as a precedent for the incarceration, without trial, of other enemies of the Left."[27] Still, Welch began to distance himself from Walker, as did John Rousselot, who said that if Walker was found to have incited the riot, the John Birch Society should revoke his membership. Despite the JBS's threats to ostracize Walker, they were pure Welchian sophistry. Welch was not drawing distinctions between his people and extremist segregationists and interpositionists. But in distancing himself from Walker, his discourse cunningly suggested a turn away from forces that the Society did not wish to have anything to do with. He was likely prevaricating.

Welch's rhetorical habits themselves became a species of dishonesty. Although his position had been abundantly clear, Welch wrote manipulatively in the October 1962 *Bulletin*: "We take absolutely no position on the desirability, propriety, or wisdom, on the part of the University of Mississippi, of admitting a college student to enroll, or of refusing admission." "For the society as a whole would certainly be badly divided on the issue." The heart of the issue, according to Welch, was not segregation or desegregation, but the arrogant and unconstitutional efforts by the federal government "to force Mississippi to admit [Meredith]" of which "we still do not believe that the federal government should have anything to do." In other words, he was not in the camp of the segregationists, but neither was he on the other side. He said he was in limbo, but his heart was deep within the segregationist camp as nothing up to this point suggested otherwise.[28]

21

Revolution in the Streets and the Paranoid Style in Belmont, 1963

Because it had so much to teach Americans about the civil rights struggle, Algeria was very much on Welch's mind in 1963. Welch thought what happened in Algeria foreshadowed what was going to happen in America. French President Charles De Gaulle supported Algerian independence, but Welch believed that de Gaulle had betrayed the French living there. Welch believed Algerian independence was a tragedy on par with the loss of China and Eastern Europe; it relegated France to "the first of three or four great powers like ourselves to fall under the Communist tyranny."[1]

Algeria had always been a pet project of President John F. Kennedy, who Welch thought was as corrupt as he was charismatic. According to Welch, the president had learned from his father—a man who made his fortune running liquor during Prohibition and hiding the profits—that honesty did not pay. As Robert saw things, Joseph Kennedy trained Jack to be amoral; he sent him to the London School of Economics, which Welch believed to be established by the Fabian Society to train Marxists. As a senator, Kennedy awakened the country to the crusade of Algeria's Ahmed Ben Bella's Communist National Liberation Front, or FLN. Welch panned Kennedy for presenting the sadistic Ben Bella as a humanitarian. As Kennedy extolled his virtues, Ben Bella tortured Muslims, cutting off their ears, noses, and lips, while portraying himself as their liberator.[2]

As in the civil rights movement, for Welch, things were not what they seemed in Algeria, and the Communists were to blame. Far from attacking the French imperial overlords, the Communist guerrilla fighters of the FLN feigned to represent the Algerian people but actually terrorized them while blaming the French: "With their usual exact reversal of the truth, the Communists have used pictures of the horrible results of *their own* tortures and murders to 'document' their charges against the French—exactly as the Soviets charged the Germans with the Katyn Forest massacre which they themselves had perpetrated."[3] Similarly, thought Welch, did the Communists harm Black Americans while claiming to support them.

Welch came to support colonization *because* it was anti-racist. Welch had met with Samuel L. Blumenfeld, the Jewish journalist and a founder of the anti-FLN American Committee for France and Algeria. Organizer of the Jewish Society of Americanists, which was sponsored by the John Birch Society, Blumenfeld was instrumental in driving out many of the older anti-Semitic members of the JBS. He also developed an alternative explanation for de Gaulle's support of Algerian independence: de Gaulle wanted to purify France by ridding it of Muslims, so as to "build his Europe of fatherlands from the Atlantic to the Urals." Welch concurred and bought into this peculiar anti-racist argument for colonization.

Although Welch thought Kennedy actively stood on the wrong side concerning Algeria, by the spring of 1963 he found him to also be at least an unknowing dupe of the Communists, who he believed were exploiting racial tensions nationwide.

In April and May in Birmingham, or as Black citizens called it "bombingham," civil rights activists squared off against the police forces under Eugene T. "Bull" Connor for a series of marches, sit-ins, and preach-ins.[4] From a jail cell there, Martin Luther King wrote his famous letter in which he claimed that it was impossible to wait any longer for desegregation. King was right. Many civil rights activists concluded that if reform could occur in Birmingham, it could happen anywhere, and the movement grew more militant. Civil rights groups such as the Student Nonviolent Coordinating Committee (SNCC) and the Congress for Racial Equality (CORE) were now open to abandoning their nonviolent strategies.[5]

The scene in Birmingham reminded Welch of Algeria, where he believed gangs of Muslims were terrorizing the people in the name of "freedom"; in Birmingham, Blacks were supposedly fighting for the same cause of freedom but were really dupes of the Communists. In both places, the real victims, as he saw things, were the Muslims and Blacks who were allegedly rebelling. According to Welch, the Communists were aware that most people, whether Black or White, Christian or Muslim, had no desire for social disruption. Therefore, the Communists knew that terror was necessary to coerce them into it.[6] Accordingly, Robert had concluded that King was nothing but a Communist agitator, and his activity in Birmingham was a Communist-directed smear campaign targeting the Birmingham Police Department. In reality, King was bravely launching a campaign in the most segregated large urban area in the United States. King knew the stakes. Since 1957, the attempt to break down the racial barriers led to eighteen bombings and at least fifty cross burnings. King said to his organizers: "Some of the people sitting here will not come back alive from this campaign." He was right. Birmingham's commissioner of public safety unleashed snarling German shepherds, used electric cattle prods, and employed high-pressure fire hoses that stripped bark from trees, tore bricks from buildings, and blasted children down city streets like human tumbleweeds.[7]

Despite Blacks being assaulted by snarling dogs and children launched into the air by fire hoses, Welch embraced a worldview completely divorced from reality. Bull Connor was simply maintaining order in the face of a dangerous situation. Connor was being careful. According to Welch, the Communists had planned for the vulturous liberal press to capture the scene at an inopportune moment for the police. "Cameras were poised and ready to catch the show at the right instant," Welch said. That moment came: "One or more hotheads or dupes among the Negroes," Welch reported, "deliberately kicked one of the dogs." The cameras flashed as the dogs snarled. "The result was a picture, plastered in the papers all over the United States." The Communists had their "glorious piece of propaganda."[8] Foreshadowing Alex Jones's pronouncements in the twenty-first century, Welch characterized the violence perpetrated against Blacks by Whites in Birmingham as a false flag. It paved the way for the Communists to introduce a Soviet-style dictatorship to the United States. But Welch wove a tapestry of sophistry. Bull Connor called the shots in Birmingham, not the

Communists. Welch failed to see reality and believed that Communists provoked the dogs despite the lack of any evidence whatsoever.

But President Kennedy saw the reality of Birmingham for what it was. He was shaken by the violence, like most Americans. Birmingham jolted the president from his slumber concerning civil rights. Kennedy's worldview completely changed because of Birmingham. He realized Bull Connor was actually helping the Communists to win the Cold War. The violence perpetrated against American Blacks by White police officers was making the America a land of intolerance from the perspective of the Soviet Union. It was calamity for the United States and grist for the Russian propaganda machine. Kennedy demanded television time and delivered an important address calling civil rights a "moral issue" that "is as old as the Scriptures and is as clear as the American Constitution."

Why was Robert Welch unable to grow in such a way? Two factors perhaps held Welch back. First was the company he kept. He may have come of age in a diverse community where African Americans were a majority, but Welch's present company included unapologetic racists and diehard segregationists, and he simply had a tougher time than some casting off dear friends, despite their pernicious and outdated line of thinking. This probably had something to do with his Southern Baptist fundamentalist background, which extolled the virtue of loyalty toward friends, even dying for them. To be sure, Welch abandoned this inerrant view of the Bible, but this tendency remained with him perhaps because it represented southern honor at its very best, and he never considered Massachusetts or the Northeast home anyway. Whether his mother's religion was at play, Welch was stunted and lacked a capacity to grow on the racial front when, as Kennedy put it in his June address, "a great change was at hand."

Another more central factor played a more instrumental role. His penchant to indulge in inane conspiracy theory prevented him from accepting the reality of police brutality and supporting the Civil Rights Act of 1964, the Voting Rights Act of 1965, or any federal intervention in the arena of civil rights. His statement that dogs attacked Blacks in Birmingham because the Communist Blacks kicked the dogs while a photographer waited for the perfect moment stretches the imagination. That he viewed the civil rights movement as a Communist plot not only suggests an inability to soften on civil rights but highlights how conspiratorial thinking inhibited his ability to grow as a human being. His adamant belief, from his youth on, that greater federal intervention was the road to serfdom and one-world government also made it difficult for him to see other points of view, much less call out people as racists. His southern ancestors, who owned slaves and feared the Yankee merchant elite and the loss of their slaves, played an important role in his conspiratorial thinking, which later blinded him to the suffering of Blacks. The Birmingham campaign was an important moment in American history because King's courage resulted in Kennedy's advocacy for what became the 1964 Civil Rights Act. Yet Birmingham highlights the danger that conspiratorial thinking poses to democratic norms. Birmingham was a moment when the soul of the nation was essentially saved, and everything included in the Declaration of Independence was held to be important, but Welch's ludicrous conspiracy theory whittled down the event to a minor story of Black rage at a dog—something that not only was completely meaningless and divorced from any semblance of the truth, but also struck a blow at the democratic experiment. If Welch's version of reality was embraced by President Lyndon Johnson rather than John Kennedy's version of what happened in Birmingham in May 1963, the Fourteenth Amendment would still not have any teeth to support the rights of Blacks, but also women—what the 1964 Civil Rights Act accomplished.

This was a long-standing theme of Welch's, as in the Eisenhower letter. By 1963, Welch had determined that it was impossible to disconnect *The Politician* from the John Birch Society. Inspired by the trailblazing discourse of Dan Smoot and *The Invisible Government,* which invigorated anti-Communist conspiracy theory without mentioning Communism, Robert decided to lean into the identification and sell the Eisenhower letter as a book, after replacing any language about Eisenhower's supposed Communism with a vaguer indictment of the "left-wing establishment." In the new version, Welch had removed the most contentious passage. But he downplayed the scrubbing as simply addressing "typographical errors corrected and a few other" issues. Beyond the shift in villain, Welch also added an abundant crop of endnotes, supposedly to offer more credibility for his case. Clarence

Manion expressed so much enthusiasm about the new version that he called it the "book event of our generation, because it will take just that to turn the Red tide."

To the great disappointment of the genuinely anti-Semitic Revilo Oliver, sections that he interpreted as anti-Semitic were cut. Oliver called the new version a "shabby hoax" since it was "thoroughly censored to eliminate all of the many references to Jews." Ironically, the original version was never as anti-Semitic as Revilo contended, and Welch cut only descriptions of John Floberg, Edward Greenbaum, and Maxwell Gluck, on the basis that they "were no longer of any importance in the context."[9]

John Rousselot, recently promoted to JBS public relations director, was tasked with selling the book, though he didn't always agree with Welch's analysis. In March 1963, Rousselot addressed an Atlanta crowd. First, he said, Eisenhower was a New Deal, left-wing Democrat. He had been offered the Democratic nomination in 1948 by Harry Truman, and his domestic and foreign policies resembled those of the New Deal and the Fair Deal. Second, Eisenhower was not "a strong anti-Communist." He counted as evidence Eisenhower's support for "Operation Keelhaul," which involved the return of Soviet refugees after World War II. That Eisenhower was a left-wing establishment man was also demonstrated by his opposition to the Bricker amendment, his refusal to investigate Communists in government, his persecution of Joseph McCarthy, and his inviting Nikita Khrushchev to the United States. In short, Rousselot said, Eisenhower was one of three things: a dupe, a Communist, or an astute politician "who is smart enough to see that the tide of the Left is very strong." Eisenhower would go wherever the wind blew him.[10]

Along with *The Politician,* Welch and the JBS were also publishing the Society's version of what happened the year before in Oxford, Mississippi. Written by conservative Dallasite Earl Lively and published in October 1963, *The Invasion of Mississippi* held that the American people had been brainwashed by the government and the media. "Shakespeare's famous observation has seldom been so appropriate as in the months of September and October 1962," Lively said. "Oxford, rather than the world, was the stage, but the players in the wings were scattered across the land." Lively alleged that an ambitious photographer had carried a crucifix to the campus and tried to pay students to set it on fire. When they refused, the photographer did it himself.

Lively wrote of the increasingly common application of the Carl Braden technique, a ploy practiced by civil rights activists. In 1954, Anne and Carl Braden, who battled segregation in residential neighborhoods, helped a Black couple, Andrew and Charlotte Wade, purchase a home in an all-White community near Louisville, Kentucky. Segregationists supposedly fired gunshots into the new abode, burned crosses on the lawn, and threw rocks through the windows before blowing it to bits. The terrorists were not charged; Carl Braden was, with sedition, and then arrested, convicted, and sentenced to fifteen years in prison. But Lively said that it was all a staged affair: Braden was a Communist, despite his denial, and the Communists had bombed the Wades' home to create the appearance that White supremacists had.

Lively said the same thing had happened at Ole Miss. Edwin Walker was a victim of the Braden technique. Walker, Lively said, was interested in peaceful protest and wanted to showcase the unlimited boundaries of federal power, but the national media—run by liberals—turned him into an "advocate of rebellion and insurrection." The dictatorial federal government then arrested Walker and put him in a mental asylum.[11]

The message from Lively and Welch was clear: fake news was real. Things were not as they seemed. Much as Alex Jones reports nonsensical realities today, any political violence, whether beatings or assassinations or bombings, were not the work of the White South but Communists seeking social control, power, and world domination. These were delusions.

Real violence was perpetrated by the proponents of racial segregation at Ole Miss. Before the riots began, racists drove their cars through Oxford. They yelled, "The South shall rise again." They waved Confederate flags. They attacked Blacks. The violence was perpetrated by Whites. A violent crowd swelled to 3,000. The White rioters roamed the campus. They learned that James Meredith was in Baxter Hall. So the Whites assaulted it. Hearing of the violence, President Kennedy sent in reinforcement under Brigadier General Charles Billingslea, the commanding general of the US Army's 2nd Infantry Division. When he arrived in the morning, the mob set his car on fire, and Billingslea, Deputy Commanding General John Corley, and Captain Harold Lyon broke out of the burning car and crawled to safety while being fired upon by the white throng. When the violence came to an end, 166—one-third of the federal agents—suffered casualties.

But Welch did not see things as they actually happened. The rush of events in Birmingham, on the heels of Mississippi, convinced him to dedicate the JBS more forcefully to the civil rights issue. In the coming years, he moved JBS books that explicitly addressed civil rights, such as Gary Allen's *Communist Revolution in the Streets* and Alan Stang's *It's Very Simple: The True Story of Civil Rights*. Some in the Society questioned Welch's move into the book business. "Welch has turned what claimed to be a militant anti-communist movement into a book-selling operation," observed the highly critical Slobodan Draskovich. "His notion that the Birch Society is going to save America by getting people to read books is absurd." But the book-selling operation was very impressive. By the end of the decade, there were 400 Birch-owned bookstores.

Welch was initially very reluctant to go all in against the civil rights movement, partly because he knew that meant deeper alliances with racists, which would hurt the conservative movement. But Roger Milliken helped him soften. Milliken was a big backer of the Society's 1959 Committee Against Summit Entanglements, and he told Welch that things looked different after Birmingham. "Temperate conservative Southerners were signing up for the John Birch Society 'in droves,'" he said; joining the JBS was a lot less controversial than joining the Klan or a Citizens' Council. Welch saw an incredible opportunity to grow the JBS in the South and ultimately did not resist the impulse.[12] Again, Welch's conspiracy theory—that the Communists controlled the civil rights—forged alliances that were morally wrong in the first place.

Along with external events, the influence of Alan Stang contributed to Welch's belief that JBS must mount a strong offensive that Communism lay behind the civil rights movement. In June 1963, *American Opinion* published Stang's "The New Plantation," which developed into his book *It's Very Simple: The True Story of Civil Rights*. Stang began the book with James Baldwin, who eloquently expressed his fury in *The Fire Next Time* for being refused a cup of coffee in an American diner. Baldwin was viewed by the mainstream press as the new face of a more militant Black movement comprising Malcolm X and Stokely Carmichael. In "The New Plantation," Stang wondered how the more radical "current Negro revolt" was going to satisfy Baldwin's desire for a cup of coffee. The "only legitimate function of government," Stang said, was to protect property. Civil rights legislation was abominable, Stang said, because it interfered with "the absolute and inviolable power to dispose of a specific property—one's own property." Anybody who does not have that power is "a slave"—hence his title. The NAACP, Stang said, was "probably not a Communist organization, nor even a Communist front," but was "gulled" by the Communist conspiracy, which was "captur[ing] the American government through a "process of internal corruption and dissolution." The civil rights movement, Stang said, was producing "the very thing it claims to oppose, not freedom for the Negro, but slavery for all."[13]

Welch was also inspired by African American anti-Communists who had lived inside the belly of the beast as Communists in the 1930s. Many of these Blacks were now anti-Communists eager to disclose what they had been doing. They were also highly reputable, very eloquent, and compelling, as they thought they were risking their lives to tell the truth. They wholeheartedly rejected the concept of race consciousness and, like Welch, believed that interracial violence and Communism were the real reasons for the civil rights movement. They highlighted that, contrary to what his critics said about him, Welch was no segregationist.

Manning Johnson was the most important Black conservative who brought to the John Birch Society the message that Communist agitators were promoting violent revolution all over the world in the name of nonviolence and peace. Johnson wrote that comity and civil harmony were not what the civil rights activists were interested in; they wanted to sow seeds of destruction and hate. Desegregation of public restrooms and schools were never meant to bring the races together but to tear them apart.

Like many well-respected conservatives, Johnson began his political career in the Communist Party, which he joined in 1930. By the end of the decade, he was a prominent voice in it, but he lost confidence in its mission. He eventually testified against his comrades before HUAC, relaying the sensational story that the CPUSA sought to establish a "Negro Republic" in the South. "Across nine states in 219 counties, the Negro Republic ran from Maryland to Texas," and "revolution and armed insurrection" in that area were the means to the end. Johnson explained that the plan fit with Lenin's anti-imperial program to provide "national minorities" a system of self-government. According to Johnson, during training in New York, he learned all about the theory of "world revolution" and how to organize "the workers, the farmers, the intellectuals, the artists, the professionals, and the middle-class elements into various types of groups," and exploit "the grievances among them for the purpose of drawing them into the Communist world general movement." He told Congress he quit the CPUSA because he learned that integration was never a true aim of the Communists, but the Southern Negro Republic was.

Teaming up with Archibald Roosevelt, the son of Theodore Roosevelt, Johnson formed the Alliance, which published his book *Color, Communism, and Common Sense* in 1958. The JBS later reprinted it. Johnson alleged that monstrous displays of racial antipathy were created by the NAACP, which sought to humiliate the United States and assist Soviet Russia in the conquest of Asia and Africa.[14] Johnson concluded that integration would hinder the progress that folks like him had made with Whites. The Communists wanted to promote a "persecution complex" among southern Blacks, Johnson charged, fostering racism in them. "Interracialism" would be "deadening . . . for Negro projects," he said, and the integration promoted by the Warren Court and the NAACP ruined "race pride." Johnson observed that Polish Americans, Chinese Americans, and German Americans benefited magnificently from spatial segregation; why should Blacks be any different? The CPUSA ended its program for Black self-determination in 1959, but Johnson insisted it never ceased to be a goal.[15]

After leaving the CPUSA, Johnson lived in a state of perpetual fear, praying every time he turned the keys in his car. In 1959 Johnson was killed in an automobile accident, and some followers thought foul play was involved, perhaps by the Soviets. While highly unlikely, the allegations seemed not as farfetched as they do today. Communists-turned-anti-Communists lived as fugitives, and many remembered the story of Leon Trotsky, who was murdered by a Stalin-sent assassin with an ice pick in Mexico. In the United States, there was nothing so notorious, but there were tales of anti-Communists being murdered or persecuted or simply disappearing. Whether the tales were real or not did not really matter. Herbert Philbrick, a former G-man who spied on the Communist Party for the agency, told Robert Welch in 1959 that the Johnson case was "just too damned quiet"; he warned Welch to "watch for almost anything."[16]

This likely did little to settle Welch's mind, but Robert handled stress very well overall. He was an expert compartmentalizer. He could nap anywhere at anytime. He was a rare combination of composure and nervous energy. If anything perturbed him, he rarely showed it. And when he did worry, Robert never questioned that it was for good reason. But given how much he believed in a Communist conspiracy, it is a wonder he remained so calm and relaxed. Robert was a cool character and, while eccentric, never suffered any physical, mental, or emotional breakdown. His blood pressure was perfect for a man in his sixties, and he was as relaxed and happy as ever, despite working two to three times as many hours a day as the average American male. Free from want, deeply in love, treasured by JBS members, and finding meaning in the fight against Communism, he was living the life he wanted to live. He believed the Communists were watching him, but it didn't appear to faze him. He liked the attention from watchers because it gave his life meaning. And it was what he signed up for. He was an affluent male enjoying his White privilege during the period of America's economic zenith.

Robert found Johnson's book illuminating. "Because of its timeliness in connection with the rising storm in the South," Robert promoted the book throughout 1963. Johnson, Welch believed, saw "through the massive and cruel deception being practiced by the Communists." Welch was absolutely convinced that Johnson, had he lived, would have led the anti–civil rights movement and perhaps eclipsed Martin Luther King and other civil rights leaders. More immediately, Johnson's race helped the John Birch Society distance itself from White supremacists to some extent.[17]

Welch seemed influenced by FBI Director J. Edgar Hoover's congressional testimony that the civil rights movement was swarming with Communists, just as it had been in the 1930s. Welch often drew on the works of Hoover. Here, he echoed Hoover's conclusion that Communists had infiltrated civil rights organizations. But Welch added a conspiratorial dimension: social action sought violence and chaos, but upheaval was not an end in itself. The real goal was to create an emergency that required the government to forcefully alleviate the chaos. In essence, Welch believed, chaos was the Communists' objective because it justified the government's assumption of autocratic powers, and empowered the Communists already ensconced within the government.

Welch's thinking on the civil rights movement was also shaped by his exposure to the pamphlet "American Negro Problems," written by Hungarian Communist and strategist Joseph Pogany in 1928 under the pseudo-name "John Pepper." Pogany had outlined the entire Communist struggle for civil rights and advised stirring "up racial riots" and advancing "the Communist cause through racial agitation."[18] Pogany's plan was happening all over the world right now, Welch said—though Pogany had been murdered in 1938 on Stalin's orders.

Pogany supported abolishing Jim Crow and ending prohibitions on interracial marriage. He also wanted federal anti-lynching laws and legislation prohibiting discrimination in employment. In essence, he provided a laundry list for the activists of the "long civil rights era." Anti-Communists like Welch then said the goals of the civil rights movement were the goals of the Communists. Yet Pogany further argued that such reforms were only the appetizer for a much larger and richer main course. For him, capitalists, rather than segregationists, presented the bigger problem because they dominated the working class. Pogany said that Black Americans needed to free themselves from "capitalist exploitation," but they first needed to abolish legal and social segregation. After that, American workers—both Black and White—would develop class consciousness, become a united force, and achieve paradise.

Most important for his influence on Welch, Pogany placed the civil rights struggle in the larger context of the international fight to throw off the European colonialist yoke. Both in the colonized world and in America, Pogany wrote, it "is necessary" to combine "full racial, social, and political equality of the Negroes" with their right for self-determination. According to Pogany, and then to Welch, the battle for an all-Black Soviet state was being fought in the streets of Oxford, Birmingham, Harlem, and soon Detroit and Watts. The Communists were behind both movements inside and outside the United States.[19]

Welch's dip in the sordid waters of colonialism created a strange brew. It provided a justification to align with southern segregationists while denying any racism. But so long as the goal was defeating the Communist conspiracy, Welch had no compunction about finding bedfellows with racist views. By the mid-1960s, Welch was working closely with southern segregationists, including Billy James Hargis and Kent Courtney, because they viewed anti-colonialism abroad and civil rights on the home front through the same lens as Welch did. Not only did Welch send money to Hargis, but Birch members frequented Hargis's Christian Crusade Convention. There, in August 1962, one popular conversation concerned the Kennedy administration's policy on Africa. Eviscerating the idealism of the New Frontier, speaker Martin Camacho of the Portuguese American Committee on Foreign Affairs derided JFK as foolish to assert that the African people had "the yearnings, the hopes, the aspirations, and the rising expectations" to "desire national existence" and throw off the yoke of "their alleged colonial oppressors." The same sorry canard, Camacho observed, was manufactured by the Communists in the 1920s. The Communists, he said, simply wanted to oppress the African people, just as they wanted to enslave Blacks marching in the streets for civil rights. The Communist persecutors, Camacho argued, wanted to present the colonial powers as oppressive masters, but he held that Goa, Mozambique, and Angola, for example, were as much an "integral part" of Portugal as Alaska and Hawaii were of the United States. To Welch and Hargis, the proud colonial power was not a force for racism, but only sought national interests, "human decency," and "law and order."[20]

As the civil rights movement gained power, many Birchers remained unmoved, or worse. When Martin Luther King Jr. stirred the cause of freedom with his magnetic and magnificent "I Have a Dream" speech in August 1963—"I have a dream that my four little children will one day live in a nation where they will not be judged by the color of their skin but by the content of their character"[21]—many Birchers were horrified by King's image of Black and White children walking hand in hand. For Slobodan Draskovich and others, such contact was a nightmare, and King's words were Communist propaganda from the global conspiracy designed to produce revolutionary violence in the streets. The nonviolent civil rights strategy of King was a charade, thought Draskovich, designed to lull the American people to sleep before the shooting started. Draskovich thought that focusing on "law and order" and anti-Communist education was the best way to curtail the coming revolutionary violence.

Draskovich peddled a murky mixture of racist pseudoscience. He opposed civil rights not only because the movement was a Communist plot but because he sought to preserve Western civilization from "mongrelization" and barbarism. The March on Washington, Draskovich complained, was "a challenge to the rule of law and order" and "the natural climax of a series of moves which the Communist conspiracy has minutely planned, prepared and executed in the last few years." America's continuation as a nation was "gloomier than ever" given the march, "the test ban treaty," and the Kennedy's administration's "fraternization with Khrushchev."[22]

But Welch was not on board with Draskovich's apocalyptic worldview. He did not believe in the March on Washington, but then again, neither did President Kennedy. Welch's efforts to halt civil rights seemed to have nothing to do with maintaining apartheid in the South or preserving its racial caste system. In the modern world, scientific racism was outré, the stuff of Nazis, and Welch was no Nazi—leftist aspersions notwithstanding. Welch didn't think genetic traits made Black and White intellectual inequalities inevitable. His views were distinct from the Citizens' Councils that defended segregation according to scientific racism. Welch even prohibited members of the Citizens' Councils from joining JBS. Of course, he could not control members of the Citizens' Councils from voicing their support for the JBS, and some did. At no point did the civil rights movement threaten "racial purity," according to Welch. He was not obsessed, as some White southerners were, with interracial intercourse.[23] For Welch, every American, Black or White, had a right to citizenship and should have a chance to rise. Racial inequality was based in social and cultural differences, fomented by Communists, he thought. Welch did not oppose integration but believed in gradualism. He thought that things were moving too fast, and he certainly did not want desegregation by federal fiat. That said, his all-Black JBS groups *were* segregated, and this reality puts him in the same league with President Eisenhower, who also believed progress was moving too quickly and himself opposed the desegregation of the army in 1948. Because of zealous belief in conspiracy, Welch, sadly, could not embrace the fact that a great change in racial relations was essential.

Welch faced allegations of racism for his outspoken opposition to a civil rights law, but he categorically deemed it as the product of "malicious imagination."[24] Welch maintained that the John Birch Society was far from racist; it contained "all white chapters, all Negro chapters, and integrated chapters. . . . For us to lay down some rule, and tell our members everywhere that they must be sure to have a cross-section of the community in each chapter," which would be the result of any civil rights law, "would be as stupid on our part as the Federal Government is now pretending to be."[25]

Like Draskovich, Welch argued that JBS members were simply protecting civilization from the Communists who would ruin everything that had been built over two millennia. He wanted to keep the enduring values that made America great, but he suffered from a serious blind spot when it came to recognizing that African Americans also made America great. It was his mission to save America from the Communists who were colonizing the world and bringing on a new dark age.

But generally Welch and Draskovich did not agree. Welch had to keep a close eye on Draskovich, who did conspire with fellow racist Revilo Oliver to remove Welch from the John Birch Society. Draskovich wanted Welch's job, and Robert knew it. Sometimes being paranoid does not mean you aren't being watched. Draskovich wrote Oliver in April 1962 of "a clamor to remove or replace Bob" that was growing every day. Welch eventually fired Oliver for his anti-Semitism. Oliver, "whose anti-Semitic feelings are probably as strong as those of anybody in America (even including Westbrook Pegler)," observed Welch, "and which bias of his we have always had some trouble keeping under wraps, has been so stirred up by every other violent anti-Semite in the country writing to him that I was wrecking the Society, or allowing it to be wrecked by refusing to countenance open anti-Semitic activities." Welch concluded this infighting within the leadership resulted in the *New York Times* reporting "about my being retired as an 'elder statesman' of the Society."[26] While false, the article held that the JBS council had kicked Welch upstairs, diminishing his role, even as the JBS was fading away into obscurity. The reality was that most of the National Council remained loyal to Welch and was convinced that the membership was too.[27] And it never possessed the authority to remove him anyway. Welch was aware that some council members "do listen to such continued suggestions as that I simply must have a team of people like Draskovich and Oliver to help me actively in running the society—which would of course only add to my labors and pressures to the point of breaking me down. So keeping the real situation sufficiently understood has taken a lot of time and energy." This only contributed to his feeling of being absolutely beleaguered.[28]

According to Welch, Los Angeles council member Paul H. Talbert spearheaded the original drive to remove him in 1961, and never gave up. Welch believed that Talbert "wanted to take over the Society himself and still thinks this might be possible." Talbert, Welch said, "has always had and still has some help from Coleman Andrews, who was beguiled by William Buckley into the original drive" to oust him.[29] Clarence Manion seemed in his corner, or at least not on the other side of the ring. Manion, according to Welch, "was very much with [Talbert] at one time, but I believe is pretty well—though not completely—changed over." Welch regretted that Manion was too political, however: "Manion still thinks entirely in political rather than educational terms, and that the Society should become an adjunct to the political action of some party or candidate." Welch disagreed and wanted to continue to build an educational organization.[30]

Increasingly, Welch simply did not know whom to trust. He drew more inward, hired more deferential, imperfect figures who would at least demonstrate loyalty and affection. The more semi-incompetents he hired, the further the Society fell.

In the 1960s and 1970s, the day-to-day manager at Belmont was Tom Hill, the director of field activities, who was with the JBS for twenty-five years. The *American Opinion*'s prolific writer Gary Allen once observed that, according to "nearly one hundred former Coordinators and Major Coordinators . . . [e]very creative idea which would help build the Birch Society and/or damage the Conspiracy died on Tom Hill's desk." Some concluded that Hill was a mole. Allen continued:

"There has been a great deal of debate as to whether Tom Hill is a plant—or a vegetable. Actually it makes little difference. The bottom line is that Tom Hill stifles creativity and activity regardless of what his motives may be."[31]

Whether or not Hill was a plant, he was certainly a sycophant of Welch. He took advantage of the fact that the JBS council members had little influence and served primarily as window dressing. According to Allen, "by withholding information and coloring the facts, [Hill] managed to play Mr. Welch like a Stradivarius." "Hill has no leadership capacity. He could not inspire thirsty sailors just home from 90 days to go into a bar." Allen once said to JBS coordinator Bill Murray that Hill should be a bureaucrat in the Social Security Administration. He was not meaning to pay a compliment. Murray replied that he was overrating him. "Tom Hill should be taking quarters at a toll bridge." The one known major disagreement that Marian Welch ever had with Robert concerned Hill.

By the 1960s, the introverted Hill, Allen said, "was a mackerel out of water" and was miscast as, "in essence, the national sales manager of a nationwide organization." At the time of Hill's appointment, Allen said, "the Society had many creative and aggressive Coordinators and members. Rather than provide training and leadership to keep these people out of trouble, all problems wound up on Tom Hill's desk. Naturally human beings try to avoid pain. Hill soon discovered, perhaps subconsciously, that by telling people to do little more than read, write letters, and pass out literature, the number of problems arriving at his desk greatly diminished. The result, however, was to smother growth, activity, and morale in the society."[32]

Welch felt beset by his former friends, the press, and the Communists. He sounded like a victim, a persecuted figure. "In all American history only the persecution of the Mormon church during the middle of the nineteenth century has ever equaled in ferocity and duration the attack that was turned on the John Birch Society," he later said.[33] The press was conspiring against him, he thought, with the "worst of all media" being CBS. "They not only carried all kinds of falsehoods and smears over the national network, and over local stations which they controlled," but "CBS men resorted to all kinds of physical tricks and harassments against me."[34] And yet, "CBS was by no means alone in manifesting such bitter hostility to any anti-Communist speaker who was reaching sizable audiences. . . . [Once], I was bodily pushed around by some of the reporters present. And after one later speech, in some college town in western Wisconsin, where there were 3000 students and teachers on hand, the manhandling to which I was subjected on the platform after my speech reached physically dangerous proportions."[35] It is not hard today to imagine a major public figure claiming persecution by the national press and by individuals deep within the organization he himself led. In his talk of persecution and unfairness, Welch foreshadowed the style of populism that Donald Trump applied against a "deep state" and electoral disappointments. Playing the victim was not an endearing trait for either.

But Welch and Draskovich, for all their differences, foreshadowed another aspect of twenty-first-century conservative populism. Presaging Steve Bannon and his circle of acolytes who attempted to decouple Communist China, socialist regimes, and supranational organizations like the United Nations and NATO from former president Trump's nationalist agenda, Draskovich was a populist who sought to make anti-Communist activism more international. "The problem of our strategy and tactics," Draskovich said, is "that they do not exist. . . . We cannot destroy a world-wide conspiracy of traitors without a world-wide conspiracy of patriots." He said the JBS was not reaching out to enough citizens in other countries that were besieged by Communist movements. "Our work in Latin America, Europe and Asia cannot wait. . . . [I]f the whole world goes, the US cannot stand alone," Draskovich warned. He wanted international JBS chapters, and others suggested the same. "The natural climax of a series of moves which the Communist conspiracy has minutely planned, prepared, and executed in the last few years" made going global imperative.[36] Draskovich augured Steve Bannon's twenty-first-century vision of global populism.

Welch was reluctant to go global. He knew Draskovich wanted to be "running all over the world forming such branches." Draskovich also wanted the John Birch Society to be a "secret organization, passing our 'instructions' down to our members through our Major Coordinators to our Coordinators to our Section Leaders to our Chapter Leaders to the members themselves, instead of mailing bulletins." Welch thought Draskovich's suggestions "impracticable nonsense."[37] He was deeply dismayed when Draskovich typed a twenty-two-page letter claiming that Welch was "betraying American youth" for failing to adopt his suggestions.[38]

Welch did not want to follow this route because he was busy putting out fires with other conservatives at home. Yet he was nothing if not a compulsive analyst of foreign affairs. He remained deeply concerned by the global Communist conspiracy that lay behind the mask of the nonviolent civil rights movement, fomenting revolutionary violence not only in the streets of the United States but all over the world. Only anti-Communist education and "law and order," he thought, could turn back the tide against these civil rights marauders and quash the disorder erupting in Newark, Philadelphia, Los Angeles, and around the globe.[39]

Robert's writings on events in Congo embodied his belief that the civil rights movement was just one finger on the hand of a worldwide Communist conspiracy. He came to compare the "Invasion of Mississippi" (which was, in reality, a segregationists' riot), in which James Meredith tried to enroll at the University of Mississippi in October 1962, with the UN's role in Katanga, a province of the Congo. After Congo received independence from Belgium, Katanga, a region full of rich resources, became a breakaway province due to the efforts of Moise Tshombe, a Congolese politician and businessman still loyal to commercial interests in Belgium. But between 1961 and 1963, the Kennedy administration was instrumental in helping the UN defeat Katangan forces and reunifying the Congo. Welch was indignant about Katanga's loss of independence.

In both Katanga and Mississippi, Welch said, a nefarious supergovernment had overextended its power and brought chaos to a pacific people, who followed the rule of law and embraced Christianity. Welch carefully juxtaposed a capitalist, civil, and Christian Katanga against the chaotic, primal, atheistic, and Communistic Congo led by Patrice Lumumba. Unlike the Congo, which was in arrears and ruins, Katanga was a thriving economic paradise. According to Welch, it was "the one part of the former Belgian Congo that preserve[d] law, order, and decency." Katanga received a raw deal from Kennedy and the UN, said Welch. And its unjust and brutal subjugation by that supranational body demonstrated "the hypocrisy of the 'anti-colonialism' propaganda, which the Communists have been using for 40 years." Kennedy's vicious decision, said Welch, to send federal troops to Mississippi was an equally seminal and analogous moment.[40]

The August 1963 *JBS Bulletin* contained the Society's most comprehensive treatment of the worldwide revolution of civil rights yet. Robert stated unequivocally that what was going in the American South was going on around the world. He also declared that the nuclear test ban treaty, the March on Washington, and Kennedy's newfound support of the civil rights movement demonstrated the president's allegiance to the Communist conspiracy. Welch made his case by quoting from Communists, including an article in *Political Affairs*, a Communist monthly, which Welch declared was the playbook that Kennedy was following. The July 1963 article read: "The key to the future, in fighting both for peace and civil rights, clearly lies in the strengthening and advancement of the mass movements and struggles. . . . The fight for Negro freedom has become the focal point" and "holds the key to all other struggles, including the fight for peace."[41]

In that *Bulletin*, Welch located a date when it all started. Likely drawing on Pogany's chronology, Welch declared that in approximately 1920, the Communists started the movement to end European imperialism by establishing "guerrilla bands in one so-called colonial area after another." At the same time, European powers gave "the 'colony' both enlightened and beneficent rule." Quality of life improved under imperialism, Welch claimed. The "standards of living, of education, and of native participation in government" surged, Welch alleged. But as with the civil rights movement, the federal government destroyed what was very good progress. That he was wrongheaded did not mean that he was insincere.

Welch and the Society's leaders wrote innumerable articles and gave many speeches highlighting the Communists' control of the civil rights movement. John Rousselot, the erstwhile California congressman, said the Communists had "betrayed a good cause" in disrupting amicable racial relations. Civil rights was a Communist program "as part of a world revolution against what they have elected to call 'colonialism,'" wrote Medford Evans, a contributor to *American Opinion*. They are establishing a "beachhead ready for exploitation in the final struggle," he added.[42]

In December 1963, Manion formalized the turn toward civil rights as the central issue of the JBS. Manion established a committee that reported on the major changes already underway in the direction of the Society. It concluded that remaining an "educational organization" was simply no longer an option. "Truth can be successfully used to defeat a false ideology," Manion's report read, but truth "does not suffice to defeat a conspiracy." The conspiracy that controlled the civil rights movement made it imperative, Manion suggested, to make the JBS an action-based organization that produced real results.

Manion's report expressed much concern with Robert's leadership style. Members were also unhappy with the projects Robert supported, found Manion. There was also some dissatisfaction with Robert's conspiratorial pamphlet *The Neutralizers*. In the pamphlet, Welch found that after the 1961 attacks by liberals and Communists failed to destroy the JBS, the conspiracy began a new strategy: it started to infiltrate the organization with anti-Semites to convince the American people that the JBS was an anti-Semitic organization. Along with the other cabals, real or otherwise, against the Society, Welch said the Neutralizers picked up speed in 1963. "Bill Richardson, John Rousselot, Tom Hill, and I, all separately became absolutely convinced from careful study" that the Neutralizers were real and meant business, Welch wrote. The Neutralizers included folks like the Reverend Cotton, who was "actually an enemy infiltrator" and had "been tearing chapters to pieces in California by persuading enough members to go off on an anti-Semitic binge" by writing "letters running to thousands of words."[43] "The Neutralizers, Welch lamented, "created terrific problems and pressures, because it is all done with such an appearance of spontaneity and sincerity."[44] Again, that Welch permitted such members to remain, let alone enter in the first place, suggests that the JBS failed to take a strong enough stand against anti-Semitism in a century haunted by the Holocaust. In admitting anti-Semites, Welch stood up to be counted with the enemy, threatening everything the allies in WWII fought against.

That said, anti-Semitism, Welch believed, distracted members from fighting Communism. Welch characterized anybody who dabbled in anti-Semitism or spoke of an "international Jewish conspiracy" as a Communist agent provocateur. Note that Welch also wrote of a "Zionist conspiracy" that was periphery to the Communist conspiracy. Thus, depending on his audience, Welch peddled in deception.

The Manion report protested that publishing *The Neutralizers* might drive away anti-Semitic members: "It sets us on a collision course that must bring us into conflict with some of the oldest, most powerful, and most influential patriotic organizations in the nation, including several retired Admirals and Generals." In the final analysis, Welch could not run a society based on theories about shadowy string pullers without attracting anti-Semites—which was what happened.

Despite Manion's protests that the characteristics of the Old Right were acceptable as late as the early 1960s, to some extent, in publishing *The Neutralizers,* Welch seemed to be admitting that a house cleaning of anti-Semites was desirable. Welch's *The Neutralizers* seemed to be dumping the anti-Semitic remnants of the Old Guard and the last vestiges of anti-Semitism from the JBS, but his inconsistency on the question presents challenges for historians trying to reach a definitive answer. He tried to be too clever by half when addressing the problem of anti-Semitism, but, in the last analysis, every letter of Welch's should have made it abundantly clear that such hatred had no place in his Society.

Manion's report provided the John Birch Society with a formal blueprint for an institutional response to the civil rights movement. The Society opposed the southern civil rights movement and civil rights bills as symptoms of a worldwide Communist conspiracy. Civil rights agitators, Welch further argued, wanted to end the rule of law by enlarging the power of the state and make way for a one-world government. But at the same time, he saw the civil rights movement as one arm of the worldwide anti-colonial movement against civilization.[45] Consequently, as the race for the 1964 presidential election heated up, the JBS prioritized its opposition to the civil rights movement and civil rights legislation, lamented the decline of law and order and the growth of the federal government, while keeping a close eye on anti-colonial movements throughout the world.

22

Two Novembers, 1963–1964

President Kennedy watched television closely in June 1963 as blasts from fire hoses violently forced men, women, and children down the streets of Birmingham. In response, Kennedy appeared on television to label civil rights "a moral issue"; he then called for a new civil rights bill. That night, a sniper shot and killed civil rights leader Medgar Evers in Jackson, Mississippi.[1] Welch thought the Communists were behind Evers's assassination, just as they had murdered Emmett Till and countless other Blacks.[2] Soon after his address, Kennedy's approval rating plummeted from 70 percent to 55 percent. Conversely, Welch's program to impeach Earl Warren grew only more popular after JFK introduced the civil rights bill.

The summer of 1963 saw an ebbing of the irrationally exuberant self-confidence of the 1950s and the high hopes of the early 1960s. For many Americans in 1963, JFK represented American confidence. For one brief moment, it seemed that Kennedy's promises to lower taxes while providing health insurance for a larger number of Americans and increasing the size of the military were plausible. He boldly wanted to put a man on the moon by the end of the decade. He called for the elimination of poverty and racial discrimination. He signed a treaty banning atmospheric testing of nuclear weapons. At American University, Kennedy called for "not merely peace for Americans but peace for all men and women—not merely peace in our time but peace for all time" because "we all inhabit this small planet. We all breathe the same air. We all cherish our children's future. And we are all mortal." Some said he had learned the limits of martial rhetoric after bringing the world to the brink of nuclear holocaust in the Cuban missile crisis. Rumors abounded in Washington that Kennedy was experimenting with LSD, which was broadening his horizons and making peace a priority.

Robert Welch shared none of his countrymen's romantic sentiments toward Camelot on the Potomac. Kennedy grew more corrupt every day, Welch thought, spending the hard-earned dollars of the voters and moving the country to the left, or worse. When Kennedy expressed his unequivocal support for civil rights, Robert concluded that a Republican opposed to civil rights was needed. He believed that Republicans could attract southern conservatives who had been Democrats, combine them with the conservative strength in the Middle West and Far West, offset the liberalism of the Northeast, and finally prevail. Robert continued to believe that Barry Goldwater was the man for the job.

Goldwater came to agree. After Nixon lost the Black vote to Kennedy in 1960, Goldwater told Atlanta Republicans that the GOP was "not going to get the Negro vote . . . so we ought to go hunting where the ducks are." He meant the South. Although Goldwater was not yet committed as a candidate, Republican strategists stood ready to draft him if necessary. By the time the Draft Goldwater Committee held its first press conference in 1963, its leaders, Peter O'Donnell and F. Clifton White, had already lined up chairs in thirty-three states and had nationwide support from precinct chairs to national committee members.[3]

Despite his commitment to Goldwater, Welch remained preoccupied with educational and organizational matters, not with political ones. "For the past year," he wrote, "I have had a rough time, far rougher than anybody else could realize. . . . For one thing, I have had to face a continuous, renewed, and increasing behind the scenes effort to have me step aside and let somebody else run the Society."[4] By the fall of 1963, Robert clearly needed a break. "I was worn out and run down so that it was taking me much longer to do everything." "After nearly seven years of working seven days and nights per week," Welch was "finally able to squeeze in [a] vacation."

Then at 12:30 p.m. on November 22, 1963, Lee Harvey Oswald fired three shots into the presidential limousine and revolutionized the political landscape. When President Kennedy was assassinated in Dallas, a "storm hit us," Welch said.[5]

In Phoenix, two shots were fired into the local office of the John Birch Society. The gunman yelled: "You killed my man." At the time, the national press presented the JBS as dangerous extremists, and many people concluded that the organization obviously had something to do with the assassination, which was inaccurate. Robert Welch received threatening phone calls. "Shouting college-age youngsters," he said, circled the Birch Society headquarters in Belmont yelling "insults and catcalls." Someone threw a brick through his office window. Protests encircled the Society's building in Los Angeles; the office closed for the day.[6]

Welch remained composed during the "storm." He telegrammed Mrs. Kennedy saying that the John Birch Society shared in the country's "deep sorrow" for the loss of the president. Welch also canceled the Society's fifth-anniversary dinner that weekend in Boston.[7] Welch wrote that the "terrible tragedy" was "everything which the JBS has feared for our country and to which we have been so bitterly opposed." "For several years Communist pressures have increasingly made the assassination of heads of state a weapon of political action." In 1961, it was the murder of General Rafael Trujillo in the Dominican Republic. In 1963, it was the military coup of Iraq's Prime Minister General Abd al-Karim Qasin, and a few weeks before, South Vietnam's President Ngo Dinh Diem. Welch was "horrified to see that weapon used in our own country."[8]

But people blamed Welch and the Far Right. Conservative Texas Senator John Tower received multiple threats after Kennedy's murder and holed up his family in a hotel. Richard Nixon embodied the spirit of many when he called J. Edgar Hoover after hearing of the shooting, and asked "What happened, was it one of the right wing nuts?"[9] By December 12, Welch stated: "the assassination of the president was not only to have been blamed in a general way on the spirit of hatred supposedly created by the so-called 'right wing extremists.' But it was to be proclaimed loudly and emphatically that the actual assassin was a member of some right-wing group which was directly responsible for the crime." Welch was correct in his analysis about an effort to tie the Right to Kennedy's killing. Welch fought back, explicitly claiming in a full-page advertisement that "Communism Killed Kennedy"; he placed it from December 15th to the 18th in the *New York Times,* the *Washington Post,* the *Chicago Tribune,* and the *Los Angeles Times.* Welch pointed out that Oswald had renounced his citizenship to live in the Soviet Union, was photographed giving the Communist salute, and was married to the niece of a KGB colonel.[10]

Many Americans who were glued to their television sets and perusing *Time, Life,* and the mainstream national newspapers did not see things the way Robert Welch hoped. Many blamed the Right despite the fact that a Communist killed the president. The media and political leaders reflected that belief. It was the responsibility of arch conservative H. L. Hunt, said US senator Maurine Neuberger from Oregon. Walter Cronkite reported, incorrectly, that Barry Goldwater said: "No comment" when hearing of the shooting.[11] Right-wingers, Bishop James A. Pike said, "have consistently supplied fuel which would fire up such an assassin." We may never know why Oswald killed President Kennedy, observed Chief Justice Earl Warren, "but we do know that such acts are commonly stimulated by forces of hatred and malevolence, such as today are eating their way into the bloodstream of American life. What a price we pay for such fanaticism!"[12] Professor Donald T. Rowlingson of Boston University put it: "Having watched Hitler grasp power in Germany in 1932–33 on the pretext of protecting the nation from the menace of communism, I am less than convinced that right-wing extremism is any less dangerous here than left-wing extremism."[13]

The assassination reinforced the idea that the radical Right and the John Birch Society were agents of extremism, and the murder cast a long shadow over the Goldwater campaign.[14] A study by Dallas Republican Peter O'Donnell conducted a month before the assassination concluded that "neither Republicans nor Democrats identify Goldwater as part of the radical right." That was not the case soon after. By demonstrating that extremism was a problem in the body politic, the assassination recast Goldwater as a trigger-happy warmonger, an extremist, and a danger to the country. Right-wing extremism did shape the 1964 election. The Democratic nominee, President Lyndon Johnson, said five days after the murder: "let us put an end to the teaching and the preaching of hate and evil and violence. Let us turn away from the fanatics of the far left and the far right, from the apostles of bitterness and bigotry, from those defiant of law, and those who pour venom into our Nation's bloodstream."[15]

Welch was deeply disappointed by the national reaction to the Kennedy assassination. He had argued that the socialism and Communism advocated by the dashing and seemingly vigorous leader had promoted violence and disorder; indeed, the assassination only buttressed his theory about the consequences of failing to stand up to the Communism and socialism at the highest levels of power. Welch believed the fact that an American leader was cut down by a dedicated Communist who defected from the United States and lived in the Soviet Union provided the best evidence that Communism killed Kennedy. Welch believed that despite the various conspiracy theories surrounding the assassination, his own theory was best and should have had wider purchase. But somebody liked what the Society was doing. In December 1963, Welch wrote, "we are now up to over thirty-thousand members," and "we are now tremendously stronger than ever before."

Compounding the problem of leading a Society being blamed for the assassination of a president, Robert was beset by new problems with anti-Semitism. Westbrook Pegler had written a blatantly anti-Semitic article for *American Opinion,* but Robert thought he had headed it off. As he explained, I went "over with Scott Stanley [the editor of *American Opinion*] repeatedly, what I wanted in the magazine and the pitfalls to be guarded against." Welch would not tolerate anything in the magazine that smacked of anti-Semitism. "I had so carefully guarded against the worst features of the Pegler problem, that it was thoroughly understood the Pegler article was to be a factual review of the rise of the labor-union movement," but "these directions lasted for about three paragraphs, and Pegler went off worse than ever into the very kind of 'hate-mongering' that is so contrary to the spirit of the Society, and so dangerously destructive of what we are trying to do." Stanley covered himself by having the article read by several people—but not by Marian, or Miss Lovett or Mrs. White, and that convinced "him that the article was all right to run." Welch had been in California at the time, and when he returned, "the damage was done, or at least the magazine was printed" and "only the responsibility, good sense, loyalty and determination of Miss Lovett kept it from being already in the mails before I even had a chance to see it or do anything about it." Welch held back the issue, costing the Society a "dead investment of about $15,000." There never was a December issue. And Marian would thereafter, by his order, have to approve "every single paragraph in every issue before Scott sends it to the printer."[16]

There were other problems. The printer they used was being "harass[ed] and smear[ed]" for doing business with them. "I cannot be positive that the total effect of these and other considerations and pressures might not be to weaken this printer for having us for such a large customer" with bills "running at the rate of over half a million dollars per year." Welch "put about $40,000 of my own [money] into the breach during" 1963 "in order to sustain our growth in staff and inventories and equipment." "On top of all that," Welch said, "the Allen Bradley Company, from which we have been drawing about $10–$15,000 per month . . . is under so much pressure from the Internal Revenue Service over similar patriotic activities of the company that they have held up payments to ourselves." "And we have had other blows pile up on us in rather heartbreaking fashion." Welch requested from Olive Simes, a wealthy Bostonian, "a loan of at least $50,000 to either the John Birch society, or *American Opinion*, or to myself personally for two years, at 5% interest. . . . I need the money now. . . . I have given up practically everything else in this struggle, or at least certainly expect to do so before it is over."[17]

On the positive side of the ledger, though, Welch and the John Birch Society became central to the Goldwater campaign. Goldwater never condemned the Society because, as one Republican strategist wrote, "fortunately, or unfortunately, the Birchers are contributing a substantial portion of our workers and some of our leaders in many important areas and can be increasingly in evidence as the campaign progresses." Many GOP leaders concluded the Society was necessary for success because grassroots campaigns were needed to win elections. And right-wing activists like Birchers, GOP leaders eventually conceded, were necessary in state and local and party institutions. More often than not, Robert Welch himself was rejected while members received a pass and were considered well-intentioned, passionate conservatives.[18]

Further, many of Goldwater's closest advisors—Arizonans Denison Kitchell and Frank Cullen Brophy, and law school dean Clarence Manion—were members of the Society. Goldwater's own views certainly dovetailed nicely with those of the Society. Goldwater believed the Constitution protected property rights and restricted democracy to safeguard privilege. He understood the Constitution as a restrictive document that protected property rights and prioritized the state power over federal control. He assailed the 1964 Civil Rights Act for giving rise to "a federal police force of mammoth proportions." He attacked the *Brown v. Board of Education* decision, arguing that it was "not based on law" because it directly violated southern traditions of White entitlement and Black exclusion. Goldwater said, "I am firmly convinced—not only that integrated schools are not required—but that the Constitution does not permit any interference whatsoever by the federal government in the field of education." It was pure Bircher catnip.[19]

Goldwater called Birchers the "finest people in his community" and believed the Society played a "decisive role" in the California primary.[20] And yet, Goldwater's Arizona advisors embraced a "don't ask, don't tell" strategy when organizing Birchers.[21] Concerned that Goldwater had already been labeled as extremist, they "were trying to avoid any further repercussions."[22] Increasingly, Birchers were quiet about their affiliation—or were encouraged to hide it. T. Coleman Andrews was prohibited from active participation in the Goldwater campaign: "I have been told right straight out that they don't want the cooperation of any official of the John Birch Society except on a very quiet basis."[23]

Welch himself hoped for a Goldwater victory, but knew the odds were long. Lyndon Johnson, a master politician, had ascended to the presidency with a strong understanding of Congress and a desire to secure his fallen predecessor's legislative program. In a seemingly magnanimous gesture, Johnson shrewdly identified the 1964 Civil Rights Act as primarily John Kennedy's priority, rather than his own, to get broad bipartisan support, avoid backlash, and build upon his reputation as a man of steady moderation.[24]

Welch, of course, saw in this strategy a hidden red hand. Nothing is spontaneous from the perspective of a conspiracy theorist. Everything is completely premeditated. Pursuing the Civil Rights Act could lead to only chaos in the streets. By the spring of 1964, Welch was hearing reports, especially from Alan Stang, that "many of the same things seemed to be happening in Harlem, . . . as had happened in Algeria before the Communists grabbed it in 1962." Stang continued: "As in Algeria, several terrorist gangs were in operation. In Algeria, they had been composed of Moslems who allegedly were fighting 'for freedom.' In Harlem, they were composed of Negroes who were allegedly fighting for the same thing. What was happening, of course was that the Communists were terrorizing into line the Negro people they planned to use as cannon fodder in their plan to create chaos." On July 18, 1964, Harlem was ablaze. Bands of young men roamed the streets looting stores, while police used force to restore a semblance of equanimity. For six long nights, 4,000 participated in the riots that engulfed Harlem and Brooklyn's Bedford-Stuyvesant neighborhood. The New York Police Department severely beat looters, and by the end of the conflict 465 were arrested and 118 were injured. Stang declared that he saw the whole tragedy playing out before his very eyes: "It is still eerie to recall that as I finished the manuscript for [*American Opinion*] with a warning that riots might break out, as in Algeria, police sirens screeched past, indicating that the riots had already begun."[25] While Welch believed the riot was planned weeks if not months in advance, making it as premeditated by the Communists as the Kennedy assassination, in truth the riot began when police Lieutenant Thomas Gilligan shot and killed fifteen-year-old James Powell in front of dozens of witnesses.

But Welch was not the only one who believed that a conspiracy accounted for the Harlem riot. The president directed J. Edgar Hoover to investigate the cause and to give careful consideration that the Communists instigated the rioting. The president said the FBI has "got to stop these riots" since "every time one occurs, it costs me 90,000 votes." The Communists and the right-wing extremists like Texas millionaire H .L. Hunt were both involved, said Johnson. "Both sides are in on these riots," Johnson said. "Hell, these folks have got walkie-talkies. . . . Somebody's financing them big."[26] As riots came to dominate Johnson's thinking and threaten his reelection, he grew conspiratorial too.

He didn't have much to worry about. Kennedy's murder had dampened Goldwater's enthusiasm for the campaign. More important, perhaps, as Goldwater's running mate, William Miller, summed it up: "The American people were just not in the mood to assassinate two Presidents in one year." Johnson won handily.

23
Nadir, 1965–1966

After his resounding victory, Lyndon Baines Johnson led the charge for the Great Society, passing laws for Medicare, the National Endowment for the Arts, the National Endowment for the Humanities, and the Corporation for Public Broadcasting. Johnson saw his Great Society as accomplishing what his "political daddy" Franklin Delano Roosevelt had only dreamed of. For Robert Welch, these social engineering projects not only failed to work as promised but solidified the control of globalist eastern elites.

During and after World War II, Whites benefited from low-interest mortgages, defense jobs, and new highway construction projects. Johnson now expanded these opportunities to African Americans and other minorities. Yet civil rights leaders and progressives became impatient for more liberal reform, especially economic reform, and called for strong programs against poverty, racism, and voting discrimination. Despite being the most liberal president in history, Johnson was assailed by the New Left and others for not doing enough. And at the same time, Republicans embraced a nominally color-blind discourse that championed the "hard-working" who were being robbed by the "undeserving," and backlash resulted.

Johnson believed that a civil rights revolution was inevitable, but was uncertain whether it would manifest peacefully or violently. In an effort to ensure peaceful change, he waged a War on Poverty by redistributing wealth through legislation. Welch, however, called this War on Poverty a cancerous revolution that would "take from the haves, and give it the have-nots." It was not a novel venture, he said, but a program the Communists had been implementing for years. Welch became convinced that, despite any evidence, the real purpose of Johnson's Office of Economic Opportunity (OEO) was to steal tax dollars from paychecks and distribute them to various revolutionary groups. Readers of *American Opinion* learned that Harlem's Black Arts Repertory Theater, founded by Black nationalist playwright LeRoi Jones, spent $115,000 in anti-poverty funds on a production in which the Black chauffeur kills all the White characters. "I don't see anything wrong with hating white people," Jones observed. "Harlem must be taken from the beast and gain its sovereignty as a black nation."[1] Welch exposed other federal boondoggles, such as the case of the Blackstone Rangers, a 1,500-member-strong Chicago street gang that squandered more than $927,000 in job-training funds from the OEO. Notoriously violent, the Rangers were allegedly responsible for twenty-six murders between 1966 and 1968 and various outbreaks of violence with their chief rival, the Gangster Disciples. The Rangers were led by Eugene Hairston, whose tenure was marred after his conviction of soliciting a fourteen-year-old to commit murder. Conservative leaders of *American Opinion* winced upon learning that radical Saul Alinsky's Woodlawn Organization, an umbrella organization of community groups, was sympathetic to Hairston's plight.[2]

As the bad publicity and police raids increased, the gangs stepped up their warfare. Six teachers in the OEO program were indicted for rape or murder. But the greatest public controversy arrived when the police raids discovered that Reverend John Fry, the pastor of Illinois's oldest Presbyterian church, was storing an arsenal of gang weapons in his church basement. Welch used the Blackstone Rangers to embarrass the Johnson administration and highlight abuse, mismanagement, and misuse of War on Poverty funds.[3]

Meanwhile the Voting Rights Act of 1965 contributed to the elections of more liberal Democrats who were even more zealous than LBJ in their commitment to societal transformation, racial amity, and the implementation of more entitlement programs. The traditional Democratic Party became unmoored by the New Left, which argued that the underprivileged were being ignored. The party's longtime emphasis on growing individual opportunities became complicated by the infusion of more constituencies to satisfy. The New Deal Coalition was falling apart, just as inner cities started to fall apart as well.[4]

Days after the signing of the Voting Rights Act, Watts exploded. Lasting a full week, the Watts riot killed 34 people, injured 110, and caused $40 million in property damage. It began on August 11, 1965, with an act of police brutality and soon was out of control. The Los Angeles Police Department was outmanned, and rioters overran the streets.[5] Government officials did not see it coming, and President Johnson was reportedly paralyzed to act, but Robert Welch saw things completely differently. Watts, Welch asserted, was a premeditated rehearsal for revolutionary race war. He thought a board of revolutionary strategists had planned the entire riot and brought in approximately fifty African American Communists to stage the production. Drawing from Black Nationalists, Black Muslims, and paramilitary groups, the Communist insurgents were an intellectual elite comprising professors, attorneys, and businesspeople. They were all highly intelligent, shared a hatred toward Caucasians, were committed to the Communist conspiracy. As Gary Allen observed, the Watts riots were "about as spontaneous as the New Year's Day Rose Parade." Welch believed that a crucial component of the rehearsal for bigger things to come was conditioning the populace to the myth of police brutality. After this conditioning, an "incident" was manufactured—a traffic violation, in this case—that specified even the type of material to be looted. Liquor stores were chosen because intoxication supposedly made looters more amenable to suggestion. Supermarkets were popular because well-fed looters were likely to have the stamina to take on the "power structure." Pawn shops yielded guns. The purpose of Watts, according to Welch, was to determine whether revolutionaries could maintain a riot and acquire enough guns, money, and merchandise for a subsequent one.[6] Welch certainly had an imagination.

In 1966, there were thirty-eight riots, leaving 7 dead and 500 injured. The next year was even more deadly. Rioting in Newark and Detroit left 64 dead, and, as Michael Flamm observed, "discredited the liberal enterprise"—specifically Great Society programs.[7] But Welch saw conspiracy in the Detroit riots too. When Communist instigators there set fire to Black neighborhoods, Welch said, other conspirators were on the phone from Washington and urging local officials and police to stand down. More destruction was necessary, the conspiracy cried. That way, the violence and disorder could get out of hand and chaos could reign in the streets, unmatched by the local police. The only solution, the conspirators wanted people to learn, was that the federal government was the exclusive body that could "do something" to end the nightmare in the streets. Martial law and the end of American sovereignty were waiting in the wings, suggested Welch.

Welch called civil rights actions "civil turmoil," whether rioting in Watts, Detroit, or Newark; demonstrators marching from Selma to Montgomery; or Blacks registering to vote during the Student Nonviolent Coordinating Committee's Freedom Summer. Idealistic northern college students who joined these efforts were "brainwashed youngsters," he said. In the summer of 1965, Welch established The Truth About Civil Turmoil (TACT) Committees, a series of local groups to "expose" the "fraud" of civil rights. By 1968, 500 TACT Committees in three states were putting "on a massive and continuous educational program."[8]

Welch denied that TACT advocated White supremacy. The committees, he said, had "no position with regard to integration or segregation" and did not admit "purveyors of hate" as members. In the *JBS Bulletin,* he implored members to "find some hardworking Negro American whose store has been burned down by rioters" and tell that person to join TACT.[9] The African American former Communist Leonard Patterson was a member. He said that Moscow's Lenin school had trained him in urban guerrilla warfare, and the Watts riot was "just a continuation of what was done back in the 1930s" when he learned in Russia how to make Molotov cocktails and start riots.

After the Watts riot, local chapters of Welch's ad hoc group Support Your Local Police (SYLP) also grew in number. SYLP members did not always belong to the JBS; sometimes, in fact, they opposed it. But most felt disenchanted by the urban riots and campus protests that they associated with the rise of the New Left, Students for a Democratic Society, and the Black Power movement. They supported law and order, and they rejected the conclusions of California's McGone Commission that the Black community's "resentment, even hatred of the police" accounted for the violence in Watts, along with structural poverty, chronic cultural problems, and lack of educational opportunities. Because of what Welch called "a subtle, but now increasingly bolder, and more extensive effort, to harass and discredit local police forces and their individual members," SYLP set out to expose the myth of police brutality and dispel any drive for civilian review boards. According to Welch, police brutality was "as fraudulent as the lying pictures on the same subject published by *Life* magazine."[10] Julia Brown, a Black former Communist who became an FBI informant, spoke before TACT Committees on the subject of police brutality. The John Birch Society commissioned her memoir, *I Testify*, which described police brutality as a "familiar divide and conquer tactic." "I [have] never witnessed any instance of police brutality to Negroes," Brown said. "On the other hand," she continued, "I have witnessed incidents where every effort is made by misguided Negroes to provoke law enforcement into some action which might be propagandized as police brutality."[11]

Thus, while others argued police brutality was a genuine problem in the Black community, Welch and the John Birch Society concluded it was little more than Communist propaganda that sought to delegitimate the police, break down the rule of law, and cause societal turmoil. Communists, Welch believed, had started the original drive for civilian review boards and supported the replacement of local police forces with a centralized force under the control of the federal government. "The Communist press of America has been screaming for years," Welch wrote, "to have local police forces discredited, shunted aside, or disbanded, and replaced by Federal Marshals, or by similar agents and personnel of a nationalized federal police force." He felt the Kennedy administration's "invasion" of Mississippi under the guise of desegregating Ole Miss was powerful evidence of this.[12]

Events such as the 1962 turmoil at Ole Miss, the 1963 conflagration at Birmingham, and the 1965 riots at Selma and Watts convinced Welch that a race war would begin soon, likely in the South. The war would be horrific, he believed. Black Nationalists had a roster of police to kill, along with their families. They would start fires in oil fields, diverting the attention of thousands of firefighters. Meanwhile, murderous mobs would circulate, killing as many White men and children as possible. They would rape White women. There were simply not enough National Guardsmen to put down an insurrection of this size. Then, Whites would conclude that they needed to band together both in defense and to invade Black neighborhoods. The Communists concluded that the 90 percent of Blacks who were unwilling to get involved sooner would be forced to join if Whites invaded their homes. And from there the chain reaction would set the stage for the ineluctable merger between the Soviet Union and the United States. Welch saw racial confrontation as international in scope and sparking worldwide Communist revolution. "Our TACT Committees . . . ," Welch later said, "also argued that the civil rights struggle was part of the Communist's drive for decolonization in Africa."[13]

Welch and other members of the Republican Right saw themselves as supporting colonialism abroad for the same reasons as opposing civil rights at home: safeguarding property, upholding natural law and the rule of law, and saving civilization from the barbarians. To Welch, the White anti-Communists who fought against the end of apartheid in South Africa and Rhodesia were not to be condemned as racist practitioners of the same kind of segregation that pervaded the South but celebrated for safeguarding free-market capitalism and civilization and saving the benighted from the tangles of Communism.

For Welch, Rhodesia's White minority government was a quintessential example. In October 1964, Northern Rhodesia declared its independence from England, becoming the Republic of Zambia. In October 1965, in an effort to postpone rule by the Black majority, Southern Rhodesia also declared its independence and became the Republic of Rhodesia. England and the United States did not recognize the White government of Rhodesia because of its practice of segregation. Robert Welch, among others on the Far Right, protested this on the basis that Rhodesia's leaders were fiercely anti-Communist. "If there had been a United Nations in 1776, do you honestly believe it would have been on the side of Freedom?"[14] Welch asked. Rhodesian Prime Minister Ian Smith, a White man who allied himself with prominent conservatives, also portrayed Rhodesia's independence as akin to the American Revolution. The patriots of 1776 and 1965, Smith wrote, were trailblazing pioneers who built a civilization in the wild and fought oppression from distant rulers. "In each case a government thousands of miles away [was] convinced it knew better than those on the spot," Smith observed. Far from keeping at bay the rights of the Black majority,

Rhodesia was maintaining civilization, supporting law and order, and fighting Communism at home.[15]

John Birch Society council member Tom Anderson was the organization's authority on Africa. He supported Ian Smith. On the John Birch Society radio show in 1966, Anderson said "the issue is not color, but capacity; not race, but fitness to shoulder responsibility." Anderson continued: "one man, one vote Rhodesia would produce a black government, which would produce another Congo: chaos hunger and communism."[16] Two years earlier, Anderson called the civil rights bill "part of the grand design that the collectivists for their One World: one race, mongrel; one church, apostate and antichrist; one government under the Beast."[17]

Similarly, Welch believed that what was going on in Africa foreshadowed the denouement of the civil rights struggle in the United States. In his essay "Two Revolutions at Once," Welch concluded that the civil rights movement was both an anti-colonial movement and a proletarian revolution. Welch said that imperialists "were giving their subjects a very enlightened and benevolent rule" in 1920. So "separatist movements had to be artificially created" by the Communists, who sought to trick the very beneficiaries of colonial rule into rebelling against capitalism.[18] It was an unconvincing and ultimately embarrassing argument. It was also a dangerous one because followers believed it.

But Welch wasn't the only conservative who seemed to be floundering. The Goldwater rout convinced the Republican Party of the need to repackage conservatism. Messaging became a bigger priority and came to be considered crucial to success. Soon, they were making every effort to paint liberals as extremists outside the mainstream. Conservatives grew more populist and mainstream because they successfully depicted liberalism as a radical ideology. External events like the urban riots helped in this. So did the rise of new, skillful communicators.

24
Avenging the Insiders, 1966–1968

In California in 1966, Ronald Reagan was running an effective campaign for governor. Echoing Robert Welch and the John Birch Society, a practice he would continue even into his presidency, Reagan concluded that the Watts riots, the student free speech movement at Berkeley, and waning morals in broader society were all related products of liberalism. Affable and smiling, Reagan energized the Right with an easy victory over Edmund "Pat" Brown. The Right was on the rise in Congress too. Under the guidance of party chair Peter O'Donnell, Senator John Tower, who had embraced Welch's vision that civil rights and African decolonization were part of a single Communist conspiracy, won reelection. Republicans won forty-seven seats in the House and three seats in the Senate. Claude Kirk became the first Republican governor of Florida since Reconstruction. As riots engulfed cities, the public came to associate liberalism with lawlessness and conservatism as the mooring of civilization and law and order.

Robert was repackaging the Society too, admitting privately that the Goldwater loss in 1964 had caused a tremendous loss of momentum: "The morale of the Birchers and of all other anti-Communists was badly shattered." Worse, "very strong impetus was given to the widespread view being so sedulously created that political support of any candidate by the Birchers amounted to a kiss of death. During the spring of 1965, the Society was adding about ten chapters per day, but only one chapter per week by the summer of 1966." But as he put it, we had "no slightest intention" of "sink[ing] into a mere shell" or "fad[ing] away altogether."[1] Welch did limit some of his undemocratic and absolutist rhetoric amid changing national discourse. And he made it a priority to restrain the militancy and fanaticism of some in the Society. He doubled his efforts to jettison doctrinaire, undiplomatic, and divisive Society leaders, including Revilo Oliver, the anti-Semite and racist, as well as Robert DePugh for organizing the Minutemen, which fomented armed resistance to Communism. (Of course, that they belonged in the first place does little to raise the reputation of the Society.) DePugh led a dangerous underground army that was scattered throughout the United States. The Minutemen built up a large store of weapons, including machine guns and high-powered rifles, and trained secretly for guerrilla warfare. DePugh was convinced, like Welch, that the Communists had already taken over the government, but DePugh, unlike Welch, concluded that the only way to stop it was to arm his band of zealots to the teeth. Welch still believed that education gave the American people at least a fighting chance.

Robert Welch was a salesman who understood very well that if a product had a bad reputation, the public would reject it. Welch was far more a politically skilled salesman than a charlatan. He was also far more flexible than some have recognized, as well as more important within the Republican Party than historians have realized. He faced mighty headwinds in turning back the image of the John Birch Society as a band of crackpots, but he persevered with a new strategy. In the late 1960s and into the 1970s, Welch changed course and spun a richer tapestry for the Society beyond patriotism and conspiracy. While never completely abandoning the impeachment of Earl Warren or the narrative of the grand conspiracy, Welch made the Society sound more sensible and reasonable. To a greater degree, Welch appealed largely to a commonsense argument that liberal programs failed. Welch held that self-help and autonomy worked, and unbalanced budgets for untested social programs simply did not. Voters, registering unprecedented defiance of liberalism, agreed. And the Society began to grow again after 1966.

With its field staff, in the late 1960s the John Birch Society built the infrastructure for greater circulation for its two magazines, *The Review of the News* and *American Opinion*. "The going was rough," Welch said, "because we could not count on any newsstand sales except those created by some of our most dedicated members through acting as volunteer distributors to drug stores in similar outlets in their local communities."[2] Most issues were well produced and timely.

The John Birch Society continued to develop its chain of American Opinion Bookstores, "With the 9000 commercial retail outlets for books and magazines, as well as all of the regular wholesale channels, practically closed to us by pressures of all kinds from the left-wing forces—including sabotage of our publications at all levels of distribution," Welch said, we "creat[ed] our own methods of moving books and pamphlets into the hands of our own members and as much of the public as we could reach." We set "up nearly 400 of these very useful, encouraging, and visible physical outposts of our educational progress. Some of them were little more than an otherwise empty garage or a room in somebody's house. And almost all of them had to be staffed by volunteers, because there was not sufficient volume of sales to keep them open otherwise."[3]

Like Dan Smoot, Welch came to the conclusion in 1966 that a larger conspiracy existed beyond the Communist cabal. What he was fighting was not what he originally thought it was. A gradual revolution in his thinking was occurring. The Communist conspiracy based in Moscow was only one branch of a much more pernicious cabal running from New York, London, and Paris. This cabal was more long-standing, secretive, and dangerous than the Russian Communist Party, which he said "is only a tool of the total conspiracy." Welch determined that folks could be part of the conspiracy while not necessarily members of the Communist Party. But he began to understand the Communists as the conspiracy's hit men, ready to do the dirty work.

Welch's speech on this, "The Truth in Time," drew heavily from Smoot's *The Invisible Government*.[4] Smoot discovered a cohort of high-level government officials and establishment figures who were not Communists but members of the Council on Foreign Relations, which was the conspiracy's nerve center. They included Secretary of State Dean Rusk, CIA Director Allen Dulles, and Secretary of Defense Robert McNamara. According to Smoot, these appointed public officials generally favored the United Nations, backed foreign aid, and supported the expansion of the federal government. Welch also drew from John Stormer's *None Dare Call It Treason,* which envisioned a State Department clique intent on disarmament.[5]

Highly educated, immensely wealthy, and highly cultured, the Insiders came from the highest social strata and had a long-standing philanthropic reputation. They controlled the media, and any group aiming to expose them, as the JBS was doing, would be ridiculed by newspapers, radio, and television, as well as socially ostracized, and perhaps eliminated.[6]

The Insiders were not Communists loyal to Moscow or Peking. They were interested only in the aggrandizement of their own power. According to Welch's new vision, power-grasping billionaires created Communism not as a movement for the down-trodden but for themselves. They planned to control the world by creating socialist governments in each nation-state. Then in the "Great Merger," the United Nations would consolidate all these governments into an omnipotent socialist superstate. One of their greatest accomplishments, Welch said, was "turning one nation after another over to Communist tyranny—as in Czechoslovakia, and China, and Cuba, and the Congo," using the power of the federal government. They exploited socialism for their own ends, using it as their hammer and finance capitalism as their anvil to take over the world. Welch reported that the Insiders claimed they were building a paradise on earth, when they were actually constructing a prison planet.

Just as Smoot laid out, the Council on Foreign Relations, comprising 1,500 elite members in labor, government, and business, was the Insiders' key vehicle. Staffing key positions in government since the early days of the New Deal, the Council's first purpose was to control the State Department and remain as secretive as possible. Obviously it was succeeding because few Americans even knew of its existence, according to Welch. With the exception of James Byrnes, Cordell Hull, and William Rogers, all secretaries of state for thirty-eight years were members of the council. According to Welch, the council was responsible for founding the United Nations.

Welch found an even more secretive organization that served as the Council on Foreign Relations' international equivalent: the Bilderbergers, named after the Hotel de Bilderberg in Oosterbeek, Holland, where it first met in May 1954. Founded by the Netherland's Prince

Bernhard and with holdings in Royal Dutch Petroleum (Shell Oil), the Bilderbergers comprised important financial and political figures from Western Europe and the United States, who met once or twice a year.

Welch saw the hands of the Insiders and the Bilderbergers at work in the American misadventure in Vietnam, though he did change his analysis over time. Initially, he believed that the Vietnam War was a "phony war" run by the Insiders. He said that it was illegal because a formal declaration of war had never been made. He grew angry when Dean Rusk declared that the United States entered Vietnam because it was obligated to live up to the South-East Asian Treaty Organization Treaty—a regional UN subsidiary. For Welch, that meant that the United Nations was running the war. Welch was under some delusion that the man actually running the war for the United States was Alexi E. Nesterenko, a Soviet Communist and the UN undersecretary for political and Security Council affairs, which ran all UN military activities. Without any foundation whatsoever, Welch alleged that Alger Hiss and John Foster Dulles had agreed at a UN conference in London in January 1946 that a Communist would always run that department. He also saw the Vietnam War as a Communist plot because, he alleged, President Johnson in 1965 and 1966 was sending to the Vietcong, through the Soviet Union and its satellites, "non-strategic commodities like aluminum, oil, and wheat, as well as jet engines, guidance systems, navigational equipment, and advanced computer technology." The Insiders, he said, wanted the war to keep going, regardless of the costs in life and money. He claimed they had tricked the American people into four major wars since Woodrow Wilson took the oath of office. Yet the masters of war, he said, ironically were the loudest voices for peace.[7]

Welch believed there were other reasons for the conspiracy too. The longer the war continued, the more American soldiers would need governmental care. Also, more men would become addicted to the heroin that was readily available and increasingly popular each year among the troops. Welch claimed that Mao Tse-tung was manufacturing the heroin to destroy American morale and waste more American tax dollars. The Insiders and their hypocrisy had riddled the nation with drug abuse, exorbitant debt, and an inability see the truth.

For all this, Welch decided not to foreground these conspiratorial assertions, on the grounds that making a positive case for winning the war would be more popular among his followers. Welch called for "Victory in Vietnam Instead of Defeat." By embracing a "win or go home" stance, Welch was able to capitalize on how the war was unraveling the liberal consensus. Welch assailed the mismanagement of both the war and the Great Society, as the Democratic Party fractured under these pressures.[8]

With the publication in the February 1967 *Bulletin* of "The Truth About Vietnam" Welch had become a hawk. It was time to win, he said. Why can't our forces "lick a bunch of half-starved guerillas in a country the size of Missouri?" It was time to remove the "many incredible handicaps on our men." The rules under which the United States was waging the war were making it impossible for US ground forces to do their jobs. Bombers were unable to inflict the type of casualties needed to win. Welch denigrated the craven draft dodgers who would not fight for their country the way John Birch and Welch's own son had. In March 1967, Welch and the Society sent a petition to Congress requesting the administration to "stop, promptly and completely, giving aid in any form, directly or indirectly, to our Communist enemies." JBS members gathered signatures and recruited more members—an eventual total in 1967 of 33,017 petitions with 551,908 signatures. Welch called it the "Greatest Petition Drive in American History." In 1970, the Society had collected 1.8 million signatures. In April 1967, Welch issued "More Truth About Vietnam," calling for an end to aid to Communist nations.

Then in March 1968, under the provocative title "If I Were President," Welch published a speech calling for the removal of the United States from the United Nations, the end of foreign aid, and victory in Vietnam. Robert had no intention of running for president, but his speech, delivered before a friendly Birch Society audience, caused some internal problems. Council member Robert Love of Wichita, Kansas, who called not for victory in Vietnam but for immediate withdrawal, resigned from the Council. He placed a full-page ad in his local newspaper and mailed it to fellow council members, encouraging them to do the same. Fred Koch's son, Charles, resigned his membership in the Society. Welch was concerned because the Kochs had deep pockets. He urged Charles to reconsider and even offered him the chance to serve on the council, as his father had. But Charles never returned.[9]

The Society was experiencing a number of small victories in 1968. The petition drive was signing up new recruits. Chief Justice Earl Warren announced his retirement, and his handpicked successor, Abe Fortas, was not confirmed. Georgia governor Lester Maddox declared August 23, 1968, "John Birch Day," proclaimed the young Georgian a national hero, and praised the "national patriotic organization" named after him. In December, the Society celebrated its tenth anniversary, with Welch declaring that the Society's greatest accomplishment "has consisted of staying alive" despite all the efforts "to destroy us." The mood was jovial. When the emcee, William Grede, asked Robert, "Have you ever actually filled out an application and joined the John Birch Society?" Robert joked: "No, I always thought I could be more effective on the outside."

Meanwhile the Left was in disarray. On March 12, Eugene McCarthy stunned the nation by nearly defeating Lyndon Johnson in the New Hampshire primary. Johnson soon announced that he would not seek nor accept another term as president. Robert Kennedy, whom Alan Stang called "vicious as a wolverine," announced in March as a presidential candidate to the chagrin of many McCarthy supporters. When Kennedy was assassinated on June 5, Stang thought he was a victim of the Communists, as his brother had been: "Sirhan had been trained by Communists at a camp in Communist Syria. The conspirators had decided to write Kennedy out of the script. As usual, the phony 'Liberals' began bleating that a gun had killed Kennedy, and therefore that guns, and not Communists, should be outlawed."[10]

Kennedy's murder came closely on the heels of Martin Luther King's assassination on April 4, which Welch attributed in part to the indefatigable efforts of Julia Brown: "One of our very patriotic Negro women speakers, Julia Brown, who previously worked nine years for the FBI, completely ruined Martin Luther King's usefulness to the conspiracy as a lying agitator, by simply telling the truth about the Communist hands and plans behind all of our racial problems, month after month, to sizable audiences in the very towns where King spoke, shortly before or after he made his appearances." According to Welch, "Julia Brown's year or two of speeches along these lines" and everything "we had done to expose the whole early 'civil rights' fraud" were "important factor[s] in leading the [Communist] Conspirators to have King assassinated because he would be more value to them as a dead martyr than he ever could be again as a live militant." Welch couched his extraordinary statement: King's "murder was certainly no part of our plan, expectation, or desire." In essence, Welch thought that King was a liability to the Insiders, who decided they could get "more mileage" out of King dead than alive.[11]

Ronald Reagan was equally unsympathetic. The "assassination," Reagan declared, "was part of the great tragedy that began when we began compromising with law and order, and people started choosing which laws they'd break." "White America killed Dr. King," said Stokely Carmichael, "and declared war on black America." "Go home and get your guns," he added.[12]

Things continued to improve for the Society. In 1967, Welch reported that the Society had raised $5 million that year and a lifetime total of $20 million from dues, benefit dinners, book sales, contributions, pamphlets, records, and films. Welch accurately boasted that he had the country's best-financed organization on the Far Right. The sound financial condition of the John Birch Society was due in part to the generosity of dog-food magnate D. B. Lewis, who bequeathed it $1 million. Welch had 270 paid employees, the thriving publishing house Western Islands, as well as its flourishing American Opinion Speakers' Bureau, which he called "perhaps the most immediately and spectacularly successful of" any JBS program. Welch claimed that the bureau was the "largest such agency in the world (when measured by either the number of engagements sponsored or the total audience reached in any one year.)" In addition, the Society had recently formed an affiliate: the American Opinion Study Club's Association, which was open to nonmembers. The association was a great boon to the Society because nonmembers could support issues that members cared about without having to be associated with an institution many deemed extremist.[13]

To be sure, there were setbacks, as in any large organization. John Rousselot, long considered a possible heir to Robert Welch, resigned in 1967 as the public relations director. That he was receiving $30,000 a year is testament to the financial viability of the Society at the time. But he wanted more. He had three children, and said he had to consider their financial concerns and "long term obligations." He also was questioning his impact and said, "I did not feel I was adding enough weight." Welch also faced the resignation of his publicity directors for the midwestern and eastern divisions. Longtime member T. Coleman Andrews, along with two others, resigned from the National Council.[14]

Slobodan Draskovich, who had quit the council and the Society in August 1966, was also still assaulting the JBS as futile and Welch as ineffective. "You know about the man who built the marvelous machine? When he turned it on, gears would grind, pistons pump, and lights flash. People would admire it and then ask what it did. 'Nothing,' the inventor said, 'absolutely nothing.' That's the John Birch Society today, spinning around and doing nothing," he observed. "Welch is a man of strong talk and weak action. Welch built a fifty foot cabin cruiser in his basement, but could not get it out of his house." Considering their reputations, that Draskovich, Revilo Oliver, and others of their ilk continued to attack probably redounded to the benefit of Welch and the Society, diluting charges of anti-Semitism and racism.[15]

Meanwhile Welchian logic was becoming popular in some parts of the Left. "The idea that everything was a lie," observed the historian Jill Lepore, "became a fashionable faith. Poststructuralism and postmodernism suffused not only American intellectual life, but American politics, too. If everything is politics, and politics is a series of lies, then there is no truth."[16]

And beyond the suffusion of Birch-like thinking among intellectuals of the Left, larger events continued to create opportunities for Welch. Identity politics soared in the late 1960s, further fracturing the liberal consensus. When the American Indian movement became active, Welch responded with a strong attack, calling it a "garish uprising of criminal agitators," which he strongly believed was funded and encouraged by perfidious elements inside the federal government. He credited his Speakers' Bureau with "squelching of the American Indian Movement, for which the Communists obviously had such pretentious and sinister revolutionary plans." The John Birch Society had one of its own Native Americans "on our role of speakers who risked his life many times in so dramatically opposing such a murderous gang."[17]

In 1968, North Korean Communist forces seized the American USS *Pueblo* on the high seas. The crew was held in captivity for nearly a year. It was a downcast moment for the Johnson administration, but a public relations victory for the John Birch Society. When radio shipman Navy Petty Officer Lee Hayes was asked by reporters what he would do when he returned to the United States, he crowed, "I'm going to join the John Birch Society."

A strange domestic story benefited the Society as well. In the small New Mexico town of Tierra Aramilla, the revolutionary Reies Lopez Tijerina led a motley gang, shot some victims, and took hostages before running for the mountains, chased by the National Guard. Tijerina declared his secession from the United States, in the name of "justice" for the theft of his ancestors' land. *American Opinion*'s Alan Stang was hot on Tijerina's trail. Like a reactionary and sober Hunter S. Thompson, Stang found Communists at work and the Great Society at fault in New Mexico. Stang compared Tijerina to a cross between Lenin and Castro. He said Tijerina and the Confederation of Free City States "have secretly been using the mailing list of the 'The Worker,'" the official newspaper of the Communist Party, USA. The moment provided the JBS the chance to introduce conservative readers to the Chicano movement and portray it in a predictably terrible and conspiratorial light. The Insiders, after manipulating African Americans to strive for civil rights, were now trying to hoodwink Latinos, asserted Welch. In an echo of the Black Republic that Joseph Pogany said was to be carved out of the Southeast, the Chicano movement was to partition the Southwest and establish a nation for Latinos whose lands had been stolen by the White man. According to Stang, "Tijerina's movement petered out—as a consequence of the educational campaign to expose it conducted by members of The John Birch Society in the Southwest."[18]

Then came Chicago and the 1968 Democratic Convention, which was a catastrophe for the unity of the Democratic Party. Stang, properly dusted off from New Mexico, bought two gas masks. "We knew that the violence would be 'spontaneous,' as it always is," declared

Stang sarcastically. The convention opened and "the revolutionaries," as Stang called them, gathered in Grant Park across from the Democratic National Headquarters in the Conrad Hilton Hotel. "It was not necessary to bring one's own marijuana," Stang said. "All one had to do was breathe." From Stang's vantage point: "On the night Hubert Humphrey was nominated, the revolutionaries attacked the hotel. They assaulted the police." They threw rocks, bottles, balls with nails, potatoes with razor blades, and plastic bags with human waste at the police. "Despite days of constant attacks on the police, the television screen showed us nothing but the police retaliating, for no apparent reason, thereby creating the phony impression that they had gone berserk. Once again, the conspirators at the very top, who completely control our national press, were collaborating with their employees at the bottom, in the streets, to get the effect the Conspiracy wanted."[19]

The 1968 election, Welch thought, left the American people little choice between the two major candidates, Hubert Humphrey and Richard Nixon—or "Tweedledick and Tweedledumphrey" as one Birch writer put it. Both were members of the Council on Foreign Relations. Both were willing to obey the Insiders. Both held the same fuzzy principles. But Welch believed a prewritten script decreed that Nixon was to be president. Part of the production was for Nixon to run as a conservative and then govern as a liberal. The plan, according to Welch, was to scare the American people into rejecting Humphrey's radicalism. The Insiders also promoted the fear of another four years—on top of eight already—of Democrats running the economy. Soaring debt, irresponsible social experimentation with untested programs, and higher taxes would destroy the economy, said the Insiders, according to Welch. Compared to Humphrey, Nixon was the responsible choice.

Still, Welch viewed Nixon as a Nelson Rockefeller toady and the choice of the Insiders. According to Welch, it was Rockefeller who resurrected Nixon's political fortunes after Nixon moved to New York, where he purchased an apartment in the same 810 Fifth Avenue address as Rockefeller. Nixon became a partner in the law firm of Rockefeller's attorney John Mitchell and rebuilt his reputation before vying for the 1968 nomination. Welch was convinced that Rockefeller was also responsible for Nixon's soaring wealth.[20] According to Welch, when

Nixon won the presidency, he would proceed to pay back Rockefeller, the kingmaker of the eastern liberal establishment.[21]

And yet, Welch benefited from Nixon's pledge to restore law and order—a huge issue because of the rioting, the counterculture, and the protests over Vietnam. Law and order were core JBS concerns because they encompassed the cultural issues that appealed to their members and potential recruits: more prisons, tighter prisons, private prisons, and less gun control, which Welch saw as aimed at confiscation. During the campaign, Nixon merged an ostensibly color-blind rhetoric of civil rights with a "law and order" discourse. Color-blind rhetoric played far better with suburbanites than overt claims of White supremacy or Goldwater's tirades against the 1964 Civil Rights Act. Middle-class suburbanites could embrace Republicans' calls for home ownership, neighborhood schools, residential class distinctions, minimal diversity, and taxpayers' rights. Nixon called for "greater opportunity for all Americans, justice for all, renewed respect for law, and peaceful resolution of conflicts that mar society."[22] This rhetoric proved effective because the intervening years had exacerbated anxieties about violent crime and societal breakdown. National Republicans charged that Democrats and liberals were the real extremists.

The JBS had a strict policy of refusing to endorse political candidates, even when their goals matched. Welch never publicly backed any candidate in 1968, though he thought that George Wallace was the most effective one. He had long backed Wallace; in 1965, he quietly began working with Selma's sheriff, Jim Clark, relaying lists of prominent Birchers nationwide committed to helping Wallace "save our country from being taken over by the Communists," as Welch said.[23] Welch justified the turn to the Alabama governor who once defiantly stood in the schoolhouse door to oppose the desegregation of the University of Alabama by pointing out that Wallace had abandoned his penchant for yelling "Nigger-Nigger-Nigger" for "Commie-Commie-Commie." Following the passage of the Voting Rights Act of 1965, Wallace did emphasize segregation less and adopted a discourse that drew directly from the John Birch Society playbook. Just as Welch did, Wallace highlighted the social consequences of the untested social programs of the Great Society and determined that rising crime, decline of morality, and usurpation of state power by the federal government were the consequences of liberalism. His message appealed to working-class southerners, but also drew the support of blue-collar workers in the North. His lack of support in the Sunbelt in 1968 testified that his appeal attracted voters who were more racially motivated than Nixon. Wallace's 1968 presidential campaign depended on much support from John Birch Society members, especially in Texas and California.[24]

Why didn't Robert back Ronald Reagan? The answer is simple: he no longer thought Reagan was a conservative. "About two thirds of our members in California, who originally supported Reagan, have now come to the conclusion he is not a Conservative at all."[25] Ironically, it was Reagan's victory in 1966 that contributed to the Birch Society's turn away from the Republican Party in 1968. Reagan never brought any Birchers into his administration, and his aides scoffed at the notion the Birchers were instrumental in their success.[26] Moreover, Reagan had moved to the center on some matters. He became concerned with problems among African Americans, preoccupied with cutting the budget in California, and moderate on open housing. He also appointed Caspar Weinberger, a moderate who made Reagan listen to State Controller Houston Flournoy, a liberal Republican. To the ire of the John Birchers, Reagan also ended a feud with Thomas Kuchel, whom they loathed.[27] Nevertheless, despite Welch's disavowal of Reagan, especially in his presidency, the former Californian came more and more to act like Robert Welch in his political style.

Welch was not disappointed with Nixon as president. That is to say, he saw Nixon fulfilling everything that the Insiders wanted him to do. Welch knew Nixon was a phony who would do anything to attain and maintain power. That meant living up to every project that the Insiders had in mind. When Nixon ran as a conservative and governed as a liberal, Robert saw this as Nixon simply being Nixon.

When Nixon appointed Henry Kissinger, the embodiment of the eastern establishment and himself a member of the Council on Foreign Relations, as national security advisor, Robert was convinced that Rockefeller forced Nixon to do it. (Kissinger had served loyally for five years as the governor's advisor on foreign relations.) Robert viewed Kissinger as the real secretary of state, despite the presence of William P. Rogers. In Kissinger, Welch knew that the Insiders had their plant, and expected him to pursue a defeatist foreign policy. Welch was unsurprised by the decision to withdraw half a million men from Vietnam. Far from the "just and lasting peace" that the president claimed, Welch saw it as a one of the biggest retreats in American history. Candidate Nixon had promised not to send any more supplies to Communists, who were killing our boys in Vietnam. But President Nixon increased the supplies.

The reversals continued. Welch was nonplussed when Nixon—who had made his career on the prosecution of Alger Hiss—visited the State Department and promised not to remove supposed Soviet agents there, despite his declarations otherwise on the campaign trail. Another early Nixon initiative that Welch bemoaned was his Family Assistance Program (FAP), which provided a Guaranteed Annual Income. Welch was irked that Nixon paid lip service to decentralization, while under his "New Federalism" increased the number of welfare recipients and the power of the executive branch. Welch had serious problems with Nixon's revenue sharing program as well. He saw revenue sharing as erroneously touting the decentralization of federal power, but it actually made the states depend more on federal largesse because money went from the states to Washington, where it was distributed. Candidate Nixon had called Johnson and Humphrey magnificent spenders of the taxpayers' money, but then President Nixon spent more than any president in history and publicly announced to journalist Howard K. Smith that he was "now a Keynesian in economics." Shocked, Smith retorted: "That's a little like a Christian Crusader saying: 'All things considered, I think Mohammed was right.'" Welch considered Nixon one of the greatest frauds the country had known, without any moral compass whatsoever. After a long investigation, Welch's research team concluded that Nixon was lying when his lips moved.[28]

What Robert could not have known (in fact, few outside the president's inner circle knew this) was that Nixon was sounding a lot like Robert Welch inside the White House. Nixon was growing more cynical and paranoid. Kevin Phillips's *The Emerging Republican Majority* came out in 1969. Nixon read the book and told his chief of staff H. R. Haldeman, "Go for Poles, Italians, Irish, must learn to understand Silent Majority . . . don't go for Jews and Blacks." Nixon and the GOP were moving to capitalize on the civil rights backlash, but many suggested moving the Democratic Party to the left. Democratic strategists Richard M. Scammon and Ben J. Wattenberg wrote in their 1970 book *The Real Majority* that moving leftward was a terrible idea. "Under the banner of New Politics, there is talk of forming a new coalition of the left, composed of the young, the black, the poor, the well-educated, the socially alienated, minority groups, and intellectuals—while relegating Middle America and especially white union labor to the ranks of 'racists.'" "The great majority of the voters in America are unyoung, unpoor, and unblack; they are middle-aged, middle-class, middle minded," read *The Real Majority*. Who was the average voter? A Catholic, forty-seven years old, and a housewife who was married to a machinist from Dayton, Ohio.

Scammon and Wattenberg wanted the Democrats to go to the center, but the Democrats did not heed their advice and were crushed in the 1972 election.[29] Democrats were defeated because Nixon was reading the *Real Majority*. Haldeman wrote in his notes the president "talked about *Real Majority* and need to get that over to all our people" and "wants to hit pornography, dope, bad kids." "We should aim our strategy primarily at disaffected Democrats, at blue-collar workers, and working-class white ethnics" and set out to capture the vote of the forty-seven-year-old Dayton housewife." Instead of calling Democrats "big spenders," in the 1970 congressional campaigns, Nixon would go for the votes of blue-collar workers through social issues like pornography and marijuana. Welch was doing the same thing. Nixon ordered Spiro T. Agnew, his vice president, to push the Democrats away from the political center by calling Edward Kennedy and his ilk "radical liberals." Nixon was using domestic policy to divide his opponents. "Building outhouses in Peoria" was how Nixon referred to the welfare state.[30] Nixon was dividing the American people, and many Americans were not trusting one another anymore.

The president was embracing the paranoid style of Robert Welch. His predecessors—Johnson, Kennedy, among others—had abused their power during the Cold War too. They used the CIA to undergo covert operations, including assassinations. The IRS audited political opponents. The FBI spied on American citizens. But Nixon went further, and got caught in the Watergate affair, partly due to his own Welch-like paranoia and conspiracy-minded need to micromanage.

Sure, other Cold War presidents had sophisticated recording systems in the White House, but Nixon wanted his system to turn on automatically. A small noise turned on the play button and the tape started to record. Only Nixon and Haldeman knew about the system, which recorded telephone calls and meetings.

In June 1971, the *New York Times* published excerpts from the so-called Pentagon papers, providing a history of American decision making in Vietnam since World War II. Daniel Ellsberg, a former Defense Department advisor, had leaked segments of the Pentagon papers to the *New York Times*. When Nixon heard about it, the president said it was a "Jewish cabal" and called the *Times* "the same media that supported [Alger] Hiss." The president's men concurred. "If this thing flies, they're going to do the same to you," said Kissinger, a German Jew. Kissinger persuaded Nixon to ask the Justice Department to prohibit the *Times* from publishing any more of the Pentagon papers, but the *Washington Post* then began publishing Ellsberg's leak. But even though the tapes were the property of the American people, Nixon continued to block attempts to release what he saw as his tapes. In April 1974, he released 1,200 pages of transcripts, which recorded the depths of his paranoia, anti-Semitism, racism, pettiness, and rage. Former chief justice Earl Warren, who had been a target for impeachment by Welch, observed, "if Nixon is not forced to turn over tapes of his conversations with the ring of men who were conversing on their violations of the law, then liberty will soon be dead in this nation." The Supreme Court finally delivered a unanimous opinion that Nixon needed to release the tapes.

Despite Welch's aversion to Nixon, the two men shared many similarities: their fascination for global affairs, their deep suspicions, their conspiratorial styles, and their deep intelligence. Perhaps Welch's knowledge that the two shared so much in common, but that Nixon—being a younger man who served in WWII, achieved electoral success, and attained the offices that Robert coveted—accounts for Robert's dislike of Nixon. Perhaps Welch envied Nixon.

25

The Fifty-Foot Cabin Cruiser, 1969–1975

Despite Welch's reports that the Society had between 60,000 and 100,000 members, it's likely the membership peaked "in the fall of 1965" at 30,000. Like any former political candidate or businessperson running a private company, Welch was inexact about the numbers. He was beholden to no shareholders because the John Birch Society was not a public enterprise. But numbers alone are not really important. Members were passionate. Members were committed.

And despite a sharp decline around 1966 and a "total decline of some fifteen thousand members," the Society grew thereafter and solidified its position as the primary institution on the rightmost edge of acceptable conservatism. In the January 1970 *Bulletin,* Welch called the last quarter of 1969 "the most encouraging, in every respect, which we have had in over three years." If the mid-1960s were the years of decline, the Society was on the rise at the end of the decade and the early 1970s. Significant numbers of new members were joining. Satisfactory, albeit imperfect, financial backing was being secured. By 1973, the Society, Welch said, had gained back "eight or nine thousand members" since its nadir, probably taking it to 24,000—not a mean feat for a band of zealots.[1]

Fault lines in the management began to show in the early 1970s, especially as Robert entered his ninth decade on earth. Robert had never handled criticism well, and his letters tended to exacerbate problems that more skilled managers would handle more deftly. He still tried to bring everybody together, but that propensity sometimes led him to invite some extremely eccentric individuals into the circle of leadership.

The Nord Davis Jr. imbroglio epitomized this tendency. Davis, who lived in New Hampshire, was a former IBM executive who specialized in antique cars and studied the Kennedy assassination. Davis believed that twenty-one bullets were fired in Dealey Plaza on November 22, 1963, by numerous assassins. Davis was a wingnut who published the pamphlet "Pardon Me, but . . . ," which Welch unfortunately promoted in a 1968 *JBS Bulletin*. Welch soon came to regret the decision, but went about expressing it the wrong way. In a letter to Davis, Welch wrote in exasperation: "What in heaven's name has gone wrong with you? . . . Frankly, Nord, we believe that the exhortation to 'grab your guns and your groceries, boys, and take to the hills,' shows a very poor understanding of how the Communists operate when they take over any country." Welch called Davis's philosophy a "futile course" and admonished his "silly antics" as "contrary to the beliefs of the Society." Welch also brought up that Davis had run for the US Senate in 1968 against Edward M. Kennedy, which "made you look extremely foolish"; indeed, wrote Welch, "I doubt very much if Kennedy ever even knew that you were in the race." Nord also got under Welch's skin by claiming "there being 'a serious problem' at The John Birch Society, because 'Mr. Welch is isolated' by the staff" and relies on Tom Hill too much. But Welch could not bring himself to sever ties with Davis, despite the latter's eventual role as an anti-government religious extremist and leader of the Christian Identity Movement, which practiced vicious White supremacy and operated from a compound chock-full of automatic weapons.[2] The tie to Davis testifies to the networks that Robert Welch never should have forged. Friendships and associations reveal the identity and character of complicated individuals, and moving in circles with Davis, notwithstanding Welch's criticism, demonstrated Welch's propensity to engage with villainy and lie down with some of the worst in humanity: in other words, another case of bad judgment and poor mismanagement.

A crisis always seemed afoot in the tense Belmont offices. There was no water-cooler dallying allowed there. Welch once included in the *Bulletin* a photo of an employee taking a catnap, with a reminder for all employees: "Don't forget, Communism is 120 years old—the John

Birch society is only 12 years old. . . . We've got a lot of catching up to do." But leaders continued to disagree over tactics and overall goals. To be sure, every large-scale operation has problems. But some second-rate hires turned out to be third rate. Silly matters received far too much attention. Complaints poured in about members who caused ruckuses during school board meetings and badgered city councillors and town officials. Welch sometimes himself wrote tactless letters that never should have been sent, producing more angry letters from smoking typewriters and accusations that JBS members were being unfair to their opponents. Far too much ink was spilled "to get the facts straight" when a misunderstanding was really not the problem; a long-standing animus, grudge, or personality quirk probably was. Rather than settling the matter, response letters ran on for pages and produced only new dilemmas and novel problems. In the October 1973 *Bulletin*, Welch disclosed that there was a spy in the John Birch Society. Somebody—apparently Director of Public Relations Rex Westerfield, who had recently resigned—had absconded with the Society's membership lists, the magazines' subscription list, and bookstore lists with their contributors.[3]

The John DeFriend case is a typical example of the infighting and mismanagement within the Society in the 1970s, as well as a window onto the chaos that reigned in the field. As a staff fundraiser, DeFriend traveled often, predominantly throughout the Southeast. On his peregrinations, he had "first-hand contact" with JBS coordinators; he found "little or no training and less guidance from the Major Coordinators." John described Paul Shetter, the coordinator for southern Florida, which covered Miami and Palm Beach, as "a dedicated country boy from Georgia," who "was plunked into this environment and given absolutely no guidance and cast off on his own." Of Don Foster, the coordinator for northern Florida, DeFriend recounted, "I entered his territory for the first time and ran into 4 members in that first day who besought me to 'do something' about the Coordinator since I was 'from Belmont.' They proceeded to unload their troubles on me."

DeFriend admitted that he did not "kow-tow to the boys from Belmont." He claimed that he and others "saw too clearly the deliberate stunting of the growth of the JBS which was being carried on from the offices." Soon, he was fired for "the most personally galling set of accusations (wasting money, not doing my assigned job, and being a smart-aleck)." Although DeFriend "agree[d] with the last charge totally," his vociferous and undiplomatic protests against the charges attest to the fact, at the very least, that leadership positions at the grassroots level were simply not being filled by the best men. Tom Hill, who was running daily operations at Belmont, and Welch and others in the office were responsible for their share of infighting, of course, but they were dealing with some second raters, third raters, problem children, and miscreants in the field.

DeFriend had come to the ridiculous conclusion that because the Society failed to implement the reforms that he favored—supporting the anti-abortion crusade and tax reform movement with greater vigor, finding a more "judicious use of funds" or resources, and positioning his associates as he recommended—Belmont was insincere in fighting the conspiracy. DeFriend thought Belmont interested solely in building a bureaucracy and raising money. He believed it had a downright nefarious purpose behind its frequent practice of shuffling out coordinators and bringing in new ones.

"Yes Virginia," DeFriend said, "the conspiracy really is there, but it is obvious that the top leadership of this body provides no solutions, except to help that same conspiracy." Belmont was running "a clandestine, conspiratorial, behind-the-back-operation." "May God Forgive" the Belmont conspirators "the treachery that has been committed and the betrayal of so many good men and women." DeFriend thought the conspiracy had run amok and infiltrated Belmont. He discovered a conspiracy within a conspiracy. Or so he thought, at least.

Tom Hill spent too much time addressing DeFriend's charges and producing more problems. "In nearly fifteen years as an employee of The John Birch Society, I have never seen the likes of a letter such as yours," Hill began before "getting the facts straight" for six single-spaced pages and then adding DeFriend's goal was to "weaken the Society wherever and whenever you can." Sometimes it seemed the purpose of letter writing at Belmont was not to reconcile but to inflame.[4]

Throughout the 1970s, this same dynamic recurred. Some members anxious about fighting the conspiracy came to the sorry conclusion that they were part of it. And they wanted out. This was a major problem since Welch relied on members' loyalty. Despite attacking others' loyalty to America, Welch always assumed that neither his nor any council member's commitment to the cause of Americanism would come under suspicion.

Then Nicholas Bove, a bright young zealot, arrived on the scene. Welch took a liking to him, and Bove became his research assistant. According to Robert and some other members, Bove had a falling out with one of the female staff members at Belmont. Soon he was harboring much bitterness. In 1974, Bove sent a booklet to JBS members showing that many council members were affiliated with the institutions of the establishment, the body running the conspiracy. According to Bove, council members had deep ties to the Federal Reserve Bank, the Newcomen Society, the Council on Foreign Relations, and the National Council of the YMCA. Bove said Freemasons in the Illuminati were running the National Council and manipulating JBS members. The "ordinary Bircher," Bove said, had "to sit up and take an honest look at what is really happening." Livid and also worried that a conspiracy-minded membership would believe Bove's charges, Welch wrote Bove a scathing letter to convince him to repudiate everything he said.

According to Welch, the real trouble with Nick began one day in the 1975 when he, "without any warning or any slightest interest in how many urgent pressures there might be on my time, had burst into my office without any prior notice, imperially closed the door, and proceeded to tell me what a rotten stinker I was in the way I was running the Society." "Finding that there was not going to be any other way to terminate or postpone the interview, I undertook to straighten out Nick's thinking and misunderstanding about several matters. Also, I was quite happy to feel when the conference finally broke up, and to find from Nick's attention to his own job and his greatly improved general attitude the next day, that I had apparently been successful."

What perturbed Robert more than Nick's two-hour interruption of his work was that Nick called Robert a liar. After Robert sent Bove his letter, Bove wrote to others that it "contained 70 lies in its four short pages." Robert went on a fresh attack, calling Bove a "twenty-three-year-old arbiter and protector of morality." Tim, Welch said, "is remarkable for having no understanding for how little he understands. It seems to me that he has been swept even further off balance by the heady excitement of showing how much damage he personally, . . . can do to The John Birch Society and me; and how important he can thereby make himself, no matter how much harm he does to the lives and careers of entirely innocent people in the process," Welch said. Welch told him his "whole destructive campaign" of besmirching council members made him appear a "pompous, vain, overbearing, condescending, 'sophomore,' with a paranoidal imagination, whom it would be very easy to make appear ridiculous."

Welch implored Nick to repudiate everything he had said because he simply did not know whom he was up against. "If absolutely necessary (which I hope it will not be) I can fight too," Welch warned. "Goodness knows Nick," Welch threatened, many "former friends, neighbors, girl friends in two states, and one-time associates in college and church and job, all on their own initiative—have provided me with enough ammunition. . . . I do not feel that I can simply sit still and permit these inordinately vicious diatribes to be circulated any longer." "We are suggesting that you call it off, and let all the noisy excitement that Nick loves disappear." He hoped Nick would "go to work seriously at some job for which he is at present really suited, put his mind and his abilities into doing that job well, and grow up from a bumptious, self anointed prodigy into a level-headed and mature young man."[5]

But even as organizational and administrative problems piled up, the Society was more influential and effective than ever. Between 500 and 1,000 members were added each month in the 1970s. Why? Quite simply, Welch and the issues he endorsed—taxation relief, ending abortion, deregulation, supporting the local police, stopping the Equal Right Amendment—came to match the time and the mood and the values of the country. Robert championed new and less conspiratorial issues to retain membership, foster growth, and refashion the Society. "Rather than retrenching any," as Welch put it, "we pushed right on ahead in the same crusading spirit, while actually managing to expand materially." "The chief factor and method in this expansion was a steady increase in the number" of our field staff. The paid circulation of the two JBS magazines doubled from approximately 25,000 in 1970 to 50,000 in 1977.

JBS's book publishing division, Western Islands Press, also doubled in reach and size in the same period, despite lacking any national consumer advertising whatsoever and being marketed exclusively through JBS channels. The books were very popular among the Far Right, sold well, and, as Robert said, contributed to "the awakening and resistance by an appreciable fraction of the American people." JBS books were hawked at myriad booths at county fairs, business conventions, and similar venues. One book, *Teddy Bare*, about Ted Kennedy and Chappaquiddick, made the *New York Times* bestseller list for three months.

The Society thrived in other media as well. By 1976, 140 newspapers carried the Birch Log, a syndicated feature by John McManus, the Society's long-standing and loyal public relations director. The "Alan Stang Report," a five-minute radio broadcast, grew from 10 stations in 1974 to 117 in 1976. The Speakers' Bureau grew in size and popularity, despite a virtual blackout from the mainstream media.[6] In 1975, the JBS established a research arm. Birch Research sold Fourth of July speeches and provided services for political candidates, who could pay $25 per hour for opposition research. "We can really get to the nitty gritty of an incumbent," observed the research director, Pat Mahoney.[7]

And then there were the John Birch Society summer camps. Between backpacking and canoeing, youngsters learned how the tentacles of the Insiders were strangling free enterprise and shackling other American institutions. In 1970, the Society had only one summer camp with 80 students. By 1973, there were camps in six states—California, Colorado, Michigan, Minnesota, Tennessee, and Washington—with 1,000 students overall.[8]

The Society started a highly successful campaign against Cesar Chavez and his boycott of California grape growers. JBS distributed thousands of articles, including Rex Westerfield's book *Sour Grapes*, highlighting that the real purpose of Chavez's movement was to stop American agriculture in its tracks: "The object of the boycott is to unite American agricultural workers in a single union under the control of revolutionary leaders—known Marxists and identified Communists," including Students for a Democratic Society, the Student Nonviolent Coordinating Committee, the Black Panthers, and the W. E. B. DuBois Clubs. Welch's role in the movement was so considerable that many came to think that he was not a former candyman but the self-interested owner of the Welch Company that made grape jelly.

The Society also invested heavily in billboards. Members dedicated labor, money, and time to cover the cost of such ventures in their earnest belief that they were helping to roll back or at least keep at bay sinister occurrences nationwide. For them, they were making great sacrifices with a patriotic determination no other anti-Communist group possessed.[9]

By 1971, the glory days for the John Birch Society appeared to be returning. But while Welch was happy that things were moving awfully fast on his battle against the conspiracy, "a great deal more than what we were doing to inform and alarm the American people was desperately needed." "Some people wish we were dead, but I can assure one and all, we are not. The society is growing like Topsy. That's Topsy. Not Trotsky." Welch bragged that the Society was spending approximately $5 million annually to support its 3,000 to 4,000 chapters, comprising between 60,000 and 100,000 men and women. But now "number one on our agenda is to double the membership. We want 150,000 to 200,000 members." He continued to obfuscate the numbers, however. Welch claimed that the Society was in the process of "doubling everything." "Since the first of the year, for example, the circulation for one of our magazines *American Opinion* has doubled from 22,000 to nearly 45,000."[10]

At the same time, Robert was no longer a happy warrior. He grew more strident with age. He wanted to smash Communism and openly advocated an unpremeditated first strike on the Soviet Union.[11] By 1973, he was proposing war with China: "The Chinese have nothing to fight with if we want to fight them. Red China won't even feed its people. Don't forget Mao-tse-Tung and Chou-En-lai murdered some 60 million of their own countrymen going back to 1924." By 1973, Welch's position on Vietnam resembled an upside-down cake because he saw the Insiders running every aspect of the conflict. He urged more aggressive action. "We haven't been allowed to attack North Vietnam," he said. "Our wars are designed to help the Communists. . . . North Vietnam wanted to take over South Vietnam. But they couldn't just invade. The North needed some excuse. So we go in there pretending to aid the South while at the same time we were supplying the North with the actual equipment they needed to fight us with."[12]

In a more traditional mode, Welch took to blasting the ecology and energy movements as Communist cabals. "The ecology and energy scares provide for government controls that lead to totalitarianism. It's the purpose of our government to create shortages and scarcity in order to have us merge comfortably with the Communist nations. The Communists live on a philosophy of scarcity and we live on a philosophy of abundance. And we've got to change before there can be a one world communist government."

By 1972, the Nixon administration was supporting economic and welfare policies that many on the Right called "socialistic." Nixon had traveled to Peking and Moscow. The United Nations admitted China. The United States was withdrawing from Vietnam. But Welch claimed he was not discouraged: "On the contrary, the more these things happen, the more people are beginning to listen and to realize that our warnings were right on target. What we are talking about is the survival of the United States." When JBS had started out thirteen years ago, "I said the odds were about one to 100 that America could resist the takeover. Today I think the odds of a communist takeover are about 3 to 2 and I think what we have done has played an important part in shortening them." In 1972, Welch was confident in the future of the John Birch Society: "We are now stronger than ever before. I think the mass of people have come to see we are here to stay, they accept that, and we are getting a more objective, even press from some of the liberal newspapers, which say they are still against the John Birch Society, but acknowledged that they are for some of the things we believe in." "I think it is significant that we got signatures on approximately 1 million letters asking the president not to go to Peking and that there were 4 to 5 signatures on each letter."

At no point in the 1970s did Welch have any intention of stepping aside as the leader of the John Birch Society, as much as he loved to play chess and read and travel. "I am 72 but I have no present plans for retirement. I intend to keep on going for several more years anyway. My mother died last month at the age of 98."[13] Welch reported he was in good health and more alarmed than ever before. The Insiders have "been getting more and more power, more and more influence, more and more control, all over the world." In 1975, Welch published a schedule of the Insiders' machinations, postulating that they would follow the pattern established by the original thirteen states, laid out in the Articles of Confederation from 1776 to 1789. The Insiders "would soon go to work" and acted "as if the future over-all government . . . already existed in nebulous shadow from under the present reaches of the United Nations; just as the 'United States' after 1776, through the unsubstantial authority of the Continental Congress and then the tenuous shell of the Articles of Confederation, began to act in many ways as if it were already a nation."[14]

Most startlingly, Robert had concluded that "the Insiders have planned to revamp the United Nations into a strong one world government by 1976—both the 200th anniversary of the founding of the conspiracy in Bavaria and the birth of the United States, its biggest enemy. It all fits in so beautifully." Anniversary dates carried great psychological value and were grand morale builders for the Insiders, Welch said. He believed that since "their Conspiracy began with the founding of the Order of the Illuminati in Ingolstadt, Bavaria on May 1, 1776," July 4, 1976, the bicentennial of the American Republic, would mark the beginning of the new world order.[15] At that time "the ruling regime would have the power to demand and enforce the obeisance of all the people on earth." They would do this, Welch concluded, "under and through the United Nations, with all other governments to be converted into, or replaced by, merely provincial agencies of this one-world despotism."[16]

When July 4, 1976, came and went without the establishment of a world government, Welch credited the Birch Society with stopping, or at least delaying, the event. "Although 1976 was originally the target date, little by little, the Society broke down the standing of the United Nations."[17] Moreover, Welch discovered that the Insiders had concluded that the plan for 1976 was too aggressive and "impracticable"; they "would require about fifteen more years for completion." Welch became convinced that "our Birch activities and exposures were having quite a bit to do with this postponement." The new target date, Welch surmised, was July 14, 1989, 200 years after the storming of the Bastille during the French Revolution. "By 1989, exactly as happened in America in 1789, the new and formally very central government would be functioning quite positively, though still under the name of the United Nations; just as the American central government had begun functioning in 1789 under the same name as the United States which it had been using." The die was cast.[18]

Welch became more confident that the press was reporting his words more accurately, but that worked against him because his discourses on the rise of the Illuminati or the Insiders made him sound strange to some, or worse. In September 1973, he sat for the *Boston Globe* and just purged. He told the reporter that it all began in Bavaria on May 1, 1776, when Baron Adam Weishaupt founded the Order of the Illuminati. It's all in a book by John Robinson, Welch explained. But the Illuminati were forced underground when Bavarian authorities raided their headquarters. The reporter's eyes probably widened. But by 1840, the Illuminati was strong and produced the Great Revolution of 1848 and the League of the Just Men, which hired Karl Marx to draft *Das Kapital.* The conspiracy was on the doorsteps of Russia by 1905, Welch continued, and in 1917, the agents of the Illuminati, Lenin, Stalin, and Trotsky, threw over the czars, with funding from the Rothschilds. Welch was on fire now. The Insiders, he continued, went to Yale or Harvard, grew up with all the advantages, controlled American politics and international banking, and wanted to enslave everyone else. In 1912, the Insiders brought in Woodrow Wilson to drag the country into World War I. They convinced America to fight World War II with assistance from Insiders like President Roosevelt and George Marshall. They master-planned the civil rights revolution, and they work through the UN, the Council on Foreign Relations, and tax-free foundations. Perhaps the reporter nodded now and then, encouraging him on.[19]

During other visits with reporters, Welch explained the real purpose of the income tax and the federal reserve, as well as Nixon's role in the Insiders' plans. "Then there was the Federal Reserve System, which started central banking, the income tax, which is directly out of the Communist Manifesto, and the 17th amendment, which provides for the direct election of Senators. This last event was the first great step in the breakdown of our republic into a democracy. . . . Now you have mob rule." "The Insiders began to climb ahead with Communist influence in our government" after Franklin Roosevelt became president, "and that climb has been extremely accelerated under the Nixon administration." "Every important thing Nixon has done leads toward totalitarian government." The "best illustration," Welch said, was the Occupational Safety and Health Act, "the worst piece of tyranny ever imposed on any people by any government." "You've given thousands of inspectors the right to put anyone out of business anywhere they want to."[20]

As Watergate threatened to drive Nixon from office, Welch's analysis became even more fantastical. "Nelson Rockefeller planned the whole thing behind the scenes. He wants to get rid of Nixon and become president in 1976." According to Welch, "Nixon's life ambition is to be the first ruler of the world." That ambition, Welch said, "is the key to his support for Communist regimes." Nixon "won't be elected" world president, but the "United Nations will make him president." "Rockefeller had to discredit Nixon so he could become a powerful president and possibly world president himself."[21]

Nelson's brother, David, was on Welch's mind more than ever in the 1970s. Welch became convinced that David had fired Nikita Khrushchev. "He [Rockefeller]," Welch observed, "made that trip over there and came back. Nobody ever thought there was anything wrong with Khrushchev and Khrushchev retires soon. He didn't have to get shot or anything. He retired to a comfortable place to live and became an elder statesman." He later held that David Rockefeller had made Jimmy Carter an Insider. "I think he was taken inside by David Rockefeller three years ago in London," said Welch in 1976 about the president-elect. "You know he was invited into Rockefeller's Trilateral Commission when it was founded."[22]

Even as Welch grew more conspiratorial, the JBS grew more effective. In 1966, Welch started to use the members he had "as the dedicated leadership for gathering into and behind our whole educational program three or four times as many patriotic Americans as were on [his] membership rolls." "We simply faced realities instead," Welch said. "Aware that all of the colossal smearing of the Society . . . had created a public attitude which would make it practically impossible for us to bring in . . . new members for quite a while to provide any significant growth," and aware "that most of our members already enrolled would remain completely loyal," and confident that "our field staff was quite capable of directing its professional abilities and activities into new channels," Welch shifted his emphasis into organizing "ad hoc committees instead of the recruitment of fully fledged members." The John Birch Society field staff served as the "cohesive guiding force at work on all fronts" and accomplished much during the next six years.[23]

The ad hoc committees helped bridge the chasm between capitalist libertarians who wanted smaller government, lower taxes, and less regulation, and the social conservatives concerned with societal transformations in gender rights, the liberalization of sexuality and pornography, and civil rights reforms. The groups worked like a prong of a fork: each had its own objectives, but together they stabbed the liberal leviathan mercilessly throughout the 1970s. In this way, the John Birch Society—the handle of the fork—constructed the scaffolding of what became the new conservative coalition. Through the ad hoc committees, many of the doctrinal differences that divided religious conservatives were patched over. Protestants found issues, such as abortion, that Catholics were already concerned with. Ideological dissimilarities that divided libertarians and social conservatives were often set aside. Together, they forged alliances against liberals and reacted to their proposals with counterproposals. Issues that preoccupied these ad hoc groups in the 1970s included abortion, the Equal Rights Amendment, homosexuality, the United Nations, sex education, and tax reform.

This helped set the stage for Ronald Reagan's election as president in 1980 and the remaking of the Republican Party. To be sure, the JBS did not create the Reagan revolution, but it did charge up many of the issues that dominated the Right's rise to power. The Society was but one force in a broad coalition including right-wing intellectuals, conservative think tanks, and rank-and-file members of the GOP.[24]

The cost of establishing and running ad hoc organizations such as the Movement to Restore Decency, Tax Relief Immediately, and To Restore American Independence soon ran to more than a million dollars per year. Welch said that the "pressures against us steadily grew as the Insiders became aware that we were causing their treasonous projects far more problems and failures" in the 1970s than in the 1960s. As he put it, "we spent at once, for such urgent needs . . . every dollar we could get our hands on; and sometimes considerably more."[25] One coordinator in the state of Washington suggested asking for $250 from every member, on the assumption that there were 100,000 of them. The problem was, as Robert put it, "the plain fact was that we did not have 100,000 members, or anywhere near it." "Also tens of thousands of the members we did have consisted of couples, where one contribution (if any were made at all) had to serve for both man and wife. And thousands of our members were children, whose parents had done all they could afford by bringing these youngsters into the Society at so early an age." "Thousands of our most dedicated and hard-working members were policemen or secretaries or widows or other splendid citizens who didn't have $250 which they could fork over to the Society at one time."[26]

The society's finances were genuinely dire. Deficit spending throughout the early 1970s was approximately $1 million each year. Reports from the Massachusetts attorney general's office showed that the John Birch Society Inc. had a cumulative deficit of $5.3 million at the end of 1975. One report on the financial condition of the JBS observed that "continuation of the company as a going concern appears to depend upon future profitable operations or securing additional capital as required."[27] Welch was even blunter in an open letter "to about 900 friends," published in the *Bulletin*, calling the situation "rather desperate."[28] Welch mentioned that a heavily increased membership could avert the crisis, but even the "net gain of a few thousand members" could not balance the books. He doubled membership dues in September 1976. But he said he would not "cut back on the size and reach of this laboriously constructed total operation when our prospects for so much greater influence and achievement on behalf of our basic purposes seem so much better than before."

By 1976, the John Birch Society was a miniconglomerate of five corporations spending $8 million each year, with a staff of 240. Robert Welch, Inc., which included *American Opinion* and the retail sales of Society pamphlets, was in the black. Review of the News, Inc., which produced *Review of the News*, was also in the black. General Birch Services, Inc., which comprised the JBS's book division and Speakers' Bureau, was "somewhat marginal," according to Charles Humphries, the Society's comptroller. Birch Research, Inc. was "still trying to get into the black," he said. As a whole, said Humphries, "we're marginal. We've been hanging in there by the skin of our teeth."[29]

Welch was able to raise some money through "many kinds of voluntary contributions from many wonderfully patriotic people," including Clint Murchison, Fred Koch, and Olive Simes. But by far the Society's most generous benefactor was one man: Nelson Bunker Hunt.

26

Bunker, 1970–1978

The John Birch Society's financial woes lessened once it was anointed with the oil money of the booming Sunbelt, especially Dallas. There, Welch found a burly savior. In the 1970s, the Sunbelt, with its thriving oil sector, stood in stark contrast to the rusting economies of the Midwest and Northeast. American businesses were moving west and south, out of states like Michigan, Ohio, Pennsylvania, and Wisconsin and into business-friendly states without unions, high taxes, or much regulation, especially Texas and California. Part and parcel of this regional boom was the oil business. Even as the country as a whole fell into an inflationary spiral, oilmen celebrated this turn of events. Inflation meant that people had to pay more money for oil.[1]

Robert traveled to Dallas to seek an infusion of money into the Society from one of the richest men—likely *the* richest man—in the world: Nelson Bunker Hunt. With holdings in international offshore wells, thoroughbred farms, grazing land, skyscrapers, cattle ranches, and approximately 8 million acres of oil fields in Libya, Hunt was estimated to be worth $16 billion at one point. And he had become politically vocal. Over two days, Welch reviewed with Hunt "what we were doing, where we stood, and our plans and outlook for the future." Afterward, Welch happily observed that Hunt was "generous" and "had enough confidence in the value and wisdom of our work to provide me with some very substantial immediate help; and to give me a firm assurance of similarly substantial support at recurrent intervals for an indefinite period ahead"—which he took to mean at least two years.[2]

No other figure contributed as much to the viability of the John Birch Society as Hunt.

From his birth in 1926 as a twelve-pound bouncing baby, Nelson Bunker Hunt—long known as Bunker—was never afforded much interest from his father, H. L. Hunt. His father sent Bunker off to Culver Military Academy at the age of twelve.[3] Over time, H. L. was annoyed not just by Bunker's poor work ethic but his diet. H. L. was an early promoter of something like what became the Paleo diet, but Bunker was a snack-food junkie. His diet consisted of pizzas, cheeseburgers, and his personal favorite: Fritos topped with chili and cheese. Bunker ate ice cream by the gallon and was often sighted by employees at his desk gobbling down his favorite snack while perusing documents on oil production. Yet Bunker, while portly at 300 pounds, was also athletic and healthy. Throughout the 1960s and 1970s, the sweaty, moon-faced figure with thick black glasses jogged regularly—pounding the streets of North Dallas and Highland Park in his extra-sized Adidas tracksuit. An evangelical Christian, Bunker was a teetotaler and did not smoke. His cardiovascular system apparently remained in excellent condition, and he lived a long life.[4]

Sons of censorious fathers, especially rich oilmen, have to make it on their own to receive their fathers' approbation. Plucky and lucky, H. L. Hunt was a billionaire many times over, having discovered one of the world's largest oil deposits in East Texas. He formed Facts Forum, a conservative media empire central to the Goldwater presidential effort, and pumped millions of dollars into conservative organizations. Bunker wanted to land an oil prize even larger than his father's and put significant pressure on himself to find it. In the 1950s, Bunker hired a University of Illinois geologist to find an "elephant," a massive oil field. He spent most of that decade drilling dry holes in North Africa and losing millions of dollars of his family's fortune.[5]

In 1961, Bunker's luck turned. He made a deal with British Petroleum (BP), which agreed to sink a wildcat well in Libya.[6] On a piece of desert called the Calansho Sand Sea, Bunker hit a gusher that blew 3,910 barrels a day. He had discovered the Sarir Fields, which contained approximately 8 to 11 million barrels—one of the largest known oil fields at the time, nearly three times as large as East Texas. Overnight, Bunker was richer than H. L., with a value on paper of $6 to $8 billion.[7]

But getting the Sarir Field oil to market presented a big problem. A 300-mile pipeline needed to be constructed across the desert to an oil port, which itself would have to be built. The pipeline was finally completed in 1965, and oil began to flow by January 1967. But when the pipeline finally went online, it pumped only 100,000 barrels of oil per day, a rate that Bunker said deliberately underestimated the potential of the Sarir Field. Bunker leaked to the *Oil and Gas Journal* that the delay and insufficient production were due to foot dragging by British Petroleum, which was concerned with poor market conditions. Bunker also told the journal that BP was concerned about a rising generation of Libyan nationalists. Most of the Libyan population lived in extreme poverty, and the aging King Idris faced pressure from nationalists and socialists to seize and distribute the new oil wealth. After Bunker's strategic leak, production rose to 300,000 barrels a day and eventually reached 470,000 barrels. His yearly profit from the Libyan oil play was a hefty $30 million in tax-free cash.[8]

His newfound wealth allowed him to invest in right-wing causes himself throughout the late 1960s and 1970s. He gave to the Manion Forum and the Southern States Industrial Council, which attacked unions, foreign aid, and civil rights. Bunker also donated to other conservative organizations and political candidates. Senator Strom Thurmond received $1,000 for his 1964 reelection campaign. New Hampshire native Harrison Thyng, an aviator and retired brigadier general, received a $1,000 check from Bunker in his unsuccessful bid for the US Senate in 1966. Bunker also helped bankroll the 1968 presidential campaign of George Wallace and gave $1 million to his running mate, the hawkish General Curtis LeMay.[9] (Today, Hunter's contributions would equal approximately $8,400, $8,100, and $7.6 million, respectively.)

But Bunker's true ideological home was the John Birch Society, and he was by far its largest benefactor, as well a member of the governing board. Attesting to his avidity, when a Dallas reporter told Bunker that Barry Goldwater, Clare Boothe Luce, and Carl Brandt had established a conservative organization, the Free Society Association, he retorted: "They don't strike me as any so-called conservatives. They're not Robert Welch or H. L. Hunt."[10] Bunker and Robert were cut from the same cloth. Both were suspicion-minded conspiracy theorists.

Both believed that an international Communist conspiracy comprising members of the Council on Foreign Relations and controlled by the Rockefellers wanted nothing less than world government.

When in September 1969, Muammar al-Qaddafi, a twenty-seven-year-old nationalist, socialist, and army colonel overthrew King Idris and threatened nationalization of Bunker's Libyan oil fields, Bunker grew even more suspicious than Robert. He began to operate with extreme caution. He hired detectives and security guards. He traveled under a false name. When flying commercially, he booked seats on multiple flights to sow confusion about his whereabouts. Employees picking him up at the airport were not told which flight he was on. Bunker's imagined enemies were vast, but he could have had real enemies too, like Libyan security agents, terrorists, and others motivated by Qaddafi's calls for pan-Arab pride. But some were simply imaginary, friends claimed, products of Bunker's love of mystery and intrigue.[11]

Religion played an important role in how he spent his money. A very conservative Presbyterian, Bunker believed in the inerrancy of the Bible and embraced premillennial dispensationalism, which proposed that the Bible foretold the end of the world.[12] In Dallas, he was not alone, as throughout the 1960s and 1970s, it produced many popular prognosticators of Armageddon. Dallas Theological Seminary president John Walvoord and faculty members J. Dwight Pentecost and Merrill Unger wrote many books heralding the last days. These books had a common story: at any moment, Jesus Christ was going to call his true believers, who would disappear into thin air and enter heaven. After the disappearance of all the world's infants in the Rapture, the Antichrist would rule for seven years and assemble his armies for the final battle of Armageddon.

That contemporary events in the world foreshadowed a satanic new world order was not just the stuff of a handful of cranks. As fantastical as these stories sound, books by Hal Lindsey and other dispensationalists sold hundreds of thousands and even millions of copies in the late twentieth century. A Dallas Theological Seminary graduate, Lindsey wrote *The Late Great Planet Earth*, a bestseller in 1970, which foretold that the Rapture was imminent and that we were living through the earth's last days. Lindsey made the connection between politics and prophecies explicit. For him, the Antichrist was a necessary evil, making possible the return of Jesus Christ. The Antichrist would need "nations" to rule over. Lindsey identified supranational organizations like the United Nations with the Antichrist, who would use them in his run-up to power.

Lindsey's work attracted folks who already equated liberalism with moral decay, the rise of United Nations, and the dissolution of the culture. He provided a popular religious bulwark for the John Birch ad hoc organization TRAIN (To Restore American Independence Now), which sought American independence from the UN, where the Antichrist was going to establish his world government. Although Robert Welch was no premillennial dispensationalist—he had abandoned his mother's fundamentalism in his teens—evangelical support bolstered membership in the 1970s.

For individuals who did not hold his religious worldview, Lindsey made the efforts to get the United States out of the United Nations appear banal compared with his fantastic story. Yet for most people, the lesson of the twentieth century, with its two world wars, was the need for a United Nations. "It is sadly true we have not come anywhere near actually getting us out," Welch admitted, though he did claim that the United States was not under the control of the UN, and gave the JBS the credit. The task was difficult because the threat was enormous. "In this endeavor we are trying to wipe out the very core of the long-range plan of the most powerful Conspiracy in all of human history," Welch said. Over time, TRAIN did seem to convince many Americans that the UN was nefarious at worst and ineffective at best. When polled by Gallup in 1955, 55 percent of Americans said the UN was doing a "good" job. That number fell to 50 percent in 1967, 44 percent in 1970, 32 percent in 1975, and 31 percent in 1980.[13]

Lindsey had graduated Dallas Theological Seminary before relocating to southern California to work with Bill Bright's Campus Crusade for Christ, to which Nelson Bunker Hunt donated generously. Bunker helped that organization become a global one.[14] Bright's parachurch ministry became one of the most successful evangelical organizations in the world and drew in many West Coast Birchers. Many who found a seat in the evangelistic Campus Crusade and in the more secular John Birch Society joined both organizations to escape political liberalism, the hedonism of many Californians, and the growing secularism of the Sunbelt's universities. Campus Crusade engaged in activities promoting spiritual growth and saving one soul at a time, but also encompassed evangelical Christians of the 1970s who were turning toward electoral politics, motivated by their opposition to abortion, the Equal Rights Amendment, and sex education. Welch certainly tolerated and encouraged followers who embraced the premillennialism and Baptism of the burgeoning Christian Right.[15]

In the 1970s, the politics of civil rights and Vietnam became less tumultuous. The politics of religion—family values, sexuality, and morality—became central in an increasingly metropolitan, affluent, and business-friendly region replete with upwardly mobile homeowning middle-class families. Religious issues and cultural concerns rose as a force in American life. Fundamentalists, preachers, radio hosts, and other evangelists grew in number. With Bob Dylan, Black Panther Eldridge Cleaver, and convicted Watergate lawyer Charles Colson proudly declaring to be "born again," *Newsweek* and *Time* called 1976 "the Year of the Evangelical." The most famous "born again" Christian in the United States that year, however, was president-elect James Earl Carter.[16]

That same year, Francis Schaefer wrote *How Should We Then Live,* explicitly arguing that proliferating pornography, accelerating abortion rates, prohibitions of prayer in public school, and other examples of "secular humanism" were the work of Satan. It was the mission of evangelical Christians to save the country from Satan by taking back their government.[17] Schaefer was central in bringing evangelical Christians to politics, but he was a reclusive intellectual theologian living on a mountaintop in Switzerland. His clarion call would not have been distributed so extensively without an infusion of money from Nelson Bunker Hunt. The rotund international oilman bankrolled a documentary film adaptation of *How Should We Then Live.* A phenomenal success, the film convinced thousands of evangelical Christians that a culture war was afoot, and they had an obligation to take the fight to Satan by abandoning any past reluctance to engage in politics.[18]

The premillennialist bent fit Bunker's apocalyptic and conspiratorial view of the politics, especially his loathing of the Soviet Union, the UN, and the Trilateral Commission, which was begun in 1972 by David Rockefeller and Zbigniew Brzezinski, a Columbia University specialist in international affairs for the purpose of strengthening ties between political and economic elites in Europe and the United States. Bunker believed that the Council on Foreign Relations was the political arm of the Trilateral Commission. He hired researchers and spent a lot of money to establish the connections between the Trilateralists and the editors of *Time*, the *New York Times*, the *Wall Street Journal*, and the *Washington Post*. He also detailed the numerous individuals serving at the highest levels of government with Trilateralist connections. Like-minded Hal Lindsey wrote that the Trilateral Commission sought "changes of global significance . . . with no public consultation, no debate, no election" and set "the stage for the political-economic one-world system the Bible predicts for the last days."[19]

While not a fundamentalist or a premillennialist, Welch also believed that the Trilateral Commission was a potent force for evil in the world and a way station on the road to UN global domination. The Trilateral Commission, Welch wrote, was "the bellwether organism that led and pressured all other temporary governmental cooperations on earth into the inescapable corral of an all-powerful United Nations." Confusingly, he held that the efforts of the John Birch Society actually led to the creation of the Trilateral Commission. "Until a very few years ago, bringing our country and all other countries directly under complete control of the United Nations had been the route counted on by the Insiders of that Conspiracy for soon arriving at their goal of absolute tyranny over the whole human race." But the Society had exposed "the real function and purpose of the United Nations," which "caused quite a setback and eventually prompted the creation of an intermediate stage, called the Trilateral Commission, in their progress towards the same ultimate objective." Welch exclaimed that members were ecstatic because the establishment of the Trilateral Commission proved that the "Get US out!" campaign was having its desired effect.[20]

Whether Bunker read Hal Lindsey or heard of the Trilateral Commission through Welch, these teachings affirmed his view that things were growing worse.[21] America was coming apart. Protesters were burning the flag over Vietnam. War and rumors of war were running rampant in the Middle East. Runaway inflation was inevitable. Dope was everywhere. In 1970, Alvin Brodsky, a New York commodities broker, visited Bunker at his Circle T Ranch in Dallas and appealed to his pessimism and apocalyptic thinking. As the two sat in Bunker's kitchen, Brodsky pointed to the utensils, the food, the tablecloth. "Bunker," he asked, "do you believe you're going to have to pay more for these things next year than you did this year?" Bunker nodded. "Well then," replied Brodsky, "you should consider silver." Bunker's brother Herbert had recently devoured Jerome A. Smith's *Silver Profits in the Seventies,* which predicted catastrophe for the economy and recommended silver as a safe harbor.[22] Bunker and Herbert began buying silver. In December 1973, Bunker made a 20-million-ounce silver order. By 1974, Bunker had stockpiled 55 million ounces—7 to 9 percent of the entire world's supply.[23]

Bunker had continued to support the John Birch Society, including a generous contribution in 1975. But both he and Welch had made a series of financial mistakes, and no more money was forthcoming between 1975 and 1977. Welch pleaded for a further infusion of cash. "I need $200,000 very badly this week, Bunker. You can imagine how badly from the fact that I am willing to ask for it in this fashion."[24] "Let me repeat most emphatically that I am not voicing any complaint about your action under the circumstances" and "have only deep appreciation for so much that you did to help us." "But I do need badly to let you know how our affairs were affected by such delays and curtailment as did take place."

Welch continued: "I believe that both physically and mentally, I am a fairly hardy soul. But the incredible combination of blows and pressures that have struck me over the past twelve months have almost certainly taken at least five years out of my life, or I most assuredly would not yet be looking for any more help from you." "I still intend and expect to live long," Welch said, "to see the tide turned against the lying, bluffing, murdering, treasonous conglomeration of evil forces that is out to destroy our whole civilization and to reduce most of the human race to the level of barnyard animals."

"One of those disastrous developments," Welch admitted, "was my own fault." "I was so encouraged over the visible increase in our influence and effectiveness on the contemporary scene that I could not resist taking just one more final but important step in the spirit of a crusade." In 1975, he had authorized the hiring of ten more paid coordinators, bringing the total to ninety "extremely hardworking officers in our educational army." By that fall, "I began to wish that we had never" hired them. "Various unexpected blows began to hit us, which became worse and worse throughout 1976" and into 1977.

As Welch explained, in 1976, there was $600,000 in "'big money' from various people, on which we had counted, but never arrived, as expected." By 1977, the John Birch Society was "running just about" $600,000 behind in accounts payable. Contributing to the revenue problem was the fact that it was an election year; money that would have come to the JBS was likely diverted to other political causes. In one case, Welch said, a $100,000 donation "not only had been definitely promised to us in 1975 by our prospective benefactor, but he had called me aside later to assure me that he meant it, and that I could count on receiving the check around the end of the year." But the check never came because the benefactor became a political candidate. "I really had counted on" that $100,000," Welch exclaimed.

But "this is only the beginning," he told Hunt, "of our tale of woe." In the summer and fall of 1966, when Welch had developed his strategy of ad hoc committees to combat the Insiders, he borrowed more money than during any other year, most in the form of ten-year notes, due in 1976. Most of those who lent at the time did not want the money back, Welch said. But by 1976, the economy had turned sour with massive inflation, slow growth, high unemployment, and long gas lines. The lenders were still loyal to the Society, but they now wanted or needed the notes to be paid. Consequently, the JBS was on the hook for another $200,000.

"Then there was the computer problem," Welch said. Welch was a nineteenth-century man and was not familiar whatsoever with computers. But he acquiesced to "the extremely insistent urging" by his chief accountant and administrative associates, and agreed to purchase a "state-of-the-art" computer for $250,000. Welch explained that the sophistication of the newly adopted "incentive program," which provided a commission for field staff who were able to drum up new memberships, made the case for the computer convincing to him, as it would manage the "tremendously extensive allocation of different commissions payable on their so variegated laborers and accomplishment."

By early 1977, Welch "hoped and believed we were seeing some decrease in the darkness ahead." Then "we suffered probably more than any other nationwide organization in America all the impact of the most severe, extensive, and long continued storm conditions in our country's history." The Blizzard of 1977 blanketed the Atlantic Seaboard, and the snow was so high and the damages so great that major factories closed. Two-thirds of the country suffered delays in payments or lost payrolls for extended periods of time. The implications for the JBS were dire because members concentrated on essentials and ignored membership dues. Welch reported the John Birch Society lost $300,000 because of the storm and its economic impact.

Welch launched an austerity program and cut back on expenses. His goal was to "get on a sound business footing." The incentive program was part of this, aimed at making every member of the field staff completely self-supporting. But the program was an unmitigated disaster. As Welch admitted, the coordinators "each went rapidly thousands of dollars behind," and "we had to reduce our field staff from 90 men down to about 60 men today." Survival required that membership dues be doubled at every level. That decision, Welch declared, "has cost us at least the temporary loss of a few thousand members. And perhaps even half of them will never return, mostly because they simply cannot afford it after all of the leveling between wages and welfare payments, which subversive and destructive development is being so brazenly carried out by the Conspiracy."

By 1978, Welch was having more difficulty than ever finding good men. He admitted that many simply "have not been anywhere near the best in those characteristics of salesmanship needed for getting subscriptions to our magazine, or selling advertising, or even for recruiting new members." Welch sought men who had "far-reaching self-education," "psychological insight," "levelheaded judgment," "inspiring leadership," and an "unshakable will to win this struggle despite all obstacles and pitfalls." He had spent many long years in business and benefited from much experience and observation at every level, but the new leadership was simply not acquiring the necessary tools: confidence in delivery, camaraderie in relationships, the pleasure of other men's company, and admiration of their peers. Robert Welch demanded a great deal from his employees because his own abilities were extraordinary. He was a demanding boss because he could do the work of several men in his late seventies.

Paradoxically, the Society was achieving its ideological goals like never before. Robert was absolutely accurate in stating that "our whole educational program has never before had so much visible effectiveness as during" the mid-1970s. Welch's personal papers show that the Society's influence peaked in the 1970s, not earlier as often claimed. Welch's focus on cultural issues that became important to conservatives throughout the 1970s—the ERA, sex education, abortion, pornography, and tax reform—was the key. All of these "confrontations [with] members of the Left," he said, "have been . . . decidedly helpful, on behalf of the Americanist cause."

27

Making Morning in America . . . , 1970–1985

It was no wonder that the 1970s was the best decade in the John Birch Society's history. For many, events began to affirm the veracity of Robert Welch's seemingly spurious claims. Conspiracies abounded, and the number of people who said they trusted the government plummeted, from 55 percent in 1972 to 30 percent in 1978.[1] John McManus reported that many people became aware of conspiracies in high places at the same time that they came to agree with the John Birch Society on a whole host of issues, including regulation, burdensome taxes, federal controls, and bloated government spending. The American people, wrote McManus, realized that the JBS had "a lot to say."[2]

Welch had been telling his members that the government was lying to them since the late 1950s. In the 1970s, Americans began finding out that he was correct. In 1973 and 1974, Watergate demonstrated that a president could abuse his constitutional authority egregiously. Welch had been arguing that cover-ups were common, and Richard Nixon's secretly recorded Oval Office tapes affirmed this suspicion. Even more, a suspicious eighteen-minute gap in one key recording became fodder for conspiracy theorists and lowered confidence even further. Some even concluded that the gap concealed who killed President Kennedy. In a cryptic comment, Nixon observed that a substantial investigation of Watergate may "open up the whole Bay of Pigs thing," which H. R. Haldeman, Nixon's trusted aide, said was a code for the Kennedy assassination. An investigation by a select committee of the House of Representatives concluded there were "probable" conspiracies in the assassinations of both President Kennedy and Martin Luther King. Welch never had the slightest doubt about either case because he believed the Communists had killed both men.[3]

Watergate also revealed the White House effort to destroy the credibility of staffer Daniel Ellsberg, whose release of the Pentagon Papers proved that members of Kennedy and Johnson administrations lied to the public about the progression of the Vietnam War, lowering confidence in the presidency even further.[4] Robert had thought Vietnam a staged affair that the Communists were going to win eventually. Kennedy, Johnson, and Nixon were just going through the motions for the inevitable defeat, Robert said. He felt affirmed in April 1975 when Saigon fell to the Communists, along with American confidence in its military might, an infectious disease that came to be termed the Vietnam Syndrome. For many, the grand expectations that the United States could stop Communism in East Asia seemed to fade away along with the certainty that America could "bear any burden," "oppose any foe," and come out on top.

Americans were also learning that more government officials had spied for the Soviet Union, had worked with mobsters to kill a foreign head of state, and had, without informed consent, conducted LSD experiments on Americans.[5] Democratic US senator Frank Church's investigations in 1975 and 1976 demonstrated—contrary to Welch's beliefs—that American leaders had been too aggressive, if anything, in their determination to kill Communist heads of state. The congressional committee also showed that American agencies had even spied on their own citizens. Still, the Church committee contributed to conspiracism only because it proved that government conspiracies were real. Faith in American intelligence agencies plummeted, part of a larger slide in trust in government institutions from 80 percent in 1966 to 25 percent in 1981.[6]

Paranoia filled American popular culture, whether in the movie version of *All the President's Men* or *The Parallax View*. In the latter, Warren Beatty's character realizes that he may be the only person who saw the real killer of a US senator. Fearing for his life, he goes down his own rabbit hole. A figure appearing to be Earl Warren announces that, like Lee Harvey Oswald, the killer was a lone gunman: "There was no evidence of a conspiracy," a claim meant to be seen as a cover-up. Other great films, including *The Conversation*, starring Gene Hackman, made Americans question whether their understandings of everyday reality bore any resemblance to the truth.[7]

Americans watched as Vice President Spiro T. Agnew, who was charged with extortion, bribery, and conspiracy, resigned in infamy. When Agnew's replacement and Nixon's eventual successor, Gerald Ford, pardoned Nixon, Robert Welch may have been nonplussed, but others concluded that a corrupt bargain had been forged: the presidency for a pardon. Ford took office in August 1974 with an approval rating of 71 percent, and finished the year at 42 percent.

Americans were learning that their government was not only corrupt but also incompetent. In July 1975, facing a sanitation strike, 70,000 tons of rotting garbage on the streets, and impending bankruptcy, the government of New York City begged for a congressional bailout and embraced an emergency austerity program.[8] The incompetence of fallible human beings, rather than conspiracy, better explained events, but where some saw ineptitude, Robert characteristically saw intentional perfidy and cabals. Increasingly, Americans agreed.

An energy crisis plagued the American economy throughout the 1970s when the Organization of Petroleum Exporting Countries (OPEC) imposed an oil embargo on the United States. Oil shortages gripped the East Coast, and drivers waited in long lines to fill up. But, like Welch, more Americans blamed not Arab sheiks but the Carter administration for the shortage, arguing that the scarcity was a fraud committed by advocates of Carter's energy-efficiency program. According to the *Wall Street Journal*, if the Carter administration truly sought to safeguard consumers, "it is only necessary to remove the mind-boggling federal array of price ceilings, price tiers, incremental prices, fuel use restrictions, fuel allocations, fuel use barriers, crude oil entitlements, drilling restrictions and other entanglements that result in so much of the human energy of the energy industry being immobilized and wasted by regulation."[9] Could Robert Welch have said it any better?[10]

These concerns displaced anti-Communism as a core political issue, and Welch shifted his messaging accordingly. As evangelicals and Catholics became drawn to cultural issues, they significantly influenced local, state, and national GOP politics. And they participated in these issues in part through the John Birch Society's ad hoc committees. Evangelicals and Catholics found a forum in the pages of *American Opinion* and the *JBS Bulletin*.[11] Welch thus helped transform the GOP into a party of conservatism. He was an early proponent of the cultural issues that the moderates in the establishment wanted to eschew, and these issues eventually became central to the social conservative wing of the Reagan revolution. Robert fiercely battled liberals who he said wanted to eradicate Christianity in the public schools, and he assailed homosexuals who wanted equal rights and sought to decriminalize sodomy. In Birch Society bulletins, feminists were labeled "feminoids" who wanted to pass the Equal Rights Amendment and supported what Welch called "abortion on demand." The threefold issues of sex education, abortion, and the ERA lit a fire for social conservatives, and Welch and the Birch Society were early assailants of all three concerns.

While Welch adopted a more secular message, he had long encouraged his members to heed the messages of Christian patriotic nationalism and anti-Communism of Carl McIntire and Billy James Hargis.[12] Both McIntire and Hargis were popular among the Christian Right across the Bible Belt.[13] Although Welch still considered Communism a crisis, he came to adopt the view of many fundamentalists that liberalism—because of its promotion of relativism and secularism—represented a more dire threat than first supposed. Like socially conservative activists, Welch backed single-issue campaigns focusing on traditional values. "The family is being destroyed as the solid building block of our social structure," Welch said. He defended the family and "family values" by assailing pornography, sex education, abortion, and the ERA.

Perhaps the support of Dwight Eisenhower in 1957 for the ERA helped make Robert into a fierce opponent of it. In 1972, the House and Senate passed it, giving the states seven years to ratify it—or not. Within a year, thirty states had. The eventual ratification failure of the ERA demonstrated the growing power of grassroots action; it was the greatest victory the John Birch Society ever had.

The ERA campaign marked a surge of interest among social and religious conservatives who valued Christian morality, patriotism, and family. Welch rallied Christian conservatives who wanted to preserve traditional gender roles, maintain family values, loathed "cultural socialism," and embraced living a life of Christ. Birchers made the case that ERA would have frightful consequences, such as the inclusion of female troops in combat units and unisex bathrooms. For Welch, women were meant to be doting wives and nurturing mothers. He wholeheartedly embraced the nineteenth-century belief in "separate spheres," which confined a woman's proper place to the home. For Welch, the ERA was "a combination of cruel joke and criminal idiocy." In the first year of its consideration by legislatures, "we did not see how it could be taken seriously by anybody except possibly a very few old female battleaxes who could find no other way to convince anybody that they were women except by standing up for 'women's rights.'" "But we were wrong," Welch admitted, and momentum for the ERA grew along with "the evil forces which are so determined to destroy the American family as the very building block of our civilization."[14]

In 1975, Betty Ford sat down for an interview with Morley Safer on CBS's *60 Minutes*. She backed the ERA. "I feel the equal rights amendment ought to probably pass in our bicentennial year." The First Lady then celebrated—to the chagrin of her husband, President Ford—the outcome of *Roe v. Wade*: "I feel very strongly that it was the best thing in the world when the Supreme Court voted to legalize abortion, and in my words, bring it out of the backwoods and put it in the hospitals where it belongs. I thought it was a great, great decision." When the president saw the interview, he declared to his wife: "Well honey, there goes about 20 million votes."[15]

Ford was correct because both Robert Welch and Phyllis Schlafly had wound the two issues together. Catholic Phyllis Schlafly, already popular on the Far Right for her bestselling tract *A Choice Not an Echo*, fought the amendment by founding STOP ERA.

Now the traditional, albeit, incomplete narrative is that Schlafly stopped the ERA. To be sure, the former Goldwater promoter and JBS member was a force to be reckoned with. Schlafly possessed formidable organizational skills to slow down the passage of the ERA. Schlafly liked to speak of herself as a housewife first. Petite and blonde, her finely pressed pink suits and pumps were her trademark.[16] But Schlafly's 1964 *A Choice Not an Echo* drew from the same conspiratorial wheelhouse that Welch had been building since *May God Forgive Us*. Self-published, Schlafly wrote that "secret kingmakers," as the historian Geoffrey Kabaservice put it, were "a shadowy group made up of internationalist New York investment bankers" who "dominated the media." These kingmakers, Schlafly wrote, selected presidential nominees and stole the election from Robert Taft, who would have campaigned "on the issues" and won. They duped the United States into getting involved in World War II and buttressed Communist regimes throughout the world. Yet Welch had been saying the same thing for decades before. As Geoffrey Kabaservice wrote, "her pamphlet essentially restated" Welch's own words from 1961: "the establishment that has been running the Roosevelt–Truman–Eisenhower–Kennedy administration . . . those tremendous forces which, throughout all of this one continuous administration under different names and fronts, have been striving 'so to change the economic and political structure of the United States so that it can be comfortably merged with Soviet Russia in a one-world socialist government.'"[17] *A Choice Not an Echo was* an echo—and the voice was Welch's own. In other words, Schlafly was savvy and smart, but Welch was cunning and brilliant as well. Both mobilized their respective organizations to defeat the ERA by tying it closely to the social issue of abortion.

Robert praised Schlafly and Jaquie Davison, the founder of Happiness of Womanhood (HOW), for doing a "superb job of rallying opposition, mostly by women" and slowing "almost to a standstill the very rapid progress the ERA was making towards ratification." But, he said, Schlafly "did not have . . . any organization with the cohesiveness and experience . . . which the Birch Society could supply."[18] "By November [1972], we had realized how serious and how extensive was this threat to the quality and health and sanity of American life. We had plunged into the fight with full force. Our members rallied to the call with an enthusiasm and determination and quick grasp of how to proceed. . . . Within five months their efforts had been victorious in enough states to bring the total to 16 that had refused ratification," Welch added.[19] He remarked that ERA was being relegated "to the classification of an Entertainingly Remembered Absurdity."[20]

On December 21, 1972, JBS members organized an opposition meeting in a small town in Utah and formed a short-term organization. Robert observed that the group yielded to "acronym temptation, as well as some keen psychological insight," and named the group

HOT DOG, or Humanitarians Opposed to Degrading Our Girls." The female leader of HOT DOG wrote in her John Birch Society MMM, or members' monthly memo, that in December, "we plan to petition, telegram, correspond and telephone the Utah legislators to pieces until they're converted. Hope name and purpose is catchy enough to go statewide." On January 24, 1973, the Utah legislature voted against ratification of ERA.[21]

Meanwhile "in Oklahoma," Welch reported, "a similar fight, initiated by our members, and converted by them with the cooperation of many other patriotic groups into a statewide organized opposition," began. "The patience, determination and labor" that "was done by these Oklahoma Birchers" ended in a surprisingly "clear-cut victory, when the Oklahoma legislature voted against ratification by 53 to 45."[22]

Within two months, Robert was growing confident that the ERA was a "dead duck."[23] In addition to Utah and Oklahoma, "we wish to add earnest congratulations and sincere thanks to our members in Nevada, Missouri, Montana, Nebraska, and North Carolina." Meanwhile, a JBS member informed Welch that the amendment was being held in committee in the Georgia and Arizona legislatures because its "proponents know it would be defeated in a floor vote." In North Carolina, a newspaper reported that a massive campaign of letter writing by opponents turned the tide; the final tally there was sixty-two to fifty-seven against ratification. One leader there remarked: "This could not have been done without education as the key." The fight "resulted in know-how for ourselves and good contacts with other people who were also both dependable and informed. We had some great help—and WE WON!" Welch observed: "behind that letter writing campaign, of course, was the educational work done by so many . . . hard-working members." One opponent of the amendment who had been involved in the fight before the local Birch membership joined in, joking, "Hey, how on earth did we get so well-organized all of a sudden?"[24]

The victories kept coming. In Louisiana, Birchers put out 25,000 pamphlets on buses, car windows, lunch counters, and in morning papers. According to one local Bircher, after both the state House and Senate voted down the ERA, "we Birchers went wild! We have been starving for some solid blow against the conspiracy. This will help our recruiting and everything else."[25] The eastern Pennsylvania coordinator James McLemore was similarly ecstatic by victory in his state: "We got into it late, we fought, and we won it hands down." Even ERA supporters recognized the power of the John Birch Society. Michele Myers, a feminist active in the Philadelphia campaign, said, "there is no doubt about it." The Birch Society organized "a very effective covert campaign."[26]

The campaign included not only states that had not yet ratified the amendment but also states that had. In Rhode Island, as the Birch Society began campaigning for rescission, members of the legislature started having second thoughts. One said: "I'm not raising my daughter to serve in the Army."[27] Between late 1972 and 1982, only five additional states ratified, while five states that had ratified it rescinded their ratification. Even in states like North Carolina and Florida where President Jimmy Carter and his wife Rosalynn Carter stepped into the fight, Welch observed that "the prestige and pressures of the White House behind them, our people had done such thorough work in creating an understanding of the really subversive nature and purpose of this Communistic monstrosity that enough members of both legislatures stood firm against it." ERA was never able to gain the support from the thirty-eight states that it needed. By 1982, it was moribund.

"Before we got into the fight at all," Welch observed, "I had been stupid enough to believe that this country could not possibly take seriously any such an idiotic proposal. But then we did plunge in and with full force, by having members of our field staff start organizing specific local groups, to educate their fellow citizens and especially the members of their respective state legislatures, in every state where ratification was still to come up in the future."[28] In the end, Robert Welch shared credit with Phyllis Schlafly for stopping the ERA, concluding that neither could have done it without the other.[29]

Welch also took on sex education in schools, forming the Movement to Restore Decency (MOTOREDE) in 1969. Welch's goal was to resist the "breaking down of modesty, cleanliness, good manners, good taste, moderation in appetites, restraint in behavior, morality, and tradition." MOTOREDE members showed home movies to potential recruits and held letter-writing workshops. A MOTOREDE packet of a dozen articles included Professor E. Merrill Root's "What to Tell Your Children," JBS council member Rev. Francis Fenton's "A Priest on

Sex Education," and a staff member's sharp eight-page denunciation of popular advice columnist Ann Landers.

The drive against sex education was led by both the John Birch Society and Billy James Hargis's Christian Crusade. Each advised the other, endorsed the other, and reprinted the other's material. For instance, in January 1969, the John Birch Society republished the Christian Crusade's pamphlet *Is the Schoolhouse the Proper Place to Teach Raw Sex* as *Sex Education in the Schools*. The two organizations formed a formidable alliance and foreshadowed a methodological change for some fundamentalist organizations. In the future, many allied with secular organizations when the issues aligned.[30]

Welch campaigned against pornography as well. In 1964, in *Jacobellis v. Ohio*, the Supreme Court made the prosecution of obscene material more difficult, ruling that questionable literature must be without "redeeming social importance" to be censored.[31] Partly as a result, pornography became more accessible in America than ever before. Mailboxes became full of advertisements for pornography, and pornographic movie advertisements appeared in newspapers. More Supreme Court decisions protected pornographers under the First Amendment. In 1973, the Court defined obscenity in *Miller v. California* as material violating "community standards and not possessing serious literary or artistic value."[32]

The American Right saw the liberalization of pornography within a milieu of moral decline, the abandonment of traditional values, and complete abandonment of personal responsibility. A hedonistic culture of self-indulgence was growing. Hippies experimented with new drugs, libertine sexual practices, and alternative communal environments. Many rejected the materialistic values, politics, and lifestyles of their parents. The pill and other new forms of artificial contraception changed attitudes toward sex and marriage. Once "in the closet," homosexuality became increasingly socially acceptable and overt.

These developments, coupled with sex education in the public schools, increased Robert Welch's fear that the Communists were succeeding, destroying traditional moral standards and rotting the minds of the young. Welch was highly successful in convincing people that the Left had a coordinated plan to make sexual lifestyles and obscene material completely acceptable, even within public schools. Welch also helped popularize the belief that disseminating smut to minors was one of the chief objectives of progressive educators and sex educators.

For Welch, Mary Calderone, the founder of the Sexuality Information and Education Council of the United States (SIECUS), perfectly encapsulated the moral decay inherent to secular humanism. Imperious, gray haired, and tall, Calderone rejected evangelical sexual morality, preached a nonabsolutist attitude toward values, and encouraged sexual neutrality. She said: "What I'm trying to do is to free people—free society really, . . .—from the horrible incubus that we've been carrying for years of looking upon sexuality as evil instead of a gift from God." Calderone and SIECUS, like Alfred Kinsey and Masters and Johnson, wanted to eradicate sexual guilt and cultural anxiety about sex. In its programs and education, SIECUS advocated sexual pleasure—"We cannot talk about human sexuality without talking about values, but they're not, the 'no' values, they're the 'yes' values," observed Calderone—which came under attack from social conservatives, who saw in this a threat to America's children. "I was so incredibly excited when I heard about the fetal erection," Calderone once said, concluding that young children were sexual beings. She also wrote letters to the pope to explain that masturbation is innocuous. Welch believed that the sex hygiene educators were in a cabal with pornographers to not only exploit lust for monetary purpose but also to subvert the morals of children for Communist subjugation.[33]

For this crusade, Welch drew on the older argument of John Birch Society council member E. Merrill Root and others who feared Communist indoctrination in public schools. The Birch Society reissued Root's most prominent works for the culture wars of the 1970s, including *Brainwashing in the High Schools* and *Collectivism on Campus*, fostering the thesis that sex education was pornography and that Mary Calderone peddled smut and sexual depravity. These arguments echoed those published in *American Opinion* over the years by Gary Allen, the John Birch Society's most prolific chronicler of the counterculture, the civil rights revolution, and other social movements. Allen started writing in 1965 (four years before the establishment of SIECUS) and contributed more than 200 articles, one of which made the case that in May 1919, the Allies found the Communists' book *Rules for Revolution* in Dusseldorf, Germany. That document—which was more likely a product of post–World War II England—declared that Communists wanted to "corrupt the young, get them away from religion, get them interested in sex, make them superficial [and] destroy their ruggedness." It was cited in the anti-Communist newsletter *FACTS in Education* alongside the tale that a Los Angeles sex instructor had asked his students to discuss sexual experiences with animals.[34]

The Communists wanted to "destroy the moral character of a generation" observed George Schuyler, an African American erstwhile Communist, MOTOREDE activist, and writer for *American Opinion*. According to him, the SIECUS crowd was working with the National Council of Churches to brainwash American children with pornography and rot their minds and morals. Schuyler also propounded another tale about Communists in either Poland or Russia who enlisted "hundreds of sex criminals, perverts, and prostitutes" for a ten-day orgy in an unidentified town. Pictures were taken and distributed—"Millions of prints," Schuyler said, "poison[ed] the minds of countless young Americans."[35]

Hargis's Christian Crusade was essential to the MOTOREDE program. In 1968, Christian Crusade's Gordon V. Drake published *Blackboard Power: NEA Threat to America*, which conflated Black radicalism with progressive educational reforms and concluded that the National Education Association (NEA) sought to turn teachers into Communists. According to Drake, the NEA was aligned with the nefarious World Confederation of Organizations of the Teaching Profession (WCOTP), which assaulted nationalism and celebrated world citizenship, the United Nations, and its auxiliary United Nations Educational Scientific and Cultural Organization (UNESCO).[36]

An entire chapter of *Blackboard Power* was dedicated to sex education. Drake expanded it into the pamphlet *Is the Schoolhouse the Proper Place to Teach Raw Sex*, which essentially made the same case as Welch and MOTOREDE: sex education sought to spread pornography to schoolchildren. Drake showed that SIECUS board members were on the editorial board of the magazine *Sexology*, which claimed to be educational in focus but which Drake said hawked "sex-sensationalism." Drake said that SIECUS wanted such *Sexology* articles as "Do Sex Change Men Want to be Mothers?," "Group Sex Orgies," and "The Prostitutes of Ancient Greece" taught in the classroom. Drake also red-baited the board members. Albert Ellis, Drake wrote, was not only a "leader in one of the dozens of left-wing political groups in New York City" but also depraved sexually because he wrote *The American Sexual Tragedy*, in which he attacked "men who cannot be sexually satisfied with any form of sex activity but coitus."

Sex education by SIECUS was "a final assault upon the family as a fundamental block in the structure of our civilization," Robert Welch declared. Under the guidelines of SIECUS, the state was usurping all parental "responsibility for the education of their children." SIECUS, Welch added, actively encouraged "such universal sexual promiscuity—and perversion—that the family will become, as the Communists have always wanted, merely a temporary arrangement for economic convenience."[37]

Robert initially hoped that MOTOREDE members would be Birchers, but most members were concerned not with conspiratorial arguments but with the rights of parents. As Welch put it: MOTOREDE consisted of "good citizens drawn from every level and division of American life, who were seriously concerned about the future of their children and of their country." Welch recognized that religious men and women were interested in the new social issues the John Birch Society was promoting, and he hoped to tap that lode for new members. In 1969, MOTOREDE produced the film *The Innocents Defiled*, which foreshadowed the rise of the religious Right. "He that shall scandalize one of these little ones," the film began with the Bible verse, "it were better for him that a millstone should be hanged around his neck, and he should be drowned in the depths of the sea."[38]

MOTOREDE was the primary and only organized opposition to SIECUS and its drive to implement sex education in secondary schools. Welch and the John Birch Society successfully convinced many Americans who would never join the Birch Society that SIECUS actually wanted to promote legalized pornography and permissive immorality. Powerful evidence of the significant impact of MOTOREDE came from an organization that opposed the John Birch Society: the Anti-Defamation League of B'nai B'rith. The league reported: "if the sex education campaign has proved nothing else, it has demonstrated the [Birch] Society's ability—given the right issue—to mount a nationwide campaign that can have an impact on community life throughout the United States, as school districts and more than 30 states have recently learned. The campaign against sex education in the schools . . . became a nationwide phenomenon of disturbing proportions only after [Robert] Welch threw the Society's efforts into the drive. It is clear from the results that of all the groups on the radical Right only the Birch Society has the kind of nationwide, continuing organization apparatus that can sustain such an ongoing campaign."[39]

Welch organized no particular auxiliary movements against homosexuality, but the pages of the *JBS Bulletin* were full of evidence suggesting that JBS members and MOTOREDE members also regarded homosexuality as an attack on traditional values, a symptom of moral degradation, and akin to bestiality and promiscuity among heterosexuals. MOTOREDE declared, too, that homosexuality threatened national security because Communists targeted—and thus favored—gay men in the State Department, believing their sexual orientation made them more susceptible to blackmail.[40] Welch averred that Communists more broadly encouraged "homosexuality and every other form of sexual perversion, as smart and normal and acceptable from the classroom to the White House." The ascendancy of Sumner Welles and John Maynard Keynes was not due to any talent they possessed in their service to the public, Welch argued, but "because they [were] flagrant homosexuals."[41]

By the mid-1960s, Welch was concerned that homosexuality was spreading across the United States like wildfire. Welch, George Schuyler, and a number of public officials became obsessed with homosexuality and what they considered deviant sexual activity within the civil rights movement. Congressman William L. Dickinson, on the House floor, explained the Selma-to-Montgomery march was a motley crew of "Alabama Negroes, do-gooders, Communists, adventurers, beatniks, and prostitutes."[42] At a Montgomery church, he said, the marchers engaged in an all-night orgy. Schuyler echoed Dickinson and called the march "notoriously homo-infested" and involving the "sex deviates" Bayard Rustin and James Reuben Reid. Communism was to blame for the debauchery and the debacle of traditional morality, Schuyler claimed: "A sure sign of society down the drain, of the failure of manhood and womanhood, of a jaded slump into death" were "wrist danglers" bragging of their "indiscretions" and when "a neighboring butch tells of her latest conquest."[43] In 1969, Medford Evans wrote in the *American Opinion* that pornographers "were usually homosexuals" and "had a special hatred for women" because they can bear children.[44]

Sex education and more open acceptance of homosexuality were not the only social issues that drove some evangelicals and Catholics to the right—and that Welch capitalized on. He attacked both the expanded availability of birth control and the rise of abortion "on demand." John McManus, Robert Welch's formidable right hand at the time, gave voice to the Catholic community's rejection of liberalized abortion laws, which struck at the heart of the Catholic belief system.[45] Catholics represented a significant portion of John Birch Society membership, and they viewed life as God's gift. Conception—the moment that life happened—was that one instant when God clasped hands with a human being. It was a fundamental moment of nexus between the divine and the mortal. Any encroachment—let alone murder—on this evanescent connection was an affront to the divine. Roman Catholic theologians saw the temporal phase of life as central to everlasting life in heaven. Because abortion interrupted this necessary phase for salvation and eternal life, it encroached on God's work and was fundamentally nefarious. Accordingly, Catholics attacked the lenient abortion laws being passed throughout the nation in the 1970s.[46]

But feminists argued that this worldview belonged to the male-dominated ivory tower of Catholic intellectualism. Moreover, these feminists, or feminoids—female hemorrhoids—as Robert Welch called them, argued that such scholastic nitpicking imposed a belief system everybody did not hold. Deriving their worldview from Jean-Jacques Rousseau's *Rights of Man* rather than John Locke's, which held that rights came from God, these essentially libertarian feminists argued "My Body Belongs to Me."

Many feminists held that the ability to terminate life was their right. While some called for more radical solutions, most feminists held that abortion should be permitted at least in cases of incest, rape, endangerment to the life of the mother, or deformation of the child. They supported liberalization of abortion laws and were successful. Hawaii became the first state to repeal its restriction on abortion in 1967. New York was next, with Governor Nelson Rockefeller signing legislation to abolish restrictions on abortion for the first twenty-four weeks of pregnancy. Welch refused to call Ronald Reagan a conservative because as governor he signed California's law to liberalize abortion in 1967. Liberalization of abortion laws became reality in fourteen other states. Early on, the John Birch Society actively tried to stop this trend, joining the Right to Life League and Mothers Outraged at the Murder of Innocents. Female Birchers made up a most important cohort of foot soldiers in fighting the liberalization of abortion laws. Many also belonged to the National Right to Life Committee (NRLC).[47] They enjoyed some success. In the spring of 1971, one member of Congress who was also a JBS council member obtained a presidential order forcing military installations to adhere to the abortion laws of the states in which they are located. The number of abortions fell in military hospitals.[48]

The Supreme Court's 1973 decision in *Roe v. Wade* beckoned even more evangelicals to join the ranks of a Republican Party increasingly committed to anti-abortion platforms. Welch, too, displayed even greater conviction on the issue. "We can think of no matter more compelling . . . than the murder of tens of thousands of unborn infants each month," he observed. Political pragmatism and pressure from anti-abortion groups like the John Birch Society, the Christian Crusade, the Campus Crusade for Christ, as well as the NRLC pushed the Republican Party to the right on the issue.[49] The strong performance of George Wallace in 1968 showed that anti-abortion Republicans could get the Catholic vote. James Buckley's election as senator from New York sent a similar message in 1970. Republicans who once espoused population control through contraception and abortion embraced instead a pro-life position. Richard Nixon shifted, too, declaring in May 1972, "I consider abortion an unacceptable form of population control. In my judgment, unrestricted abortion policies would demean human life." Nixon's "Catholic Strategy" paid off, as he won 60 percent of the Catholic vote in the 1972 election.

The fight against "abortion on demand" was also a central priority of MOTOREDE. In 1970, McManus observed, "MOTOREDE believes that abortion is murder. When, therefore we note the cries for relaxation of laws prohibiting abortion, liberalized attitude toward abortion, or abortion on demand, we read instead, relaxation of laws prohibiting murder, liberalized attitude toward murder, or murder on demand." Welch was less absolutist than McManus on the matter of abortion. He urged members "not to get into the controversy over birth control, but to confine their efforts to opposing the legalization, encouragement, and subsidization of 'abortion on demand,' especially by the federal government."[50]

Like Alex Jones in the twenty-first century, Welch believed that the Insiders wanted to control the size of the American population through infanticide. "Visibly planned to come right behind the drive for abortion," Welch said in 1970, "will be similar drives for infanticide to be practiced on the very young and euthanasia to be practiced on the very old—with government determining who shall be allowed to live and who shall be killed. From this it would be a short step toward deciding that anybody hostile to government should be done away with, for the good of society." MOTOREDE spokesman Jack Moore observed that the federal government advocated an abortion policy to "establish population controls as brutal and restrictive as those of Hitler's Germany and modern Russia."[51] MOTOREDE members echoed the beliefs of the JBS. In 1972, one citizen of El Paso viewed the JBS film *License to Kill* and remarked "One Worlders" were using "birth control, sterilization, abortion" to decimate the middle-class and were "trying to destroy our youth by drugs, pornography, etc. to bring about a complete moral breakdown." John Schmitz, a US representative from California and John Birch Society member, ran for president on the American Party ticket in 1972 as a culture warrior. One West Coast JBS district governor suggested that Schmitz should highlight the issue of "people control," a category that included "ecology, population control, abortion, and education bussing [*sic*], and education into the whole effort of the Insiders to control people and their environment."[52]

The religious Right of the late 1970s was primed by the Birch Society's campaigns against the ERA, sex education, and abortion.[53] On this foundation, more social conservatives entered the fray. In 1977, James Dobson established his Focus on the Family, which attacked sex education and gay rights. In 1979, Beverly LaHaye, the wife of Timothy LaHaye, founded Concerned Women for America, which enjoyed a larger budget and membership than its nemesis, the National Organization for Women. Son of a US senator, fundamentalist minister Pat Robertson established the Christian Broadcasting Network in

1977 and hosted the popular religious program *The 700 Club*.[54] W. A. Criswell, a Dallas Baptist preacher, led a purge of liberal and moderate factions in the Southern Baptist Convention and stepped up his involvement in GOP politics.[55] In 1979, Jerry Falwell developed the "pro-family" Moral Majority and railed against abortion as "America's original sin" and the ERA as "a definite violation of the Holy Spirit," while also assailing gay rights and the decline of the nuclear family. In 1981, Nelson Bunker Hunt, who had supported Robertson's flirtation with a presidential run in 1980, donated $1 million to the Moral Majority.[56] But the Birch Society was way ahead of many of these groups.

Before the 1980 election, Falwell asked, "What can you do from the pulpit? You can register people to vote. You can explain the issues to them. And you can endorse candidates, right there in church on Sunday morning."[57] Falwell, along with Robertson and Criswell, served on the executive board of the Religious Roundtable, a more ecumenical counterpart to the Moral Majority that fostered evangelical political activism. James Robison became executive director of the Religious Roundtable. A handsome and fiery Baptist preacher who vilified feminists and the movements for women's and homosexual rights, Robison evinced a growing contentiousness among the Christian Right. Bunker's father, H. L. Hunt, praised Robison as "the most effective communicator I have ever heard."[58]

On August 21, 1980, before the Religious Roundtable in Dallas, Ronald Reagan, the Republican presidential nominee, addressed 15,000 people. Criswell, Falwell, and Robertson sat on the stage. Robison spoke immediately before Reagan, declaring that "not voting is a sin against Almighty God!" Robison testified that he was "sick and tired about hearing about all the radicals and the perverts and the liberals and the Communists coming out of the closet! It's time for God's people to come out of the closet, out of the churches, and save America!" Reagan won the day when, following Robison, he declared, "I know you can't endorse me because this is a nonpartisan meeting, but I endorse you." He went on to compare the persecution that Jesus Christ predicted for all Christians with the state in which his audience found itself, "persecuted together by Democrats and liberals." But he brought down the house when he said of the Bible, "All the complex and horrendous questions confronting us have their answer in that single book." Robison later said that on the day Reagan was elected president, "God gave us grace."[59]

Welch was not consumed by issues of sex and religion. He also added economic issues to the Birch Society's agenda in the 1970s. Throughout the 1970s, the Society's publishing house, monthly magazine, reading rooms, and bookstores extolled the virtues of the free-market philosophy and fostered an alternative program to the welfare state.

While he had once backed the Liberty Amendment, which sought to abolish the income tax, Welch now supported more measured proposals to limit taxes. When he was active in the National Association of Manufacturers in the 1950s, NAM helped develop a tax plan calling for the gradual reduction of the top rates of both corporate and individual income taxes to 35 percent within five years.[60] Thirty-five percent is approximately what the marginal tax rate was in 2020. Also in the 1950s, Welch served on the advisory council of the taxpayer association the Campaign for 48 States, which included Howard Buffett, William F. Buckley, Frank Chodorov, J. Evetts Haley, Henry Hazlitt, Clarence Manion, J. Howard Pew, Dan Smoot, and Robert E. Wood. Calling itself "a program for patriots . . . that can be supported and recommended by any banker, businessman, or professional man without fear of political repercussion," the Campaign for 48 States sought a "limitation of the power of Congress to tax" through passage of the Reed-Dirksen amendment, which lowered the marginal tax rate and granted to the states the sole power to tax gifts and estates.[61] Welch supported T. Coleman Andrews for the presidency in 1956 in part because of his strong advocacy of lowering income taxes. Andrews observed that "the number one thing wrong" with the graduated income tax was "it was conceived in vengeance rather than as a revenue measure."[62]

Welch helped push the country to the right in the 1970s by providing much of the support behind the anti-tax movement at both the federal and state levels. Articles in *American Opinion* waged war on labor unions, opposed government intervention in the economy, but most importantly advocated tax cuts for those in the highest tax brackets. The Birch Society's campaign influenced tax relief for the rich at the federal level—especially Reagan's most consequential legacy: the 1981 tax law, which reduced the marginal tax rate for the wealthiest Americans from 70 percent to 50 percent. At the state level, Birch Society member Lewis Uhler founded the National Tax Limitation Committee, which was instrumental in passing Proposition 13 to reduce California's property taxes in 1978. That proposition cut property taxes by 57 percent, slashed tax rates, and established that taxes would rise no more than 2 percent in any given year. Proposition 13 also established that legislators in Sacramento needed a two-thirds majority to increase state taxes. Other states soon followed the California example, with twenty-eight of them lowering income taxes and thirty-seven lowering property taxes.[63]

Significantly, Welch did not call for abolishing the income tax because he wholeheartedly supported the allocation of federal dollars to the national defense. Welch warned against civil disobedience, frowning upon those anti-tax protesters who refused to pay their income taxes. As he put it, he avoided the instincts of tax revolters who "let[] their enthusiasm run way with [their] judgment in falling for every cockeyed scheme." Welch was seriously worried about members getting in trouble with the IRS. "One of our outstanding members in San Diego," Welch explained, "was pulled in by IRS agents, along with about a dozen real hotheads with whom he had been briefly associating, on some kind of charge to violate the law." "It took him over a year to recover from the shock and expense."[64]

Welch heavily criticized Liberty Lobby founder Willis Carto for both his anti-Semitism and his irresponsible attitude on tax revolts. Carto, Welch said, "would have to look the words 'morality' or 'ethics' up in the dictionary to have the slightest idea of what was being talked about." Moreover, Carto was peddling a "half-baked concoction of sophomoric drivel." Before he knew of Carto's budding anti-Semitism, Welch hired him at Belmont in 1959, but fired him after a few months. By the 1970s, Welch was continuously annoyed with Carto because of his affinity for using "our people to turn his [tax-revolt] concept into a reality." "We have been under increasing fire" Welch wrote in 1975, "because we would not 'cooperate—' which means do practically all of the work—in making" tax revolt a goal of the anti-Communist cause. Welch advised members to "stay out of the tax revolt trap." "I was lambasted all over the map by Carto's supporters as having condemned the tax revolt, and having refused to let Birchers cooperate in it as all patriotic organizations should."[65]

Welch instead provided a more responsible, legal way to protest high tax rates. As he put it when establishing the ad hoc group TRIM (Tax Relief Immediately), "the main thrust of our campaign will be simply and directly against the enactment of higher taxes, and in support of the reduction of present taxes." As early as 1973, Welch wrote that TRIM sought to "become a watchdog with regard to state income taxes" and "prevent any new state income taxes from being implemented."[66] By 1977, the Society had more than 200 active TRIM committees throughout the country, producing factual bulletins detailing the positions on tax policy of members of Congress and candidates for their jobs. Rather than avoid paying income taxes, members aimed to vote out legislators who were raising taxes. Welch called TRIM "the most effective ad hoc operation we have ever undertaken" and boasted that in 1976 the program "was directly responsible for, or very helpful to, the election of several new conservative members of Congress, and of at least one new conservative Senator." TRIM provided a potent vehicle for business conservatives. "One quite successful former business man," Welch boasted, "sold his business and is putting his whole effort into the promotion and sale of our TRIM bulletins, at his own risk and expense, to other business firms." What made TRIM extraordinary was that it marked the first time an ad hoc group became self-supporting, becoming, as Welch put it, "a clearly enough defined and permanent enough organization to call for the regular payment of any dues."[67]

TRIM and the tax revolts of the 1970s gave rise to the New Right, a more secular coalition than the religious Right, concerned with tax cuts, decreasing the size of the state, and reducing regulation of business. Armed with the names of folks—many Birchers or ex-Birchers—who had signed up for the Goldwater and Wallace presidential campaigns, Richard Viguerie, a conservative Catholic from Wisconsin, created an enormous database of conservative voters and a large-scale direct-mail program. Without Viguerie's list and database, there would have been no Reagan revolution. But without Birchers, it is highly likely there would have been no list.

With Welch, TRIM, and JBS rank-and-file providing momentum, the 1970s saw not only conservative intellectual organizations that decried the nation's sordid culture and weak economy but also a renewed focus on electoral success. After losing the 1976 Republican presidential nomination to the incumbent President Ford, former California governor Ronald Reagan took to the airwaves with daily syndicated radio addresses assailing illegal immigration, welfare, President Carter's weak foreign policy, and the poor economy, which he blamed on the Democrats. In April 1979, Reagan declared, sounding very much like a member of TRIM, "when we talk of these problems all of us seem to do so in the context of what government should do about them." "May I suggest that government has already done too much about them and that's why we have the problems." Reagan said massive tax cuts—the kind that Robert Welch long fought for—were necessary to get the economy moving again. Reagan became the national mouthpiece for the cuts that California tax revolters, TRIMMERS, and Birchers had been calling for all decade. Reagan discovered that taxation was front and center for many Americans. Proposition 13 "triggered hope in the breasts of the people that something could be done. It was a little bit like dumping those cases of tea off the boat in Boston Harbor," he said. The tax revolt forged tighter bonds between libertarian conservatives and GOP businesspeople.[68]

Reagan's 1980 presidential campaign conjoined the religious Right and the New Right. One reporter remarked: "There is no formal Christian caucus at the Republican national convention.... None is needed. Overlap between the Reagan campaign and evangelical Christians is substantial."[69] Reagan's acceptance speech at the Republican convention promised the lightening of the tax burden and concluded with a silent prayer. Once in office, Reagan moved quickly to secure the promised tax cut. His fierce anti-Communism and support for broad-based tax reform that assailed the state and "starved the beast," as his budget director David Stockman observed, attracted every cohort of his coalition. The "supply-side" tax cut would power the economy by putting more money in the hands of the people to invest in their families, the president claimed. Lightening the tax load for the more affluent would "trickle down" to all Americans, Reagan promised. Rejecting any criticism from Keynesian economists and political opponents, Reagan said—just as Welch and TRIM did—that tax cuts, even without a corresponding decrease in spending, would advance economic growth and actually increase tax revenues. Reagan's budget totaled more than $40 billion in domestic spending cuts and included a 30 percent tax cut over three years, primarily to the benefit of the richest Americans. On August 13, 1981, Reagan signed into law the Economic Recovery Tax Act.[70]

Among those affluent Americans celebrating the tax cut was Nelson Bunker Hunt. Come 1984, Dallas hosted the National Republican Convention, and during that week, Bunker hosted a "California gold rush party" for 1,650 people at his Circle T Ranch at $1,000 a plate. He hoped to raise $1 million for the National Conservative Political Action Committee. The *New York Times* called it "certainly the most elaborate of many social extravaganzas related to the Republican National Convention." Attendees included Bob Hope, Pat Boone, Charlton Heston, Mickey Rooney, Michael Landon, Glen Campbell, Arnold Palmer, Joe Frazier, Roy Rogers, and Dale Evans. Bunker's friends included southern US senators Jesse Helms, Strom Thurmond, and James Eastland.[71]

Robert Welch was not on hand. His Society depended more and more on Nelson Bunker Hunt's wealth for sustaining its own fortunes as an institution. This meant it depended on Bunker's investment acumen, and that was a mistake. Just as the Society had reached the zenith of its power and contributed to Reagan's victory, the combination of success and Bunker's insolvency spelled deep trouble for the John Birch Society, whose influence waned by 1980.

The central problem with Bunker had to do with silver. In the 1970s, he had continued to amass a sizable portion of the world's silver supply, owning about 50 million ounces as of late January 1979. But silver traded at only $6 an ounce.[72] Hunt needed it to go higher. Bunker convinced several Saudi Arabian sheikhs to support his play to invest heavily in a silver syndicate, which bought silver aggressively throughout 1979 until it peaked at $52 an ounce in January 1980.

As prices rose, silver exchanges—the Comex in New York and the Board of Trade in Chicago—began running out of silver. The Commodity Futures Trading Commission (CFTC), a federal agency, feared that Bunker and the sheikhs were playing a classic market squeeze, so as to be able to set the world silver price. Of course, Bunker and his brothers, who also were involved, denied colluding with the Saudis to illegally corner the market. The CFTC, deeply concerned, set limits on how much silver could be bought and sold. In an unprecedented decision in January 1980, the Comex prohibited any silver purchases and allowed only sales. The Chicago Board of Trade followed suit. Silver prices began to fall.

Bunker had purchased his silver on margin, or with borrowed money from banks. As silver prices dipped, Bunker was initially able to use his own cash to pay the margin calls, or the carrying costs on the loans. But with silver falling from $50.35 to $10.80 an ounce in two months—from January to March 1980—Bunker began to run out of cash and could not get it from elsewhere. His holdings and future contracts plummeted from a value of $7 billion to a $1.7 billion debt.

But the collapse was pervasive. Investors speculating alongside him on bullion and futures contracts squandered their own fortunes after being unable to exit the market. Ordinary folks whose assets were difficult to quickly liquidate—sellers of silverware and candlesticks—lost too. While Bunker was losing millions, rumors abounded that a major Wall Street investment bank was on the verge of failing. Brokerage houses and financial markets were saved when bankers and federal regulators extended Bunker a generous billion-dollar line of credit. The exodus ended, a stampede was avoided, and the meltdown was stanched. But the cost of the bailout was eventually borne by taxpayers, and the extension of a financial lifeline foreshadowed even larger bailouts for imprudent affluence in the future.

In the end, Hunt correctly predicted Armageddon, but it was secular and limited to the silver markets. It was hardly divine. Bunker avoided any criminal liability, but in the years ahead, the bankruptcy proceedings, damage claims, lawsuits, and civil charges devoured thousands of hours of his time and ate greedily into his huge holdings in oil, gas, cattle, and horses.

Despite being bailed out by the federal government, Bunker felt only greater distrust and antipathy toward it. He became fully convinced that David Rockefeller had orchestrated the collapse of the silver market, along with the international Communist conspiracy and the Council on Foreign Relations. Yet even as his belief in conspiracies was strengthened, he weakened the John Birch Society, the group most responsible for foisting such ideas on the American public, by being unable to support it.[73]

The Society also suffered financially when in 1983, it needed to cut a check for $400,000 after losing what became a seminal Supreme Court case. The case began fourteen years prior when Alan Stang published an article in the *American Opinion* about a Chicago police officer who was convicted of murder. In it, Stang called Elmer Gertz, one of the victim's lawyers, "a member of the Communist National Lawyers Guild." Gertz sued the Society for libel. The Society tried to claim Gertz was a public figure, who would have to prove that Stang's characterization was malicious, not just defamatory. The Supreme Court ultimately ruled that Gertz was not a public person, and suddenly the Society was in the hole for nearly half a million dollars.[74]

As the Society moved into the 1980s, a continuing barrage of letters and telephone calls inundated the headquarters at Belmont from staunch and longtime members complaining of internal dissension within the group. Older members increasingly felt isolated from the decision-making process. Some members canceled their membership and joined other organizations that had more dynamic and inspirational leadership. Dues-paying members likely sank from 30,000 to 12,000 by 1985.

Recordkeeping at Belmont had become dodgy, as Welch celebrated birthdays in his eighties. Improved business methods were much needed. The JBS was hemorrhaging from legal costs and efforts to avoid further litigation. Telephone charges were soaring. Travel expenses were not itemized. Many failed to keep receipts. According to Gary Allen, American Airlines had cut off credit because of delinquent bills.

Staffers were unhappy too. Some of the most talented folks were not promoted. As in many male-dominated organizations in the postwar United States, women were never given opportunities to serve in top management positions—one of Welch's chief failures as founder. Scott Stanley, the eagle-eyed editor of both *American Opinion* and the *Review of the News*, and his editorial staff, comprising Elise W. Clark, Bill Hoar, Jim Graves, Lee Clark Graves, and Jim Drummey, were performing yeoman's work, but they were a small team. The meticulous Clark was the only editor who had been on staff since 1961. Stanley enjoyed great respect among conservatives and journalists. He had served Welch for two decades, demonstrating sound judgment while seeking few plaudits or rewards. Because of Stanley's indefatigable efforts to produce high-quality publications, the goals that Robert Welch conceived in the 1950s and 1960s were embraced in the 1970s. If Welch had planted and nurtured the seeds, Stanley was collecting the fruits of the harvest. But management was simply ineffective in ensuring that the machinery was strong enough to reap and gather the crops.

For sure, the magazine had low circulation and lost money, but it was still the Society's best revenue source. Stanley stressed the need to promote the magazine, but his arguments continually fell on deaf ears. Management continued to promise that marketing would improve. Management promised that the process for subscription renewal would become easier for readers, but such promises were never fulfilled.

This was partly Welch's fault. That said, he was in his ninth decade on the planet. He remained a loyal friend or colleague to individuals who may not have deserved it. He hired some individuals who were toadies and whose views departed from the goals of the *Blue Book* of the John Birch Society. Whether he was too old to serve as gatekeeper or too reluctant, his unwillingness hurt the Society. Welch's libertarian instinct kept him from kicking out members he should have kicked out. He refused to bring himself to fire long-standing members of the team. He wanted individuals to police themselves according to the goals. Contrary to what his critics said of him, he was so anti-authoritarian, he found the idea of telling people how to behave repellent. But the individuals that he hired, especially Tom Hill, failed to do their work. Hill's failure had a cascading effect throughout the Society.

By 1985, *American Opinion* and *Review of the News* had become inferior products, at least compared with past decades. Alan Stang, Gary Allen, Medford Evans, Sue Huck, John Rees, Jim Graves, and Elise Clark were replaced with freelance writers and syndicated columnists. No assets remained. Lifetime subscription money was long gone. Long-term advertising funds were spent. Nelson Bunker Hunt resigned from the council, taking away the Society's meal ticket. The field staff meanwhile imploded as coordinators throughout the country resigned.

In 1983, the best writer in the JBS—eighty-three-year-old Robert Welch—suffered a serious stroke and never recovered. Larry McDonald, a conservative Democratic US representative from Georgia, succeeded Welch as the chair of the John Birch Society. According to member Charles Provan, the John Birch Society covered the cost of

Welch's hospitalization and stay in the Winchester Convalescent and Nursing Home. The total cost amounted to less than $40,000. That said, Welch never accepted any salary from the Society for the twenty-six years of his involvement. Welch gave every dollar he ever made to the John Birch Society. Royalties from the *Blue Book* and *The Politician* covered the maintenance of his home, which was the only asset he left his wife. He gave his life and fortune to the Society.

According to Jack McManus, Welch converted to Catholicism on his deathbed in 1985, but the story is not accurate because Welch was unable to recognize even his wife during the final months of his life. Welch likely died a Unitarian.

After his death, Marian needed to sell the home for income. Welch once wrote, "I have given up practically everything else in this struggle, or at least certainly expect to do so before it is over."[75] For this, he would be prophetic. But throughout their marriage, Marian had stood by his side and enjoyed the fight. Nothing suggests that she ever changed her mind about any of it after Robert passed.

The businessman, in the end, had failed to balance the books. But his influence on American conservatism cannot begin to be measured. Robert H. W. Welch will continue to influence American politics deep into the twenty-first century and beyond—when all of us who are among the living are long dead and gone. The candyman, despite what they say of him, will continue to dish out his tasty morsels in print and media for years to come.

Epilogue

Despite the predominant argument that a "responsible Right" purged conspiracy theory and Welchian logic from the conservative movement, Robert Welch was never excommunicated by William F. Buckley Jr., and his conspiratorial style of politics remained extremely potent after his death.

Even more so than in the early 1960s, when Robert was considered an eccentric, Robert Welch is important today because beginning in the 1980s and continuing to the present, his world has become ours. His world seems no longer so strange. We, the living, inhabit it.

Events began to accelerate in the 1980s. American leaders began to embrace a Welch-like worldview. Of course, no one exactly napped through the 1970s, which witnessed the US withdrawal from Vietnam, Watergate, Nixon's resignation, and congressional committee findings that the CIA worked with the mafia to murder a world leader, among other nefarious dealings. But then, in the mid-1980s the American people experienced the Reagan presidency.

Remembered today as the avatar of the Republicans' lost respectability, Reagan in 1971 described African United Nations delegates to a chortling Richard Nixon as "monkeys . . . uncomfortable wearing shoes."[1] He espoused conspiracy theories like the claim that Gerald Ford staged assassination attempts against himself to win sympathy votes in the 1976 presidential primaries and that the Soviet Union had removed 20 million young people to the countryside to practice for reconstructing their society after launching an offensive nuclear war.

The newsletter of Reagan's political action committee advocated the quack cancer cure (a pet Bircher cause of Larry McDonald) laetrile, which "may be efficacious against cancer but which government in its wisdom wants to keep people from using." (The reason was that it didn't work and frequently killed people.)

Then Reagan became president—and the only thing that changed was the people around him worked harder to keep his wackiness from the public.

They were frequently frustrated—for instance when Reagan claimed the nuclear freeze movement that drew a million protesters to Central Park in 1982 had been engineered in the Kremlin or the time he told reporters that apartheid South Africa had "eliminated the segregation that we once had in our own country." There was also the moment when he quoted to a group of college students visiting the White House Vladimir Ilyich Lenin's "eloquent statement" of his plan to conquer America: that he would first take Eastern Europe, then "organize the hordes of Asia," then "move into Latin America"; then "we will not have to take the last bastion of capitalism, the United States. It will fall into our outstretched hand like overripe fruit." Lenin never said any such thing, but Robert Welch did, at the first meeting of the John Birch Society.[2]

From the vantage of President Ronald Reagan, the "evil empire," as he called the Soviet Union, was engulfing Central America "in a sea of red, eventually lapping at our own borders." The left-wing government in Nicaragua, Reagan said, was "a cruel clique of deeply committed Communists at war with God and man from their very first days." Communism was coming to a town near you, Reagan suggested.[3]

Acting upon Welch-style thinking, Reagan wanted to protect the invasion of America by funding anti-Communist Nicaraguan counterrevolutionaries known as the Contras, but Congress refused. Reagan became obsessed with helping the Contras, whom he called the "moral equal of our Founding Fathers." Reagan's administration found a shocking way to thwart Congress's ban on military assistance to the rebels. In 1985, American officials sold arms to Iran in exchange for the return of American hostages who had been captured in Lebanon by Muslim extremist groups. Iran's money was then quietly diverted to the Nicaraguan Contras. For two years, Lieutenant Colonel Oliver

North and CIA director William Casey developed a sophisticated apparatus to use the proceeds of the sale of arms for hostages to purchase military supplies for the Contras. Reagan had enjoyed the nickname "the Teflon president"—until the Iran Contra scandal came out. He thereafter lost the public's confidence, and his administration was tarnished. But Welch would have approved.

Apocalyptic rhetoric, another feature of Robert's conspiratorial style, also became more predominant on the Far Left—though it has been present in American politics since the beginning of the republic. When John Adams ran against Thomas Jefferson, for instance, Adams's backers claimed that a Jefferson victory would mean Americans would live in a world without God.[4]

Apocalyptic rhetoric only grew on the Far Right. A division within the Republican Party was aired in 1992, when Patrick Buchanan, who challenged President George H. W. Bush for the presidency in 1992, delivered a divisive address that defined what was ultimately at stake in that race. According to Buchanan, Democratic nominee Bill Clinton would impose "abortion on demand, a litmus test for the Supreme Court, homosexual rights, discrimination against religious schools, women in combat units. That's change, all right, but that's not the kind of change America needs, it's not the kind of change America wants, and it's not the kind of change we can abide in a nation we still call 'God's country.'" The crowd thundered, "Go, Pat, go!" If Robert Welch were alive and present, he would likely have cheered along with the Republican crowd.[5]

As Bill Clinton took the oath of office, the Left embraced a politics of sensitivity and self. The Right also adopted identity politics that cultivated the resentments of privileged White males grieving their loss of potency and hegemony in an America experiencing vast demographic change. The Right began to feed on a resentment of immigrants and the rising status of African Americans. Rather than embracing a politics of amity, both sides indicted the other with animus and antipathy.[6]

Second Amendment rights divided the country, and domestic terrorists seemed to be more ubiquitous and more ominous.

As the seas rose and climate change became a new reality, Americans became embattled in fierce combat over guns. Battle lines were drawn. Pistols were sometimes not left outside the door. For each side, every confrontation seemed to matter more than the last. What America stood for was all that was at stake.

As Arthur Schlesinger put it, "one set of hatreds gives way to the next." Partisanship became more central, ideology more crucial. The other camp was an enemy of the state.[7]

In the 1990s, on the radical fringe of the Far Right, private militia members who believed the government represented a grave threat to freedom armed themselves to the teeth. "Christian Patriots," including the Aryan Nation and Posse Comitatus, embraced anti-Semitism and racism. The Militia of Montana, a private army, committed itself to resisting federal gun control laws. They saw owning a gun as a symbol of American liberty. They embraced the language of the American Revolution. They read Thomas Paine. They read Patrick Henry. Both major parties, they claimed, wanted to cede power to the United Nations and end American sovereignty. (Sound familiar?) After Ruby Ridge and Branch Davidian incidents in 1992 and 1993, the militia movement grew even more conspiratorial about the reach of the federal government. In protest, in 1996, Timothy McVeigh exploded a bomb outside a federal building in Oklahoma City, killing 168, including many children in a daycare.

McVeigh observed that the American dream was in "serious decline." The rural White middle class was getting crushed by globalization and the failure of wages to rise since the 1970s. The Right blamed the Left. The Left blamed the Right, but on the Right especially, but not exclusively, conspiracy theory offered an alternative explanation for the death of the American dream. Possessing an enormous imagination, harboring potent powers of illusion and delusion, conspiracy theorists provided a welcome escape. The dream was dead, they said, because globalists and elites in the government wanted it to be.

In 1996, Alex Jones brought his conspiracy theory to the American public with his radio show *The Final Edition*. Jones asserted Welch-like conclusions without any evidence whatsoever, such as that the government planned the Oklahoma City bombings and plotted to murder David Koresh and his Branch Davidian followers. As Jones grew more paranoid, he grew more affluent. "I don't care if it's Bill Clinton or Governor Bush, they are all elitist filth if you ask me," he said.[8] Jones's rhetoric seemed sheer lunacy—at first. But the lines between what distinguished normal political dialogue and hate-filled rhetoric were deteriorating quickly.[9] The new social media fueled an emerging intolerance for different political opinions.

In 1987, the FCC abolished the fairness doctrine; broadcasters were no longer required to present opposing views, and conservative radio grew by leaps and bounds. Rush Limbaugh, who declared that he possessed "talent on loan from God," was the most popular of the conservative talk radio hosts. Limbaugh vented hatreds and White resentment of a changing America for three hours in important timeslots every day, giving his opinions of "the way things ought to be" with occasional Welchian forays into conspiracy theory, all the while drawing one important caveat: he was only asking questions.

Limbaugh's incessant attacks on Bill and Hillary Clinton embraced Welch-like qualities in that imaginations were often stretched and illusions were created on the fly. Whether the charges had merit seemed not to matter. Hillary covered up the murder of Vince Foster, Limbaugh suggested, for one. Did Limbaugh have evidence? Covering himself from the legal consequences of slander, he declared, well, "that's what it said in the fax," whatever that was. Under the new conspiracism, the evidence was not what mattered. What mattered was the assertion, and its continuous repetition.[10]

Such was the complex dance that has always been at the heart of Republican politics in the conservative era. The extremist vanguard shopped fantastical horror stories about liberal elites in the hopes that one might break into the mainstream, such as the "Clinton Chronicles" VHS tape distributed by Jerry Falwell in the early 1990s. The stories included the Clintons not only covering up the murder of Vince Foster, but also murdering witnesses to their drug smuggling operation, and participating in a crooked land deal at a development called "Whitewater."[11]

Television networks also became more partisan and more popular. In July 1996, MSNBC, which later became the partisan network Democrats watched, was followed later that year by Fox News, the partisan network that Republicans watched. Owned by the Australian tabloid newspaper magnate Rupert Murdoch, Fox News was managed by Roger Ailes, a neophyte to the field of journalism who said he didn't respect journalists. Still, he established a powerful media empire.[12]

During the period from 1950 to 1970 when three broadcast networks—ABC, CBS, and NBC—ruled, an age of consensus prevailed and partisanship reached its nadir. But with hyperpartisan cable news and then social media, hoary platitudes and conspiracy theories replaced vigorous discussion.

These forces relegated democratic deliberation to theater. But it was a theater of war. Hiram Johnson astutely observed that the first casualty of any war is truth; in this war, Congress was second. Soon, prevarication became a means of survival on both sides of the aisle. The next casualty was the electorate. The American people, locked inside their echo chambers—Twitter, Facebook, Fox News, MSNBC—became partisan warriors. Families split over politics because allegiance to party mattered more. Perhaps most troublingly, moderate voices disappeared.[13]

America had become Welchland. Just as Welch called Eisenhower a Communist and demanded the impeachment of Earl Warren, by the 1990s every presidency was investigated by hyperpartisans and their allies in the cable news networks. With Bill Clinton, it was the "Whitewater" land deal. Then it was the Paula Jones sexual harassment case, backed by the National Conservative Political Action Committee. When it was revealed that Clinton had an affair with a White House intern, the hyperpartisan atmosphere grew hotter. The affair was a grand ratings success for Fox News. The electorate found it completely engrossing and altogether human. Battle lines were drawn. Eighty-four percent of Democrats opposed Clinton's eventual impeachment; 67 percent of Republicans backed it. The coverage was sensationalized down to every unpleasant detail, just as Welch had examined every nook and cranny of Eisenhower's nefarious career and detailed them in *The Politician*.

But the entire spectacle—the nation's theme park journey into Welchland—backfired for the Republicans. They not only lost seats in the 1998 midterms, the politics of morality had a boomerang effect. Republican Speaker Newt Gingrich, already married twice, resigned in disgrace when his affair with an intern twenty-three years his junior became public knowledge. Gingrich bitterly blamed "cannibals who had blackmailed him into quitting."[14]

Robert Welch would have recognized these politics of mutually assured destruction. Cynicism ran rampant. Americans began to abhor

Congress even more. Attempted coups d'état became standard practice. Americans had come to embrace the scorched earth policies of life in Welchland, where presidential leadership was illegitimate at best. Opponents of George W. Bush, Barack Obama, and Donald J. Trump all called the holder of the nation's highest office "unconstitutional." As Jill Lepore observed, "the nation had its lost its way in the politics of mutually assured epistemological destruction. There was no truth, only innuendo, rumor, and bias. There was no reasonable explanation; there was only conspiracy."[15]

Donald J. Trump was born in 1947. His father was a real estate man from Queens, New York. Donald graduated from college during a year marked by political assassinations, chaos at the Democratic National Convention, and the political comeback of Richard Milhous Nixon. In the 1970s, Trump gave lavishly to the Democratic Party. He earned a reputation as either a huckster or a hustler, but he was never at a loss for words and loved the limelight, and it loved him. He possessed an amazing television and radio personality. He could garner immediate ratings for any host. He was viewed as an endearing charlatan when he offered to serve as an arms negotiator for the United States with the Soviet Union. Rumors abounded in 1987 that he had his sights on the presidency.

In 1988, in New Hampshire, he showed up in a stretch limousine. He was surrounded by Trump for President signs. "I'm not here because I'm running for president. I'm here because I'm tired of our country being kicked around." But he didn't actually run for president. In the "go-go 90s," when wealthy people were revered and the stock markets were booming, Trump was lionized as a sort of teetotaling fun-loving magnificently wealthy man-child playboy. He relished even the bad press. He was a cultural icon.

And many Americans wanted to hear what this playboy had to say about Bill Clinton's affair with Monica Lewinsky. Trump said he would have more respect for the president if he had sex with a supermodel instead. Soon, it looked like Trump was eyeing a 2000 presidential run. He published the book *The America We Deserve*, replete with the chapter entitled "Should I Run?" He declared "the major parties have lost their way." He was already playing the role of the populist. "I don't hear anyone speaking for the working men and women in the center."[16] Mark

Shields, the Washington-based syndicated columnist, wrote: "the only thing standing between Donald Trump and the presidency is the good judgment of the American people." And for a while, that prevailed.

In the summer of 2001, Alex Jones had been telling his listeners, "Please! Call Congress. Tell 'em we know the government is planning terrorism." To his followers, Jones was a modern-day Nostradamus. On the afternoon of September 11, 2001, Jones declared to more than 100 stations during five hours of ranting, "Well, I've been warning you about it for at least five years, all terrorism that we've looked at from the World Trade Center in Oklahoma City to Waco, has been government actions. They need this as a pretext to bring you and your family martial law. They're either using provocateur Arabs and allowing them to do it or this is full complicity with the federal government; the evidence is overwhelming." Days later he would tell his listeners: "98% chance this was a government orchestrated control bombing."[17] American conspiracism was about to kick into a higher and much more dangerous gear, on the country's fantastic voyage into Welchland.

Welch-like logic popped up everywhere. The George W. Bush administration suggested—and perhaps even believed—that links existed between the September 11 hijackers, al Qaeda, and Iraq's Saddam Hussein. In his State of the Union address of 2002, President Bush called Iraq, along with Iran and North Korea, an "axis of evil." Although no strong evidence connected Iraq to the attacks of 9/11, much less any investigation into Bush's Welch-like assertion that Saddam Hussein unquestionably possessed weapons of mass destruction, his team sought regime change in Iraq, and the march to war began. The myths that drove it and that it created swept up even those, like Secretary of State Colin Powell, who did not initially endorse them. By 2003, some 70 percent of Americans believed in the administration's conspiracy theory.[18] On March 19, 2003, on the basis of a myth, America, the British, and other nations invaded Iraq. When US search teams were unable to find the weapons of mass destruction that President Bush promised existed, administration insiders charged the White House and the Pentagon with deliberately misusing intelligence and misleading the American people. Americans' faith in the president fell precipitously, and alternative 9/11 conspiracy theories became widespread.

And in the meantime, thousands of American soldiers and hundreds of thousands of Iraqis, including children and women, died.

By 2006, at least one-third of Americans thought their government had either planned the attacks of 9/11 or allowed them to happen.[19] The grassroots alternative theorists called themselves "truthers." The internet was their medium. And conspiracy theories began to thrive on the new social media sites.

Americans were increasingly getting their news from the internet and the social media it enabled. In 2004, Facebook arrived. In 2005, YouTube. In 2006, Twitter. By 2014, Twitter had 284 million users. Two of every three Americans were using cell phones. Conspiracy theories exploded in popularity. But why?

People are social animals. They love to shoot the breeze. The new sources of news were unedited. Facts went unchecked. But the people kept passing on to others what "a lot of people are saying." Soon, alternative political communities arrived. The Right had 4Chan and 8Chan. The Left had Tumblr. But everybody in this land of confusion found hatred everywhere they went on the internet. They found apocalyptics. They found hysteria. Meanwhile, nefarious trolls and hackers from Russia were stirring the pot. They established fake accounts to delegitimize the fact-checked news, incite violence, foster racial divide, and make sure Americans were at each other's throats twenty-four hours a day.[20]

The chatter about what really happened on September 11, 2001, continued. Some truthers said Osama bin Laden was a pawn used by Dick Cheney and George W. Bush to repress the American people, expand America's empire, and tap into an Afghanistan oil pipeline. Some said that a missile, rather than a plane, struck the Pentagon. Some said secret agents piloted the plane using remote control. *Loose Change,* a documentary, became an internet and international sensation and garnered 10 million viewers in its first eighteen months. *Loose Change* drew on ludicrous theories to present a gargantuan conspiracy. The film suggested the plotters used "candy"—explosives—to topple the towers. Like Kennedy assassination conspiracy theorists, many truthers became engrossed with the physical evidence, into which they read ludicrous meanings. They wondered why the Twin Towers fell so fast and right into their own "footprints," just as in a detonation. They wondered how the towers could fall when steel melts at 2800 degrees

Fahrenheit, and jet fuel burns at only 1500 degrees. Then there was the mystery of World Trade Center 7. Fire from the Twin Towers damaged WTC 7, which contained various government agencies including the CIA, but the New York Fire Department did not put out the fire and the building collapsed. Why? Did the plotters rig explosives, inside WTC 7, too, to destroy the evidence of the crime?

Truthers found evidence for the controlled demolition theory in documents that ironically had been declassified and released in 1997 when Congress created the JFK Assassination Review Board. In 1962, the Joint Chiefs of Staff proposed to Defense Secretary Robert McNamara "Operation Northwoods," an insane plan to conduct terrorist attacks on the American people and put the blame on Fidel Castro. The plan, which was scuttled by a horrified President Kennedy, involved using candy to attack US cities, shoot down an airliner filled with US passengers, and use other incendiaries to blow up a navy vessel. Operation Northwoods taught truthers that state-sponsored terrorism was not just conceivable but also likely, and it showcased the madness of Cold War military planning. Anything was possible when America was living in the world of the candyman—the world Robert Welch made.[21]

As the new social media forums grew, and as corporations and governments watched every keystroke, virtually all politics became conspiratorial. On 9/11 Jones had started the truther movement, but he soon became a "Birther," believing that Barack Obama was born in Kenya. Becoming president in January 2009, Obama knew that few Americans supported the two wars the country was bogged down in from the calamitous political, economic, and military mistakes of his predecessor. The housing market had just crashed, along with the economy and the stock market. About 33 percent of Black males in their twenties were in prison or on probation.[22] White supremacy and nationalism were on the rise globally. Populists were calling for immigration restrictions and high tariffs. On the Right and the Left, new movements were being born. On the Right, the Tea Party was born in 2009, the alt right in 2010. On the Left, Occupy was established in 2011, Black Lives Matter in 2013, and then, more loosely, Antifa. The discourse was apocalyptic. Nobody trusted anything or anyone or any authority anymore. And nobody really had any reason to, either.

The world online made little sense, but everybody looked for answers there. Like one of Welch's puzzles, detective stories, or political problems—such as why America lost China, why Eisenhower did not roll back the New Deal—everybody had to use their imagination to look for patterns and make all the pieces fit. And every piece had to fit in Welchland.

One day before Obama's inauguration in 2009, Fox News started a new political program with Glenn Beck, who compared Obama to Mussolini. Beck gave lectures about American history and told viewers Obama was a betrayal of what the Constitution stood for. Soon, the Tea Party also opposed the president's economic and healthcare programs, and members began dressing up like George Washington and Benjamin Franklin waving their Constitutions and flags. History of a certain sort was very much on the minds of the Tea Party. They thought they would make America great again by protecting the Second Amendment, bringing back prayer in schools, and opposing immigration. They argued that a conspiracy of federal government bureaucrats and Wall Street and globalists were the cause of the economic downturn. The Tea Party resembled a twenty-first century John Birch Society summer camp for adults.[23]

...

If Alex Jones was the first truther, Donald Trump was its most well known. The United States fought a Civil War over slavery, and to suggest that the first African American president of United States was not a citizen not only delegitimated everything that Obama had accomplished but it awakened a long-standing witch's brew of racial hatreds. The questions the truthers raised were ludicrous, and dangerous, and new details seemed to arrive all the time. Internet blogs contained postings that Obama was born in Nairobi. He spent time in a Jakarta madrasah. He was a furtive closet Muslim.[24] He wanted to make America all Black. In 2012, Donald Trump tweeted that "an extremely credible source has called my office and told me @BarackObama's birth certificate is a fraud."

By 2015, Trump was running for president. On December 2, Jones congratulated Trump for declaring at a campaign rally that "thousands and thousands" of Muslims had been cheering from New Jersey rooftops on September 11, 2001. Trump said he saw it on television in his penthouse. But it never happened.[25] There was never any television recording that showed that. But that did not matter. The presidential candidate had said it. And it seemed everybody was talking about it. "What you're doing is epic," Jones declared to Trump. "It's George Washington level." Trump quickly replied, "Alex, your reputation's amazing."[26]

His audience was certainly amazing. By 2011, Jones had a bigger audience than the combined audience of both Glenn Beck and Rush Limbaugh. And Trump knew what he was doing. He was speaking directly to that audience and touting a conspiracy theory.[27]

He was touting another conspiracy theory on January 6, 2021, and as president he demonstrated the power and the danger of myth. At 12:15 p.m., President Trump, refusing to embrace the reality that he lost the presidential election of 2020 to Joe Biden, encouraged a crowd of followers to head to the Capitol. "You'll never take back our country with weakness," he told them. At 12:16, one Parler user wrote: "We are going to have a civil war. Get ready." Another: "Time to fight. Civil war is upon us." By the end of that day, Trump turned an angry protest into an insurrection that killed five people.[28]

Speaking at Yale University's commencement in 1962, John F. Kennedy could have been speaking directly about Robert Welch and the John Birch Society, but his words certainly speak to our current predicament. He warned the new graduates that "the great enemy of truth is very often not the lie—deliberate, contrived and dishonest—but the myth—persistent, persuasive, and unrealistic." "Mythology distracts us everywhere—in government as in business, in politics as in economics, in foreign affairs as in domestic affairs," he added. "In recent months many have come to feel, as I do, that the dialog between the parties—between business and government, between the government and the public—is clogged by illusion and platitude and fails to reflect the true realities of contemporary American society." Kennedy knew what was going on in his day, probably better than any contemporary, and proved more prescient than we have given him credit for. Kennedy enlisted the graduates "against the spread of illusion and on the side of reality."

Robert Welch did not create alone, but he fueled this "spread of illusion" and worldview of suspicion by creating false myths that tempted the weak minded. The candyman concocted the most dangerous recipe, but we don't have to follow it.

The conspiratorial style threatens democracy because it poisons the mind and makes it difficult to see reality. It allows people to be led in dark directions, even when their actions are contrary to the better angels of their characters. The dark arts of conspiracy theory lead good people down dark paths, and make every hour of the day night. The twentieth century teaches us that the innocent and the naive can be misled by myth and commit atrocities without compunction, even despite deep reservations. Conspiracy theories are another means of authoritarian conditioning because they make the individual feel impotent and unable to change anything. They hold us back from doing our own thinking and seeking a better world for ourselves and our posterity.

As we all live our lives and decide the future for ourselves and our children, we need to enlist "against the spread of illusion," and let us never hold that the future is ordained but instead depends on the individual actions of every person, working in time. Nothing is a foregone conclusion. Our individual actions right here and right now always determine whether our future is a bright one or a dark one.

Acknowledgments

Finally, I have the opportunity to thank the individuals who made this book possible.

First and foremost, at the University of Chicago Press, I want to thank my editor Timothy Mennel for everything. He believed in my first book, and he believed in this one. In editing the manuscript, Tim was demanding, encouraging, kind, and insightful. He helped me keep my sense of humor, while writing about a fascinating but extremely challenging individual.

I also want to thank Susannah Engstrom at the University of Chicago Press. Susannah provided crucial assistance at a very important time when this book was coming into the world.

Personally, being associated with the University of Chicago Press continues to be one of my biggest professional honors. And I never take it for granted.

A supportive community of scholars and friends deserve my deepest gratitude for either laying the foundation for this work, listening to my ideas, providing keen insight, or reading and commenting on portions of the manuscript at various stages. They include, but certainly are not limited to, Patrick Allitt, Ben Alpers, John A. Andrew, Anne Applebaum, Cari S. Babitzke, Michael Barkun, Kathleen Belew, Niels Bjerre-Poulsen, David Blight, Carl Bogus, Michael Bowen, H. W. Brands, Mary Brennan, Jennifer Burns Pete Cajka, Bruce Caldwell, Robert Caro, George Cotkin, Heather Cox Richardson, Joseph Crespino, Donald Critchlow, William Cronon, Sean Cunningham,

Matthew Dallek, Ian Delahanty, Darren Dochuk, Alan Ebenstein, Thomas B. Edsall, Robert Fairbanks, David Farber, Mark Fenster, Michael Flamm, John Ganz, Mark Gelfand, Jonathan Gienapp, Laura Jane Gifford, Steve Gillon, Todd Gitlin, Larry Glickman, Robert Alan Goldberg, Linda Gordon, Andrew Hartman, Paul Harvey, Heather Hendershot, Paul Herron, Jerome L. Himmelstein, Hidetaka Hirota, William Hitchcock, John S. Huntington, Seth Jacobs, Ben Johnson, John Judis, Geoff Kabaservice, Alexander Keyssar, Rebecca Klatch, Kevin Kruse, David Paul Kuhn, Tim Lacy, Matthew D. Lassiter, Alan Lessoff, William Leuchtenburg, George Lewis, Allan J. Lichtenstein, Nelson Lichtenstein, James Livingston, Joseph E. Lowndes, David Lublin, Cynthia Lynn Lyerly, Pat Maney, George Marsden, Charles Marsh, William C. Martin, Kevin Mattson, Seth Meehan, Natalia Mehlman Petrzela, Gráinne McEvoy, Lisa McGirr, Neil McMillen, Keri Leigh Merritt, Michael W. Miles, Stephen P. Miller, John E. Moser, D. J. Mulloy, Paul V. Murphey, George H. Nash, David Neiwert, Mark Newman, Michelle M. Nickerson, Kathryn S. Olmstead, David Oshinsky, James O'Toole, Herbert Parmet, Thomas G. Paterson, James T. Patterson, Devin Pendas, Rick Perlstein, Michael Phillips, Kim Phillips-Fein, David Quigley, David W. Reinhard, Colin E. Reynolds, Sam Rosenfeld, Sarah Ross, Doug Rossinow, Katherine Rye Jewell, Catherine E. Rymph, Daniel Schlozman, Jonathan Schoenwald, Bruce Schulman, Robert Self, Jeff Sharlet, Timothy Snyder, John Spiers, Marjorie Spruill, Thomas Sugrue, Balazs Szelenyi, Joshua Tait, Calvin TerBeek, Timothy N. Thurber, Clayton Trutor, John G. Turner, David Walsh, Benjamin C. Waterhouse, Clive Webb, Sean Wilentz, Daniel K. Williams, Jeff Woods, Lawrence Wright, Robert Wuthnow, and Julian Zelizer.

My supportive deans and colleagues at Northeastern University's College of Professional Studies deserve special thanks for supporting all my scholarly endeavors. Whether serving together on the Faculty Academic Council or marching together in support of more nationwide gun legislation, Dean Mary Loeffelholz has been a treasured colleague at Northeastern University, my home away from home. Although she may not know it until now, her upcoming biography on Emily Dickinson inspired me to keep plugging along with this biography. Dean Mary Ludden, Dean Michael Gladstone, Dean David Fields,

Dean Molly Smith, and Dean Joe Griffin have provided continuous support.

I am lucky to have as my boss Dean Patrick Plunkett, a man I admire more than words can say. He inspires excellence in his teachers, values integrity above all else, and embodies the Northeastern motto "Lux, Veritas, Virtus," Latin for "Light, Truth, Courage."

My faculty director, Balazs Szelenyi, has been a mentor, boss, and also one of my dearest and closest of friends. He provided unique insight into the predilection of conspiracy theory in his native Hungary.

My colleagues, in no particular order, Ilka Kostka, Catherine Showalter, Veronika Maliborska, Natasha Watson, Crissy McMartin-Miller, Lin Zhou, and Heidi Banerjee are stellar teachers, tutors, and friends, and I have learned much from their examples. My supportive colleagues Brent Griffin and Lucy Bunning have taught me much about class and race, respectively, in the United States, and I look forward to learning more from them.

It truly makes me one of the luckiest men in the world to get to call the following people colleagues: Beth Smith, Jackie Bertman, Solange Resnik, Ethan Whittet, Jessica Dilliner, Vincent Capone, Karla Odenwald, Whitney Wotkins, Mildred Portillo, and Jeff Yu at Northeastern's NUImmerse and Global Pathways. All generously provided encouragement as well as essential advice on teaching history to international students. I also want to thank the other faculty, deans, and staff at Northeastern's College of Professional Studies. They include, but are not limited to, Jacqueline Nguyen, Jack McDevitt, Christos Zahopoulos, Harvey Shapiro, Chris Unger, Karen Reiss Medwed, Elizabeth Zulick, Kimberly Nolan, Patty Goodman, Stephen Amato, Carl Zangrel, Pamela Wojnar, Darin Detwiler, Marchev Krassimir, Lynda Hodgson, Cynthia Baron, Joe McNabb, Corliss Thompson, Alpert Shannon, Christopher Bolick, Sean O'Connell, Sara Ewell, Nancy Pawlyshyn, Martha Loftus, Lydia Young, Francesca Grippa, Earlene Avalon, Bill Ewell, Silvani Vejar, Kristen Lee, Jay Laird, Kelly Conn, Rashid Mosley, Melissa Parenti, Sandy Nickel, Joan Giblin, Uwe Hohgrawe, Amanda Welsh, Elizabeth Mahler, Connie Emerson, Kim Larson, Fiona Creed, Sean Gallagher, Mounira Morris, John Terpinas, Dave Hagen, Wendy Crocker, Mikhail Oet, Teresa Goode, Esther Tutella-Chen, Diane

Perez, Alice Mello, Quannah Parker-McGowan, Cherese Childers-McKee, Michael Dean, Lindsay Portnoy, Amy Lantinga, John Wolfe, Xiaomu Zhou, Monica Borgida, Susan Gracia, Thomas Goulding, Ed Powers, Golnoosh Hakimdavar, Robert Prior, Lori Ashline, Les Stein, Sarmann Kennedyd, Fareed Hawwa, Adel Zadeh, Alex Fronduto, Varsha Kulkarni, and Youngbok Ryu.

Outside my own college at Northeastern University, I want to thank the following faculty or staff: Victoria Cain, Paula Caligiuri, Dan Cohen, Peter Fraunholtz, Gretchen Heefner, Katherine Luongo, Heather Streets-Salter, Philip Thai, Chris Bosso, Natalie Bormann, Stephen Flynn, Costas Panagopoulos, Laura Green, Thomas Vicino, Daniel Urman, Michael Dukakis, Ted Landsmark, Francis Blessington, Barry Bluestone, Neal Lerner, and Molly Dupere.

I want to thank my undergraduate professors, Richard J. Grace, Margaret M. Manchester, and James McGovern, as well as my Weymouth High School teachers, Jack Decoste, George Ghiorse, and Gail Shields, all of whom encouraged my love of history and writing.

I have been lucky to have accumulated a great gang of friends (far too numerous to name) during my forty-five years. You keep my spirits up and I need you in my life. You are my sustenance, and I need you Dave Chepiga, Howie Bean, Kevin Botelho, Bob Bright, Jim Carnell, John Norris, Matt Norris, Paul Quinn, John Carnell, Dan McDonough, Tom Gannon, Balazs Szelenyi, John Houston, Jason Combs, Stefan Koenig, Michael O'Connor, Kurt Marcella, Michael Houston, Phirum Peang, Clayton Trutor, just for instance. You keep me writing, smiling, and laughing.

I thank my wonderful students in PLSC 1420, my Introduction to American Government course from the fall semester of 2020. They challenged me to clarify my thinking, and I learned much from their eager young minds. They include Yann Chebli, Eugenia Garza, Yu-Chen Huang, Tamara Kaminski, Antonio Kuri Gonzalez, Hongqian Lang, Haoxing Li, Yun-Jung Lu, Francesco Marzorati, Leonidas Paraschos, Haolun Qi, and Aaro Vasama. They all have bright futures.

My family deserves the most praise. The Carnell and Miller families have supported my love of history throughout my lifetime. Aunt Jeanne, a nurse at Carney Hospital for forty-eight years, offered not only incessant support for her coronavirus patients but also support for her favorite nephew. (That's a joke, John, Caroline, and Jim.) My wonderful in-laws provided not only weekly child care (at least until the pandemic made it impossible) but interest, conversation, good cheer, and great chow. The Quinn and Houston families supplied unflagging support, constructive critiques, and delicious meals at many family gatherings. Nana and Papa, whose love is infinite, deserve more praise than mere words can supply. My parents are my heroes. My wife has endured the greatest burden of living with this other man, as I have, for about six years now. I shall enjoy spending the rest of my life repaying the debt now that Mr. Robert Welch has left our household, at least as far as this project goes. He has not left my life, nor yours, and that was the whole point of the book.

Finally, I must thank my golden retriever, Sunny, already a one-year-old legend in our family. She has destroyed more articles of clothing and electronics than I care to remember since picking her up in her native New Hampshire, but I truly appreciate that she somehow avoided this laptop. But despite her aggressive chewing habit, as somebody all too familiar with the John Birch Society, a one Richard Nixon, once said: "You know, the kids, like all kids, love the dog and I just want to say this right now, that regardless of what they say about it, we're gonna keep it."

Notes

INTRODUCTION

1. Jill Lepore, *These Truths* (New York: W. W. Norton, 2018), 716.
2. Lepore, *These Truths*, 716–18.
3. Kathryn S. Olmstead, *Real Enemies: Conspiracy Theories and American Democracy, World War I to 9/11* (Oxford: Oxford University Press, 2009), 173.
4. Richard Gid Powers, *Not without Honor: The History of American Anti-Communism* (New Haven, CT: Yale University Press, 1995), 235–45, 286–93.
5. D. J. Mulloy, *The World of the John Birch Society: Conspiracy, Conservatism, and the Cold War* (Nashville: Vanderbilt University Press, 2014), 85–88, 135–36; *American Opinion*, July 1977.
6. Richard Hofstadter, *The Paranoid Style in American Politics and Other Essays* (New York: Vintage Books, 2008); Lisa McGirr, *Suburban Warriors: The Origins of the New American Right* (Princeton, NJ: Princeton University Press, 2001).

CHAPTER ONE

1. Thomas Parramore, *Cradle of the Colony: The History of Chowan County and Edenton, North Carolina* (Edenton, NC: Edenton Chamber of Commerce, 1967), 1–49; W. Scott Boyce, *Economic and Social History of Chowan County, North Carolina, 1880–1915* (London: Forgotten Books, 2015), 1–100; Troy Kickler, *The King's Trouble Makers: Edenton's Role in Creating a Nation and a State* (Edenton, NC: Edenton Historical Commission, 2013); Louis Van Camp, *Edenton and Chowan County, North Carolina* (Charleston, SC: Arcadia, 2001), 7–122.
2. *Biblical Recorder* (Raleigh, NC), December 2, 1874.
3. G. Edward Griffin, *The Life and Words of Robert Welch* (Thousand Oaks, CA: American Media, 1975), 27–46; Parramore, *Cradle of the Colony*, 1–49; Boyce, *Economic and Social History*, 1–100.
4. *Weekly Standard* (Raleigh, NC), January 25, 1837; J. T. Bynum, *History of Ballard's Bridge Baptist Church* (Raleigh, NC: Presses of Edwards and Broughton, 1908),

1–38; *Biblical Recorder* (Raleigh, NC), January 6, March 23, 1836; Thomas S. Kidd and Barry Hankins, *Baptists in America: A History* (New York: Oxford University Press, 2015), 1–97; Parramore, *Cradle of the Colony*, 1–49; Griffin, *Life and Words of Robert Welch*, 27–46; William R. Glass, *Strangers in Zion: Fundamentalists in the South, 1900–1950* (Macon, GA: Mercer University Press, 2001); George M. Marsden, *Fundamentalism and American Culture* (New York: Oxford University Press, 2006).

5. *Weekly Standard* (Raleigh, NC), January 25, 1837; *Biblical Recorder*, July 15 and 22, 1858; Bertram Wyatt-Brown, *Southern Honor: Ethics & Behavior in the Old South* (New York: Oxford University Press, 2007), 23, 37–43, 94, 101, 143, 160–61, 273–80; Bertram Wyatt-Brown, *Honor and Violence in the Old South* (New York: Oxford University Press, 2007), 23, 46, 113, 121–22; Bertram Wyatt-Brown, *The Shaping of Southern Culture: Honor, Grace, and War, 1760s–1880s* (Chapel Hill: University of North Carolina Press, 2001), 106–35; James C. Cobb, *Away Down South: A History of Southern Identity* (New York: Oxford University Press, 2005).

6. Kidd and Hankins, *Baptists in America*, 1–97; Milton Ready, *The Tar Heel State: A History of North Carolina* (Columbia: University of South Carolina Press, 2005), 50–51, 77, 81–89, 94–98, 108; Boyce, *Economic and Social History*, 1–100; Parramore, *Cradle of the Colony*, 43–72; Wyatt-Brown, *Southern Honor*, 180–84.

7. *Biblical Recorder*, July 22, 1835; *Weekly Standard* (Raleigh, NC), January 25, 1837; *Biblical Recorder*, July 15, 1858; Alan Gallay, *Voices of the Old South, Eyewitness Accounts, 1528–1861* (Athens: University of Georgia Press, 1994), 267–68; Parramore, *Cradle of the Colony*, 1–49; Boyce, *Economic and Social History*, 1–100.

8. Ready, *Tar Heel State*, 142–92; W. J. Cash, *The Mind of the South* (New York: Vintage Books, 1991), 1–188; Parramore, *Cradle of the Colony*, 50–92; Van Camp, *Edenton and Chowan County*, 7–122.

9. William L. Byrd III, *North Carolina Slaves and Free Persons of Color*, vol. 1 (Bowie, MD: Heritage Books, 2002).

10. Daniel Walker Howe, *What Hath God Wrought: The Transformation of America, 1815–1848* (New York: Oxford University Press, 2007), 532–34.

11. Jean Fagin Yellin, *Harriet Jacobs: A Life* (New York: Basic Civitas Books, 2003), 6.

12. Byrd, *North Carolina Slaves*, 1:151–86; Parramore, *Cradle of the Colony*, 43–72; Ready, *Tar Heel State*, 174–78; Wyatt-Brown, *Southern Honor*, 402–61; Wyatt-Brown, *Shaping of Southern Culture*, 137–74; Eugene D. Genovese, *The Southern Tradition: The Achievements and Limitations of an American Conservatism* (Cambridge, MA: Harvard University Press, 1994).

13. Ready, *Tar Heel State*, 210–47.

14. Parramore, *Cradle of the Colony*, 72–76; Ready, *Tar Heel State*, 174–78; *Biblical Recorder* (Raleigh, NC), December 2, 1874; *Daily Tar Heel* (Chapel Hill, NC), September 19, 1896, and August 5, 1903; *Fisherman and Farmer* (Edenton, NC), August 17, 1894, August 9, 1895, September 27, 1895, December 6, 1895, February 28, 1896, May 1, 1896, May 8, 1896, November 6, 1896, September 18, 1896, July 9, 1897, May 27, 1898, July 22, 1898, and October 7, 1898; *Weekly Economist* (Elizabeth City,

NC), October 7, 1898, July 13, 1900, and July 20, 1900; *Morning Post* (Raleigh, NC), November 27, 1898, and December 4, 1898; *Western North Carolina Times*, January 11, 1901; *North Carolinian* (Elizabeth City, NC), June 1, 1898, and August 2, 1900; *Courier* (Edenton, NC), March 29, 1900; *News and Observer* (Raleigh, NC), June 17, 1900, and March 24, 1901; *Heel* (Elizabeth City, NC), September 11, 1903; *Tar Heel* (Raleigh City, NC), December 4, 1903; *Progressive Farmer* (Raleigh, NC), April 1, 1911; *Albemarle Observer* (Edenton, NC), April 9, 1915, and May 28, 1915; *Independent* (Elizabeth City, NC), June 13, 1919, and November 11, 1921; *Daily Advance* (Elizabeth City, NC), May 10, 1923; *Daily Tar Heel* (Chapel Hill, NC), November 15, 1928; Van Camp, *Edenton and Chowan County*, 7–122.

15. Boyce, *Economic and Social History*, 41–100; Parramore, *Cradle of the Colony*, 77–82; William S. Powell, *North Carolina: A History* (New York: W. W. Norton, 1977), 144–63.
16. Donald T. Critchlow, John Korasick, and Matthew C. Sherman, eds., *Political Conspiracies in America: A Reader* (Bloomington: Indiana University Press, 2008), 49.
17. Ready, *Tar Heel State*, 284–300.
18. Ready, *Tar Heel State*, 284–300.
19. Ready, *Tar Heel State*, 284–300.
20. *Fisherman and Farmer* (Edenton, NC), August 9, 1895; September 27, 1895; February 28, 1896; May 1, 8, 1896; September 18, 1896; May 27, 1898; and October 7, 1898; Wyatt-Brown, *Shaping of Southern Culture*, 1–153; Van Camp, *Edenton and Chowan County*, 7–122.
21. *Weekly Economist* (Elizabeth City, NC), October 7, 1898; *North Carolinian* (Elizabeth City, NC), June 1, 1898; *Fisherman and Farmer* (Edenton, NC), July 22, 1898.
22. Ready, *Tar Heel State*, 284–312.
23. Ready, *Tar Heel State*, 284–312.
24. *Fisherman and Farmer* (Edenton, NC), November 6, 1896; Ready, *Tar Heel State*, 284–310.
25. *North Carolinian* (Raleigh, NC), August 2, 1900; *Albemarle Observer* (Edenton, NC), December 14, 1918; *News and Observer* (Raleigh, NC), June 17, 1900; Van Camp, *Edenton and Chowan County*, 7–122.
26. *News and Observer* (Raleigh, NC), June 17, 1900, and March 24, 1901.

CHAPTER TWO

1. Dru Gatewood Haley and Raymond A. Winslow Jr., *The Historic Architecture of Perquimans County, North Carolina* (Elizabeth City, NC: Precision, 1982), 22, 39, 48, 49, 178, 181, 184, 196; *Independent* (Elizabeth City, NC), November 11, 1921.
2. Haley and Winslow, *Historic Architecture of Perquimans County*, 22, 39, 48, 49, 178, 181, 184, 196; *Independent* (Elizabeth City, NC), November 11, 1921.
3. Haley and Winslow, *Historic Architecture of Perquimans County*, 22, 39, 48, 49, 178, 181, 184, 196; *Tar Heel* (Elizabeth City, NC), September 11, 1903; *Independent* (Elizabeth City, NC), November 11, 1921.

4. *Independent* (Elizabeth City, NC), November 11, 1921; *Progressive Farmer* (Raleigh, NC), April 1, 1911; Haley and Winslow, *Historic Architecture of Perquimans County*, 22, 39, 48, 49, 178, 181, 184, 196.
5. Haley and Winslow, *Historic Architecture of Perquimans County*, 22, 39, 48, 49, 178, 181, 184, 196; *Independent* (Elizabeth City, NC), November 11, 1921; *Progressive Farmer* (Raleigh, NC), April 1, 1911.
6. G. Edward Griffin, *The Life and Words of Robert Welch* (Thousand Oaks, CA: American Media, 1975), 25–30.
7. Bertram Wyatt-Brown, *Southern Honor: Ethics & Behavior in the Old South* (New York: Oxford University Press, 2007), 120.
8. Haley and Winslow, *Historic Architecture of Perquimans County*, 22, 39, 48, 49, 178, 181, 184, 196; *Independent* (Elizabeth City, NC), November 11, 1921; *Progressive Farmer* (Raleigh, NC), April 1, 1911; Griffin, *Life and Words of Robert Welch*, 2–150.
9. Haley and Winslow, *Historic Architecture of Perquimans County*, 22, 39, 48, 49, 178, 181, 184, 196; *Independent* (Elizabeth City, NC), November 11, 1921; *Progressive Farmer* (Raleigh, NC), April 1, 1911.
10. Griffin, *Life and Words of Robert Welch*, 2–150.

CHAPTER THREE

1. Bertram Wyatt-Brown, *The Shaping of Southern Culture: Honor, Grace, and War, 1760s–1880s* (Chapel Hill: University of North Carolina Press, 2001), 1–153; *Independent* (Elizabeth City, NC), November 11, 1921; *Progressive Farmer* (Raleigh, NC), April 1, 1911;
2. Bland Simpson, *The Mystery of Beautiful Nell Cropsey* (Chapel Hill: University of North Carolina Press, 1993), 1–170; Alex Cristopher Meekins, *Elizabeth City, North Carolina and the Civil War* (Charleston, SC: History Press, 2007), 13–134; Bland Simpson, *Little Rivers and Waterway Tales* (Chapel Hill: University of North Carolina Press), 1–189.
3. Simpson, *Mystery of Beautiful Nell Cropsey*, 1–170; Simpson, *Little Rivers and Waterway Tales*, 1–189; G. Edward Griffin, *The Life and Words of Robert Welch* (Thousand Oaks, CA: American Media, 1975), 2–150.
4. John C. Scott, *Elizabeth City: Images of America* (Charleston, SC: Arcadia, 2001), 9–128; Simpson, *Mystery of Beautiful Nell Cropsey*, 1–170.
5. Bland Simpson, *Into the Sound Country: A Carolina's Coastal Plain* (Chapel Hill: University of North Carolina Press, 1997), 1–247; Simpson, *Mystery of Beautiful Nell Cropsey*, 1–170; William E. Dunstan, *Walking with Giants: Adventures of a Southern Boyhood*, vol. 1 (Charleston, SC: Createspace, 2013), 1–33.
6. *Daily Tar Heel* (Chapel Hill, NC), November 15, 1928; Griffin, *Life and Words of Robert Welch*, 2–150.
7. Griffin, *Life and Words of Robert Welch*, 2–160.
8. Griffin, *Life and Words of Robert Welch*, 2–150.

9. Wyatt-Brown, *Shaping of Southern Culture,* 1–153; Dru Gatewood Haley and Raymond A. Winslow Jr., *History of Perquimans County, North Carolina* (Baltimore: Genealogical Publishing, 1990).
10. Elting E. Morison, *Admiral Sims and the Modern American Navy* (Cambridge, MA: Riverside Press, 1942), 520–25.
11. E. B. Potter, *Nimitz* (Annapolis, MD: Naval Institute Press, 2008), 50; Thomas J. Cutler, ed., *The U.S. Naval Institute on the U.S. Naval Academy: The History* (Annapolis, MD: Naval Institute Press, 2015), 96–117.
12. Griffin, *Life and Words of Robert Welch,* 2–150.
13. Griffin, *Life and Words of Robert Welch,* 2–150.
14. Griffin, *Life and Words of Robert Welch,* 2–200.
15. *Independent,* (Elizabeth City, NC), April 18, 1919; *News and Observer* (Raleigh, NC), August 20, 1919.
16. *News and Observer* (Raleigh NC), August 20, 1919, and July 29, 1919.
17. Donald T. Critchlow, John Korasick, and Matthew C. Sherman, eds. *Political Conspiracies in America: A Reader* (Bloomington: Indiana University Press, 2008), 69.
18. Griffin, *Life and Words of Robert Welch,* 2–200.

CHAPTER FOUR

1. James T. Patterson, *Mr. Republican: A Biography of Robert Taft* (Boston: Houghton Mifflin, 1972), 45, 48; G. Edward Griffin, *The Life and Words of Robert Welch* (Thousand Oaks, CA: American Media, 1975), 2–200.
2. Samuel Elliot Atkins, *A History of Cambridge, Massachusetts, 1630–1913* (Cambridge, MA: Cambridge Tribune, 1913), 288–305.
3. Patterson, *Mr. Republican,* 45; Arthur E. Sutherland, *The Law at Harvard: A History of Men and Ideas* (Cambridge, MA: Belknap Press of Harvard University Press, 1967), 226–99.
4. Patterson, *Mr. Republican,* 45, 48; Paul D. Carrington, *Stewards of Democracy: Law as a Public Profession* (Oxford: Westview Press, 1999), 128–55; H. N. Hirsch, *The Enigma of Felix Frankfurter* (New York: Basic Books, 1981).
5. Stanley Coben, *A. Mitchell Palmer: Politician* (New York: Columbia University Press, 1963).
6. Griffin, *Life and Words of Robert Welch,* 2–200.
7. Griffin, *Life and Words of Robert Welch,* 2–69.
8. Reay Tannahill, *Food in History* (New York: Three Rivers Press, 1988), 220, 241–42, 274, 276, 294; Tom Standage, *An Edible History of Humanity* (New York: Bloomsbury, 2009).
9. As Jeet Heer explains, Harold Gray was an important cultural conduit for right-wing ideology. This may have also attracted Welch to Gray. "The Complex Origins of Little Orphan Annie," Literary Hub, August 3, 2020, https://lithub.com/jeet-heer-on-the-complex-origins-of-little-orphan-annie.
10. Griffin, *Life and Words of Robert Welch,* 2–200.

11. Griffin, *Life and Words of Robert Welch*, 2–200.
12. Michael D'Antonio, *Hershey* (New York: Simon and Schuster, 2006), 1–147; Deborah Cadbury, *Chocolate Wars* (Philadelphia: Public Affairs, 2010), 142–48; Joel Glenn Brenner, *The Emperors of Chocolate* (New York: Broadway Books, 2000), 2–225; Tim Richardson, *Sweets: A History of Candy* (New York: MJF Books, 2002).
13. Philip P. Gott and L. F. Van Houten, *All about Candy and Chocolate* (Chicago: National Confectioners Association of the United States, 1958), 40, 42.
14. D'Antonio, *Hershey*, 148–241; Samira Kawash, *Candy: A Century of Panic and Pleasure* (New York: Faber and Faber, 2013), 6, 14, 93, 94, 144, 155–56, 193, 272, 332.
15. Wendy A. Woloson, *Refined Tastes: Sugar, Confectionery, and Consumers in Nineteenth-Century America* (Baltimore: Johns Hopkins University Press, 2002), 109–54; Jan Pottker, *Crisis in Candyland* (Bethesda, MD: Writer's Cramp, 1995), 21–238.
16. D'Antonio, *Hershey*, 148–241; Sophie D. Coe and Michael D. Coe, *The True History of Chocolate* (London: Thames and Hudson, 1996).
17. Benjamin C. Waterhouse, *The Land of Enterprise: A Business History of the United States* (New York: Simon and Schuster Paperbacks), 124–27.
18. Walter A. Friedman, *Birth of a Salesman: The Transformation of Selling in America* (Cambridge, MA: Harvard University Press), 190–254; Griffin, *Life and Words of Robert Welch*, 2–200.
19. David Greenberg, *Calvin Coolidge* (New York: Henry Holt, 2006), 70–139.
20. Louis Untermeyer, *A Century of Candymaking, 1847–1947* (Boston: Barta Press, 1947), 9–87.
21. Gott and Houten, *All about Candy and Chocolate*, 22–23.
22. Untermeyer, *Century of Candymaking*, 9–87; Cadbury, *Chocolate Wars*, 86–104; Griffin, *Life and Words of Robert Welch*, 2–200.
23. Griffin, *Life and Words of Robert Welch*, 2–200.

CHAPTER FIVE

1. Charles H. Trout, *Boston: The Great Depression and the New Deal* (New York: New York University Press, 1977), 3–49; William E. Leuchtenburg, *The Perils of Prosperity* (Chicago: University of Chicago Press, 1958), 241–64; Frederick Lewis Allen, *Only Yesterday: An Informal History of the 1920s* (New York: Harper Perennial Modern Classics), 251–94.
2. G. Edward Griffin, *The Life and Words of Robert Welch* (Thousand Oaks, CA: American Media, 1975), 2–200.
3. Griffin, *Life and Words of Robert Welch*, 2–200.
4. M. J. Heale, *American Anti-Communism: Combating the Enemy Within, 1830–1970* (Baltimore: Johns Hopkins University Press, 1990), 99, 120; Griffin, *Life and Words of Robert Welch*.
5. John T. Flynn, *The Roosevelt Myth* (New York: Devin-Adair, 1948), 12.

6. Michael W. Miles, *Odyssey of the American Right* (London: Oxford University Press, 1980), 30–38.
7. Griffin, *Life and Words of Robert Welch*, 2–200.

CHAPTER SIX

1. John T. Flynn, *The Roosevelt Myth* (New York: Devin-Adair, 1948), 51, 54, 387–92; Wayne S. Cole, *Roosevelt and the Isolationists, 1932–1945* (Lincoln: University of Nebraska Press, 1983), 95–112.
2. Lynne Olson, *Those Angry Days: Roosevelt, Lindbergh, and America's Fight over World War II, 1939–1941* (New York: Random House, 2013), xvii–62.
3. Jon Meacham, *The Soul of America: The Battle for Our Better Natures* (New York: Random House, 2018), 160.
4. Olson, *Those Angry Days*, 103; Alan Brinkley, *Voices of Protest: Huey Long, Father Coughlin and the Great Depression* (New York: Vintage, 1983); Leo P. Ribuffo, *Old Christian Right: The Protestant Far Right from the Great Depression to the Cold War* (Philadelphia: Temple University Press, 1983).
5. Meacham, *Soul of America*, 160.
6. Wayne S. Cole, *America First: The Battle against Intervention, 1940–1941* (Madison: University of Wisconsin Press, 1953), 188, 148.
7. Welch to Frank Graham, May 24, 1941, Welch private papers.
8. William D. Snider, *Light on the Hill: A History of the University of North Carolina at Chapel Hill* (Chapel Hill: University of North Carolina Press, 1992), 222–28; William S. Powell, *The First State University: A Pictorial History of the University of North Carolina* (Chapel Hill: University of North Carolina Press, 1992), 93–165.
9. Welch to Frank Graham, May 24, 1941, Welch private papers.
10. Robert Welch, advertisement of "One Dozen Candles" from *JBS Bulletin*, n.d., author's personal collection.
11. Rick Perlstein, "I Thought I Understood the American Right. Trump Proved Me Wrong," *New York Times Magazine*, April 11, 2017, https://www.nytimes.com/2017/04/11/magazine/i-thought-i-understood-the-american-right-trump-proved-me-wrong.html.
12. Meacham, *Soul of America*, 161.
13. "Ford's Anti-Semitism," *American Experience*, PBS, assessed March 26, 2021, https://www.pbs.org/wgbh/americanexperience/features/henryford-antisemitism/.
14. Donald T. Critchlow, *The Conservative Ascendancy: How the GOP Right Made Political History* (Cambridge, MA: Harvard University Press, 2007), 45.
15. Colin R. Reynolds, "The-So-Far Right: Radical Right-Wing Politics in the United States, 1941–1977" (PhD diss., Emory University, 2016), 19.
16. Reynolds, "The-So-Far Right," 22; Clarence Manion, "The Education of an American," address to the annual convention of the National Catholic Educational Association, Kansas City, Missouri, March 27, 1940, 4–5, 11, Clarence E. Manion Papers, Box 1, Folder 4, Chicago History Museum, Chicago, Illinois.

17. Manion, "Education of an American," 4–5, 11.
18. Reynolds, "The-So-Far Right," 20–22; Clarence Manion, "We Must Understand Freedom to Stay Free," *Chicago Herald American* (reprint), August 20, 1941, CEM, Box 1, Folder 5; Critchtlow, *Conservative Ascendancy*, 45, 46.
19. Critchtlow, *Conservative Ascendancy*, 46.
20. Welch to Frank Graham, May 24, 1941, Welch private papers.
21. Wayne S. Cole, *Charles Lindbergh and the Battle against American Intervention in World War II* (New York: Harcourt Brace Jovanovich, 1974), 134; Wayne S. Cole, *America First: The Battle against Intervention, 1940–1941* (Madison: University of Wisconsin Press, 1953); Manfred Jonas, *Isolation in America, 1935–1941* (Ithaca, NY: Cornell University Press, 1966); Selig Adler, *The Isolationist Impulse: Its Twentieth Century Reaction* (New York: Abelard-Schuman, 1957), 140; Welch to Frank Graham, May 24, 1941, Welch private papers.
22. Welch to Frank Graham, May 24, 1941, Welch private papers.
23. Adler, *Isolationist Impulse*, 298.
24. Griffin, *The Life and Words of Robert Welch.*

CHAPTER SEVEN

1. G. Edward Griffin, *The Life and Words of Robert Welch* (Thousand Oaks, CA: American Media, 1975), 50–200.
2. Griffin, *Life and Words of Robert Welch*, 133.
3. Griffin, *Life and Words of Robert Welch*, 134.
4. Griffin, *Life and Words of Robert Welch*, 44–200.
5. Joyce Mao, *Asia First: China and the Making of Modern American Conservatism* (Chicago: University of Chicago Press, 2015).
6. Griffin, *Life and Words of Robert Welch*, 135–37.
7. Friedrich A. von Hayek, *The Road to Serfdom* (Chicago: University of Chicago Press, 1944); Daniel Stedman Jones, *Masters of the Universe: Hayek, Friedman, and the Birth of Neoliberal Politics* (Princeton, NJ: Princeton University Press, 2012), 50–51; Alan O. Ebenstein, *Friedrich Hayek: A Biography* (New York: Palgrave, 2001); Edward Feser, *The Cambridge Companion to Hayek* (New York: Cambridge University Press, 2006); Bruce Caldwell, *Hayek's Challenge: An Intellectual Biography of F. A. Hayek* (Chicago: University of Chicago Press, 2004); Kim Phillips-Fein, *Invisible Hands: The Making of the Conservative Movement from the New Deal to Reagan* (New York: W. W. Norton, 2009), 34–48; Patrick Allitt, *The Conservatives: Ideas and Personalities throughout American History* (New Haven, CT: Yale University Press, 2009), 159–63.
8. Griffin, *Life and Words of Robert Welch*, 139.
9. Griffin, *Life and Words of Robert Welch*, 142.
10. Griffin, *Life and Words of Robert Welch*, 144.
11. Griffin, *Life and Words of Robert Welch*, 149.
12. Stephen E. Ambrose, *Nixon: The Education of a Politician, 1913–1962* (New York: Simon and Schuster, 1987), 128–29.

13. Kathryn S. Olmstead, *Real Enemies: Conspiracy Theories and American Democracy, World War I to 9/11* (Oxford: Oxford University Press, 2009), 83–85; M. J. Heale, *American Anti-Communism: Combating the Enemy Within, 1830–1970* (Baltimore: Johns Hopkins University Press, 1990), 99, 120; Kathryn S. Olmstead, *Red Spy Queen: A Biography of Elizabeth Bentley* (Chapel Hill: University of North Carolina Press, 2002).
14. Ambrose, *Nixon*, 148.
15. Alistair Cooke, *A Generation on Trial: U.S.A. v. Alger Hiss* (New York: Alfred A. Knopf, 1950); Alonzo Hamby, *Beyond the New Deal: Harry S. Truman and American Liberalism* (New York: Columbia University Press, 1973), 379–81; Allen Weinstein, *Perjury: The Alger Hiss Case* (New York: Alfred A. Knopf, 1978).
16. Ambrose, *Nixon*, 205. Michael W. Miles, *Odyssey of the American Right* (London: Oxford University Press, 1980), 123–28; Susan Jacoby, *Alger Hiss and the Battle for History* (New Haven, CT: Yale University Press, 2009); Sam Tanenhaus, *Whittaker Chambers: A Biography* (New York: Random House, 1997), 203–439.
17. Tanenhaus, *Whittaker Chambers*, 437.

CHAPTER EIGHT

1. David M. Oshinsky, *A Conspiracy So Immense: The World of Joe McCarthy* (New York: Free Press, 1983).
2. Ellen Schrecker, *Many Are the Crimes: McCarthyism in America* (Oxford: Oxford University Press, 1999).
3. *Salem, MA Independent*, April 29, 1950.
4. *Mattapan–Milton Tribune*, September 14, 1950.
5. Welch campaign ad, "The Rising Tide," September 21, 1949, Welch private papers; Michele Flynn Stenehjem, *An American First: John Flynn and the America First Committee* (New Rochelle, NY: Arlington House, 1976).
6. Stephen E. Ambrose, *Nixon: The Education of a Politician, 1913–1962* (New York: Simon and Schuster, 1987), 127.
7. Schrecker, *Many Are the Crimes*, 242.
8. *Boston Herald*, June 4, 1950.
9. Ambrose, *Nixon*, 307.
10. *Belmont Herald*, June 2, 1950; unidentified clipping from a Newton, MA, newspaper, May 18, 1950.
11. Welch campaign ad, "The Rising Tide," September 21, 1949; *Sunday Republican*, November 13, 1949.
12. *Independent Republican* (Attleboro, MA), March 21, 1950; *Independent* (Haverhill, MA), April 2, 1950; *Times* (Beverly, MA), May 2, 1950; *Patriot Ledger*, April 27, 1950; *Journal and Press* (Somerville, MA), March 3, 1950; *Beverly Times*, May 7, 1950.
13. Michael W. Miles, *Odyssey of the American Right* (London: Oxford University Press, 1980), 25–26.
14. *Watertown Sun*, September 14, 1950; *Boston Herald*, May 4, 1950.
15. *Cape Cod Standard Times*, May 2, 1950.

16. Welch campaign ad, "The Rising Tide," November 28, 1949.
17. *Dory News,* August 31, 1950.
18. *Stoughton News Sentinel* April 13, 1950.
19. *North Attleboro Independent,* June 1, 1950.
20. Clay Blair, *The Forgotten War: America in Korea, 1950–1953* (New York: Times Books, 1987); Miles, *Odyssey,* 152.
21. *Times* (Holbrook, MA), September 8, 1950; *Citizen* (Brookline, MA), September 14, 1950.
22. *Boston Post,* September 17, 1950; *Canton Journal,* June 9, 1950; G. Edward Griffin, *The Life and Words of Robert Welch* (Thousand Oaks, CA: American Media, 1975), 159.
23. Miles, *Odyssey,* 135, 136.
24. Griffin, *Life and Words of Robert Welch,* 160.
25. Griffin, *Life and Words of Robert Welch,* 161.
26. Griffin, *Life and Words of Robert Welch,* 161.

CHAPTER NINE

1. Richard Hofstadter, *The Paranoid Style in American Politics and Other Essays* (New York: Vintage Books, 2008), 39; G. Edward Griffin, *The Life and Words of Robert Welch* (Thousand Oaks, CA: American Media, 1975), 155.
2. Griffin, *Life and Words of Robert Welch,* 162.
3. Griffin, *Life and Words of Robert Welch,* 163–64.
4. Stephen E. Ambrose, *Nixon: The Education of a Politician, 1913–1962* (New York: Simon and Schuster, 1987), 228; Miles, *Odyssey,* 164–65.
5. Ambrose, *Nixon,* 223.
6. Michael W. Miles, *Odyssey of the American Right* (London: Oxford University Press, 1980), 155–56.
7. Joyce Mao, *Asia First: China and the Making of Modern American Conservatism* (Chicago: University of Chicago Press, 2015), 106–7.
8. Miles, *Odyssey,* 155–56, 156–57.
9. James Patterson, *Mr. Republican: A Biography of Robert A. Taft* (Boston: Houghton Mifflin, 1972), 455–59; Miles, *Odyssey,* 156–57.
10. William Stueck, *The Road to Confrontation: American Policy toward China and Korea, 1947–1950* (Chapel Hill: University of North Carolina Press, 1981), 177–220; Glenn Paige, *The Korean Decision: June 24–30, 1950* (New York: Free Press, 1968); Robert Donovan, *The Tumultuous Years: The Presidency of Harry S. Truman, 1949–1953* (New York: Norton, 1982), 187–240; Miles, *Odyssey,* 148.
11. Miles, *Odyssey,* 148.
12. Robert Ferrell, *Harry S. Truman and the Modern American Presidency* (Boston: Little, Brown, 1983), 124; Miles, *Odyssey,* 149, 150.
13. Miles, *Odyssey,* 151, 150.
14. William F. Buckley, *Getting It Right* (New York: Regnery, 2003), 47–48.
15. Richard H. Rovere and Arthur M. Schlesinger Jr., *President Truman and General*

MacArthur: The Struggle for Control of American Foreign Policy (New Brunswick, NJ: Transaction, 1992), 5, 6.

16. William Manchester, *American Caesar: Douglas MacArthur, 1880–1964* (Boston: Little, Brown, 2012), 647–49; D. Clayton James, *The Years of MacArthur*, vol. 3 (Boston: Houghton Mifflin, 1985), 476; Douglas Schaller, *MacArthur: The Far Eastern General* (New York: Oxford University Press, 1989); Donovan, *Tumultuous Years*, 268–80; David McCullough, *Truman* (New York: Simon and Schuster, 1992), 846–47.
17. Miles, *Odyssey*, 167–68.
18. Griffin, *Life and Words of Robert Welch*, 178.
19. William B. Hixson, *Search for the American Right-Wing: An Analysis of the Social Science Record* (Princeton, NJ: Princeton University Press, 1992), 4.
20. Miles, *Odyssey*, 157, 158.
21. Melvyn Leffler, "Negotiating from Strength: Acheson, the Russians, and American Power," in *Dean Acheson and the Making of U.S. Foreign Policy*, ed. Douglas Brinkley (New York: Palgrave Macmillan, 1993), 178–86; Gaddis Smith, *Dean Acheson* (New York: Cooper Square, 1972); Miles, *Odyssey*, 157.
22. Robert Welch, *May God Forgive Us* (Chicago: Henry Regnery, 1952), 56.
23. Charles Wertenbaker, "The World of Alfred Kohlberg," *Reporter*, April 29, 1952; John N. Thomas, *The Institute of Pacific Relations: Asian Scholars*, 3; Robert E. Herzstein, *Henry Luce,* Time, *and the American Crusade in Asia* (Cambridge: Cambridge University Press, 2005), 64–65.
24. Miles, *Odyssey*, 111–13.
25. George H. Nash, *Conservative Intellectual Movement in America* (Wilmington, DE: ISI Books, 2006), 135, Herzstein, *Henry Luce*, 30, 31.
26. Alfred Kohlberg to Claire Chennault, August 20, 1945, Alfred Kohlberg Collection, Box 28, Folder "Chennault, Maj. Gen. Claire Lee," Hoover Institution Archives, Stanford University, Stanford, CA; Colin R. Reynolds, "The-So-Far Right: Radical Right-Wing Politics in the United States, 1941–1977" (PhD diss., Emory University, 2016), 31.
27. Griffin, *Life and Words of Robert Welch*, 169.
28. Jonathan Schoenwald, *A Time for Choosing: The Rise of Modern American Conservatism* (Oxford: Oxford University Press, 2001), 66–67.
29. Schoenwald, *Time for Choosing*, 67.
30. *Chicago Tribune*, October 30, 1952.
31. Rick Perlstein, *Before the Storm: Barry Goldwater and the Unmaking of the American Consensus* (New York: Nation Books, 2009), 113.
32. Schoenwald, *Time for Choosing*, 67.
33. Welch, *May God Forgive Us*, 61.
34. Welch, *May God Forgive Us*, 61.
35. Welch, *May God Forgive Us*, 97–98.
36. *Los Angeles Times*, November 23, 1952; Welch, *May God Forgive Us*, 51–52.
37. Welch, *May God Forgive Us*, 60.
38. Barton Bernstein and Allen Matusow, eds., *The Truman Administration: A Doc-*

umentary History (New York: Harper and Row, 1966), 300–309; Richard Fried, *Nightmare in Red: The McCarthy Era in Perspective* (New York: Oxford University Press, 1990), 87–89; Fred Siegel, *Troubled Journey: From Pearl Harbor to Ronald Reagan* (New York: Hill and Wang, 1984), 72; David Halberstam, *The Fifties* (New York: Random House, 1993), 29–33.

39. Welch, *May God Forgive Us*, 50; Robert L. Beisner, *Dean Acheson: A Life in the Cold War* (New York: Oxford University Press, 2009), 185–89.
40. Welch, *May God Forgive Us*, 23.
41. Andrew J. Bacevich, *The Limits of Power: The End of American Exceptionalism* (New York: Holt, 2008); D. J. Mulloy, *The World of the John Birch Society: Conspiracy, Conservatism, and the Cold War* (Nashville: Vanderbilt University Press, 2014), 141; William Pfaff, *The Irony of Manifest Destiny* (New York: Walker, 2010); Peter Beinart, *The Icarus Syndrome: A History of American Hubris* (New York: HarperCollins, 2010).
42. Kathryn Weathersby, "Stalin and the Korean War," in *Origins of the Cold War: An International History*, Melvyn Leffler and David S. Painter (New York: Routledge, 2005), 274–75; Welch, *May God Forgive Us*, 65–74.
43. John Lewis Gaddis, *The Long Peace: Inquiries into the History of the Cold War* (Oxford: Oxford University Press, 1987), 97; John Lewis Gaddis, *The Cold War: A New History* (New York: Penguin Press, 2005), 42–43.
44. Chen Jian, *China's Road to the Korean War: The Making of the Sino-American Confrontation* (New York: Columbia University Press, 1994), 143.
45. Miles, *Odyssey*, 159; Welch, *May God Forgive Us*, 71–72.
46. Miles, *Odyssey*, 166–68; Welch, *May God Forgive Us*, 71–72; Ambrose, *Nixon*, 251.
47. Miles, *Odyssey*, 103–5; Tang Tsou, *America's Failure in China, 1941–1950*, vol. 1 (Chicago: University of Chicago Press, 1963), 343–45; Robert McMahon, "The Cold War in Asia: Towards a New Synthesis," *Diplomatic History* 12 (Summer 1988): 307–27.
48. Harvey Klehr and Ronald Radosh, *The Amerasia Spy Case: Prelude to McCarthyism* (Chapel Hill: University of North Carolina Press, 1996), 1–161; Stephen Whitfield, *The Culture of the Cold War* (Baltimore: Johns Hopkins University Press, 1991); Joseph Goulden, *The Best Years, 1945–1950* (New York: Atheneum, 1976), 276–88; Robert Ferrell, *Harry S. Truman and the Modern American Presidency* (Boston: Little, Brown, 1983), 134–35; David Caute, *The Great Fear: The Anti-Communist Purge under Truman and Eisenhower* (New York: Simon and Schuster, 1978), 55–56.
49. William Stueck, *The Wedemeyer Mission: American Politics and Foreign Policy during the Cold War* (Athens: University of Georgia Press, 1984); Miles, *Odyssey*, 114; Herzstein, *Henry Luce*, 97.
50. Herzstein, *Henry Luce*, 89, 92–93; Stueck, *Wedemeyer Mission*.
51. Reynolds, "The-So-Far Right," 30.
52. Richard Gid Powers, *Not without Honor: The History of American Anti-Communism* (New Haven, CT: Yale University Press, 1995), 238–39; Herzstein, *Henry Luce*, 64.
53. Miles, *Odyssey*, 112; Herzstein, *Henry Luce*, 66; Alan Brinkley, *Henry Luce and His American Century* (New York: Knopf, 2010), 344; Joseph Charles Keeley, *The China*

Lobby Man: The Story of Alfred Kohlberg (New Rochelle, NY: Arlington House, 1969); Ross Y. Koen, *The China Lobby in American Politics* (New York: Harper and Row, 1974); Lewis McCarroll Purifoy, *Harry Truman's China Policy: McCarthyism and the Diplomacy of Hysteria, 1947–1951* (New York: New Viewpoints, 1976).

54. Kathryn S. Olmsted, *Real Enemies: Conspiracy Theories and American Democracy, World War I to 9/11* (New York: Oxford University Press, 2009), 84–92; Terry Lautz, *John Birch: A Life* (Oxford: Oxford University Press, 2015), 83; *Cincinnati Enquirer*, December 14, 1952; *Orlando Sentinel*, October 19, 1952.
55. Stephen Ambrose, *Eisenhower: The President* (New York: Simon and Schuster, 1984), 100.
56. Ambrose, *Nixon*, 212.
57. Ambrose, *Nixon*, 227–48.
58. Ambrose, *Nixon*, 226–30.
59. Miles, *Odyssey*, 153, 169, 167–68.

CHAPTER TEN

1. David Caute, *The Great Fear: The Anti-Communist Purge under Truman and Eisenhower* (New York: Simon and Schuster, 1978), 45.
2. Robert Welch, *May God Forgive Us* (Chicago: Henry Regnery, 1952), 58.
3. Christopher Tomlins, *The State and the Unions: Labor Relations, Law, and the Organized Labor Movement in America, 1880–1960* (New York: Cambridge University Press, 1985); James Patterson, *Mr. Republican: A Biography of Robert A. Taft* (Boston: Houghton Mifflin, 1972), 301–68; Michael W. Miles, *Odyssey of the American Right* (London: Oxford University Press, 1980), 162–63.
4. *Berkshire Eagle*, February 5, 1952.
5. G. Edward Griffin, *The Life and Words of Robert Welch* (Thousand Oaks, CA: American Media, 1975), 164.
6. Griffin, *Life and Words of Robert Welch*, 168.
7. Alonzo Hamby, *Liberalism and Its Challengers: From FDR to Bush* (Oxford: Oxford University Press, 1985), 103.
8. Miles, *Odyssey*, 182.
9. Miles, *Odyssey*, 183.
10. Hamby, *Liberalism and Its Challengers*, 107.
11. Miles, *Odyssey*, 184–87.
12. Hamby, *Liberalism and Its Challengers*, 109–11.
13. Griffin, *Life and Words of Robert Welch*, 165–67.
14. Stephen Ambrose, *Eisenhower: Soldier and President* (New York: Simon and Schuster, 1990); Herbert Parmet, *Eisenhower and the American Crusades* (New York: Taylor and Francis, 1972); Robert Burk, *Dwight D. Eisenhower: Hero and Politician* (Boston: Twayne, 1986); R. Alton Lee, *Dwight D. Eisenhower: Soldier and Statesman* (Chicago: Burnham, 1981); Charles Alexander, *Holding the Line: The Eisenhower Era, 1952–1961* (Bloomington: Indiana University Press, 1975); Miles, *Odyssey*, 186–87.

15. Patterson, *Mr. Republican*, 509–34; Ambrose, *Eisenhower: Soldier and President*, 270–75; Paul David, *Presidential Nominating Politics in 1952*, vol. 4 (Baltimore: Johns Hopkins University Press, 1954); Miles, *Odyssey*, 187–89.
16. Griffin, *Life and Words of Robert Welch*, 165–67; Ambrose, *Eisenhower: Soldier and President*, 270.
17. Miles, *Odyssey*, 186–87, 187–89.
18. Hamby, *Liberalism and Its Challengers*, 115–17.
19. Griffin, *Life and Words of Robert Welch*, 228.
20. Roger Morris, *Richard Milhous Nixon: The Rise of an American Politician* (New York: Henry Holt, 1990), 695–736; Parmet, *Eisenhower and the American Crusades*, 102–17; Miles, *Odyssey*, 190–92.
21. Richard Polenberg, *One Nation Divisible: Class, Race, and Ethnicity in the United States Since 1938* (New York: Penguin Books, 1980); Robert Divine, *American Immigration Policy, 1924–1952* (New Haven, CT: Yale University Press, 1957); Miles, *Odyssey*, 190–93, 196.
22. Michael Bowen, *The Roots of Modern Conservatism* (Chapel Hill: University of North Carolina Press, 2011), 49–106; Miles, *Odyssey*, 194.
23. Stephen Ambrose, *Nixon: The Education of a Politician, 1913–1962* (New York: Simon and Schuster, 1987), 271–300; Morris, *Richard Milhous Nixon*, 757–808; Ambrose, *Eisenhower: Soldier and President*, 279–82.

CHAPTER ELEVEN

1. "Personnel is policy" is from Scot Faulkner, President Ronald Reagan's director of personnel. See Scot Faulkner, "Personnel Is Policy," *Washington Post*, February 2, 2016, https://www.washingtonexaminer.com/personnel-is-policy.
2. John Steele Gordon, "The Ordeal of Engine Charlie," *American Heritage*, February/March 1995, 18–22; Michael W. Miles, *Odyssey of the American Right* (London: Oxford University Press, 1980), 200.
3. William Knowland, "Be Prepared to Fight in China," *Collier's*, January 24, 1954, 120; Norman Graebner, *The New Isolationism: A Study in Politics and Foreign Policy since 1950* (New York: Ronald Press, 1956), 125.
4. Robert Welch, *The Politician* (Belmont, MA: Belmont, 1963), 226.
5. Welch, *Politician*, 225–26.
6. Wilson Miscamble, *George F. Kennan and the Making of American Foreign Policy, 1947–1950* (Princeton, NJ: Princeton University Press, 1992); Charles Bohlen, *Witness to History, 1929–1969* (New York: Norton, 1973); Miles, *Odyssey*, 202–6.
7. Miles, *Odyssey*, 200.
8. Herbert S. Parmet, *Eisenhower and the American Crusades* (New Brunswick, NJ: Transaction, 1972), 237–38; 241–46; Stephen Ambrose, *Eisenhower: The President* (New York: Simon and Schuster, 1984), 33, 47, 51–52.
9. Heather Cox Richardson, *To Make Men Free: A History of the Republican Party* (New York: Basic Books, 2014), 221–38.
10. Fred I. Greenstein, *The Hidden Hand Presidency: Eisenhower as Leader* (New York:

Basic Books, 1982), 50; Alonzo Hamby, *Liberalism and Its Challengers* (New York: Oxford University Press, 1985), 122, 124–25; and Stephen E. Ambrose, *Eisenhower: Soldier and President* (New York: Simon and Schuster, 1990), 545.

11. Ambrose, *Eisenhower: The President,* 219.
12. Abraham Hoffman, *Unwanted Mexicans in the Great Depression* (Tucson: University of Arizona Press, 1974).
13. Ambrose, *Eisenhower: The President,* 38.
14. Welch, *Politician,* 136–38.
15. William I. Hitchcock, *The Age of Eisenhower* (New York: Simon and Schuster, 2018), 103–7; Ambrose, *Eisenhower: The President,* 14–15, 30–32.
16. Ambrose, *Eisenhower: The President,* 101–10; Joyce Mao, *Asia First: China and the Making of Modern American Conservatism* (Chicago: University of Chicago Press, 2015), 89–92.
17. Ambrose, *Eisenhower: The President,* 68.
18. Welch, *Politician,* 91–93. Ambrose, *Eisenhower: The President,* 70.
19. Hitchcock, *Age of Eisenhower,* 136–38; Ambrose, *Eisenhower: The President,* 66–69, 124–131; Karl B. Pauly, *Bricker of Ohio: The Man and His Record* (New York: G. P. Putnam's Sons, 1944).
20. Welch, *Politician,* 148–49; Miles, *Odyssey,* 202–6.
21. Ronald Pruessen, *John Foster Dulles and the Road to Power* (New York: Free Press, 1982); Frederick Marks, *Power and Peace: The Diplomacy of John Foster Dulles* (Westport, CT: Praeger, 1993); and Richard Immerman, ed., *John Foster Dulles and the Diplomacy of the Cold War* (Princeton, 1990).
22. Miles, *Odyssey,* 202.
23. Richard Rovere, *The Eisenhower Years: Affairs of State* (New York: Farrar, Straus, and Cudahy, 1956), 277, 285.
24. Ambrose, *Eisenhower: The President,* 39.
25. Welch, *Politician,* 147; Miles, *Odyssey,* 202–6.
26. Hitchcock, *The Age of Eisenhower,* 178–81; George Herring, *America's Longest War: The United States and Vietnam, 1950–1975* (Philadelphia: Temple University Press, 1986), 3–42; Stephen Ambrose, *Rise to Globalism: American Foreign Policy since 1938* (New York: Penguin Books, 1985), 140–45; Welch, *Politician,* 145–46; Miles, *Odyssey,* 204–6.
27. Walter LaFeber, *America, Russia, and the Cold War* (Boston: McGraw Hill Higher Education, 2006), 166–69; Welch, *Politician,* 145–46; Miles, *Odyssey,* 204–6.
28. David Anderson, *Trapped by Success: The Eisenhower Administration and Vietnam, 1953–1961* (New York: Columbia University Press, 1991), 154; Lloyd Gardner, *Approaching Vietnam: From World War II through Dienbienphu, 1941–1954* (New York: W. W. Norton, 1988).
29. Welch, *Politician,* 77.
30. Welch, *Politician,* 256.
31. Ambrose, *Eisenhower: The President,* 39.
32. Ambrose, *Eisenhower: The President,* 82.
33. Hitchcock, *Age of Eisenhower,* 129–41.

34. Welch, *Politician*, 286–87; Miles, *Odyssey*, 207.
35. Ambrose, *Eisenhower: The President*, 14–15, 30–32.
36. Hitchcock, *Age of Eisenhower*, 137–138; Welch, *Politician*, 249.
37. Welch, *Politician*, 81.
38. Welch, *Politician*, 81.
39. Greenstein, *Hidden Hand Presidency*, 195.
40. Richard Fried, *Nightmare in Red: The McCarthy Era in Perspective* (New York: Oxford University Press, 1990), 139–41; Welch, *Politician*, 86.
41. Welch, *Politician*, 80–85.
42. Ambrose, *Eisenhower: Soldier and President*, 334.
43. *JBS Bulletin*, January 1961; Mary Dudziak, *Cold War Civil Rights: Race and the Image of American Democracy* (Princeton, NJ: Princeton University Press, 2000), 107–17.
44. G. Edward Griffin, *The Life and Words of Robert Welch* (Thousand Oaks, CA: American Media, 1975), 11.

CHAPTER TWELVE

1. John B. Judis, *William F. Buckley Jr.: Patron Saint of the Conservatives* (New York: Simon and Schuster, 1988), 112.
2. Rick Perlstein, *Before the Storm: Barry Goldwater and the Unmaking of the American Consensus* (New York: Nation Books, 2009), 9–10.
3. Perlstein, *Before the Storm*, 113.
4. Darren Dochuk, *From Bible Belt to Sunbelt: Plain-Folk Religion, Grassroots Politics, and the Rise of Evangelical Conservatism* (New York: W. W. Norton, 2011), 46–47.
5. Barry Hankins, *Gods Rascal: J. Frank Norris and the Beginnings of Southern Fundamentalism* (Lexington: University Press of Kentucky, 1996), 100.
6. Colin R. Reynolds, "The-So-Far Right: Radical Right-Wing Politics in the United States, 1941–1977" (PhD diss., Emory University, 2016), 21.
7. Robert E. Herzstein, *Henry Luce,* Time, *and the American Crusade in Asia* (Cambridge: Cambridge University Press, 2005), I, 2; Jonathan Schoenwald, *A Time for Choosing: The Rise of Modern American Conservatism* (Oxford: Oxford University Press, 2001), 67.
8. Terry Lautz, *John Birch: A Life* (Oxford: Oxford University Press, 2015), 25.
9. Dochuk, *Bible Belt to Sunbelt*, 47; Reynolds, "The-So-Far Right," 26.
10. Lautz, *John Birch*, 25.
11. Lautz, *John Birch*, 87, 93–95, 92; Robert Welch, *The Life of John Birch: In the Story of One American Boy, the Ordeal of His Age* (Chicago: Henry Regnery, 1954), 2.
12. Reynolds, "The-So-Far Right," 25–35.
13. Dochuk, *From Bible Belt to Sunbelt*, 48–49.
14. Lautz, *John Birch*, 139–57.
15. Joyce Mao, *Asia First: China and the Making of Modern American Conservatism* (Chicago: University of Chicago Press, 2015), 109.
16. Perlstein, *Before the Storm*, 113.
17. William Knowland, "United States Policy in the Far East—Admission of Com-

munist China to United Nations," *Congressional Record*, September 5, 1950, 14204; Reynolds, "The-So-Far Right," 27–46.

18. Clarence Manion to Robert Welch, 1954, Clarence E. Manion Papers, Box 2, Folder 8, Chicago History Museum, Chicago, IL; Reynolds, "The-So-Far Right," 46.
19. Reynolds, "The-So-Far Right," 25–47.
20. Reynolds, "The-So-Far Right," 46.
21. Welch, *Life of John Birch*, 33, 45, 110.
22. G. Edward Griffin, *The Life and Words of Robert Welch* (Thousand Oaks, CA: American Media, 1975), 202.
23. Schoenwald, *Time for Choosing*, 236.
24. Reynolds, "The-So-Far Right," 25–47.
25. William Stueck, *The Wedemeyer Mission: American Politics and Foreign Policy during the Cold War* (Athens: University of Georgia Press, 1984); Albert C. Wedemeyer to George S. Birch, December 24, 1962, 2, Albert C. Wedemeyer Collection [ACWC], Box 115, Folder 10, Hoover Institution Archives, Stanford University, Stanford, CA; Albert C. Wedemeyer to Robert Welch, October 10, 1961, ACWC, Box 115, Folder 9; Reynolds, "The-So-Far Right," 45–52.

CHAPTER THIRTEEN

1. G. Edward Griffin, *The Life and Words of Robert Welch* (Thousand Oaks, CA: American Media, 1975), 229.
2. Robert Welch to "Dear Mr. ——, December 18, 1954, private Welch collection.
3. Addendum to the black book 1958; pasted in Welch's collated copies, private Welch collection.
4. Robert Welch to "Dear Mr. ——, December 18, 1954, private Welch collection.
5. Robert Welch to "Dear Mr. ——, December 18, 1954, private Welch collection.
6. Robert Welch to "Dear Mr. ——, December 18, 1954, private Welch collection.
7. D. J. Mulloy, *The World of the John Birch Society: Conspiracy, Conservatism, and the Cold War* (Nashville: Vanderbilt University Press, 2014), 142.
8. Colin R. Reynolds, "The-So-Far Right: Radical Right-Wing Politics in the United States, 1941–1977" (PhD diss., Emory University, 2016), 106.
9. Jonathan Schoenwald, *A Time for Choosing: The Rise of Modern American Conservatism* (Oxford: Oxford University Press, 2001), 70–71, 72, 72–73.
10. Donald T. Critchlow, *The Conservative Ascendancy: How the GOP Right Made Political History* (Cambridge, MA: Harvard University Press, 2007), 41–48.
11. Robert Welch to Clarence Manion, November 25, 1959, Clarence E. Manion Papers, Box 62, Folder 1, Chicago History Museum, Chicago, IL; Robert Welch, "The Politician" (unpub. vers., 1958), 267, Herbert A. Philbrick Papers, Box 210, Folder 4, Manuscript Division, Library of Congress, Washington, DC; Reynolds, "The-So-Far Right," 107.
12. Alfred Kohlberg to Robert Welch, September 2, 1958, Alfred Kohlberg Collection [AKC], Box 200, "Welch, Robert H. W., 1957–58" Folder, Hoover Institution Archives, Stanford University, Stanford, CA; Robert Welch to Alfred Kohlberg, Sep-

tember 4, 1958, AKC, Box 200, "Welch, Robert H. W., 1957–58" Folder; Reynolds, "The-So-Far Right," 107.

13. Alfred Kohlberg to Robert Welch, September 2, 1958, AKC, Box 200, "Welch, Robert H. W., 1957–58" Folder; Robert Welch to Alfred Kohlberg, September 4, 1958, AKC, Box 200, "Welch, Robert H. W., 1957–58" Folder; Reynolds, "The-So-Far Right," 107.
14. December 10, 1962, letter from Robert Welch, private collection.
15. John B. Judis, *William F. Buckley Jr.: Patron Saint of the Conservatives* (New York: Simon and Schuster, 1988), 111; *U.S. News & World Report*, August 6, 1954; Schoenwald, *Time for Choosing*, 68–70.
16. Judis, *William F. Buckley Jr.*, 111.
17. Alvin S. Felzenberg, *A Man and His Presidents: The Political Odyssey of William F. Buckley Jr.* (New Haven, CT: Yale University Press, 2017), 138.
18. Stephen Ambrose, *Eisenhower: The President* (New York: Simon and Schuster, 1984), 97; Robert Welch, A Brief Report to Friends on My Trip for the Far East on the Plane Returning Friday, September 2, 1955, Welch papers, private collection.
19. Robert Welch, Brief Report.
20. Griffin, *Life and Words of Robert Welch*, 180–82.
21. Griffin, *Life and Words of Robert Welch*, 180–82; Welch, Brief Report.
22. Welch, Brief Report.
23. Welch, Brief Report; Griffin, *Life and Words of Robert Welch*, 182–85.
24. Ambrose, *Eisenhower: The President*, 229, 230–45.

CHAPTER FOURTEEN

1. Robert Welch, A Brief Report to Friends on My Trip for the Far East on the Plane Returning Friday, September 2, 1955, Welch papers, private collection.
2. Benjamin Waterhouse, *Land of Enterprise* (New York: Simon and Schuster, 2017), 138–40; Jonathan Soffer, "The National Association of Manufacturers and the Militarization of American Conservatism," *Business History Review* 75, no. 4 (Winter 2001): 775–805.
3. Alan Lichtman, *White Protestant Nation: The Rise of the American Conservative Movement* (New York: Atlantic Monthly Press, 2008), 137.
4. Rick Perlstein, *Before the Storm: Barry Goldwater and the Unmaking of the American Consensus* (New York: Nation Books, 2009), 113; Benjamin Waterhouse, *Lobbying America: The Politics of Business from Nixon to Nafta* (Princeton, NJ: Princeton University Press, 2014), 43–59.
5. Lichtman, *White Protestant Nation*, 138, 194, 195.
6. Robert Welch to James Welch, 1955, Welch private papers.
7. Robert Welch to James Welch, 1955, Welch private papers.
8. Jonathan Schoenwald, *A Time for Choosing: The Rise of Modern American Conservatism* (Oxford: Oxford University Press, 2001), 68.
9. D. J. Mulloy, *The World of the John Birch Society: Conspiracy, Conservatism, and the Cold War* (Nashville: Vanderbilt University Press, 2014), 137–40; Robert Welch,

The Blue Book of the John Birch Society (Belmont, MA: Western Islands, 1961), 15–16; Robert Welch, *May God Forgive Us* (Chicago: Henry Regnery, 1952); and Robert Welch, *The Life of John Birch: In the Story of One American Boy, the Ordeal of His Age* (Chicago: Henry Regnery, 1954); G. Edward Griffin, *The Life and Words of Robert Welch: Founder of the John Birch Society* (Thousand Oaks, CA: American Media, 1975), 179–87; Richard Gid Powers, *Not without Honor: The History of American Anticommunism* (New York: Free Press, 1995), 104–6, 125–26, 230–33.

10. Schoenwald, *Time for Choosing*, 69.
11. Stephen Ambrose, *Eisenhower: The President* (New York: Simon and Schuster, 1984), 249–50.
12. Ambrose, *Eisenhower: The President*, 253, 255.
13. John McManus, *The John Birch Society: Its History Recounted by Someone Who Was There* (Wakefield, MA: Overview Productions, 2018), 35–38.
14. Griffin, *Life and Words of Robert Welch.*
15. Griffin, *Life and Words of Robert Welch*, 193.
16. Robert Welch to James Welch, 1955, Welch private papers.
17. Griffin, *Life and Words of Robert Welch*, 195.
18. *One Man's Opinion*, February 1956.
19. Ambrose, *Eisenhower: The President*, 422–24; Charles Alexander, *Holding the Line: The Eisenhower Era, 1952–1961* (Bloomington: Indiana University Press, 1975), 178–81; Dwight D. Eisenhower, *Waging Peace, 1956–1963* (Garden City, NY: Doubleday, 1965), 62–69.
20. *One Man's Opinion*, February 1956.
21. Ambrose, *Eisenhower: The President*, 328, 354–56.
22. *One Man's Opinion*, November 1956.
23. Alexander, *Holding the Line*, 172–78; Ambrose, *Eisenhower: The President*, 421–22, 424–26, 430–33; Diane Kunz, *The Economic Diplomacy of the Suez Crisis* (Chapel Hill: University of North Carolina Press, 1991).
24. William I. Hitchcock, *The Age of Eisenhower* (New York: Simon and Schuster, 2018), 306–17; Ambrose, *Eisenhower: The President*, 356–59.
25. Ambrose, *Eisenhower: The President*, 90–99, 373.
26. Stephen B. Oates, *Let the Trumpet Sound: A Life of Martin Luther King, Jr.* (New York: Harper Perennial, 1982), 206–32.
27. Ambrose, *Eisenhower: The President*, 305–28.
28. Mulloy, *World of the John Birch Society*, 107; *One Man's Opinion*, September 1956.
29. Sara Diamond, *Roads to Dominion: Right-Wing Movements and Political Power in the United States* (New York: Guildford Press, 1995), 86; Mulloy, *World of the John Birch Society*, 107–9; *One Man's Opinion*, September 1956; Martin Durham, *White Rage: The Extreme Right and American Politics* (London: Routledge, 2007); Alan F. Westin, "The John Birch Society: Fundamentalism on the Right," *Commentary* 32, no. 2 (August 1961); Seymour Martin Lipset and Earl Raab, *The Politics of Unreason: Right-Wing Extremism in America, 1790–1977* (Chicago: University of Chicago Press, 1978), 269; Schoenwald, *Time for Choosing*, 89–90.

30. "Racism and the John Birch Society—Part 3," rev. February 5, 2021, https://sites.google.com/site/aboutxr/home/jbs-racism3.
31. John A. Farrell, *Richard Nixon: The Life* (New York: Doubleday, 2017), 132–36.
32. *One Man's Opinion*, April 1956.
33. Harry McPherson, *A Political Education* (Boston: Little, Brown, 1972).
34. *One Man's Opinion*, September 1957, April 1956.
35. Colin R. Reynolds, "The-So-Far Right: Radical Right-Wing Politics in the United States, 1941–1977" (PhD diss., Emory University, 2016), 52; Committee of Endorsers, "A Program to Govern Our Foreign Relations," *New York Times*, February 28, 1955.
36. William Stueck, *The Wedemeyer Mission: American Politics and Foreign Policy during the Cold War* (Athens: University of Georgia Press, 1984); Reynolds, "The-So-Far Right," 71; Committee of Endorsers, "A Program to Govern Our Foreign Relations," February 28, 1955, reprint, Alfred Kohlberg Collection, Box 89, "Edward Hunter, 1956" Folder, Hoover Institution Archives, Stanford University, Stanford, CA.
37. Reynolds, "The-So-Far Right," 51; For America, "News Release," June 5, 1954, Clarence E. Manion Papers [CMP], Box 2, Folder 7, Chicago History Museum, Chicago, IL; Clarence E. Manion, "Revive American Independence," *Manion Forum*, Weekly Broadcast No. 1, October 3, 1954, 1, CMP, Box 81, Folder 11; Committee of Endorsers, "A Program to Govern Our Foreign Relations," February 28, 1955.
38. Perlstein, *Before the Storm*, 114.
39. Donald T. Critchlow, *The Conservative Ascendancy: How the GOP Right Made Political History* (Cambridge, MA: Harvard University Press, 2007), 58, 57.
40. Ambrose, *Eisenhower: The President*, 376–79.
41. *American Opinion*, April 1959.
42. Hitchcock, *Age of Eisenhower*, 443–44, 451–53, 489–504; Ambrose, *Eisenhower: The President*, 498–500, 516–17, 538–39.
43. Schoenwald, *Time for Choosing*, 70.

CHAPTER FIFTEEN

1. Soviet refugee Nicholas Goncharoff testified in 1954 before the Internal Security Subcommittee that Lenin said it, and conservatives repeated it to make the case that Americans were growing vulnerable to Communism. Colin R. Reynolds, "The-So-Far Right: Radical Right-Wing Politics in the United States, 1941–1977" (PhD diss., Emory University, 2016), 93–94.
2. Reynolds, "The-So-Far Right," 99–100; J. Howard Pew to Dr. Robert L. Johnson, March 29, 1954, J. Howard Pew Personal Papers [JHPP], Box 38, "J, 1954" Folder, Eleutherian Mills Historical Library, Hagley Library and Museum, Wilmington, DE; J. Howard Pew to Robert Welch, October 27, 1954, JHPP, Box 112, "Welch, Robert, H. W., Jr., 1954" Folder.
3. Reynolds, "The-So-Far Right," 99; Robert Welch, *The Blue Book of the John Birch Society* (Belmont, MA: Western Islands, 1961), 47–49.
4. D. J. Mulloy, *The World of the John Birch Society: Conspiracy, Conservatism, and the*

Cold War (Nashville: Vanderbilt University Press, 2014), 137–40; Welch, *Blue Book,* 4–9; 24; Robert Welch, *May God Forgive Us* (Chicago: Henry Regnery, 1952), 9, 73.

5. Reynolds, "The-So-Far Right," 101.
6. Donald T. Critchlow, *The Conservative Ascendancy: How the GOP Right Made Political History* (Cambridge, MA: Harvard University Press, 2007), 57.
7. Critchlow, *Conservative Ascendancy.*
8. Reynolds, "The-So-Far Right," 94–95; Jonathan M. Schoenwald, *A Time for Choosing: The Rise of Modern American Conservatism* (Oxford: Oxford University Press, 2001), 62, 63, 70, 74.
9. Reynolds, "The-So-Far Right," 91–98; Welch, *Blue Book,* 73–74, 127.
10. John McManus, *The John Birch Society: Its History Recounted by Someone Who Was There* (Wakefield, MA: Overview Productions, 2018), 60–61.
11. Critchlow, *Conservative Ascendancy,* 57.
12. Schoenwald, *Time for Choosing,* 75–76.
13. *JBS Bulletin,* January 1960.
14. McManus, *John Birch Society,* 53–57.
15. G. Edward Griffin, *The Life and Words of Robert Welch* (Thousand Oaks, CA: American Media, 1975), 13–150.
16. Stephen Ambrose, *Nixon: The Education of a Politician, 1913–1962* (New York: Simon and Schuster, 1987), 245–48; Griffin, *Life and Words of Robert Welch,* 13–150.
17. Robert Divine, *The Sputnik Challenge* (New York: Oxford University Press, 1993); David Patterson, "The Legacy of President Eisenhower's Arms Control Policies," in *The Military-Industrial Complex,* ed. Gregg Walker et al. (New York: Peter Lang, 1992), 228–29; William O'Neill, *American High: The Years of Confidence, 1945–1960* (New York: Free Press, 1986), 270.
18. Robert Welch, "A Letter to Khrushchev," March 3, 1958, in *The New Americanism and Other Speeches and Essays* (Belmont, MA: Western Islands, 1976), 17–55.
19. Welch, "Letter to Khrushchev," 25–26.
20. Aleksandr Fursenko and Timothy Naftali, *Khrushchev's Cold War: The Inside Story of an American Adversary* (New York: Norton, 2006), 243–56.
21. Welch, "Letter to Khrushchev," 19.
22. Welch, "Letter to Khrushchev," 43–49; Mulloy, *World of the John Birch Society,* 143–46.
23. Welch, *Blue Book,* 79; Griffin, *Life and Words of Robert Welch,* 278; *American Opinion,* August 1959.
24. *American Opinion,* August 1959; Mulloy, *World of the John Birch Society,* 146–49; Fursenko and Naftali, *Khrushchev's Cold War,* 233–35; Carl T. Bogus, *Buckley: William F. Buckley Jr. and the Rise of American Conservatism* (New York: Bloomsbury Press, 2011), 183–84; Schoenwald, *Time for Choosing,* 40–45.
25. *JBS Bulletin,* July 1959, August 1959.
26. McManus, *John Birch Society,* 58–60.
27. McManus, *John Birch Society,* 58–60.
28. McManus, *John Birch Society,* 61–63.
29. McManus, *John Birch Society,* 56–67.

30. McManus, *John Birch Society*, 64–67.
31. Thomas Ross and David Wise, *The U-2 Affair* (New York: Random House, 1962), 98.
32. McManus, *John Birch Society*, 64–67; Michael Beschloss, *Mayday: Eisenhower, Khrushchev and the U-2 Affair* (New York: Harper and Row, 1988); *JBS Bulletin*, June 1960; James Phelan, "Mutiny in the JBS," *Saturday Evening Post*, April 8, 1967.
33. Reynolds, "The-So-Far Right," 102; Fursenko and Naftali, *Khrushchev's Cold War*, 271–89; Mulloy, *World of the John Birch Society*, 149–51.
34. Howard Jones, *The Bay of Pigs* (New York: Oxford University Press, 2008).

CHAPTER SIXTEEN

1. Fred Schwarz to Robert Welch, September 19, 1960, Herbert Philbrick Papers [HPP], Box 121, Folder 8, Manuscript Division, Library of Congress, Washington, DC; Colin R. Reynolds, "The-So-Far Right: Radical Right-Wing Politics in the United States, 1941–1977" (PhD diss., Emory University, 2016), 109.
2. G. Edward Griffin, *The Life and Words of Robert Welch: Founder of the John Birch Society* (Thousand Oaks, CA: American Media, 1975), 240.
3. Jack Mabley, "Bares Secrets of 'Red-Haters': They Think Ike Is a Communist," *Chicago Daily News*, July 25, 1960; and Jack Mabley, "Strange Threat to Democracy: Anti-Red Group Hits Leaders," *Chicago Daily News*, July 26, 1961.
4. D. J. Mulloy, *The World of the John Birch Society: Conspiracy, Conservatism, and the Cold War* (Nashville: Vanderbilt University Press, 2014), 15–19; *JBS Bulletin*, August 1960; *Chicago Sun-Times*, August 1, 1960; Reynolds, "The-So-Far Right," 108–10; Robert Welch to Fred Schwarz, September 9, 1960, HPP, Box 121, Folder 8.
5. Reynolds, "The-So-Far Right," 108–9; Herbert Philbrick to Robert Welch, August 4, 1959, HPP, Box 121, Folder 6; Memorandum from Robert Welch to Herbert Philbrick, circa 1958, HPP, Box 210, Folder 4; Memorandum from Herbert Philbrick to Frank Willette, regarding "Notes taken at John Birch Meeting, home of Harry O. King, 132 East 92nd Street, New York, N.Y.," May 28, 1959, HPP, Box 121, Folder 6; Fred Schwarz to Robert Welch, September 19, 1960, HPP, Box 121, Folder 8.
6. *JBS Bulletin*, August 1960, 6–7; Robert Welch, *The White Book of the John Birch Society for 1960* (Belmont, MA: John Birch Society, 1961).
7. John B. Judis, *William F. Buckley Jr.: Patron Saint of the Conservatives* (New York: Simon and Schuster, 1988), 194; *National Review*, April 11, 1959.
8. Rick Perlstein, *Before the Storm: Barry Goldwater and the Unmaking of the American Consensus* (New York: Nation Books, 2009), 119.
9. Michelle M. Nickerson, *Mothers of Conservatism: Women of the Postwar Right* (Princeton, NJ: Princeton University Press, 2012), 138–62; Richard Vahan, *The Truth about the John Birch Society* (New York: McFadden, 1962); Claire Conner, *Wrapped in the Flag: A Personal History of America's Radical Right* (Boston: Beacon Press, 2013); Lisa McGirr, *Suburban Warriors: The Origins of the New American Right* (Princeton, NJ: Princeton University Press, 2001), 75–79, 222–23; Jona-

than M. Schoenwald, *A Time for Choosing: The Rise of Modern American Conservatism* (New York: Oxford University Press, 2001), 62–99; Richard Gid Powers, *Not without Honor: The History of American Anti-Communism* (New Haven, CT: Yale University Press, 1995), 288–318.

10. Perlstein, *Before the Storm*, 101–2, 114–18.
11. *JBS Bulletin*, February 1961.
12. *JBS Bulletin*, February 1961.
13. *JBS Bulletin*, April 1960; Adam Winkler, *Gun Fight: The Battle over the Right to Bear Arms in America* (New York: W. W. Norton, 2011).
14. Mulloy, *World of the John Birch Society*, 109–10; Robert Welch, *The Blue Book of the John Birch Society* (Belmont, MA: Western Islands, 1961), 19; Robert Welch, *The Politician* (Belmont, MA: Belmont, 1963), 267; *JBS Bulletin*, January 1961.
15. *JBS Bulletin*, January 1961; Edward Cain, *They'd Rather Be Right: Youth and the Conservative Movement* (New York: Macmillan, 1963), 86.
16. Bernard Schwartz, *Super Chief: Earl Warren and His Supreme Court—A Judicial Biography* (New York: New York University Press, 1983), 204–52; Ed Cray, *Chief Justice: A Biography of Earl Warren* (New York: Simon and Schuster, 1997), 329–41; Jim Newton, *Justice for All: Earl Warren and the Nation He Made* (New York: Riverhead Books, 2006), 345–57; Mulloy, *World of the John Birch Society*, 111–13; Pennsylvania v. Nelson, 350 U.S. 497 (1956); Konigsberg v. State Bar, 33 U.S. 252 (1957); Watkins v. United States, 354 U.S. 178 (1957); and Sweezy v. New Hampshire, 354 U.S. 234 (1957); David Caute, *The Great Fear: The Anti-Communist Purge under Truman and Eisenhower* (New York: Simon and Schuster, 1978), 207–9; Patrick Allit, *The Conservatives: Ideas and Personalities throughout American History* (New Haven, CT: Yale University Press, 2009), 181–83.
17. Cray, *Chief Justice*, 338; Rosalie M. Gordon, *Nine Men against America: The Supreme Court and Its Attack on American Liberties*, rev. ed. (New York: Devin-Adair, 1960); *JBS Bulletin*, July 1961, April 1961, June 1962; Mulloy, *World of the John Birch Society*, 113–17; *JBS Bulletin*, May 1961, August 1961; "The Unveiling," *Time*, February 16, 1962; *New York Times*, February 6, 1962, November 9, 1963.

CHAPTER SEVENTEEN

1. D. J. Mulloy, *The World of the John Birch Society: Conspiracy, Conservatism, and the Cold War* (Nashville: Vanderbilt University Press, 2014), 82.
2. *Bridgeport Post*, October 25, 1959.
3. *Bedford Daily-Times Mail*, December 4, 1959.
4. *Deseret News*, October 26, 1959.
5. *Daily Oklahoman*, October 25, 1959; *Tucson Citizen*, October 24, 1959.
6. Donald T. Critchlow, *The Conservative Ascendancy: How the GOP Right Made Political History* (Cambridge, MA: Harvard University Press, 2007), 45.
7. *JBS Bulletin*, July 1977.
8. Critchlow, *Conservative Ascendancy*, 58–59.
9. Robert Welch, *The Blue Book of the John Birch Society* (Belmont, MA: Western

Islands, 1961), 109; *American Opinion,* August 1960; *JBS Bulletin,* May 1960; Mulloy, *World of the John Birch Society,* 79.

10. Critchlow, *Conservative Ascendancy,* 41–48.
11. *Bulletin,* April 1960; David Farber, *The Rise and Fall of Modern American Conservatism* (Princeton, NJ: Princeton University Press, 2010), 89–92; William A. Rusher, *The Rise of the Right* (New York: William Morrow, 1984), 88, 233.
12. Critchlow, *Conservative Ascendancy,* 45; Greg Barnhisel and Catherine Turner, eds., *Pressing the Fight: Print, Propaganda, and the Cold War* (Amherst: University of Massachusetts Press, 2010), 50–70.
13. A. J. MacDonald, *Kangaroo Court versus the John Birch Society* (Los Angeles: A. J. MacDonald and Associates Political Research Bureau, 1963), 70; Mike Newberry, *The Yahoos* (New York: Marzani and Munsell, 1964), 17, 18, 45, 57, 148.
14. *JBS Bulletin,* April 1960.
15. *JBS Bulletin,* April 1960.
16. Robert Welch, *The White Book of the John Birch Society, 1960* (Belmont, MA: John Birch Society, 1960), 7.
17. *JBS Bulletin,* September 1960.
18. *JBS Bulletin,* August 1960.
19. *JBS Bulletin,* October 1960.

CHAPTER EIGHTEEN

1. Carl Brauer, *John F. Kennedy and the Second Reconstruction* (New York: Columbia University Press, 1977), 1–86.
2. Michael Beschloss, *The Crisis Years: Kennedy and Khrushchev, 1960–1963* (New York: HarperCollins, 1991), 48.
3. *JBS Bulletin,* December 1960.
4. *JBS Bulletin,* January 1961.
5. Donald T. Critchlow, *The Conservative Ascendancy: How the GOP Right Made Political History* (Cambridge, MA: Harvard University Press, 2007), 52–53.
6. Thomas Paterson, ed., *Kennedy's Quest for Victory: American Foreign Policy, 1961–1963* (New York: Oxford University Press, 1989), 3–23.
7. Paterson, *Kennedy's Quest for Victory,* 123–55.
8. Critchlow, *Conservative Ascendancy,* 53.
9. Critchlow, *Conservative Ascendancy,* 64–65; John A. Andrew, *The Other Side of the Sixties: Young Americans for Freedom and the Rise of Conservative Politics* (New Brunswick, NJ: Rutgers University Press, 1997), 151–68; Arnold Forster and Benjamin R. Epstein, *Danger on the Right: The Attitudes, Personnel, and Influence of the Radical Right and Extreme Conservatives* (New York: Random House, 1964), 11–46; Daniel Bell, ed., *The Radical Right: "The New American Right" Expanded and Updated* (Garden City, NY: Doubleday, 1963); Benjamin R. Epstein and Arnold Forster, *Report on the John Birch Society* (New York: Vintage Books, 1966).
10. Robert Welch, *The Blue Book of the John Birch Society* (Belmont, MA: Western Islands, 1961), 9–11.

11. Jonathan Schoenwald, *A Time for Choosing: The Rise of Modern American Conservatism* (Oxford: Oxford University Press, 2001), 63, 80.
12. Welch, *Blue Book,* 64; Michelle Nickerson, *Mothers of Conservatism: Women of the Postwar Right* (Princeton, NJ: Princeton University Press, 2012), 138–39.
13. Critchlow, *Conservative Ascendancy,* 54.
14. John H. Rousselot, Speech to the Fourth Annual Christian Crusade Convention, Tulsa, Oklahoma, August 4, 1962, John Birch Society Sound Recordings Collection, Manuscript, Archives, and Rare Book Library, Emory University, Atlanta, GA.
15. US Department of State, *Freedom from War: The United States Program for General and Complete Disarmament in a Peaceful World* (Washington, DC: US Government Printing Office, 1961).
16. Colin R. Reynolds, "The-So-Far Right: Radical Right-Wing Politics in the United States, 1941–1977" (PhD diss., Emory University, 2016), 146.
17. *JBS Bulletin,* March 1960; Crichtlow, *Conservative Ascendency,* 50–54; *JBS Bulletin,* April 1960.
18. *JBS Bulletin,* July 1960, December 1960.
19. Rick Perlstein, *Before the Storm: Barry Goldwater and the Unmaking of the American Consensus* (New York: Nation Books, 2009), 100.
20. Welch, *Politician,* xix–xxi; Thomas Paterson, "Fixation with Cuba: The Bay of Pigs, Missile Crisis, and Covert War," in Paterson, *Kennedy's Quest,* 123–55; Trumbull Higgins, *The Perfect Failure: Kennedy, Eisenhower, and the CIA at the Bay of Pigs* (New York: W. W. Norton, 1987); Beschloss, *Crisis Years,* 29–30, 100–108; Giglio, *Presidency of JFK,* 48–63; Thomas Reeves, *A Question of Character: A Life of John F. Kennedy* (New York: Free Press, 1991), 256–76.
21. Aleksandr Fursenko and Timothy Naftali, *Khrushchev's Cold War: The Inside Story of an American Adversary* (New York: Norton, 2006), 339; *JBS Bulletin,* June 1961; Robert Welch, *The Politician* (Belmont, MA: Belmont, 1963), xvii–xxi; D. J. Mulloy, *The World of the John Birch Society: Conspiracy, Conservatism, and the Cold War* (Nashville: Vanderbilt University Press, 2014), 151–55; *New York Times,* April 22, 1961, and January 2, 1962.
22. *JBS Bulletin,* December 1960.
23. *JBS Bulletin,* July 1977.
24. Mulloy, *World of the John Birch Society,* 19–20; *Santa Barbara News-Press,* January 22, 1961, January 23, 1961; *JBS Bulletin,* August 1960; *JBS Bulletin,* September 1960.
25. Mulloy, *World of the John Birch Society,* 20–21; *Los Angeles Times,* March 5, 6, 7, 12, 1961.
26. *Time,* March 10, 1961; Mulloy, *World of the John Birch Society,* 21–22.
27. *New York Times,* April 20, 1961; Mulloy, *World of the John Birch Society,* 57–61; Mike Newberry, *The Fascist Revival: The Inside Story of the John Birch Society* (New York: New Century, 1961), 7–18; *New York Times,* November 19, 1961.
28. Reynolds, "The-So-Far Right," 101; *JBS Bulletin,* April 1961; Robert Welch, *The White Book of the John Birch Society for 1961* (Belmont, MA: John Birch Society, 1962).

29. Critchlow, *Conservative Ascendency*, 64–65.
30. Heather Hendershot, *Open to Debate: How William F. Buckley Put Liberal America on the Firing Line* (New York: Broadside Books, 2016), 14–15.
31. Reynolds, "The-So-Far Right," 118; Welch, *Politician*, 26–34.
32. Reynolds, "The-So-Far Right," 118–20; *JBS Bulletin*, April 1961; Welch, *White Book 1961*; David Nirenberg, *Anti-Judaism: The Western Tradition* (New York: W. W. Norton, 2013); Benjamin W. Segal, *A Lie and a Libel: The History of the Protocols of the Elders of Zion* (Lincoln: University of Nebraska Press, 1995).
33. Mulloy, *World of the John Birch Society*, 11.
34. Robert Welch to Verne P. Kaub, February 9, 1961, Ernie Lazar Collection.
35. Robert Welch to Verne P. Kaub, February 9, 1961, Ernie Lazar Collection.
36. Jon Meacham, *The Soul of America: The Battle for Our Better Natures* (New York: Random House, 2018), 161; Ribuffo, *Old Christian Right*, 19–24.
37. Robert Welch to Verne P. Kaub, February 9, 1961, Ernie Lazar Collection.
38. Robert Welch to Verne P. Kaub, February 9, 1961, Ernie Lazar Collection.
39. Robert Welch to Gerald L. K. Smith, April 14, 1962, Ernie Lazar Collection.
40. Robert Welch to Gerald L. K. Smith, April 24, 1962, Ernie Lazar Papers.
41. Robert Welch to Lawrence Lacey, February 10, 1961, Ernie Lazar Collection.
42. Robert Welch to Lawrence Lacey, February 10, 1961, Ernie Lazar Collection.
43. Robert Welch to Lawrence A. Lacey, February 10, 1961, Ernie Lazar Collection.
44. Robert Welch, *The Neutralizers* (Belmont, MA: John Birch Society, 1963); Robert Alan Goldberg, *Enemies Within: The Culture of Conspiracy in Modern America* (New Haven, CT: Yale University Press, 2001), 45–46; Arthur Goldwag, *The New Hate: A History of Fear and Loathing on the Populist Right* (New York: Pantheon Books, 2012), 132; Mulloy, *World of the John Birch Society*, 62–64; Alan Brinkley, *Voices of Protest: Huey Long, Father Coughlin and the Great Depression* (New York: Vintage, 1983), 281; Ribuffo, *Old Christian Right*, 19–24.
45. In 1968, when Gore Vidal called Buckley a "pro-crypto-Nazi" at the Democratic Convention, Buckley snapped, "stop calling me a crypto-Nazi or I'll sock you in the goddamned face and you'll stay plastered."
46. John B. Judis, *William F. Buckley Jr.: Patron Saint of the Conservatives* (New York: Simon and Schuster, 1988), 196.
47. California Senate, *Twelfth Report of the Senate Factfinding Subcommittee on Un-American Activities* (Sacramento: Senate of the State of California, 1963), 62; *New York Times*, March 29 and March 26, 1961; Mulloy, *World of the John Birch Society*, 22–27; *New York Times*, April 2, 1961; *JBS Bulletin*, January 1961; *New York Times*, March 21, 1961; *JBS Bulletin*, July 1977.
48. *New York Times*, April 1, 4, 1961; *JBS Bulletin*, August 1961; Mulloy, *World of the John Birch Society*, 34–35.
49. *JBS Bulletin*, July 1977.
50. *JBS Bulletin*, March, April 1961; September 1960.
51. Mulloy, *World of the John Birch Society*, 36–37; *JBS Bulletin*, April 1961.
52. Leo Reardon, "Welch Statement," attached to Clarence Manion to Robert Welch,

March 28, 1961, Clarence E. Manion Papers [CEMP], Box 62, Folder 1, Chicago History Museum, Chicago, IL.

53. Clarence Manion to Robert Welch, September 27, 1961, 1, CEMP, Box 61, Folder 7; Reynolds, "The-So-Far Right," 111–13.
54. *Meet the Press*, Washington, DC, May 21, 1961, John Birch Society Sound Recordings Collection, Manuscript, Archives, and Rare Book Library, Emory University, Atlanta, GA.
55. Reynolds, "The-So-Far Right," 113.

CHAPTER NINETEEN

1. Heather Hendershot, *What's Fair on the Air: Cold War Right-Wing Broadcasting and the Public Interest* (Chicago: University of Chicago Press, 2011), 65–69; Dan Smoot, *People along the Way: The Autobiography of Dan Smoot* (Tyler, TX: Tyler Press, 1996), 141–86; Dan Smoot, *The Hope of the World* (Dallas: Miller, 1958); Dan Smoot, *The Invisible Government* (Belmont, MA: Western Islands, 1962).
2. Dan Smoot, "Invisible Government," Ninth Symposium on Freedom, Los Angeles, CA, 1961, John Birch Society Sound Recordings Collection, Manuscript, Archives, and Rare Book Library, Emory University, Atlanta, GA; Smoot, *Invisible Government*, 3–51; Colin R. Reynolds, "The-So-Far Right: Radical Right-Wing Politics in the United States, 1941–1977" (PhD diss., Emory University, 2016), 114–17.
3. Mark Fenster, *Conspiracy Theories: Secrecy and Power in American Culture* (Minneapolis: University of Minnesota Press, 1999); Michael Barkun, *A Culture of Conspiracy: Apocalyptic Visions in Contemporary America* (Berkeley: University of California Press, 2003); Robert Alan Goldberg, *Enemies Within: The Culture of Conspiracy in Modern America* (New Haven, CT: Yale University Press, 2001).
4. D. J. Mulloy, *The World of the John Birch Society: Conspiracy, Conservatism, and the Cold War* (Nashville: Vanderbilt University Press, 2014), 27–31, 34–35; *New York Times*, April 7 and August 20, 1961; Stanley Mosk, *Report to the Governor on the John Birch Society* (Sacramento: California Department of Justice, 1961), 1–11.
5. Shawn Francis Peters, "'Did You Say That Mr. Dean Acheson Is a Pink?' The Walker Case and the Cold War," *Viet Nam Generation* 6, nos. 3–4, (1995): 20; Jonathan Schoenwald, *A Time for Choosing: The Rise of Modern American Conservatism* (Oxford: Oxford University Press, 2001), 102–4; Rick Perlstein, *Before the Storm: Barry Goldwater and the Unmaking of the American Consensus* (New York: Nation Books, 2009), 146.
6. Chris Cravens, "Edwin A. Walker and the Right Wing in Dallas, 1960–1966" (master's thesis, Southwest Texas State University, 1991); Daniel Bell, ed., *The Radical Right: "The New American Right,"* expanded and updated ed. (Garden City, NY: Doubleday, 1963), 526; Curtis Spears to John F. Kennedy, Box 2910, "Edwin A. Walker Correspondence" Folder, White House Central Name File, John F. Kennedy Presidential Library, Boston, MA.
7. Clive Webb, *Rabble Rousers: The American Far Right in the Civil Rights Era* (Athens: University of Georgia Press, 2010), 141–49; Donald T. Critchlow, *The Conservative*

Ascendancy: How the GOP Right Made Political History (Cambridge, MA: Harvard University Press, 2007), 60.

8. John A. Andrew, *The Other Side of the Sixties: Young Americans for Freedom and the Rise of Conservative Politics* (New Brunswick, NJ: Rutgers University Press, 1997); Darren Dochuk, *From Bible Belt to Sunbelt: Plain-Folk Religion, Grassroots Politics, and the Rise of Evangelical Conservatism* (New York: W. W. Norton, 2011), 234–37; Kent Courtney and Phoebe Courtney, *The Case of General Edwin A. Walker: The Muzzling of the Military Who Warn of the Communist Threat* (New Orleans: Conservative Society of America, 1961), 135; *New York Times*, April 14, 18, and 23, 1961; *Dallas Morning News*, June 4, 13, 1961; Cravens, "Edwin A. Walker," 81; Department of Defense Directorate for News Services, June 12, 1961, Box 2910, "Edwin A. Walker Correspondence" Folder, White House Central Name File, Kennedy Presidential Library; *Dallas Morning News*, June 13, 1961.
9. *Dallas Morning News*, June 10, 1961.
10. Box 2910, "Edwin A. Walker Correspondence" Folder, White House Central Name File, Kennedy Presidential Library; Cravens, "Edwin A. Walker," 81.
11. Peters, "'Did You Say?'" 13.
12. George and Jack Salish to John F. Kennedy, May 8, 1961, Box 2910, "Edwin A. Walker Correspondence" Folder, White House Central Name File, Kennedy Presidential Library.
13. Schoenwald, *Time for Choosing*, 100–123; Peters, "'Did You Say?'"
14. Victor G. Reuther, *The Brothers Reuther and the Story of the UAW* (Boston: Houghton Mifflin, 1976), 437–40; John A. Andrew III, *Power to Destroy: The Political Uses of the IRS from Kennedy to Nixon* (Chicago: Ivan R. Dee, 2002); Mulloy, *World of the John Birch Society*, 64–66; Robert Justin Goldstein, *Political Repression in Modern America: From 1870 to 1976* (Urbana: University of Illinois Press, 1978), 425; Schoenwald, *Time for Choosing*, 117.
15. John B. Judis, *William F. Buckley Jr.: Patron Saint of the Conservatives* (New York: Simon and Schuster, 1988), 197.

CHAPTER TWENTY

1. William F. Buckley, Jr., to Robert Welch, October 21, 1960, Revilo P. Oliver Papers, http://www.revilo-oliver.com/papers/.
2. Arnold Forster and Benjamin R. Epstein, *Danger on the Right: The Attitudes, Personnel, and Influence of the Radical Right and Extreme Conservatives* (New York: Random House, 1964), 251.
3. William F. Buckley Jr., "The Question of Robert Welch," *National Review*, February 13, 1962, 83–88.
4. David Farber, *The Rise and Fall of Modern American Conservatism* (Princeton, NJ: Princeton University Press, 2010), 72.
5. Donald T. Critchlow, *The Conservative Ascendancy: How the GOP Right Made Political History* (Cambridge, MA: Harvard University Press, 2007), 59.

6. D. J. Mulloy, *The World of the John Birch Society: Conspiracy, Conservatism, and the Cold War* (Nashville: Vanderbilt University Press, 2014m), 215.
7. *American Opinion*, March 1962.
8. *JBS Bulletin*, March 1962; Mulloy, *World of the John Birch Society*, 82.
9. Critchlow and MacLean, *Debating the American Conservative Movement*, 137.
10. *National Review*, December 2, 1962; Alvin S. Felzenberg, *A Man and His Presidents: The Political Odyssey of William F. Buckley Jr.* (New Haven, CT: Yale University Press, 2017), 115; Nicholas Buccola, *The Fire Is Upon Us: James Baldwin, William F. Buckley Jr., and the Debate over Race in America* (Princeton, NJ: Princeton University Press, 2019), 189; John B. Judis, *William F. Buckley Jr.: Patron Saint of the Conservatives* (New York: Simon and Schuster, 1988), 209.
11. *JBS Bulletin*, July 1977.
12. On the "ostracization thesis," see Clinton Rossiter, *Conservatism in America: The Thankless Persuasion*, 2nd rev. ed. (New York: Random House, 1962); Daniel Bell, ed., *The Radical Right: "The New American Right,"* expanded and updated ed. (Garden City, NY: Doubleday, 1963); George H. Nash, *The Conservative Intellectual Movement in America since 1945*, 30th ann. ed. (Wilmington, DE: ISI Books, 2006); Judis, *William F. Buckley Jr*, 191; Jerome L. Himmelstein, *To the Right: The Transformation of American Conservatism* (Berkeley: University of California Press, 1990), 26–27; Gregory L. Schneider, *Cadres for Conservatism: Young Americans for Freedom and the Rise of the Contemporary Right* (New York: New York University Press, 1999); John A. Andrew III, *The Other Side of the Sixties: Young Americans for Freedom and the Rise of Conservative Politics* (New Brunswick, NJ: Rutgers University Press, 1997); Lisa McGirr, *Suburban Warriors: The Origins of the New American Right* (Princeton, NJ: Princeton University Press, 2001), 75–79, 222–23. That the excommunication was not a complete success but still effective, see Jonathan M. Schoenwald, *A Time for Choosing: The Rise of Modern American Conservatism* (New York: Oxford University Press, 2001), 62–99; Mulloy, *World of the John Birch Society*, 79–80; Barry M. Goldwater, *With No Apologies: The Personal and Political Memoirs of United States Senator Barry M. Goldwater* (New York: Morrow, 1979), 119; Goldberg, *Barry Goldwater*, 137; *New York Times*, February 8, 1962; *National Review*, February 13, 1962; John Rousselot, "Robert Welch and the John Birch Society," *Congressional Record*, February 15, 1962, 2, 356–57; *JBS Bulletin*, February 1962; *National Review*, February 27 and March 13, 1962.
13. Mulloy, *World of the John Birch Society*, 81–82; *JBS Bulletin*, March 1962; *New York Times*, February 8, 1962; *JBS Bulletin*, May 1962; Schoenwald, *Time for Choosing*, 18.
14. Rick Perlstein, *Before the Storm: Barry Goldwater and the Unmaking of the American Consensus* (New York: Nation Books, 2009), 111–17.
15. *JBS Bulletin*, July 1977.
16. Stephen Ambrose, *Nixon: The Education of a Politician, 1913–1962* (New York: Simon and Schuster, 1987), 657–58.
17. *JBS Bulletin*, September 1962; Robert Welch, *The Blue Book of the John Birch Society* (Belmont, MA: Western Islands, 1961), 110, 113; *New York Times*, January 9, 1962,

March 12, 1962, August 26, 1962, January 10, 1963; Mulloy, *World of the John Birch Society*, 81–82.

18. *JBS Bulletin*, July 1977.
19. Thomas G. Paterson, "Fixation with Cuba: The Bay of Pigs, Missile Crisis, and Covert War against Cuba," in *Kennedy's Quest for Victory: American Foreign Policy, 1961–1963*, ed. Thomas G. Paterson (New York: Oxford University Press, 1989), 123–55; Robert Dallek, *An Unfinished Life: John F. Kennedy, 1917–1963* (Boston: Little, Brown, 2003), 535–75; Michael Beschloss, *The Crisis Years: Kennedy and Khrushchev, 1960–1963* (New York: HarperCollins, 1991); Thomas Reeves, *A Question of Character: A Life of John F. Kennedy* (New York: Free Press, 1991), 364–86; Arthur Schlesinger, Jr., *Robert F. Kennedy and His Times* (Boston: Houghton, Mifflin, 1978), 499–532; Robert Kennedy, *Thirteen Days: A Memoir of the Missile Crisis*, ed. Theodore Sorensen (New York: W. W. Norton, 1969); Graham Allison, *Essence of Decision: Explaining the Cuban Missile Crisis* (Boston: Little, Brown, 1971); Dino Brugioni, *Eyeball to Eyeball: The Inside Story of the Missile Crisis* (New York: Random House, 1991); and Stephen Ambrose, *Rise to Globalism: American Foreign Policy since 1938* (New York: Penguin Books, 1985), 192–99.
20. Beschloss, *Crisis Years*, 557; *JBS Bulletin*, December 1962; Mulloy, *World of the John Birch Society*, 156–57.
21. Frank Lambert, *The Battle of Ole Miss: Civil Rights v. States' Rights* (New York: Oxford University Press, 2010).
22. *Dallas Morning News*, March 21, 1962.
23. Edwin A. Walker to John F. Kennedy, April 22, 1962; Walker to Kennedy, September 26, 1962—both in Box 2910, "Edwin A. Walker Correspondence" Folder, White House Central Name File, Kennedy Presidential Library, Boston, MA.
24. James C. Cobb, *Away Down South: A History of Southern Identity* (New York: Oxford University Press, 2005), 208; Critchlow, *Conservative Ascendancy*, 62–63.
25. Chris Cravens, "Edwin A. Walker and the Right Wing in Dallas, 1960–1966" (master's thesis, Southwest Texas State University, 1991), 98; Bell, *Radical Right*, 526.
26. Mulloy, *World of the John Birch Society*, 119.
27. Mulloy, *World of the John Birch Society*, 116–20; *JBS Bulletin*, September 1962.
28. *New York Times*, October 4, 1962; Clive Webb, *Rabble Rousers: The American Far Right in the Civil Rights Era* (Athens: University of Georgia Press, 2010); Mulloy, *World of the John Birch Society*, 120–21; *JBS Bulletin*, October 1962.

CHAPTER TWENTY-ONE

1. Robert Welch to Frank Cullen Brophy, May 29, 1962, Clarence E. Manion Papers [CEM], Box 61, Folder 7, Chicago History Museum, Chicago, IL; Colin R. Reynolds, "The-So-Far Right: Radical Right-Wing Politics in the United States, 1941–1977" (PhD diss., Emory University, 2016), 171–73.
2. *American Opinion*, October 1973; Thomas Paterson, ed., *Kennedy's Quest for Victory: American Foreign Policy, 1961–1963* (New York: Oxford University Press, 1989), 160; Arthur M. Schlesinger Jr., *A Thousand Days* (Boston: Houghton, Mifflin, 1965),

564–65; Odd Arne Westad, *The Cold War: A World History* (New York: Basic Books, 2017), 261–312.

3. *JBS Bulletin*, January 1960; Robert Welch, *The White Book of the John Birch Society for 1960* (Belmont, MA: John Birch Society, 1961), 21.
4. Samuel L. Blumenfeld, "About De Gaulle" (Belmont, MA: John Birch Society, 1962); Reynolds, "The-So-Far Right," 172–74; Carl Brauer, *John F. Kennedy and the Second Reconstruction* (New York: Columbia University Press, 1977), 1–86; Giglio, *Presidency of JFK*, 159–88.
5. Stephen Ambrose, *Nixon: Triumph of a Politician, 1962–1972* (New York: Simon and Schuster, 1989), 36–37; Taylor Branch, *Parting the Waters: America in the King Years, 1954–1963* (New York: Simon and Schuster, 1989), 673–845; D. J. Mulloy, *The World of the John Birch Society: Conspiracy, Conservatism, and the Cold War* (Nashville: Vanderbilt University Press, 2014), 122; James T. Patterson, *Grand Expectations: The United States, 1945–1974* (New York: Oxford University Press, 1989), 480–81; Robert Dallek, *An Unfinished Life: John F. Kennedy, 1917–1963* (Boston: Little, Brown, 2003), 594–600.
6. Gary Allen, "Since Camelot," *American Opinion*, unidentified clipping.
7. Clayborne Carson, *In Struggle: SNCC and the Black Awakening of the 1960s* (Cambridge, MA: Harvard University Press, 1981), 34–37; Branch, *Parting the Waters*, 419–21, 673–845; Robert Weisbrot, *Freedom Bound: A History of America's Civil Rights Movement* (New York: W. W. Norton, 1990), 57–63; Aldon Morris, *The Origins of the Civil Rights Movement: Black Communities Organizing for Change* (New York: Free Press, 1984), 229–74; David Lewis, *King: A Biography* (Urbana, IL: Praeger, 1970), 171–209; Adam Fairclough, *Martin Luther King, Jr.* (Athens: University of Georgia Press, 1995), 71–82; Glenda Elizabeth Gilmore, *Defying Dixie: The Radical Roots of Civil Rights, 1919–1950* (New York: W.W. Norton, 2008).
8. *JBS Bulletin*, July 1963; Welch, *The White Book of the John Birch Society for 1963* (Belmont, MA: John Birch Society, 1964), 12–13; Reynolds, "The-So-Far Right," 160–61; Mulloy, *World of the John Birch Society*, 120–21.
9. Reynolds, "The-So-Far Right," 124–27; Welch, *The Politician* (unpub. vers., 1958), 67, 210, 223–36, 266–67; Robert Welch, *The Politician* (Belmont, MA: Belmont, 1963), 77, 52–53, 130–37, 140–45; Revilo Oliver, *America's Decline* (London: Londinium Press, 1984), 199; *American Opinion*, unidentified clipping.
10. Reynolds, "The-So-Far Right," 123; Clarence Manion to Robert Welch, March 15, 1963, CEM, Box 61, Folder 7; Clarence Manion to Robert Welch, August 25, 1964, CEM, Box 61, Folder 7; John H. Rousellot, "Disarmament: Blueprint for Surrender," Biltmore Hotel, Atlanta, GA, March 18, 1963, John Birch Society Sound Recordings Collection, Manuscript, Archives, and Rare Book Library, Atlanta, GA.
11. Earl Lively Jr., *The Invasion of Mississippi* (Belmont, MA: American Opinion, 1963), 4; Reynolds, "The-So-Far Right," 146–58.
12. Joseph Crespino, *Strom Thurmond's America* (New York: Hill and Wang, 2012), 144–45.
13. *American Opinion*, June 1963; Alan Stang, *It's Very Simple: The True Story of Civil Rights* (Belmont, MA: Western Islands, 1965), 72; James Baldwin, *The Fire Next*

Time (London: Michael Joseph, 1963); Gary Allen, *Communist Revolution in the Streets* (Belmont, MA: Western Islands, 1967).

14. Manning Johnson, *Color, Communism and Common Sense* (New York: Alliance, 1958).
15. John Pepper, *American Negro Problems* (New York: Workers Library, 1928), 4; Whittaker Chambers, *Witness* (New York: Random House, 1952), 247; Reynolds, "The-So-Far Right," 172–75; John Pepper, "American Negro Problems," *Communist*, October 1928, 628; Stang, *It's Very Simple*; *Manchester Union Leader*, May 5, 1964.
16. Herbert Philbrick to Robert Welch, August 10, 1959, Herbert A. Philbrick Papers, Box 121, Folder 6, Manuscript Division, Library of Congress, Washington, DC; Reynolds, "The-So-Far Right," 145.
17. *Hearings Regarding Communist Infiltration of Minority Groups—Part 2, Before the H. Comm. on Un-American Activities*, 81st Cong. 501–7 (1949) (testimony of Manning Johnson); Reynolds, "The-So-Far Right," 142–46; Ellen Schrecker, *Many Are the Crimes: McCarthyism in America* (Boston: Little, Brown, 1998), 43; Manning Johnson, *Color, Communism, and Common Sense* (New York: Alliance, 1958), 23–49; "What Happened to Manning Johnson?," *Soul*, September-October 1960, 19 [reprint], Radical Right Collection, Box 58, Hoover Institution Archives, Stanford University, Stanford, CA; Herbert Philbrick to Robert Welch, August 10, 1959, Herbert A. Philbrick Papers [HPP], Box 121, Folder 6, Manuscript Division, Library of Congress, Washington, DC; *JBS Bulletin*, June 1963; Welch, *White Book 1963*, 27, 15; Edgar C. Bundy to Herbert Philbrick, October 27, 1958; Reply from Philbrick to Bundy, December 31, 1958, HPP, Box 60, Folder 10.
18. *JBS Bulletin*, August 1963, September 1963; Theodore Draper, *American Communism and Soviet Russia* (1960; New Brunswick, NJ: Transaction, 2003); Adam Fairclough, *Better Day Coming: Blacks and Equality, 1890–2000* (London: Penguin, 2001); Pepper, *American Negro Problems*; *JBS Bulletin*, August 1963.
19. *JBS Bulletin*, July 1963; Welch, *White Book 1963*, 12–13; Pepper, "American Negro Problems," 628, 632; Reynolds, "The-So-Far Right," 170–85.
20. Martin Camacho, "Portugal=Angola," Fourth Annual Christian Crusade Convention, Tulsa, OK, August 5, 1962, John Birch Society Sound Recordings Collection, Manuscript, Archives, and Rare Book Library, Emory University, Atlanta, GA; Reynolds, "The-So-Far Right," 175–77.
21. Patterson, *Grand Expectations*, 482–83; Branch, *Parting the Waters*, 846–87.
22. Slobodan M. Draskovich, *Tito: Moscow's Trojan Horse* (Chicago: Henry Regnery, 1957); *American Opinion*, January 1963; Slobodan M. Draskovich to Revilo P. Oliver, April 20, 1962, 1–2, Revilo P. Oliver Papers, http://www.revilo-oliver.com/papers/; Slobodan M. Draskovich to Robert Welch, August 12, 1963, Revilo P. Oliver Papers; Slobodan M. Draskovich to Robert Welch, April 20, 1962, 2, 4, Revilo P. Oliver Papers.
23. George Lewis, *The White South and the Red Menace: Segregationists, Anticommunism, and Massive Resistance, 1945–1965* (Gainesville: University Press of Florida, 2004).

24. *JBS Bulletin*, August 1963.
25. *JBS Bulletin*, August 1963.
26. Robert Welch to Olive Simes, December 23, 1963, Welch private papers.
27. Robert Welch to Olive Simes, December 23, 1963, Welch private papers.
28. Robert Welch to Olive Simes, December 23, 1963, Welch private papers.
29. Robert Welch to Olive Simes, December 23, 1963, Welch private papers.
30. Robert Welch to Olive Simes, December 23, 1963, Welch private papers.
31. Gary Allen to Charles Provan, "Documentary History of the John Birch Society," Ernie Lazar Papers, https://7e3330be-a-62cb3a1a-s-sites.googlegroups.com/site/jbs9005a/home/Gary%20Allen%2012-4-85_1.JPG.
32. Gary Allen letter to Charles Provan, December 4, 1985, "Documentary History of the John Birch Society," December 4, 1985, Ernie Lazar Papers, https://7e3330be-a-62cb3a1a-s-sites.googlegroups.com/site/jbs9005a/home/Gary%20Allen%2012-4-85_1.JPG.
33. *JBS Bulletin*, July 1977.
34. *JBS Bulletin*, July 1977.
35. *JBS Bulletin*, July 1977.
36. Reynolds, "The-So-Far Right," 130–47.
37. Robert Welch to Olive Simes, December 23, 1963, Welch private papers.
38. Robert Welch to Olive Simes, December 23, 1963, Welch private papers.
39. *JBS Bulletin*, June 1963; Welch, *White Book 1963*, 14–15; Reynolds, "The-So-Far Right," 132; Slobodan M. Draskovich to Robert Welch, August 12, 1963, Revilo P. Oliver Papers (Kevin Alfred Strom, 2010), http://www.revilo-oliver.com/papers/.
40. Reynolds, "The-So-Far Right," 146–58; Earl Lively Jr., *The Invasion of Mississippi* (Belmont, MA: American Opinion, 1963), 18, 19, 30, 84–85; *JBS Bulletin*, January 1962; *JBS Bulletin*, October 1962; Welch, *White Book 1963*, 14, 20.
41. Reynolds, "The-So-Far Right," 157.
42. *American Opinion*, June 1963; Stang, *It's Very Simple*; Baldwin, *Fire Next Time*; Mulloy, *World of the John Birch Society*, 120–26; *New York Times*, August 20, 1964; *American Opinion*, February 1964 and November 1964; *JBS Bulletin*, August 1963.
43. Robert Welch to Olive Simes, December 23, 1963, Welch private papers.
44. Robert Welch to Olive Simes, December 23, 1963, Welch private papers.
45. Reynolds, "The-So-Far Right," 128–30; "Mr. Manion, Confidential," 1964, 1, CEM, Box 74, Folder 4; Robert Welch, *The Neutralizers* (Belmont, MA: John Birch Society, 1963).

CHAPTER TWENTY-TWO

1. Taylor Branch, *Parting the Waters: America during the King Years* (New York: Simon and Schuster, 1988), 827–35.
2. Timothy B. Tyson, *The Blood of Emmett Till* (New York: Simon and Schuster, 2017).
3. Stephen C. Shadegg, *What Happened to Goldwater? The Inside Story of the 1964 Republican Campaign* (New York: Holt, Rinehart and Winston, 1965), 62; Allan J.

Lichtman, *White Protestant Nation: The Rise of the American Conservative Movement* (New York: Atlantic Monthly Press, 2008), 246–47.

4. Robert Welch to Olive Simes, December 23, 1963, Welch private papers.
5. Robert Welch to Olive Simes, December 23, 1963, Welch private papers.
6. *Arizona Republic*, November 23, 1963; Rick Perlstein, *Before the Storm: Barry Goldwater and the Unmaking of the American Consensus* (New York: Nation Books, 2009), 248.
7. *New York Times*, December 17, 1963; *Interim Bulletin*, November 30, 1963.
8. *Interim Bulletin*, November 30, 1963.
9. Perlstein, *Before the Storm*, 247.
10. *New York Times*, December 20, 1963.
11. Perlstein, *Before the Storm*, 247–49. He was at his mother-in-law's funeral in Indiana and didn't speak to any reporter.
12. Perlstein, *Before the Storm*, 247–49.
13. David Kaiser, *American Tragedy: Kennedy, Johnson, and the Origins of the Vietnam War* (Cambridge, MA: Belknap Press, 2000), 248–84; D. J. Mulloy, *The World of the John Birch Society: Conspiracy, Conservatism, and the Cold War* (Nashville: Vanderbilt University Press, 2014), 83–90; *New York Times*, December 17, 1963; Robert Dallek, *An Unfinished Life: John F. Kennedy, 1917–1963* (Boston: Little, Brown, 2003), 400–401; George C. Herring, *America's Longest War: The United States and Vietnam, 1950–1975*, 4th ed. (New York: McGraw-Hill, 2001), 122–29; *New York Times*, December 18, 1963; *JBS Bulletin*, December 1963.
14. Donald T. Critchlow, *The Conservative Ascendancy: How the GOP Right Made Political History* (Cambridge, MA: Harvard University Press, 2007), 69–70.
15. Mulloy, *World of the John Birch Society*, 89.
16. Robert Welch to Olive Simes, December 23, 1963, Welch private papers.
17. Robert Welch to Olive Simes, December 23, 1963, Welch private papers.
18. Critchlow, *Conservative Ascendancy*, 59.
19. David W. Reinhard, *The Republican Right since 1945* (Lexington: University Press of Kentucky, 1983), 178; Nancy MacLean, *Freedom Is Not Enough: The Opening of the American Work Place* (New York: R. Sage, 2006), 73; Dan T. Carter, *The Politics of Rage: George Wallace, the Origins of the New Conservatism, and the Transformation of American Politics* (New York: Simon and Schuster, 1995), 218; Donald T. Critchlow and Nancy MacLean, *Debating the American Conservative Movement: 1945 to the Present* (Lanham, MD: Rowman and Littlefield, 2009), 123–39; Nancy MacLean, "Neo-Confederacy versus the New Deal," in *The Myth of Southern Exceptionalism*, ed. Matthew D. Lassiter and Joseph Crespino (Oxford: Oxford University Press, 2010), 308–30; John C. Calhoun and Clyde Norman Wilson, *The Essential Calhoun: Selections from Writings, Speeches, and Letters* (New Brunswick, NJ: Transaction, 1992); Irving H. Bartlett, *John C. Calhoun: A Biography* (New York: W. W. Norton, 1993).
20. Lisa McGirr, *Suburban Warriors: The Origins of the New American Right* (Princeton, NJ: Princeton University Press, 2001), 112.

21. Critchlow, *Conservative Ascendancy*, 66–76.
22. Goldberg, *Barry Goldwater*, 138; Critchlow, *Conservative Ascendancy*, 66–76; McGirr, *Suburban Warriors*, 112.
23. T. Coleman Andrews to Clarence Manion, June 15, 1964, Clarence Manion Papers, Box 58, Folder 8, Chicago History Museum, Chicago, IL.
24. Bruce J. Schulman, *Lyndon Johnson and American Liberalism: A Brief History with Documents* (Boston: Bedford/St. Martin's, 1995), 169–71.
25. *American Opinion*, October 1973.
26. Michael W. Flamm, *Law and Order: Street Crime, Civil Unrest, and the Crisis of Liberalism in the 1960s* (New York: Columbia University Press, 2005), 38.

CHAPTER TWENTY-THREE

1. "Tax Funds a 'Hate the Whites' Project," *US News & World Report*, December 13, 1965.
2. *American Opinion*, August 1973.
3. *Florida Today*, July 16, 1968.
4. Bruce J. Schulman, *Lyndon B. Johnson and American Liberalism: A Brief History with Documents* (Boston: Bedford/St. Martin's, 1995), 107–11.
5. Michael W. Flamm, *Law and Order: Street Crime, Civil Unrest, and the Crisis of Liberalism in the 1960s* (New York: Columbia University Press, 2005), 59.
6. *American Opinion*, May 1967.
7. Donald T. Critchlow, *The Conservative Ascendancy: How the GOP Right Made Political History* (Cambridge, MA: Harvard University Press, 2007), 82.
8. *JBS Bulletin*, May 1968.
9. *JBS Bulletin*, May 1968.
10. *JBS Bulletin*, July 1977.
11. Julia Brown, *I Testify: My Years as an Undercover Agent for the FBI* (Boston: Western Islands, 1966), 160–61.
12. *JBS Bulletin*, January 1964.
13. *JBS Bulletin*, July 1977.
14. *JBS Bulletin*, April 1967.
15. Ian Smith, "Rhodesia's Leader Sees His Struggle, Ours in Viet Nam as 'All the Same,'" *Daily Advance*, April 21, 1966 (reprint from American Friends of Rhodesia, Nashua, NH), Contemporary Issues Pamphlet Collection, MS 81-07-A, Box 2, "American Friends of Rhodesia" Folder, Wichita State University Libraries, Special Collections and University Archives, Wichita, KS.
16. Thomas J. Anderson, "Rhodesia," The John Birch Society Report, Transcript 6, April 10, 1966, John Birch Society Sound Recordings Collection, Manuscript, Archives, and Rare Book Library, Emory University, Atlanta, GA.
17. Thomas J. Anderson, "Here We Go Again," Key Records, 1964, John Birch Society Sound Recordings Collection, Manuscript, Archives, and Rare Book Library, Emory University, Atlanta, GA.

18. Robert Welch, *Two Revolutions at Once* (Belmont, MA: American Opinion, 1966); Colin R. Reynolds, "The-So-Far Right: Radical Right-Wing Politics in the United States, 1941–1977" (PhD diss., Emory University, 2016), 20–190.

CHAPTER TWENTY-FOUR

1. *JBS Bulletin*, July 1977.
2. *JBS Bulletin*, July 1977.
3. *JBS Bulletin*, July 1977.
4. *JBS Bulletin*, April 1966.
5. Daniel K. Williams, *God's Own Party: The Making of the Christian Right* (Oxford: Oxford University Press, 2010), 109; Lisa McGirr, *Suburban Warriors: The Origins of the New American Right* (Princeton, NJ: Princeton University Press, 2001), 135.
6. *JBS Bulletin*, April 1966, November 1966.
7. *American Opinion*, October 1973; Gary Allen, *None Dare Call It Conspiracy* (Rossmoor, CA: Concord Press, 1971), 7–18.
8. Robert Welch, *The Truth about Vietnam* (Belmont, MA: American Opinion, 1967), 20; Robert Welch, *More Truth about Vietnam* (Belmont, MA: American Opinion, 1967).
9. *JBS Bulletin*, March 1968; *American Opinion*, October 1973.
10. *JBS Bulletin*, March 1968; *American Opinion*, October 1973.
11. *JBS Bulletin*, July 1977.
12. Jill Lepore, *These Truths* (New York: W. W. Norton, 2018), 630.
13. James Phelan, "Mutiny in the JBS," *Saturday Evening Post*, April 8, 1967, https://www.saturdayeveningpost.com/reprints/mutiny-in-the-birch-society/.
14. *Shreveport Journal*, March 19, 1967.
15. Slobodan Draskovitch to Robert Welch, August 9, 1966; Ernie Lazar Papers, https://sites.google.com/site/jbs9005a/; Phelan, "Mutiny in the JBS."
16. Lepore, *These Truths*, 636.
17. *American Opinion*, July 1977.
18. *American Opinion*, October 1973.
19. *JBS Bulletin*, October 1973.
20. Nixon left the office of the vice presidency with a government pension and an Oldsmobile, along with Pat's respectable Republican cloth coat. But he had a net worth of $515,830 by 1968. *Tucson Daily Citizen*, July 23, 1973; *JBS Bulletin*, July 1977; *La Crosse Tribune*, July 11, 1971; *Fort Lauderdale News*, February 20, 1972.
21. *San Francisco Examiner*, June 13, 1971.
22. Joseph E. Lowndes, *From the New Deal to the New Right: Race and the Southern Origins of Modern Conservatism* (New Haven, CT: Yale University Press, 2008), 120–39; Matthew D. Lassiter, *The Silent Majority: Suburban Politics in the Sunbelt South* (Princeton, NJ: Princeton University Press, 2006); Sean P. Cunningham, *Cowboy Conservatism: Texas and the Rise of the Modern Right* (Lexington: University Press of Kentucky, 2010), 94–96; Edward H. Miller, *Nut Country: Right-Wing Dallas and the Birth of the Southern Strategy* (Chicago: University of Chicago Press, 2015), 138.

23. Dan T. Carter, *The Politics of Rage: George Wallace, the Origins of the New Conservatism, and the Transformation of American Politics* (New York: Simon and Schuster, 1995), 343.
24. Sara Diamond, *Roads to Dominion: Right-Wing Movements and Political Power in the United States* (New York: Guilford Press, 1995), 114, 140–46.
25. Robert Welch to Gordon E. Spencer, August 14, 1968, Welch private papers.
26. Phelan, "Mutiny in the JBS."
27. Gary Allen, *Kissinger: The Secret of the Secretary of State* (Seal Beach, CA: '76 Press, 1976), 5–139; Allen, *None Dare Call It Conspiracy*, 7–138.
28. *JBS Bulletin*, October 1973; Gary Allen, *Richard Nixon: The Man behind the Mask* (Belmont, MA: Western Islands, 1971), 1–313; *San Francisco Examiner*, June 13, 1971; *Fort Lauderdale News*, February 20, 1972; *LaCrosse Tribune*, July 11, 1971; *Tucson Daily Citizen*, July 23, 1973; *Dayton Daily News*, September 26, 1973.
29. Lepore, *These Truths*, 637.
30. Lepore, *These Truths*, 638.

CHAPTER TWENTY-FIVE

1. *JBS Bulletin*, January 1970.
2. Robert Welch to Nord Davis, December 17, 1970, Ernie Lazar Collection, https://archive.org/stream/JBS_CRITICS_INSIDE_JBS-1#page/n91/mode/2up.
3. *JBS Bulletin*, October 1973.
4. Timothy Weir to Harry Brandler, April 26, 1974; Thomas Hill to John DeFriend, May 13, 1974; Judith DeFriend and John DeFriend to Thomas Hill, May 31, 1974; Harry Brandler to Robert Koenig, April 12, 1974; John DeFriend and Judith DeFriend to Robert J. Koenig, April 30, 1974, Ernie Lazar Collection, https://archive.org/stream/JBS_CRITICS_INSIDE_JBS-1#page/n91/mode/2up.
5. Robert Welch to Nicholas Bove, October 13, 1975, Ernie Lazar Papers, https://archive.org/stream/JBS_CRITICS_INSIDE_JBS-1#page/n91/mode/2up.
6. *JBS Bulletin*, July 1977.
7. *Morning Call*, September 19, 1976.
8. *Philadelphia Inquirer*, September 16, 1973; *Boston Globe*, September 23, 1973.
9. *JBS Bulletin*, July 1977; John McManus, *The John Birch Society: Its History Recounted by Someone Who Was There* (Wakefield, MA: Overview Productions, 2018), 145–231.
10. *Akron Beacon*, July 1, 1971.
11. *La Crosse Tribune*, July 11, 1971.
12. *Tucson Daily Citizen* July 23, 1973; *Springfield Leader and Press*, February 20, 1972.
13. *Fort Lauderdale News*, February 20, 1972.
14. *JBS Bulletin*, July 1977.
15. *Boston Globe*, September 23, 1973.
16. *JBS Bulletin*, July 1977; *Clarion-Ledger*, September 19, 1976; Chip Berlet and Matthew N. Lyons, *Right Wing Populism in America: Too Close for Comfort* (New York: Guilford Press, 2000), 177–85.

17. *Courier-News,* November 5, 1976.
18. *JBS Bulletin,* July 1977.
19. *Boston Globe,* September 23, 1973; *Courier-News,* September 18, 1973; *Honolulu Star-Bulletin,* September 13, 1978; *Courier-News,* November 15, 1976.
20. *Tucson Daily Citizen,* July 23, 1973.
21. *Tucson Daily Citizen,* July 23, 1973.
22. *Courier-News,* November 15, 1976.
23. Robert Welch to Nelson Bunker, May 12, 1977, Welch private papers.
24. Kevin M. Kruse and Julian E. Zelizer, *Fault Lines: A History of the United States since 1974* (New York: W. W. Norton, 2019), 88–91.
25. Robert Welch to Nelson Bunker Hunt, May 12, 1977, Welch private papers.
26. Robert Welch to Nelson Bunker Hunt, May 12, 1977, Welch private papers.
27. *Morning Call,* September 19, 1976.
28. *Morning Call,* September 19, 1976.
29. *Newark Advocate,* September 17, 1976.

CHAPTER TWENTY-SIX

1. Kevin M. Kruse and Julian E. Zelizer, *Fault Lines: A History of the United States since 1974* (New York: W. W. Norton, 2019), 1–43.
2. Robert Welch to Nelson Bunker Hunt, May 12, 1977, Welch private papers.
3. Harry Hurt, *Texas Rich: The Hunt Dynasty from the Early Oil Days through the Silver Crash* (New York: W. W. Norton, 1981), 169–71; Bryan Burrough, *The Big Rich: The Rise and Fall of the Greatest Texas Oil Fortunes* (New York: Penguin Press, 2009), 294–97.
4. Burrough, *Big Rich,* 294–97, 349–50; Hurt, *Texas Rich,* 263–65.
5. Heather Hendershot, *What's Fair on the Air: Cold War Right-Wing Broadcasting and the Public Interest* (Chicago: University of Chicago Press, 2011), 28–19; Hurt, *Texas Rich,* 211–12; Burrough, *Big Rich,* 294–97.
6. Hurt, *Texas Rich,* 211–12, 261–62; Burrough, *Big Rich,* 348–50.
7. Hurt, *Texas Rich,* 261–63.
8. Hurt, *Texas Rich,* 261–66, 325–26; Burrough, *Big Rich,* 349–50.
9. Hurt, *Texas Rich,* 264–65; Chandler Davidson, *Race and Class in Texas Politics* (Princeton, NJ: Princeton University Press, 1990), 76–77, 211–12.
10. Davidson, *Race and Class,* 76–77, 211–12; Hendershot, *What's Fair on the Air,* 281–29.
11. Hurt, *Texas Rich,* 265–67; Burrough, *Big Rich,* 350–51.
12. Matthew Avery Sutton, *American Apocalypse: A History of Modern Evangelicalism* (Cambridge, MA: Belknap Press of Harvard University Press, 2014); Michael Phillips, *White Metropolis: Race, Ethnicity, and Religion in Dallas, 1841–2001* (Austin: University of Texas Press, 2006), 49; Paul Boyer, *When Time Shall Be No More: Prophecy Belief in Modern American Culture* (Cambridge, MA: Belknap Press of Harvard University Press, 1992), 13, 97; Robert C. Fuller, *Naming the Antichrist: The History of an American Obsession* (New York: Oxford University Press, 1995);

Stephen D. O'Leary, *Arguing the Apocalypse: A Theory of Millennial Rhetoric* (New York: Oxford University Press, 1998); Angela M. Lahr, *Millennial Dreams and Apocalyptic Nightmares: The Cold War Origins of Political Evangelicalism* (New York: Oxford University Press, 2007).

13. Robert Welch to Nelson Bunker Hunt, May 12, 1977, Welch private papers.
14. John G. Turner, *Bill Bright and Campus Crusade for Christ: The Renewal of Evangelicalism in Postwar America* (Chapel Hill: University of North Carolina Press, 2008), 176–79, 182–84; Davidson, *Race and Class*, 76–77, 211–12; Sara Diamond, *Spiritual Warfare: The Politics of the Christian Right* (Boston: South End Press, 1989), 51–54.
15. Turner, *Bill Bright*, 139–51; Lahr, *Millennial Dreams*, 171–73.
16. James C. Cobb, *The South and America since World War II* (New York: Oxford University Press, 2011), 141–43.
17. Charles Marsh, *Wayward Christian Soldiers: Freeing the Gospel from Political Captivity* (Oxford: Oxford University Press, 2007), 22; Daniel K. Williams, *God's Own Party: The Making of the Christian Right* (Oxford: Oxford University Press, 2010), 141.
18. Williams, *God's Own Party*, 141.
19. Boyer, *When Time Shall Be No More*, 266.
20. Robert Welch to Nelson Bunker Hunt, May 12, 1977, Welch private papers.
21. William C. Martin, *With God on Our Side: The Rise of the Religious Right in America* (New York: Broadway Books, 1996), 7–8; Phillips, *White Metropolis*, 49; Boyer, *When Time Shall Be No More*, 13, 84–86, 154–57, 174–76, 264–72.
22. Hurt, *Texas Rich*, 316–18; Burrough, *Big Rich*.
23. Burrough, *Big Rich*, 387–405.
24. Robert Welch to Nelson Bunker Hunt, May 23, 1977, Welch private papers.

CHAPTER TWENTY-SEVEN

1. Kevin M. Kruse and Julian E. Zelizer, *Fault Lines: A History of the United States since 1974* (New York: W. W. Norton, 2019), 1–43.
2. *Clarion Ledger*, September 19, 1976.
3. Kruse and Zelizer, *Fault Lines*, 1–43.
4. Kruse and Zelizer, *Fault Lines*, 1–43.
5. Kruse and Zelizer, *Fault Lines*, 63.
6. Kruse and Zelizer, *Fault Lines*, 1–43.
7. Rick Perlstein, *The Invisible Bridge: The Fall of Nixon and the Rise of Reagan* (New York: Simon and Schuster, 2014), 149.
8. Kruse and Zelizer, *Fault Lines*, 1–43.
9. Kruse and Zelizer, *Fault Lines*, 51.
10. Judith Stein, *Pivotal Decade: How the United States Traded Factories for Finance in the Seventies* (New Haven, CT: Yale University Press, 2010), 133–230.
11. Allan J. Lichtman, *White Protestant Nation: The Rise of the American Conservative Movement* (New York: Atlantic Monthly Press, 2008), 344; Angela M. Lahr, *Mil-*

lennial Dreams and Apocalyptic Nightmares: The Cold War Origins of Political Evangelicalism (New York: Oxford University Press, 2007), 173–75; Daniel K. Williams, *God's Own Party: The Making of the Christian Right* (Oxford: Oxford University Press, 2010).

12. Erling Jorstad, *The Politics of Doomsday: Fundamentalists of the Far Right* (Nashville: Abingdon Press, 1970), 90–91, 111–12.
13. John H. Redekop, *The American Far Right: A Case Study of Billy James Hargis and Christian Crusade* (Grand Rapids, MI: William B. Eerdmans, 1968), 185.
14. Robert Welch to Nelson Bunker Hunt, May 12, 1977, Welch private papers.
15. Jill Lepore, *These Truths* (New York: W. W. Norton, 2018), 646–57.
16. Lepore, *These Truths*, 654–67.
17. Geoffrey M. Kabaservice, *Rule and Ruin: The Downfall of Moderation and the Destruction of the Republican Party, from Eisenhower to the Tea Party* (New York: Oxford University Press, 2012), 90.
18. *JBS Bulletin*, July 1977; Robert Welch to Nelson Bunker Hunt, May 12, 1977, 215–19, Welch private papers; Catherine E. Rymph, *Republican Women* (Chapel Hill: University of North Carolina Press, 2006); Rebecca E. Klatch, *Women of the New Right* (Philadelphia: Temple University Press, 1987); Robert O. Self, *All in the Family: The Realignment of American Democracy since the 1960s* (New York: Hill and Wang, 2012), 301–5.
19. *JBS Bulletin*, July 1973.
20. *JBS Bulletin*, April 1973.
21. *JBS Bulletin*, February 1973.
22. *JBS Bulletin*, July 1976.
23. *JBS Bulletin*, April 1973.
24. *JBS Bulletin*, April 1973.
25. *JBS Bulletin*, July 1976.
26. *Philadelphia Inquirer*, September 16, 1973.
27. *JBS Bulletin*, July 1975.
28. *JBS Bulletin*, July 1977; Robert Welch to Nelson Bunker Hunt, May 12, 1977, Welch private papers.
29. *American Opinion*, November 1982; Donald T. Critchlow, *Phyliss Schlafly and Grassroots Conservatism: A Woman's Crusade* (Princeton, NJ: Princeton University Press, 2005), 212–69.
30. *JBS Bulletin*, January 1969; Janice M. Irvine, *Talk about Sex: The Battles over Sex Education in the United States* (Berkeley: University of California Press, 2002), 10, 44; Whitney Strub, *Perversion for Profit: The Politics of Pornography and the Rise of the New Right* (New York: Columbia University Press, 2011); Colin R. Reynolds, "The-So-Far Right: Radical Right-Wing Politics in the United States, 1941–1977" (PhD diss., Emory University, 2016), 197–99.
31. Lisa McGirr, *Suburban Warriors: The Origins of the New American Right* (Princeton, NJ: Princeton University Press, 2001), 226.
32. Strub, *Perversion for Profit*, 160–70.
33. Irvine, *Talk about Sex*, 22–29; Reynolds, "The-So-Far Right," 198–203.

34. *American Opinion,* March 1969; Reynolds, "The-So-Far Right," 204.
35. Jeff Woods, *Black Struggle, Red Scare* (Baton Rouge: Louisiana State University Press, 2004), 21, 230; *American Opinion,* January 1969; Irvine, *Talk about Sex,* 10; Reynolds, "The-So-Far Right," 198–205; Strub, *Perversion for Profit,* 31–32.
36. Gordon V. Drake, *Blackboard Power: NEA Threat to America* (Tulsa: Christian Crusade, 1968), 41–115.
37. James Moffett, *A Case Study of Censorship, Conflict, and Consciousness* (Carbondale: Southern Illinois University Press, 1988), 18, 103–15; Gordon V. Drake, *Is the School House the Proper Place to Teach Raw Sex?* (Tulsa: Christian Crusade, 1968), 6–31; Reynolds, "The-So-Far Right," 212–13; *JBS Bulletin,* January 1969.
38. Rex T. Westerfield, *The Innocents Defiled* (Belmont, MA: John Birch Society, 1969).
39. *American Opinion,* November 1982.
40. David K. Johnson, *The Lavender Scare: The Cold War Persecution of Gays and Lesbians in the Federal Government* (Chicago: University of Chicago Press, 2004); K. A. Cuordileone, *Manhood and American Political Culture in the Cold War* (New York: Routledge, 2005).
41. *JBS Bulletin,* January 1968; Reynolds, "The-So-Far Right," 221.
42. "Dickinson Claims March Misconduct," *Alabama Journal,* March 31, 1965.
43. Reynolds, "The-So-Far Right," 221.
44. *American Opinion,* April 1969.
45. *JBS Bulletin,* November 1970.
46. Donald T. Critchlow, *Intended Consequences: Birth Control, Abortion, and the Federal Government in Modern America* (New York: Oxford University Press, 1999); James T. Patterson, *Restless Giant: The United States from Watergate to Bush v. Gore* (New York: Oxford University Press, 2005), 136–38, 177.
47. Donald T. Critchlow, *The Conservative Ascendancy: How the GOP Right Made Political History* (Cambridge, MA: Harvard University Press, 2007), 135–37.
48. *JBS Bulletin,* July 1975.
49. Critchlow, *Conservative Ascendency,* 135–37.
50. *JBS Bulletin,* November 1970.
51. Reynolds, "The-So-Far Right," 226.
52. Reynolds, "The-So-Far Right," 226; Charles R. Armour to John Schmitz, August 2, 1972, John G. Schmitz Papers, Box 66, Folder 3, Wichita State University Libraries, Special Collections and University Archives, Wichita, Kansas.
53. Jerome L. Himmelstein, *To the Right: The Transformation of American Conservatism* (Berkeley: University of California Press, 1990), 97–128.
54. David Edwin Harrell, *Pat Robertson: A Life and Legacy* (Grand Rapids, MI: William B. Eerdmans, 2010); Pat Robertson and Jamie Buckingham, *Shout It from the Housetops* (Plainfield, NJ: Logos International, 1972); David John Marley, *Pat Robertson: An American Life* (Lanham, MD: Rowman and Littlefield, 2007); Alec Foege, *The Empire God Built: Inside Pat Robertson's Media Machine* (New York: John Wiley, 1996).
55. Curtis W. Freeman, "Never Had I Been So Blind: W. A. Criswell's 'Change' on Racial Segregation," *Journal of Southern Religion* 10 (2007): 1–12; Barry Hankins,

Uneasy in Babylon: Southern Baptist Conservatives and American Culture (Tuscaloosa: University of Alabama Press, 2004), 242; Mark Newman, *Getting Right with God: Southern Baptists and Desegregation, 1945–1995* (Tuscaloosa: University of Alabama Press, 2001); Darren Dochuk, *From Bible Belt to Sunbelt: Plain-Folk Religion, Grassroots Politics, and the Rise of Evangelical Conservatism* (New York: W. W. Norton, 2011); Williams, *God's Own Party*, 141; Chandler Davidson, *Race and Class in Texas Politics* (Princeton, NJ: Princeton University Press, 1990), 201–3; Sean P. Cunningham, *Cowboy Conservatism: Texas and the Rise of the Modern Right* (Lexington: University Press of Kentucky, 2010), 155–77.

56. Steven P. Miller, *The Age of Evangelicalism: America's Born Again Years* (New York: Oxford University Press, 2014), 51–108.
57. Frank Lambert, *Religion in American Politics: A Short History* (Princeton, NJ: Princeton University Press, 2008), 184–204; Kruse and Zelizer, *Fault Lines*, 90–94.
58. Williams, *God's Own Party*, 115–19, 182–90; William Martin, "God's Angry Man," *Texas Monthly*, April 1981, 223.
59. Edward H. Miller, *Nut Country: Right-Wing Dallas and the Birth of the Southern Strategy* (Chicago: University of Chicago Press, 2015), 144.
60. NAM Memo to Members, September 28, 1955, Welch private papers.
61. Undated Campaign for the 48 States, Welch private papers.
62. Undated pamphlet entitled T. Coleman Andrews, "Tax Relief and Who Needs It," Welch private papers.
63. Robert Kuttner, *Revolt of the Haves: Tax Rebellions and Hard Times* (New York: Simon and Schuster, 1980), 13, 43, 68–69, 277–80; Isaac William Martin, *The Permanent Tax Revolt: How the Property Tax Transformed American Politics* (Stanford, CA: Stanford University Press, 2008), 115–16; Molly McLemore, *Tax and Spend: The Welfare State, Tax Politics, and the Limits of American Liberalism* (Philadelphia: University of Pennsylvania Press, 2012).
64. Robert Welch to ——, August 17, 1975, Welch private papers.
65. Robert Welch to ——, August 17, 1975, Welch private papers; Sara Diamond, *Roads to Dominion: Right-Wing Movements and Political Power in the United States* (New York: Guilford Press, 1995), 86, 148.
66. *JBS Bulletin*, February 1973.
67. Daniel A. Smith, *Tax Crusaders and the Politics of Direct Democracy* (New York: Routledge, 1998), 1–84; *JBS Bulletin*, July 1977; Robert Welch to Nelson Bunker Hunt, May 12, 1977, Welch private papers; Isaac William Martin, *Rich People's Movements: Grassroots Campaigns to Untax the One Percent* (New York: Oxford University Press, 2013), 153–56.
68. Bruce J. Schulman, *The Seventies: The Great Shift in American Culture, Society, and Politics* (Boston: Da Capo Press, 2002), 229–40.
69. Kruse and Zelizer, *Fault Lines*, 104.
70. Monica Prasad, *Starving the Beast: Ronald Reagan and the Tax Cut Revolution* (New York: Russell Sage Foundation, 2018).
71. Davidson, *Race and Class in Texas Politics*.
72. Hurt, *Texas Rich*, 323–27; Burrough, *Big Rich*, 387–405.

73. Hurt, *Texas Rich*, 349–420; Burrough, *Big Rich*, 387–405.
74. Elmer Gertz, *Gertz v. Robert Welch, Inc.: The Story of a Landmark Libel Case* (Carbondale: Southern Illinois University Press, 1992).
75. Robert Welch to Olive Simes, December 23, 1963, Welch private papers.

EPILOGUE

1. Tim Naftali, "Ronald Reagan's Long-Hidden Racist Conversation with Richard Nixon," *Atlantic*, July 30, 2019, https://www.theatlantic.com/ideas/archive/2019/07/ronald-reagans-racist-conversation-richard-nixon/595102/.
2. Rick Perlstein and Edward H. Miller, "The John Birch Society Never Left," *New Republic*, March 8, 2021, https://newrepublic.com/article/161603/john-birch-society-qanon-trump.
3. Kathryn S. Olmstead, *Real Enemies: Conspiracy Theories and American Democracy, World War I to 9/11* (Oxford: Oxford University Press, 2009), 178.
4. Jill Lepore, *These Truths* (New York: W. W. Norton, 2018), 688.
5. Lepore, *These Truths*, 691–92; Patrick Buchanan, "Culture War," Republican National Convention, Houston, TX, August 17, 1992.
6. Lepore, *These Truths*, 702.
7. Arthur M. Schlesinger Jr., *The Disuniting of America: Reflections on a Multicultural Society* (New York: W. W. Norton, 1991), 11.
8. Lepore, *These Truths*, 702.
9. Jonathan Kay, *Among the Truthers: A Journey into the Growing Conspiracist Underground of 9/11 Truthers, Birthers, Armageddonites, Vaccine Hysterics, Hollywood Know-Nothings and Internet Addicts* (New York: HarperCollins, 2011), 27–29; Lee Nichols, "Libertarians on TV," *Austin Chronicle*, August 7, 1998.
10. Philip Seib, *Rush Hour: Talk Radio, Politics, and the Rise of Rush Limbaugh* (Fort Worth, TX: Summit Group, 1993), 4, 27, 59; Charles J. Sykes, *How the Right Lost Its Mind* (New York: St. Martin's Press, 2017), 135.
11. https://newrepublic.com/article/161603/john-birch-society-qanon-trump.
12. Gabriel Sherman, *The Loudest Voice in the Room: How the Brilliant, Bombastic Roger Ailes Built Fox News—and Divided a Country* (New York: Random House, 2014), 175, 183.
13. Markus Prior, *Post-Broadcast Democracy: How Media Choice Increase Inequality in Political Involvement and Polarizes Elections* (New York: Cambridge University Press, 2007); Benjamin Ginsberg and Martin Shefter, *Politics by Other Means: Politicians, Prosecutors, and the Press from Watergate to Whitewater*, rev. and updated ed. (New York: W. W. Norton, 1999).
14. Haynes Johnson, *The Best of Times: America in the Clinton Years* (New York: Harcourt, 2001), 328–30, 373–74, 397; Steven M. Gillon, *The Pact: Bill Clinton, Newt Gingrich, and the Rivalry That Defined a Generation* (New York: Oxford University Press, 2008), 249.
15. Lepore, *These Truths*, 711.
16. Lepore, *These Truths*, 715.

17. *The Alex Jones Show on 9-11-2001*, Internet Archive, October 22, 2008, https://archive.org/details/TheAlexJonesRadioShowOn9-11-2001; Alexander Zaitchik, "Meet Alex Jones," *Rolling Stone*, March 2, 2011; Lepore, *These Truths*, 723–24.
18. Olmstead, *Real Enemies*, 208.
19. Olmstead, *Real Enemies*, 229.
20. Angela Nagle, *Kill All Normies: The Online Culture Wars from Tumblr and 4chan to the Alt-Right and Trump* (Washington, DC: Zero Books, 2017); Lepore, *These Truths*, 723–56.
21. Olmstead, *Real Enemies*, 205–31.
22. Marc Mauer, *Young Black Americans and the Criminal Justice System: Five Years Later* (Washington, DC: Sentencing Project, 1995); Lepore, *These Truths*, 726.
23. Lepore, *These Truths*, 755–56.
24. David Maraniss, *Barack Obama: The Story* (New York: Simon and Schuster, 2012), xxiii.
25. "Fact-Checking Trump's Claim That Thousands in New Jersey Cheered When World Trade Center Tumbled," PolitiFact, November 21, 2015, https://www.politifact.com/factchecks/2015/nov/22/donald-trump/fact-checking-trumps-claim-thousands-new-jersey-ch/.
26. Lepore, *These Truths*, 700–729.
27. Eric Hananoki and Timothy Johnson, "Donald Trump Praises Leading Conspiracy Theorist Alex Jones and His 'Amazing' Reputation," Media Matters for America, December 2, 2015, https://www.mediamatters.org/donald-trump/donald-trump-praises-leading-conspiracy-theorist-alex-jones-and-his-amazing-reputation.
28. Aleszu Bajak, Jessica Guynn, and Mitchell Thorson, "When Trump Started His Speech before the Capitol Riot, Talk on Parler Turned to Civil War," *USA Today*, February 1, 2021, https://www.usatoday.com/in-depth/news/2021/02/01/civil-war-during-trumps-pre-riot-speech-parler-talk-grew-darker/4297165001/.

Index